LAURA LEMAY'S
WEB WORKSHOP

MICROSOFT®
FRONTPAGE™

LAURA LEMAY'S
WEB WORKSHOP

MICROSOFT®
FRONTPAGE™

Laura Lemay
Denise Tyler

201 West 103rd Street
Indianapolis, Indiana 46290

I began experimenting with creating Web pages more than two years ago. When measured in Web years (Web years, like dog years, move much faster than real years), that makes me one of the decrepit old-timers of the business. And, like many decrepit old-timers, I occasionally like to reminisce. Pull up a chair.

Two years ago, in those dark medieval times, we didn't have very many tools to help us with the process of creating Web pages. We had simple text editors like vi or emacs, command-line FTP to get the files onto a machine that could talk to the Internet, and the ability to download, compile, and install a Web server on that machine, usually subversively without the knowledge or permission of the local system administrator. And, of course, you had to know HTML or be able to crib enough from other people's pages to be able to put something together that worked. Did I mention that we had to do all our HTML editing on the back of a shovel, and cart all our files to the Web server five miles uphill in the snow?

But things are different now. With the explosion of publishing on the Web has come an explosion in tools to help you publish on the Web. FrontPage is one of those tools. It's one of the most interesting of those tools. On the box, it says it's a "Web Authoring and Management Publishing System." But marketing terms aside, what it really is is a set of tools to help you get a good-size Web site up and running quickly and easily. It'll help you write the individual pages and link them to other pages both on and off your site, whether or not you know a lick of HTML. It'll create an entire Web site for you using wizards, creating many of the typical pages and features you might want to include on that site. It'll keep track of filenames and links so if you have broken links you can fix them quickly and easily. And using the server extensions, it'll even give you a way to set up simple forms and search engines and publish the whole wad of stuff onto the server with a single button. Zap. You're done.

This book, then, most simply, teaches you how to use FrontPage to create Web pages and sites. But it's more than that. This book is also part of Laura Lemay's Web Workshop series.

The idea for the Web Workshop series came from a book I wrote in the early days of HTML, titled *Teach Yourself Web Publishing with HTML in a Week.* The continuing success of that book has been attributed to the friendly approach I took to writing it—to treat the reader like a real person who wants to learn something, to include lots and lots of very hands-on examples, and to keep a good sense of humor throughout the book.

The writers of the books in the Web Workshop series have those same goals: to use friendly, conversational writing, lots of examples, to apply the topics in the book to things that you, the reader, might actually want to do with your own Web sites, and most of all, to be interesting to read. So, for example, in this book you won't just find out about all the various menu items in the FrontPage Editor. You'll find out how to use FrontPage to create specific kinds of Web sites, to use FrontPage in the best and most efficient manner that *you*, as a Web page designer, want to accomplish. And hopefully you'll have some fun doing it.

—Laura Lemay

lemay@lne.com

http://www.lne.com/lemay/

President, Sams Publishing:	Richard K. Swadley
Publishing Manager:	Greg Wiegand
Managing Editor:	Cindy Morrow
Director of Marketing:	John Pierce
Assistant Marketing Managers:	Kristina Perry
	Rachel Wolfe

Acquisitions Editor
Christopher Denny

Development Editors
Anthony Amico
Angelique Brittingham
Andrew Fritzinger

Software Development Specialists
Brad Meyers
Steve Straiger

Production Editor
Mary Inderstrodt

Copy Editors
Fran Blauw
Greg Horman

Indexer
Tom Dinse

Technical Reviewers
Shari Held
John Jung

Editorial Coordinator
Bill Whitmer

Technical Edit Coordinator
Lynette Quinn

Resource Coordinator
Deborah Frisby

Editorial Assistants
Carol Ackerman
Andi Richter
Rhonda Tinch-Mize

Cover Designer
Alyssa Yesh

Book Designer
Alyssa Yesh

Copy Writer
Peter Fuller

Production Team Supervisor
Brad Chinn

Production
Stephen Adams, Debra Bolhuis,
Mona Brown, Jason Hand,
Daniel Harris, Sonja Hart,
Louisa Klucznik, Dana Rhodes,
Laura Robbins

Dedication

To my family and friends for believing, but most of all to Ed, for his unending support.

Overview

Contents

Part III   Advanced Techniques   253

Acknowledgments

When one looks at a painting on a canvas or listens to a musical piece, the focus is usually on the elements in the foreground. Without background scenery or instrumentation, the compositions are incomplete.

This book has its own background—a team of dedicated individuals without whom this book simply would not be. At the helm of this team are Chris Denny, Angelique Brittingham, Andrew Fritzinger, Mary Inderstrodt, and Mark Taber of Sams Publishing and Sams.net. Their skill in providing technical expertise parallels their abilities to provide moral support and friendship.

The driving force behind this book, and the series of which it is a part, is Laura Lemay, a true master in the field of Web authoring. Her clear, no-nonsense approach in her award-winning books about Web authoring are sprinkled with style and wit. This style was the inspiration throughout this book, for all involved.

About the Author

Denise Tyler is a computer graphics artist/animator and author. After a 15-year career as an engineer with technical writing and customer training experience, she left the corporate world and started her own business in 1991. She combined her technical knowledge with a lifelong interest in art and music, and developed her skills in computer art and animation. She began by specializing in the development of graphics for multimedia presentations and computer games. As the World Wide Web grew, so did Denise's interest in developing and authoring Web pages.

Using her background experience in technical writing and customer training, Denise began writing tutorials in creating computer graphics. She is a co-author of the best-selling book *Tricks of the Game Programming Gurus* and is the author of *Fractal Design Painter 3.1 Unleashed*, both published by Sams Publishing. Using the same hands-on style of writing, she is now directing her attentions to the World Wide Web.

Tell Us What You Think!

As a reader, you are the most important critic and commentator of our books. We value your opinion and want to know what we're doing right, what we could do better, what areas you'd like to see us publish in, and any other words of wisdom you're willing to pass our way. You can help us make strong books that meet your needs and give you the computer guidance you require.

Do you have access to CompuServe or the World Wide Web? Then check out our CompuServe forum by typing GO SAMS at any prompt. If you prefer the World Wide Web, check out our site at http://www.mcp.com.

NOTE: If you have a technical question about this book, call the technical support line at (800) 571-5840, ext. 3668.

As the team leader of the group that created this book, I welcome your comments. You can fax, e-mail, or write me directly to let me know what you did or didn't like about this book—as well as what we can do to make our books stronger. Here's the information:

Fax: 317/581-4669

E-mail: programming_mgr@sams.mcp.com

Mail: Greg Wiegand
          Comments Department
          Sams Publishing
          201 W. 103rd Street
          Indianapolis, IN 46290

Introduction

During the infancy of Web development, it took an Internet guru to develop Web pages. The pioneers of Web page development developed a standard program code called Hypertext Markup Language, or HTML for short. Though HTML is a relatively easy programming language to learn, the task of Web page development was usually left to the experts. Then, along came trailblazers like Laura Lemay, who developed books that clearly and effectively demonstrated the proper use of this code. As a result, the Web took off like wildfire.

The Internet is more than a phenomenon—it's rapidly becoming *the way* to communicate for the '90s and beyond. By far, the most popular area of the Internet is the World Wide Web, where corporations and individuals alike are creating home pages and Web sites that tell the world about themselves. Take a look at television advertising, movie trailers, and business cards nowadays. You'll see a home page address displayed as conspicuously as other contact information. Now, everyone wants a place on the Web. For some, though, this isn't an easy undertaking.

Despite the plethora of books on the subject, there are still many who shy away from developing their own pages. No matter how they look at it, they still see HTML as programming. Over time, software tools have been developed that make Web page development easier. Still, there are those who need more. "What we need," they say, "is a tool that will let us see what we actually get when we view the pages in our browsers—without worrying about touching any code."

We are now seeing a new generation of Web authoring tools that fulfill this need. After I evaluated several of them, FrontPage became my tool of choice. It's clearly one of the best, especially for those who want to develop a medium- to large-sized Web site. The reason for this is that FrontPage goes beyond Web page development—it combines a WYSIWYG (what you see is what you get) Web page editor with a Web server and site management tool. As you develop your site, FrontPage's bots, templates, and wizards make the job easier. You can quickly and easily verify the links in your Web, making sure they all work before the site is published. FrontPage takes all the drudgery out of Web page development, and makes it fun and easy.

Also, until the advent of FrontPage, Web page developers had to learn other programming languages in order to add interactivity to their sites. FrontPage provides a solution to this also. Using some of the bots, you can create online ordering forms, surveys, guest books, and other items that can retrieve input from those who visit your site. By selecting an Internet service provider that uses the FrontPage Server Extensions, a novice can add these advanced features to his or her Web pages without any programming.

The goal of this book is to combine the best of both worlds—FrontPage's ease of use and the straight, hands-on tutorial approach that is the Laura Lemay trademark. I hope I've succeeded in accomplishing this goal and that it opens up an exciting, interesting, and fun new world for you. Enjoy!

Who Should Read This Book

This book is designed for those of you who are familiar with browsing and surfing the World Wide Web and who want to develop pages of your own. The chapters in this book teach you how to design Web pages and complete Web sites using Microsoft FrontPage, and cover version 1.1. The chapters progress from the quick-and-easy way to develop pages toward more advanced techniques such as adding interactivity and incorporating your own code into your FrontPage Web sites. The lessons should appeal to beginners and intermediate-level authors who want to learn how to develop Web pages the FrontPage way.

This workshop book assumes that you have already surfed the Web and that you are somewhat familiar with the basic terminology of the Web. You should, at a minimum, recognize what Web pages, URLs, and links are, and what they do. Of course, this book also assumes that you use the Windows 95 operating system, and that you have or will use FrontPage as an authoring tool.

How to Read This Book

This book is divided into five sections, beginning with the easiest and quickest way to develop Web sites and progressing through more advanced techniques and publishing your Web site. The projects in the "Real-Life Examples" chapters teach you how to build complete Web sites while incorporating the majority of the features available to you in FrontPage.

❏ In Part I, "Fast Track to Webs and Pages," you learn how to use FrontPage's Web and page templates and wizards to create a Web site. In the "Real-Life Examples" chapter of this section, you learn how to combine templates and wizards to create a corporate presence on the Web, complete with public and private discussion groups.

❏ In Part II, "Basic Techniques," you learn some of the basics of Web page development. You learn how to create links, compose and edit your pages, organize information in lists, add images to your pages, and how to manage your tasks with To Do lists. In the "Real-Life Examples" chapter of this section, you begin a personal Web site project that incorporates the techniques learned in this section.

❏ In Part III, "Advanced Techniques," you learn how to design and incorporate features that are a little more advanced and state-of-the-art. You learn how to use tables to display information and enhance page layout. You step through the FrontPage Frames Wizard to build and configure frame sets. You also learn how to use some of the FrontPage bots to streamline and simplify your Web site development. Finally, you learn how to import several different types of files into your FrontPage webs. The section finishes with a "Real-Life Examples" chapter that adds more pages to your Web project, incorporating all these features in a step-by-step manner.

❏ In Part IV, "Still More Advanced Techniques," you learn how to add interactivity to your site. Three chapters teach you, from start to finish, how to create forms, edit form fields, and configure form handlers. You also learn how to insert your own code into the FrontPage Editor. The section finishes with a "Real-Life Examples" chapter that adds several types of forms and a discussion group to your Web project. After you've completed the Web project, your Web site contains nearly 30 different pages.

❏ In Part V, "Putting It All Together," you learn how to administer and maintain your Web sites. You also learn more about the FrontPage Server, the Server Extensions, and when and why you need them. Finally, you test and publish your Web on the Internet.

❏ In Part VI, the appendixes contain instructions on how to install and configure FrontPage, some FrontPage references, a directory of resources containing pages or sites on the Web where you can get further information, an HTML quick reference that displays all HTML tags and the FrontPage commands associated with them, and a list of what is included on the CD-ROM accompanying this book.

The chapters are arranged so that you can find most everything you need to know about a particular topic in one area. Margin notes direct you to other areas of the book where related information appears. Tips and notes provide you with important or interesting information that can assist in your Web page development. Cautions tell you about things that will help you stay out of trouble.

The CD-ROM contains support files for the tasks and projects in this book, as well as some additional resources that will help you make your Web sites the best on the Internet. If all this isn't enough, visit my support site for this book. In addition to a user-to-user discussion group, you'll get to see most of the FrontPage features live and in action. I'll also have some goodies and art on the site as things progress. Visit me at the following URL:

```
http://frontpage.flex.net/dtyler/FPSite/index.htm
```

Thanks for buying this book, and here's to great success in building your Web sites with FrontPage!

I Fast Track to Webs and Pages

ONE
Learning Your Way Around

If you're reading this book, you're probably already somewhat familiar with the Internet. The fastest growing part of the Internet is the World Wide Web. Most people don't become interested in designing their own web pages unless they have seen pages created by others. You realize that the Internet is a great way to tell the world about yourself or your company. This book shows you some ways to do just that. You have the right development tool in FrontPage; it's a powerful, well-thought-out product. FrontPage should satisfy the novice in its simplicity and ease of use. You'll be amazed at how easy FrontPage makes it to produce professional-looking Web pages. FrontPage should also appeal to the more experienced Web page developer in its support of extended features and custom code. Get ready to learn how to develop and manage Web sites the easy way!

You'll work primarily with two parts of the FrontPage development package—the FrontPage Explorer and the FrontPage Editor. Their screens are shown in Figure 1.1.

Figure 1.1.

*The FrontPage Explorer
and the FrontPage
Editor work together to
help you develop and
manage your Web site.*

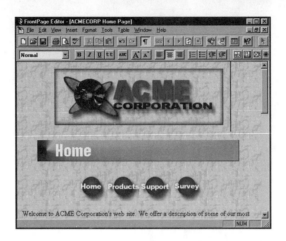

FrontPage Explorer Basics

When you installed FrontPage on your system, the first thing you probably did was open the FrontPage Editor and start designing pages. You probably then took a peek at the FrontPage Explorer and realized that was where the real power was. What sets FrontPage apart from other development tools is that it enables you to manage your web site through the FrontPage Explorer. By using the FrontPage Editor in conjunction with the FrontPage Explorer, you can manage web sites far more easily than you can with other page editors. For example:

❏ The Web templates included with the FrontPage Explorer provide several pages that are already linked together for you.

❏ If you rename or relocate a page in your web, the FrontPage Explorer asks if you want to correct all the links to the page you're moving. When you have several pages that link to each other, this feature can save you a great deal of time.

❏ Internal links to pages in your web, as well as external links to pages on the World Wide Web, can be verified quickly and easily. Broken links can be repaired with ease using the Verify Links command in the FrontPage Editor, which is shown in Figure 1.2.

With the FrontPage Explorer, you control and maintain the contents of your web. You can import and export any type of file into your web. Images are displayed on your pages or downloaded from your site. Other types of files can be placed in your site for downloading or viewing, providing that the user has the correct software to display them.

Figure 1.2.
*Links between pages in
your site as well as
those to pages on the
World Wide Web can be
verified and repaired
with ease.*

Learn how to verify and
repair links in Chapter
25, "Testing and
Publishing Your Web."

The FrontPage Explorer is also used in conjunction with the FrontPage Server
Administrator to administer your web site. Using the Web Permissions dialog box
shown in Figure 1.3, you can assign multiple web administrators or authors and allow
them access to your entire web or to only parts of it. In addition, you can provide access
to end users, providing restricted access to certain parts of your Web site if desired.
IP addresses of administrators, authors, and end users can also be restricted.

Figure 1.3.
*You can authorize
multiple administrators,
authors, and end users
to gain access to your
entire web or to only
parts of it.*

For additional informa-
tion on administering
your Web site, refer to
Chapter 23, "Web
Maintenance and
Administration."

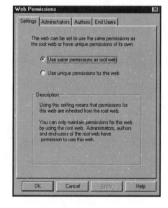

Opening the FrontPage Explorer

To open the FrontPage Explorer from Windows, choose Microsoft FrontPage I
FrontPage Explorer from the Start menu.

To open the FrontPage Explorer from the FrontPage Editor, use one of two methods:

❑ Choose Tools I Show FrontPage Explorer.

❑ Click the FrontPage Explorer button on the Standard toolbar.

About the Root Web

The first time you start the FrontPage Explorer, one web exists on the server. This is the *root web*. If you already have pages on the Internet through a local service provider, consider FrontPage's root web to be the equivalent of your home directory. Whereas the URL of the home page on your Internet service provider's server might look something like this:

```
http://www.yourserver.com/~yourdirectory/index.htm
```

the home page in the root directory of the FrontPage server on your home computer would have a URL that looks something like this:

```
http://localhost/index.htm
```

or

```
http://yourservername/index.htm
```

The root web, shown in Figure 1.4, serves some special purposes in FrontPage. Because it serves as the entryway to the other webs on your server, certain things are placed here. For example, you'll notice a couple of image map handlers in the root web—one for NSCA image maps and the other for CERN image maps. These handlers are there in case you work with a service provider that doesn't have the FrontPage Server Extensions installed. They provide an alternative set of instructions for image-map handling. Check with your service provider to see which image-map dispatcher would be the best for you to use. It's best not to delete the handlers from the root web unless you're certain you won't need them.

Figure 1.4.
The root web is the main entryway to the pages in your webs.

Learn how to create image maps in Chapter 8, "Getting from Here to There," and how to configure them for NSCA or CERN dispatching in Chapter 23, "Web Maintenance and Administration."

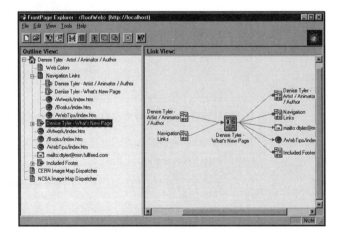

Webs—How to Make Them

There are several ways to create webs in FrontPage, all beginning with the FrontPage Explorer's File I New Web command. You can use the Web templates or Web wizards, you can create new pages based on page templates and wizards and save them to your site, or you can build your entire web site from the ground up.

You can configure the webs on your server in any way you choose. If you start off small, say a home page and a few link pages, you can place the pages in the root web. A simple diagram is shown in Figure 1.5. This method is perfectly acceptable if you don't expect your site to get too big.

Figure 1.5.

If your web is small, you can locate all the pages in the root web.

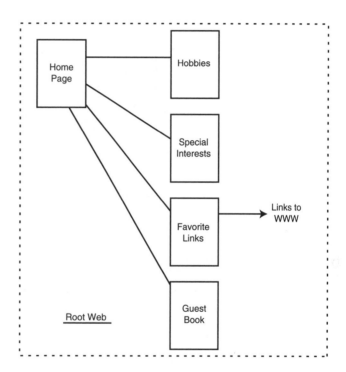

As your Web site grows, you can create new webs on your server that become subwebs of the root web. The chapters in this section show you many ways to create new webs. Each web will have a directory of its own beneath the root web, as shown in the simple example in Figure 1.6. Each new web can focus on certain topics or areas of interest. The home page in your root web links to the home pages of all the other webs on your server.

Figure 1.6.

As your web grows, you can create new webs that focus on specific topics and link them from a home page in your root web.

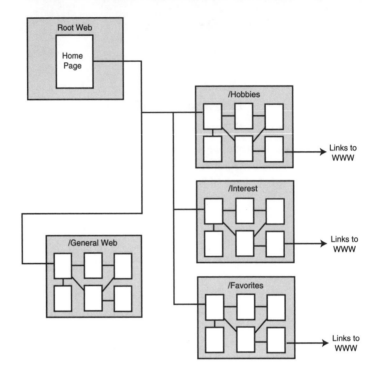

TIP: If you have already started creating all your pages in the root web, an easy way to move them from the root web into a new web on the same server is to use the FrontPage Explorer's Copy Web command. This command copies all pages, files, and images into the new web with links intact. You can then delete the original pages from your root web and create a new home page in the root web that provides a link to the home page you moved into the new web.

Webs—How to View Them

The FrontPage Explorer screen is divided into two windows, as shown in Figure 1.7. The left portion contains the Outline View of your web. The right portion can display the contents of your web in Link View or in Summary View. The following sections explain what these views do.

Figure 1.7.
The FrontPage Explorer workspace is divided into two windows.

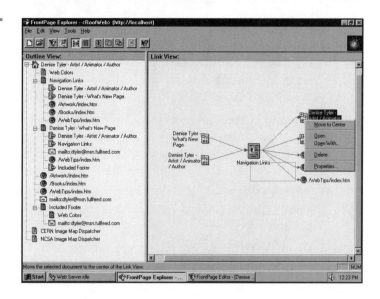

Outline View—Your Web Hierarchy

The left side of the FrontPage Explorer Window contains the Outline View, which shows a hierarchical representation of the pages in your currently opened web. The hierarchy can be expanded to show all pages that are linked to the selected page. The home page is designated by an icon that looks like a little house (appropriately).

NOTE: By default, FrontPage names your home page `index.htm`. Refer to Chapter 23, "Web Maintenance and Administration," to learn how to change the default name of the home page.

Link View—Contents at a Glance

Refer to Appendix B, "FrontPage References," for a description of the icons used in the FrontPage Explorer.

Link View, shown in the right portion of Figure 1.7, graphically displays the incoming and outgoing links to a page. Pages are displayed as icons, with the title of the page labeling the icon. Links to and from the pages are displayed as arrows, and pages that are included within the page are displayed as circles.

To display your pages in Link View on the right side of the FrontPage Explorer screen, use one of two procedures:

❏ Choose View | Link View.

❏ Click the Link View button on the FrontPage Explorer toolbar.

TIP: If you right-click on any of the page names or icons in Outline View, Link View, or Summary View, a pop-up menu appears that gives you quick access to some commonly used commands. Six commands are associated with the pop-up menus:

Move to Center (Link View only). To display this command in the pop-up menu, select one of the pages that link to or from the page displayed in the center of Link View. Then right-click to open the pop-up menu. This command moves the page that you selected into the center of the Link View and displays its links.

Find In Outline (Summary View only). Locates the selected page in Outline View.

Open. Opens the page in the FrontPage Editor.

Open With. Opens the page in another editor that is configured with the Tools I Configure Editors command.

Delete. Deletes the selected page from the web.

Properties. Opens the Page Properties dialog box for the selected page.

Summary View—Making Sense of Large Webs

Summary View, shown at the right in Figure 1.8, displays all the details of all the files in your web. It displays the title, filename, size, type, modified date, the name of the person who modified the page, the page URL, and comments for the page. The file list can be sorted in any of these categories, which is quite handy for large webs. A pop-up menu, shown in Figure 1.8, appears when you right-click on a selected filename.

To display your pages in Summary View on the right side of the FrontPage Explorer screen, use one of two procedures:

- ❑ Choose View I Summary View.
- ❑ Click the Summary View button on the FrontPage Explorer toolbar.

Displaying the Status Bar and Toolbar

The FrontPage Explorer has a status bar and toolbar that can be displayed or hidden.

The status bar is located at the bottom of the FrontPage Explorer workspace and provides brief descriptions of what each menu command or toolbar button accomplishes. To display the status bar in the FrontPage Explorer, choose View I Status Bar. Repeat the command to hide the status bar.

Figure 1.8.

Summary View is especially handy when your web contains many pages, images, and files.

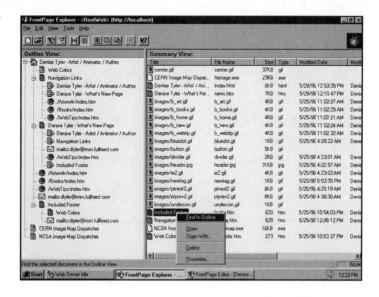

The FrontPage Explorer toolbar, shown in Figure 1.9, is located beneath the Menu List. The buttons on the toolbar provide quick access to the commands you most commonly use in the FrontPage Explorer. To display the toolbar in the FrontPage Explorer, choose View I Toolbar. Repeat the command to hide the toolbar.

Figure 1.9.

The FrontPage Explorer's toolbar provides quick access to the most commonly used commands.

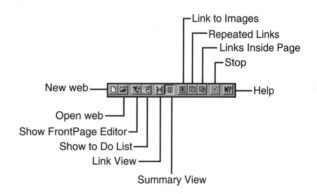

You'll find 11 commands on the FrontPage Explorer toolbar:

New Web. Creates a new web on your server.

Open Web. Opens an existing web on your server.

Show FrontPage Editor. Opens the FrontPage Editor, which allows you to create and edit pages.

Show To Do List. Displays the To Do List. If none exists, the button is disabled.

Link View. Displays a view of links to and from a page.

Summary View. Displays a list of the pages in your web and allows you to sort the list in several ways.

Links to Images. Displays links to the images on your pages in Outline or Link View.

Repeated Links. Displays repeated links on a single page in Outline or Link View.

Links Inside Page. Displays links to bookmarks on a page in Outline or Link View.

Stop. Stops the network operation that is currently in progress.

Help. Displays help for the menus, windows, and buttons in the FrontPage Explorer.

Importing and Exporting Pages

To include files in your web pages or make them available for download by end users, you need to import files into your web. To accomplish this task, perform five steps:

TIP: The easiest way to import existing pages that you have out on the World Wide Web already is to first use an FTP program to place the files in a directory or directories on your local computer. Then, you can use the File | Import command to import the pages and images into your FrontPage web.

1. From the FrontPage Explorer, choose File | Import. The Import File to Web dialog box appears. (See Figure 1.10.)

NOTE: Files already listed in the Import List are files that were previously selected for importing but have not yet been imported into your web. Files remain on the Import List until you import or remove them from the list.

2. Click the Add File button to select files to add to your Import List. The Add File to Import List dialog box appears.

3. Type the name of the file you want to import or use the Look in box to select a file from a drive and directory on your hard drive. Multiple files can be selected as follows:

    ❏ To select a contiguous range of files, press the Shift key while using the mouse or arrow keys to extend the selection.

❏ To select any of the files from the list, press the Ctrl key while clicking each file you want to select.

After you select your files from the directory, click Open to add the selected files to the Import List. You'll return to the Import File to Web dialog box.

Figure 1.10.
The Import File to Web dialog box.

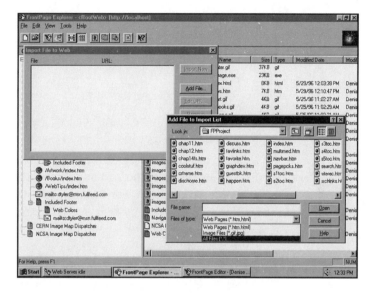

4. To import your files to the web, click Import Now. As the files are imported to your web, they are removed from the import list.

5. Click Close to exit the Import File to Web dialog box.

You should keep in mind a few important points when you import pages and images into your web. By default, web pages (`.htm` or `.html` extension) are placed into the main directory of your current web. Images are placed in an images subdirectory beneath that.

If your existing directory structure differs, it's easiest to edit the URLs of the pages before they are imported into your web. For example, assume that you have existing Web pages on the World Wide Web that do not exist on a FrontPage-enabled Web server. The main pages of this site are placed in its root directory. Beneath the root directory, you have a subdirectory called Interests, which contains pages that describe your hobbies and interests. You have another subdirectory called Inventions, which contains pages that describe some of your original inventions and creations. Your images are stored in a subdirectory called Graphics. To ensure that the links between these pages are not broken, you need to duplicate the same directory structure in your FrontPage web.

You can use the Edit URL button in the Import File to Web dialog box to place the imported files into the appropriate directories in your FrontPage web. However, the directories must already exist in your web to use this button.

NOTE:
You can also create subdirectories in your web and rename or move a page at a time after the files are imported into your web. See "Renaming or Moving Pages" later in this chapter.

To duplicate the directory structure in your FrontPage web, follow these steps:

1. Create a new web in the FrontPage Explorer. Import the main pages that exist in the root web of your original web site into this directory.

2. Switch to the Windows Explorer (Windows 95) or the File Manager (Windows NT) to duplicate the existing directory structure beneath your new FrontPage web directory. For example, your new FrontPage web is located in the C:\FrontPage Webs\Content\MyNewWeb directory on your hard drive. Create three new subdirectories beneath this directory, naming them Interests, Inventions, and Graphics.

3. Switch back to the FrontPage Explorer and use the File I Import command to import the files from your original web directories—Interests, Inventions, and Graphics—into your FrontPage web. The files are added to the import list.

4. After files are placed in your Import List, use the Edit URL button in the Import File to Web dialog box to direct each page or image to the correct subdirectory. Edit the URL of each page in the Edit URL dialog box shown in Figure 1.11. You can copy portions of a URL from the dialog box and paste them as necessary when you edit each page URL.

5. After all the URLs are correctly edited, use the Import Now button in the Import File to Web dialog box to import the files to the Web. The files are imported into your new FrontPage Web site one by one and are placed into the appropriate directories at the same time.

Figure 1.11.
You can use the Edit URL dialog box to import pages into directories that exist beneath your web directory.

To remove a file from the Import List, follow four steps:

1. From the FrontPage Explorer, choose File I Import. The Import File to Web dialog box appears.
2. Select the file or files you want to remove from the Import List.
3. Click the Remove button.
4. Click Close to exit the Import File to Web dialog box.

To save a copy of a page to a hard drive on your local or network computer, use the File I Export command in the FrontPage Explorer. The original page remains in your current web. Follow four steps:

1. From the FrontPage Explorer, choose File I Export Selected. The Export Selected As dialog box appears.
2. Use the Save In box to locate the folder on your hard drive to which you want to store the page or file.
3. Use the File Name field to change the name of the file, if desired.
4. Click Save to export the file.

Selecting Pages

You can open more than one page at a time in the FrontPage Editor. One easy way to open multiple pages is to select them from the FrontPage Explorer as follows:

❏ To select a single page, click on a page in any view. You can use the arrow keys in Outline and Summary View to change your selection.

❏ To select a contiguous range of pages in Summary View, click on one end of the range and click on the other end while pressing the Shift key.

❏ To select any set of pages, press the Ctrl key while clicking on the pages you want to select.

After you select the pages, click and drag the selection of pages into the FrontPage Editor. Release the mouse button in the FrontPage Editor window. Each page is retrieved from the server and opened in the Editor. This method allows you to work within several pages at a time.

Renaming or Moving Pages

When you rename or move a file in your web, you should follow five steps to change any links on the pages in your web that reference the file you want to rename or move:

1. In the FrontPage Explorer, select the file you want to move or rename from any view.
2. Choose Edit I Properties or right-click on the name or icon of the page and choose Properties from the pop-up menu.

3. In the Properties dialog box, select the General tab.

4. In the Page URL field, edit the URL of the page. If you want to move the file to a different directory, precede the filename by the directory into which you want to move it. If the directory does not exist in your current web, FrontPage creates it for you.

5. Click OK. If there are existing links to the page that you are moving or renaming, FrontPage asks if you want to update the links on the pages.

   ❏ Choose Yes to update the links on all the pages in your web. FrontPage corrects the links on the other pages and saves them along with the renamed or moved page. This maintains the link structure of all the pages in your web.

   ❏ Choose No to move or rename the file without updating the links. Any pages that contained a link to that page show a broken link.

Exiting the FrontPage Explorer

To exit the FrontPage Explorer, choose File I Exit. Before you exit, FrontPage closes the current web.

FrontPage Editor Basics

The FrontPage Editor is used to create your web pages. Although you can use the FrontPage Editor as a stand-alone editor, in most cases you get far more benefit from the FrontPage Editor when you use it in conjunction with the FrontPage Explorer.

NOTE: Framesets rely on creating links between other pages in your current web, so you need to have a web opened in the FrontPage Explorer. To learn more about frames, see Chapter 14, "Frames—Pages with Split Personalities."

The FrontPage Editor is a WYSIWYG editor, meaning that what you see on your page is a good representation of how the page looks on the web using the most popular browsers. Figure 1.12 shows a web page and graphics as they appear in the FrontPage Editor. Individual browsers handle certain features differently (tables are a good example), so it's wise to keep a variety of browsers on hand to fully test your pages before you send them out.

Bear in mind also, as you design your pages, that each visitor who navigates to your site can control how he or she views your page. A user can customize the text size, font, color, link colors, viewing of graphics, and more in his or her browser. There isn't much you can do about this except be aware that it happens and offer alternatives in case a user chooses to turn off the graphics.

Figure 1.12.
You create and edit pages in the FrontPage Editor.

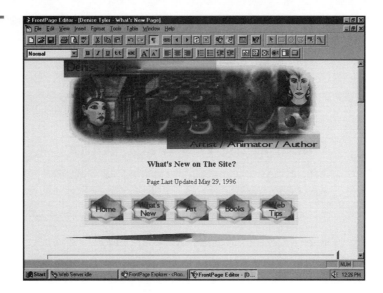

The FrontPage Editor does a great job of conforming to standards and generating "legal" HTML code. It makes your job a lot easier as a result: You can create forms and frame sets in a flash, add color and emphasis to text, add images, create image maps and transparent GIFs, and use a host of other great features, all without touching a bit of HTML code. You can view the code, though, by using the View I HTML command in the FrontPage Editor. An example is shown in Figure 1.13.

Figure 1.13.
You can view the code of your pages using the View I HTML command.

Learn how to use the HTML Markup bot in Chapter 21, "Using Your Own HTML Code."

Of course, you will occasionally want to implement features beyond those supported by the FrontPage Editor. In addition, if the pages you import contain features beyond those that are supported, you want to "protect" them from being checked for compliance in the FrontPage Editor. You use the HTML Markup bot in these cases. Insert your code into the dialog box shown in Figure 1.14, and you're on your way.

Figure 1.14.

The HTML Markup bot allows you to incorporate features beyond those supported by the FrontPage Editor.

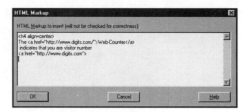

Opening the FrontPage Editor

To open the FrontPage Editor from Windows, choose Microsoft FrontPage | FrontPage Editor from the Start menu.

To open the FrontPage Editor from the FrontPage Explorer, use one of two methods:

- ❏ Choose Tools | Show FrontPage Editor.
- ❏ Click the FrontPage Editor button on the Explorer toolbar.

Pages—How to Use Them

Throughout this book, you'll use the FrontPage Editor to generate pages that can be saved to your web. You'll learn how to create pages from templates and wizards and how to create pages on your own. The pages range from simple, text-only pages to those with advanced features, such as forms, frames, and tables, that enhance your page layout. You begin each page with the File | New command in the FrontPage Editor. The rest can be as straightforward or as creative as you choose.

Windows to Your Pages

When you have several pages open at once in the FrontPage Editor, you can arrange the windows to overlap each other or to tile in the FrontPage Editor workspace:

- ❏ To display all your open pages in overlapping windows, choose Window | Cascade.
- ❏ To arrange all your open pages so that they do not overlap, choose Window | Tile.
- ❏ Use the Arrange Icons command to arrange the icons of minimized pages at the bottom of the FrontPage Editor's window. To arrange the icons, choose Window | Arrange Icons.

Displaying the Status Bar and Toolbars

Like the FrontPage Explorer, the FrontPage Editor has a status bar and toolbars that can be displayed or hidden.

❏ The status bar provides descriptions of the menu commands and toolbar buttons. To display the status bar in the FrontPage Editor, choose View I Status Bar. Choose the command again to hide the status bar.

❏ To display a toolbar in the FrontPage Editor, choose View and select the toolbar you want to display. You can tear off the toolbars and float them above your pages, as shown in Figure 1.15.

NOTE:
To return toolbars back to their positions in the FrontPage Editor menu area, click the floating toolbar and drag it back into the menu area. An outline of the toolbar follows your cursor. Position the outline where you want the toolbar to appear, and release the mouse button.

Figure 1.15.
You can float the toolbars above your pages by tearing them off the main interface.

Standard Toolbar

The Standard toolbar, shown in Figure 1.16, provides a quick way to access common page creation and editing commands. To display this toolbar, choose View I Standard Toolbar.

Figure 1.16.
The Standard toolbar.

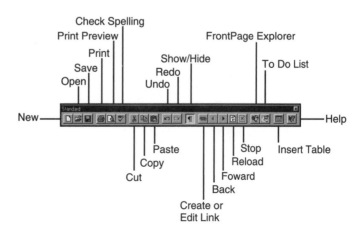

The Standard Toolbar contains 21 buttons:

New. Creates a new normal page.

Open. Opens an existing page.

Save. Saves the active page to the currently open web.

Print. Prints the active page.

Print Preview. Displays a full preview of your page.

Check Spelling. Runs the FrontPage Editor spell checker.

Cut. Cuts the selected content and puts it into the Clipboard.

Copy. Copies the selected content and puts it into the Clipboard.

Paste. Pastes the contents of the Clipboard onto your page at the current insertion point.

Undo. Reverses the last action. Up to 30 levels can be undone.

Redo. Redoes the last undone action.

Show/Hide. Shows or hides paragraph marks, form outlines, and other guides in the page.

Create or Edit Link. Creates or edits a link from the selected text or image.

Back. When using the FrontPage Editor to follow links, returns to the previous page in the Link History List.

Forward. When using the FrontPage Editor to follow links, goes to the next page in the Link History List.

Reload. Reloads the current page.

Stop. Stops the network operation currently in progress.

FrontPage Explorer. Shows or opens the FrontPage Explorer.

To Do List. Displays the To Do List. If none exists, the button is disabled.

Insert Table. Displays the Insert Table dialog box, where you specify the properties of a table that is inserted into your page.

Help. Displays help for the menus, windows, and buttons in the FrontPage Editor.

Format Toolbar

The Format toolbar, shown in Figure 1.17, contains buttons that access text and paragraph style formatting commands. To display or hide the Format Toolbar, choose View I Format Toolbar. The Format toolbar contains 15 buttons:

Figure 1.17.
The Format toolbar.

Learn how to format paragraphs and text in Chapter 9, "Composing and Editing Page Content."

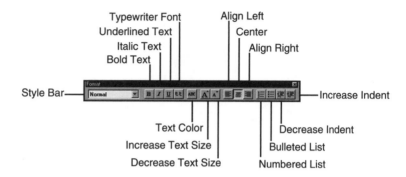

Style Bar. Allows you to choose normal text, headings, and list styles.

Bold Text. Formats text as bold (uses the <STRONG> tag).

Italic Text. Formats text as italic (uses the <EM> tag).

Underlined Text. Underlines text.

Typewriter Font. Formats text as typewriter font (uses the <TT> tag).

Text Color. Brings up the Color dialog box, which allows you to specify a different color for the text.

Increase Text Size. Increases the size of the text to a maximum size of 7. Default normal text size is 3 (12 point).

Decrease Text Size. Decreases the size of the text to a minimum size of 1.

Align Left. Aligns text or images to the left margin.

Center. Centers text or images between the left and right margins.

Align Right. Aligns text or images to the right margin.

Numbered List. Formats text as a numbered list.

Bulleted List. Formats text as a bulleted list.

Decrease Indent. Decreases the indentation of the paragraph or list item.

Increase Indent. Increases the indentation of the paragraph or list item.

Image Toolbar

The Image toolbar, shown in Figure 1.18, provides commands that allow you to create image maps and transparent GIFs. To display or hide the Image toolbar, choose View I Image Toolbar. The Image toolbar contains six buttons:

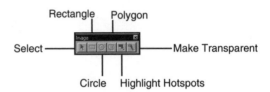

Select. Selects a hotspot on the image.

Rectangle. Draws a rectangular hotspot on the image.

Circle. Draws a circular hotspot on the image.

Polygon. Draws a polygonal hotspot on the image.

Highlight Hotspots. Highlights the hotspots on the image.

Make Transparent. Makes all pixels of a selected color in an image transparent.

Forms Toolbar

The Forms toolbar, shown in Figure 1.19, provides commands that allow you to place form fields on your page. To display or hide the Forms toolbar, choose View I Forms Toolbar. The Forms toolbar contains six buttons:

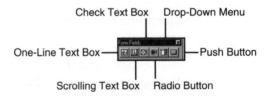

One-Line Text Box. Creates a one-line text-entry field in the form.

Scrolling Text Box. Creates a multiline text-entry box with scrollbars in the form.

Check Text Box. Adds a checkbox to the form.

Radio Button. Adds a radio button option field to the form.

Drop-Down Menu. Adds a drop-down menu to the form.

Push Button. Adds a pushbutton to the form.

Printing Your Web Pages

You can print your pages from the FrontPage Explorer. When the pages print, all text and images (with the exception of your background image) are printed. You can preview one or two pages before you print them.

Previewing a Printed Page

To preview your pages before they are sent to the printer, follow two steps:

1. Choose File | Print Preview or click the Print Preview button. The pages display in the preview similar to the way they display in a word processor, and they are paginated and assigned page numbers as required. An example is shown in Figure 1.20. You can use the buttons on the toolbar to print the page, navigate to the next and previous pages, display one or two pages in the preview, and zoom in or out from the page view.

2. Click Close when you're done previewing the page.

Figure 1.20.

You can preview one or two pages before they are printed.

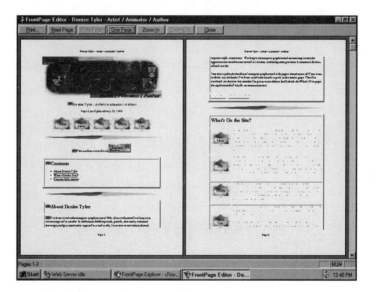

Printing Your Page

To print your page, use the File | Print command. If you need to specify margins or special printing options, complete steps 1, 2, and 3 of the following nine steps:

1. Choose the File | Page Setup command to specify a header and footer and set up the print margins for your printed pages.

2. Choose Options from the Print Page Setup dialog box to select printer options from the Print Setup dialog box shown in Figure 1.21.

3. Click OK to close the Print Setup and Print Page Setup dialog boxes.

Figure 1.21.
You can specify printer settings using the Print Setup dialog box.

4. In the FrontPage Editor, choose File I Print or click the Print button on the Standard toolbar. The Print dialog box appears.

5. If you want to print your page to a file, choose Print to File from the Printer section; otherwise, skip to the next step.

6. In the Print Range section, choose the range of pages you want to print.

7. In the Copies section, choose the number of copies of the page you want to print.

8. Click Collate if you want to collate multiple printouts (printer must support collation).

9. Click OK.

Exiting the FrontPage Editor

To exit the FrontPage Editor, choose File I Exit. FrontPage prompts you to save changes to any pages edited since the last save.

Workshop Wrap-Up

Now you have a general idea of what the FrontPage Explorer and the FrontPage Editor do and how they work together to help you manage and build your web site. You'll learn far more in the rest of this book about how to use these tools to build your own web sites.

Chapter Summary

This chapter introduced you to the FrontPage Explorer and the FrontPage Editor. You learned how you can use them together to build a web site on your local computer, how to import existing content into your webs, and how to print your web pages to your printer.

Next Steps

The chapters in this book are arranged in five sections that guide you from the most basic steps to publishing your web pages on the Internet. In brief, you learn the following in each section:

❏ Use the chapters in Part I, "Fast Track to Webs and Pages," to learn how to use the FrontPage web and page templates and wizards to generate web content quickly and easily.

❏ Use the chapters in Part II, "Basic Techniques," to learn how to add text, images, and links to your pages.

❏ Use the chapters in Part III, "Advanced Techniques," to learn how to use tables and frames in your pages, how to automate your pages with some of the FrontPage bots, and how to configure FrontPage to be used with other editors and types of content.

❏ Use the chapters in Part IV, "Still More Advanced Techniques," to learn how to design and configure forms that you can use in your site. The chapters in this section use features that require your server to have FrontPage Server Extensions installed.

❏ Use the chapters in Part V, "Putting It All Together," for information on how to administer your web, how to use the FrontPage Server Extensions, and how to test and publish your web.

Q&A

Q: Do I have to use the FrontPage Explorer while I develop my Web site?

A: You don't have to, but if you don't there will be some types of pages you won't be able to create, such as frames. The FrontPage Explorer is what sets FrontPage apart from other Web page editors. As your site grows, you'll realize how much easier the FrontPage Explorer makes it to manage your site.

Q: Why do I have to run the FrontPage Server while developing my site?

A: Think of the FrontPage Personal Web Server as your own little Internet on your own computer. As you develop your pages and links, the FrontPage Explorer uses the running server to make sure they work. You can also use your browser to connect to your internal Web site and browse through it in real, runtime mode, exactly as you would see it on the Web. This gives you the opportunity to fully test your site before you publish it on the Web. You can also use this same server software if you want people to dial in through the Internet to your local computer (you would probably want a dedicated phone line and dedicated Internet connection for this, though).

Q: What makes the FrontPage Server Extensions so special, and why are they necessary?

A: The FrontPage Server Extensions allow you to apply advanced features to your web site, including special access permissions and custom scripts that tell forms what to do and how to run. These features might otherwise require you to write custom scripts and are implemented at times by bots in FrontPage. FrontPage knows how to handle these bots, but the software on your remote server won't know how to unless the extensions exist on that side as well. Chapter 24, "Working with the FrontPage Servers," provides more details on this topic.

Q: Does this mean that to develop a Web site with FrontPage I have to use a provider that has the FrontPage Server Extensions?

A: Not necessarily, but to achieve the most benefit and ease of use with the package, that would be preferable. If you know how to write your own scripts to handle advanced features, you can do that instead. I've noted throughout this book when a feature requires the FrontPage Server Extensions.

As far as using the bots, you can use those discussed in Chapter 15, "Automating Pages with Bots," whether or not the Server Extensions exist on your remote site. Again, refer to Chapter 24 for more-detailed information on what you can and can't use without the Server Extensions.

TWO

Let's Get Personal

"Hey, do you have a home page on the Net yet?"

You probably hear this a lot. It seems that everyone wants a home page on the Internet. Today, having a home page is the greatest thing since sliced bread. It rates right up there with having your own pager as the status symbol of the decade.

If you are like me, you put it off for a long time. You look through all the shelves of books at your local computer store that focus on developing Web pages, and your eyes glaze over. "Good grief!", you think. "This stuff isn't as easy as I thought it would be. Look at all those tags and the syntax. How on earth am I going to remember all that? And when I look at my pages in my browser, they don't look at all how I thought they would. I think I'm going to give up."

Well, good news is in store. FrontPage is here. You don't have to worry about all the tags. You can say good-bye to the syntax, because you don't touch a bit of that code unless you really want to. You also work on your pages in an environment that shows you exactly how they will look in the most popular browsers. FrontPage is even kind enough to take you through the process of creating a home page. How lucky can you get?

Getting Personal the Quick Way

The quickest way to create a home page is to use FrontPage's Personal Web template to generate a web that contains a single page. It is your home page. It is a lean and mean page, void of graphics and fancy multimedia. Don't let appearances fool you, though. By the time you finish this book, you will know how to make this simple page fancier. With the Personal Web template, you can put something on the Net and finally say, "Yes, I do have a home page."

 # Creating a Personal Web

To develop a home page with the Personal Web template, first open the FrontPage Explorer. Then follow these steps:

1. From the FrontPage Explorer, choose File | New Web (Ctrl+N). The New Web dialog box appears.

2. In the Template or Wizard field, highlight Personal Web.

3. Choose OK to continue. The New Web from Template dialog box appears.

4. In the Web Server field, enter the name of the Web server on which your new web will be stored, or choose from the list of servers that you have already created.

5. In the Web Name field, enter a name for the web. Choose OK to create your Web site.

Is that it? It sure is. Once you complete these steps, the FrontPage Explorer transfers files from the `\Program Files\Microsoft FrontPage\Webs\Homepage.tem` directory into your web. While this occurs, messages in the status bar indicate that the Web server is busy. After you see the `Web Server Idle` message, the personal web appears in the FrontPage Explorer window.

One Web page is created in the personal web's root directory. This file, named `index.htm`, is titled My Home Page. It contains the following features:

Think of a bookmark as a named placeholder for a section on your page. You can use a bookmark to jump to a specific section within the same page or on another page. See Chapter 8, "Getting from Here to There," for more information.

Contents: This section contains a bulleted list of links to the other sections on your page (see Figure 2.1). This is accomplished through the use of *bookmarks*.

Employee Information: This section shows your title and key responsibilities. It has a link to your department or workgroup's home page, a link to your manager's home page, and links to the home pages of the people who work for you. (See Figure 2.2.)

Figure 2.1.
The Contents section of the home page contains links to the other sections on the page.

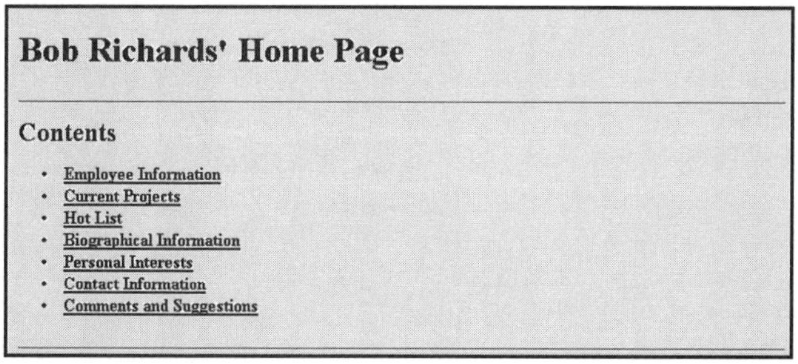

> **Bob Richards' Home Page**
>
> **Contents**
>
> - Employee Information
> - Current Projects
> - Hot List
> - Biographical Information
> - Personal Interests
> - Contact Information
> - Comments and Suggestions

Figure 2.2.
The Employee Information section displays your job title, responsibilities, and links to related pages.

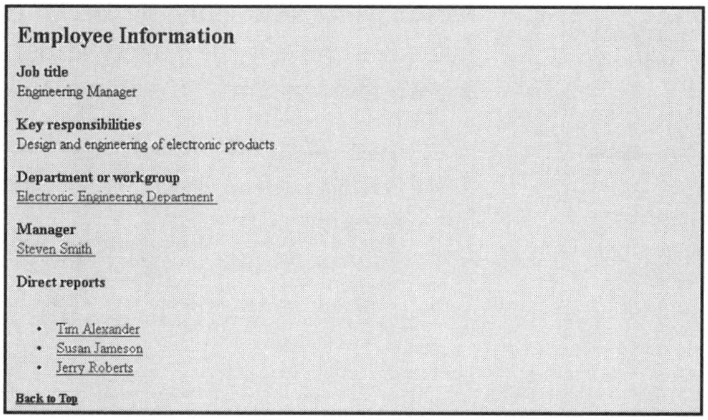

> **Employee Information**
>
> **Job title**
> Engineering Manager
>
> **Key responsibilities**
> Design and engineering of electronic products
>
> **Department or workgroup**
> Electronic Engineering Department
>
> **Manager**
> Steven Smith
>
> **Direct reports**
>
> - Tim Alexander
> - Susan Jameson
> - Jerry Roberts
>
> **Back to Top**

Current Projects: In this section, you highlight what you are currently working on. (See Figure 2.3.)

Hot List: In this section, you add links to your favorite sites on the Web. This section provides the links in a bulleted list. (See Figure 2.3.)

Figure 2.3.
The Current Projects sections shows what you are currently working on, and the Hot List provides links to your favorite sites on the Web.

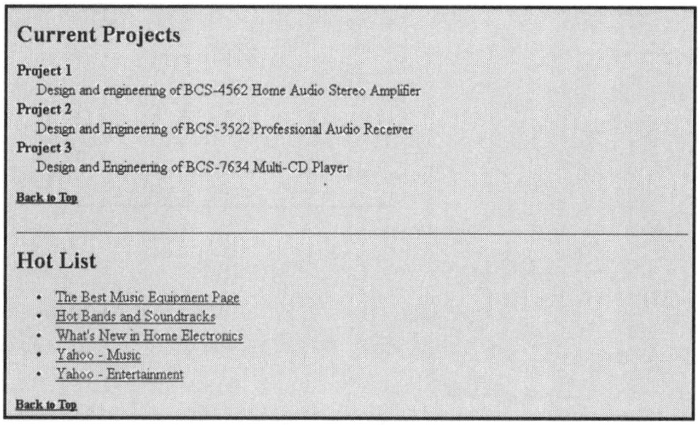

> **Current Projects**
>
> **Project 1**
> Design and engineering of BCS-4562 Home Audio Stereo Amplifier
> **Project 2**
> Design and Engineering of BCS-3522 Professional Audio Receiver
> **Project 3**
> Design and Engineering of BCS-7634 Multi-CD Player
>
> **Back to Top**
>
> **Hot List**
>
> - The Best Music Equipment Page
> - Hot Bands and Soundtracks
> - What's New in Home Electronics
> - Yahoo - Music
> - Yahoo - Entertainment
>
> **Back to Top**

Biographical Information: This section lists the companies for which you have worked and your responsibilities there. (See Figure 2.4.)

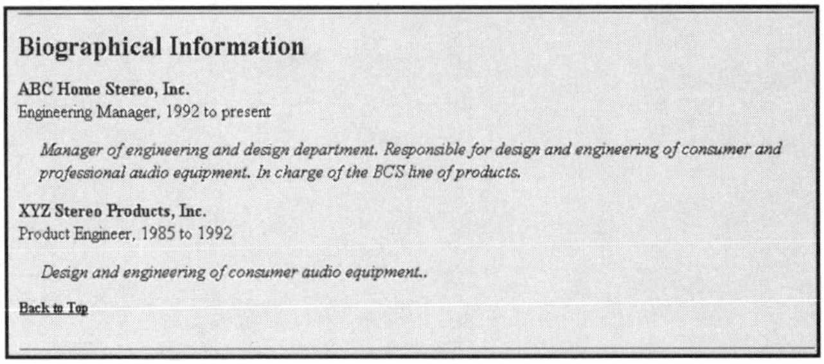

Figure 2.4.
The Biographical Information section provides your employment history.

Biographical Information

ABC Home Stereo, Inc.
Engineering Manager, 1992 to present

  Manager of engineering and design department. Responsible for design and engineering of consumer and professional audio equipment. In charge of the BCS line of products.

XYZ Stereo Products, Inc.
Product Engineer, 1985 to 1992

  Design and engineering of consumer audio equipment..

Back to Top

Use definition lists when you need to provide a description for a list item. See Chapter 10, "Organizing Information with Lists," for more information.

Personal Interests: In this section, you enter some of your interests. (See Figure 2.5.) Beneath the Interest heading, you describe what interests you and why. This information is arranged in a *definition list*.

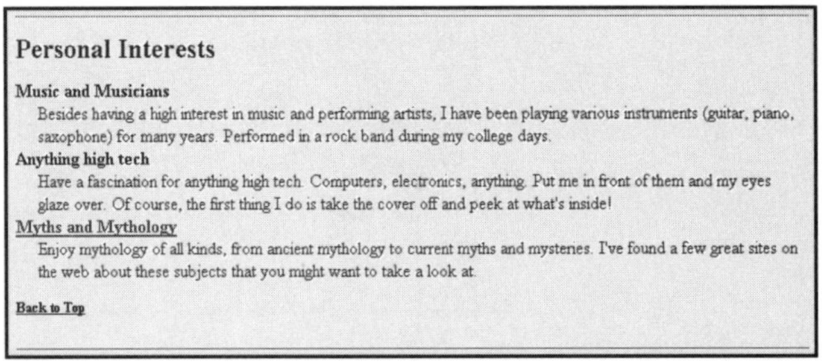

Figure 2.5.
The Personal Interests section lists your hobbies and other interests.

Personal Interests

Music and Musicians
  Besides having a high interest in music and performing artists, I have been playing various instruments (guitar, piano, saxophone) for many years. Performed in a rock band during my college days.
Anything high tech
  Have a fascination for anything high tech. Computers, electronics, anything. Put me in front of them and my eyes glaze over. Of course, the first thing I do is take the cover off and peek at what's inside!
Myths and Mythology
  Enjoy mythology of all kinds, from ancient mythology to current myths and mysteries. I've found a few great sites on the web about these subjects that you might want to take a look at.

Back to Top

Contact Information: This section provides links to your e-mail and Web addresses. It also shows your office telephone number. (See Figure 2.6.)

Figure 2.6.
The Contact Information section has links to your e-mail and Web addresses.

Contact Information

Electronic mail address
brichards@www.provider.com

Web address
http://www.bigcorp.com

Office phone
212-555-1212

Back to Top

The Save Results Bot is a form handler that requires the FrontPage Server Extensions to be present on the target server. See Chapter 20, "Runtime Bots: The Heartbeat of FrontPage Forms," for more information.

TIP: Use caution when you place contact information other than your e-mail or Web addresses. You might get telephone calls and letters that you don't expect.

Comments and Suggestions: The Comments and Suggestions section has a form that enables visitors to tell you what they think of your Web site. (See Figure 2.7.) This section uses a Save Results bot. The results of this form are stored in a text database file called homeresp.txt, which is created and updated on your Web site as comments are received.

Figure 2.7.
The Comments and Suggestions form enables people who visit your site to submit their comments to you.

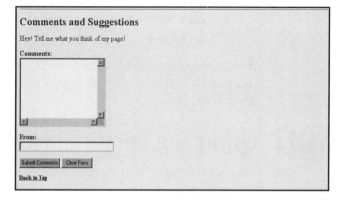

When you create a web using the Personal Web template, the FrontPage Explorer also creates a subdirectory named /images, in which any images that you import into your web are stored. An Under Construction icon is placed in this directory for you.

Getting Personal the Custom Way

Is there more in the personal web's home page than you care to share? Do you want to arrange the information differently? By using the Personal Home Page Wizard, you can customize your personal home page. For the most part, the home page contains the same content as in the Personal Web template, but the wizard enables you to display the information differently. You also can eliminate entire sections.

Most likely, you will start with a personal home page and add other pages to your Web site. To accomplish this, you can start with an empty web, to which you add your home page.

 # Creating an Empty Web

The Empty Web template creates a Web site that contains no documents. It is the best place to start when you want to design a Web site from the ground up. It is also a good web to start with if you want to import existing content into a FrontPage web.

To create an empty web, follow these steps:

1. From the FrontPage Explorer, choose File I New Web. The New Web dialog box appears.
2. From the Template or Wizard list, highlight Empty Web. Choose OK to continue. The New Web from Template dialog box appears.

3. In the Web Server field, enter the name of the Web server on which your new web will be stored, or choose from a list of servers that you have already created.

4. In the Web Name field, enter a name for the web.

5. Choose OK to create your web.

The empty web appears in the FrontPage Explorer window after you see a Web Server Idle message in the status bar. At this point, you can use the FrontPage Editor to add pages to your web.

Using the Personal Home Page Wizard

You use the Personal Home Page Wizard to create a customized home page for your Web site quickly and easily. The Personal Home Page Wizard guides you through several choices for your home page.

You are asked what types of sections you want on your page. Based on your choices, you are guided through several options to customize the appearance of your page.

To create a customized home page using the Personal Home Page Wizard, open the FrontPage Editor.

1. From the FrontPage Editor, choose File I New, or use the shortcut Ctrl+N. The New Page dialog box appears.

2. From the New Page dialog box, highlight the Personal Home Page Wizard and choose OK. The first screen of the Personal Home Page Wizard appears.

Choosing Your Sections

In the first screen of the Personal Home Page Wizard, you choose the sections that you want to appear in your home page. The section names are the same as those created with the Personal Web template. A progress bar, located beneath the options list, gives you an idea of how far along you are.

Navigation buttons appear at the bottom of the wizard screen. Click the Cancel button to exit the wizard at any time. Use the Back button to review or change the choices that you have already made. Click the Finish button from any wizard screen to generate a page with the choices that you have made so far. Click the Next button to proceed with the Personal Home Page Wizard.

Every Home Page Needs a Name

In the second screen of the Personal Home Page Wizard, you assign a URL (filename) and title to your page.

Enter a filename for the page in the Page URL field. The name `index.htm` is entered by default. Filenames are restricted to eight characters plus three letters for the extension in the Personal Home Page Wizard. Enter a title for the page in the Page Title field. The page in the previous figures is titled Bob Richards' Home Page; you might want to name yours similarly. After you assign the URL and enter your title, click Next to continue.

TIP: If you are familiar with the Internet, you have probably used Web searches to find pages. These searches typically use information from the page title. You should title your page with something descriptive so that people know whose home page they are going to.

Where You Work

If you include an Employee Information section on your home page, the wizard asks you to choose what fields you want to appear. Figure 2.2 shows a page generated with the Personal Web template; use it as a guide. The information is the same as what appears when you generate a page with the Personal Home Page Wizard. You can select any of these options: job title, key responsibilities, department or workgroup, manager, and direct reports. Click Next to continue.

Are You Busy?

If you include a Current Projects section on your home page, you can enter a list of the projects that you are working on.

TIP: If you are working on a hot Web site that you want everyone to see, provide a link to it in the Current Projects section.

After you enter the projects that you are working on, you can choose how to display the information. The default choice is a definition list, as in Figure 2.3. The information can also appear in a bulleted or numbered list. Figure 2.8 shows projects arranged in a bulleted list. Figure 2.9 shows projects arranged in a numbered list.

Figure 2.8.
Current projects are displayed in a bulleted list.

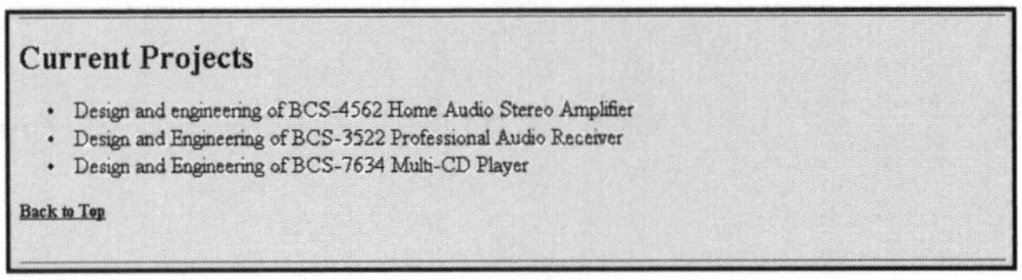

> **Current Projects**
>
> - Design and engineering of BCS-4562 Home Audio Stereo Amplifier
> - Design and Engineering of BCS-3522 Professional Audio Receiver
> - Design and Engineering of BCS-7634 Multi-CD Player
>
> Back to Top

Figure 2.9.
Current projects are displayed in a numbered list.

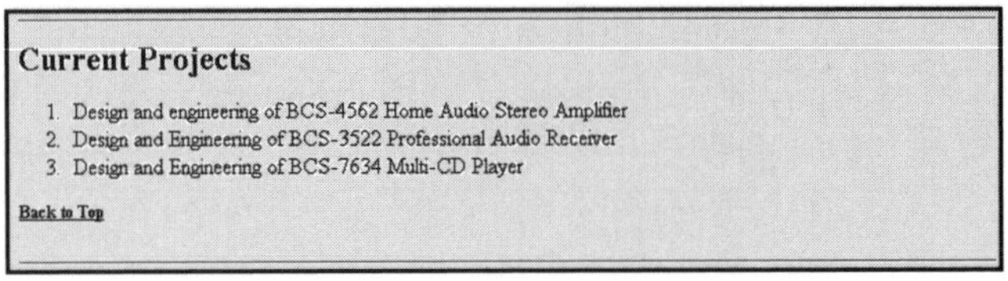

> **Current Projects**
>
> 1. Design and engineering of BCS-4562 Home Audio Stereo Amplifier
> 2. Design and Engineering of BCS-3522 Professional Audio Receiver
> 3. Design and Engineering of BCS-7634 Multi-CD Player
>
> Back to Top

How to Present Your Links

You can select the format for your hot list. You also can import a hot list from a browser that can export hot lists or favorite places into an HTM file.

You choose one of the following types of styles.

- ❑ **Bulleted list.** Hot list items appear on individual lines of a bulleted list on your page, as in Figure 2.3.
- ❑ **Numbered list.** Hot list items appear on individual lines of a numbered list on your page, as in Figure 2.10.

Figure 2.10.
You can display links in a numbered list.

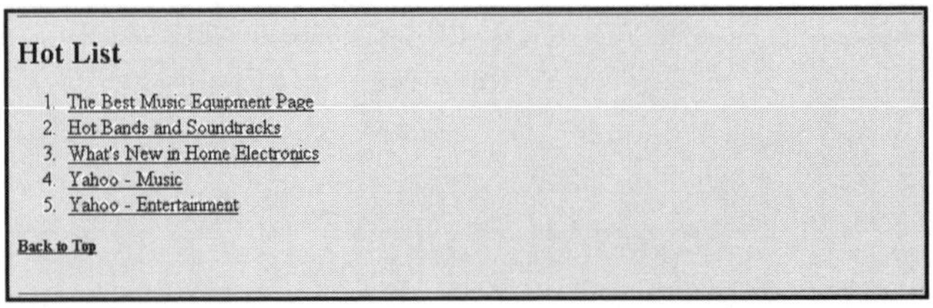

> **Hot List**
>
> 1. The Best Music Equipment Page
> 2. Hot Bands and Soundtracks
> 3. What's New in Home Electronics
> 4. Yahoo - Music
> 5. Yahoo - Entertainment
>
> Back to Top

- ❑ **Definition list.** Hot list items appear in a definition list on your page. You can add a description of each site beneath its name, as shown in Figure 2.11.

Figure 2.11.
Use a definition list to describe what you like about your favorite sites.

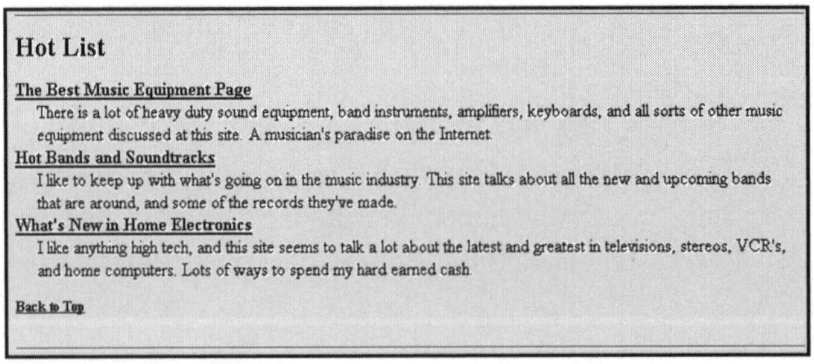

> **Hot List**
>
> **The Best Music Equipment Page**
> There is a lot of heavy duty sound equipment, band instruments, amplifiers, keyboards, and all sorts of other music equipment discussed at this site. A musician's paradise on the Internet.
> **Hot Bands and Soundtracks**
> I like to keep up with what's going on in the music industry. This site talks about all the new and upcoming bands that are around, and some of the records they've made.
> **What's New in Home Electronics**
> I like anything high tech, and this site seems to talk a lot about the latest and greatest in televisions, stereos, VCR's, and home computers. Lots of ways to spend my hard earned cash.
>
> Back to Top

❑ **Import from Web Browser.** If you choose this option, type the directory and filename of the HTM file that you want to import in the field provided, or click the File button to browse through the appropriate directory. Choose the HTM file that contains your hot list items. After the page is generated, the items appear on your page in a bulleted list.

TIP:
If you use Netscape 2.0 for a browser, you can save its bookmarks into a hot list by opening your bookmark list in Netscape with the Bookmarks I Go To Bookmarks command. Then choose File I Save As to save the bookmark list in HTM format.

Click Next to continue.

What's in the Biography?

If you have a Biographical Information section on your home page, you can choose what type of biographical information to include. The wizard has three categories of information.

❑ **Academic.** This option places headings for academic information (such as institution, dates of attendance, and degrees or positions) on your page. Figure 2.12 shows an example of academic information.

Figure 2.12.
You can place academic information on your home page.

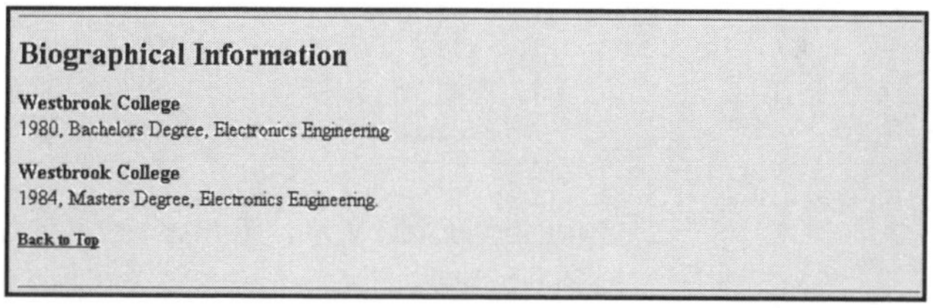

Biographical Information

Westbrook College
1980, Bachelors Degree, Electronics Engineering

Westbrook College
1984, Masters Degree, Electronics Engineering

Back to Top

❑ **Professional.** This option places professional information on the page, as in Figure 2.4.

❑ **Personal.** You can also place personal milestones or interesting events on your home page. Figure 2.13 shows an example of personal information.

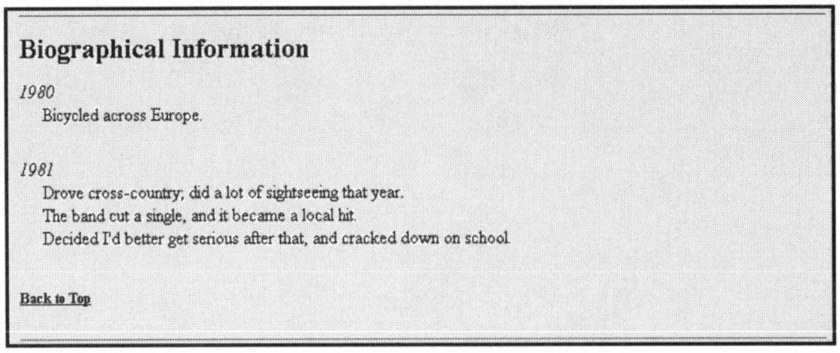

Figure 2.13.
The Personal Biographical section shows milestones or major events.

Click Next to continue.

What Else Do You Like?

If you include a Personal Interests Section on your home page, enter a list of them in the area provided. Begin each item on a separate line. Figure 2.14, for example, has three items: Music and Musicians, Anything high tech, and Myths and Mythology.

After you enter your interests, choose how you want them to appear. The three possible formats are

❏ **Bulleted list**. Your interests appear on individual lines of a bulleted list, as in Figure 2.14.

Figure 2.14.
Personal interests displayed in a bulleted list.

❏ **Numbered list**. Your interests appear on individual lines of a numbered list, as in Figure 2.15.

Figure 2.15.
Personal interests displayed in a numbered list.

❏ **Definition list**. Your interests appear in a definition list, as in Figure 2.5.

Click Next to continue.

Where Can People Reach You?

When you use the Personal Home Page Wizard, you can add contact information. Figure 2.16 shows the fields from which you can choose. They are

Postal address

Email address

URL address

Office telephone number

Fax number

Home telephone number

Figure 2.16.

Contact information can be as complete—or as sparse—as you want.

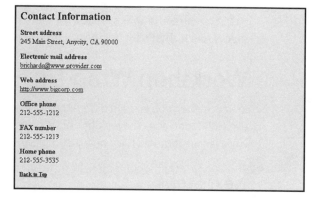

Click Next to continue.

Storing Your Visitors' Suggestions

If you include a Comments and Suggestions form on your page, you choose the format in which the data is received. You can retrieve the information from your customers in one of the following three ways:

❏ **Use form, store results in data file**. Comments and suggestions that you receive from your home page are stored in a text file on your site.

❏ **Use form, store results in Web page**. Comments and suggestions that you receive from your home page are stored in a Web page on your site in HTM format.

❏ **Use link, send e-mail to this address**. This option enables site visitors to e-mail their comments and suggestions to you. Enter your e-mail address in the data entry field. A link to your e-mail address appears on your page.

Click Next to continue.

What Do You Want First?

Examples of the various types of results files are shown in Chapter 20, "Runtime Bots: The Heartbeat of FrontPage Forms."

The Personal Home Page Wizard enables you to rearrange the order of the sections on your home page. Simply highlight the option that you want to move, and click the Up or Down button to change the location in which the section appears. Click Next to continue.

That's It! You're Done!

The final screen of the Personal Home Page Wizard informs you that you have completed all the questions required to generate your page. Click the Finish button to create your page. Use the File | Save command to save your home page to the empty web. You can add graphics, customize the information on the page, and add your own special touch. That's the fun part.

Workshop Wrap-Up

In this chapter, you learned different ways to generate a home page in the blink of an eye with FrontPage. They might not be the most eye-catching home pages that you will ever see, but you have only just begun.

Next Steps

No doubt, you want to edit the content on your personal home page. With FrontPage, you can customize your page exactly as you want it to appear. You can add or delete content, add graphics and colored text, and do a great deal more. In the next chapter, you learn how to add a discussion group—your own personal message center—to your Web site.

- ❏ To change or add to the links on your page, see Chapter 8, "Getting from Here to There."
- ❏ To edit the text content on the page, see Chapter 9, "Composing and Editing Page Content."
- ❏ To add graphics and other enhancements to your page, see Chapter 11, "Sprucing Up Your Pages."
- ❏ To learn how the Comments and Suggestions form works, see Chapter 20, "Runtime Bots: The Heartbeat of FrontPage Forms."

Q&A

Q: Do I have to name my home page `index.htm`?

A: FrontPage uses the filename `index.htm` by default for any home page. When FrontPage sees a file by that name, it knows that the file is the home page and uses a home page icon (a house) to designate it as such. Some Internet service providers require that you name your home page something other than index.htm (`index.html`, `default.htm`, and `intro.htm` are common names). Chapter 23, "Web Maintenance and Administration" outlines the procedure you use to specify a different home page name. To rename the page (especially if you have other pages in your web that are linked to it) use the Edit I Properties command in the FrontPage Explorer. This enables you to update the links on other pages in your web that point to the page.

Q: I put my home page on my Web site, and I'm getting feedback that the form doesn't work. Why?

A: The main reason might be that the FrontPage Server Extensions do not exist on your target server. For the forms to work, they need a form handler, which is explained in more detail in Chapter 20. It is common for Web developers to write their own form handlers through CGI scripts. FrontPage's form bots serve the same function and save you the tedious task of writing a form handler yourself. Your target server must know how to communicate with the bots. This is why they also need the server extensions on their end. Chapter 24, "Working with the FrontPage Servers," discusses the FrontPage Server Extensions that are available to Internet service providers.

THREE

Can We Talk?

In the "old days," people relied on bulletin boards for communicating with others in the local community. They made for a cozy atmosphere. If the local BBS sysops were savvy, they tied into larger networks that enabled users to communicate with people all over the place.

The times are changing. The Internet is changing how people communicate with one another in a big way. Newsgroups enable you to exchange messages with people from all over the world on a vast assortment of topics. There are thousands of newsgroups on topics such as business, technology, and a vast assortment of personal interests.

FrontPage offers several ways to include discussion groups on your Web site. Think of discussions as your own personal newsgroups. They enable visitors to your site to communicate with you and one another through *articles*—messages that are stored on your Web site. You can use discussion groups to reach out and touch someone on a very big party line.

In this chapter, you

- ❏ Create discussion groups on your Web site
- ❏ Examine the contents of the Customer Support Web
- ❏ Examine the contents of the Project Web
- ❏ Create discussion groups using the Discussion Web Wizard

Tasks in this chapter:

- ❏ Creating a Web with a Template
- ❏ Creating a Discussion with the Discussion Web Wizard
- ❏ Using the Discussion Web Wizard

You learn how to create a protected Web in Chapter 6, "Real-Life Examples."

What if you do want a party line, but prefer to keep the discussion quiet and closed? You do that by creating a discussion group on a protected Web, to which only registered users can gain access with a password. This opens up all sorts of possibilities for you, whether you want to reach out to the public or prefer to communicate internally with your employees on business matters.

Creating a Web with a Template

FrontPage comes with two Web templates that contain discussion groups: the Customer Support Web and the Project Web. To create either web:

1. From the FrontPage Editor, choose File I New Web. The New Web dialog box appears.
2. In the Template or Wizard field, highlight the type of web that you want to create.
3. Click OK. The New Web from Template dialog box appears.
4. In the Web Server field, enter the name of your server name or choose one from the drop-down list.
5. In the Web Name field, enter a name for the web. The name must comply with the conventions used on the server. Keep the length of the name, the character restrictions, and case sensitivity in mind when you name your web.
6. Click OK to create the Web site.

Supporting Your Customers (Without Really Trying)

The Customer Support Web template is designed to provide customer support for a software company. Of course, you can easily modify it to suit your needs. The pages created with this template demonstrate the power of many of FrontPage's features. The Web consists of two sections: general pages and discussion pages.

After you create the web with a template, the FrontPage Explorer imports several pages from the customer support Web template directory. If you installed FrontPage using the default settings, the files are located in your `Program Files\Microsoft FrontPage\Webs\Custsupp.tem` directory. Figure 3.1 shows the Customer Support Web displayed in the FrontPage Explorer's summary view.

Figure 3.1.

The Customer Support Web, shown here in the FrontPage Explorer's summary view, contains several pages that form a discussion site on your web.

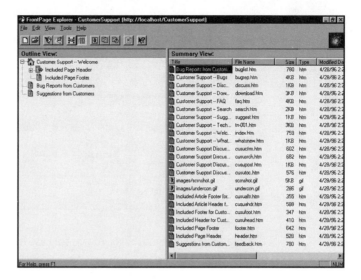

TIP: When there are several pages in a web, it is much easier to view their contents in summary view. While in summary view, you can sort the contents by title, filename, size, type of file, date when last modified, or page URL. To view Web contents in summary view, use the View | Summary View command from the FrontPage Explorer, or click the Summary View icon in the Explorer toolbar.

While in summary view, you can still see links to pages in the outline view at the left portion of the screen. To find a page in the outline, simply right-click its title in the summary view. A menu appears; choose the Find in Outline command.

On the Surface

The main section of the Customer Support Web contains several pages of a general nature. Users are welcomed to the site. They can submit and read software bug reports, ask questions about the software, make suggestions for improvements, search for topics, read technical notes, and learn what is new at the site.

Figure 3.2 shows the home page for the Customer Support Web (`index.htm`). Key features include a welcome message that contains company information. The header and footer that appear on this page are included on all the pages in the main section.

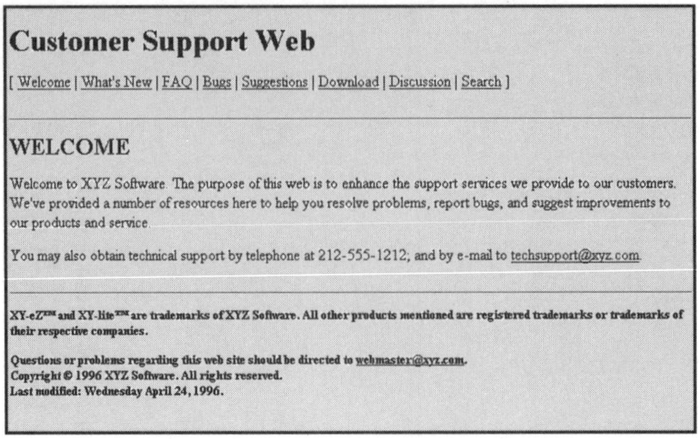

Figure 3.2.

The Customer Support—Welcome page describes the purpose of the Web site.

Customer Support Web

[Welcome | What's New | FAQ | Bugs | Suggestions | Download | Discussion | Search]

WELCOME

Welcome to XYZ Software. The purpose of this web is to enhance the support services we provide to our customers. We've provided a number of resources here to help you resolve problems, report bugs, and suggest improvements to our products and service.

You may also obtain technical support by telephone at 212-555-1212; and by e-mail to techsupport@xyz.com.

XY-eZ™ and XY-lite™ are trademarks of XYZ Software. All other products mentioned are registered trademarks or trademarks of their respective companies.

Questions or problems regarding this web site should be directed to webmaster@xyz.com.
Copyright © 1996 XYZ Software. All rights reserved.
Last modified: Wednesday April 24, 1996.

The Bugs page (`bugrep.htm`) is what visitors use to submit bug reports to the Web site. It consists of several parts. The first part, shown in Figure 3.3, states the purpose of the page.

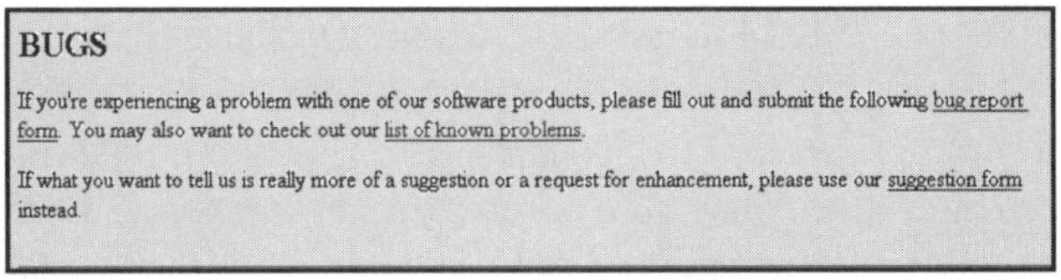

Figure 3.3.

The first part of the Customer Support—Bugs page mentions the purpose of the page.

BUGS

If you're experiencing a problem with one of our software products, please fill out and submit the following bug report form. You may also want to check out our list of known problems.

If what you want to tell us is really more of a suggestion or a request for enhancement, please use our suggestion form instead.

The next part of the page, shown in Figures 3.4 and 3.5, contains a form that visitors complete to report bugs in the software. You can change the fields to suit your particular needs.

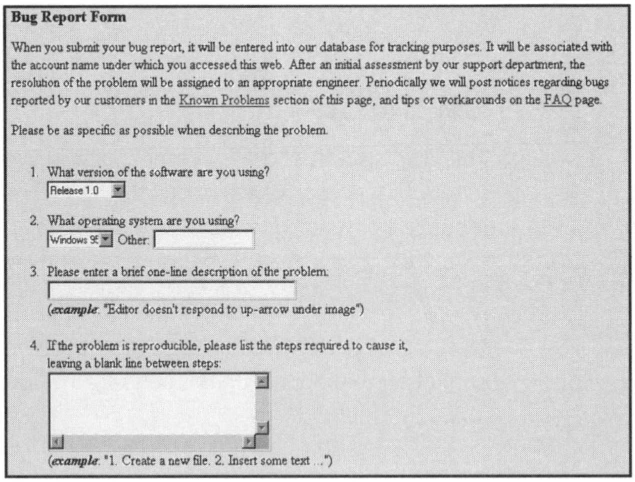

Figure 3.4.

The top portion of the Bug Report Form.

To learn how to modify the fields in a form, refer to Chapter 19, "Fields—The Building Blocks of Forms."

Bug Report Form

When you submit your bug report, it will be entered into our database for tracking purposes. It will be associated with the account name under which you accessed this web. After an initial assessment by our support department, the resolution of the problem will be assigned to an appropriate engineer. Periodically we will post notices regarding bugs reported by our customers in the Known Problems section of this page, and tips or workarounds on the FAQ page.

Please be as specific as possible when describing the problem.

1. What version of the software are you using?
   [Release 1.0 ▼]

2. What operating system are you using?
   [Windows 95 ▼] Other: [   ]

3. Please enter a brief one-line description of the problem:
   [   ]
   (*example*: "Editor doesn't respond to up-arrow under image")

4. If the problem is reproducible, please list the steps required to cause it, leaving a blank line between steps:
   [   ]
   (*example*: "1. Create a new file. 2. Insert some text ...")

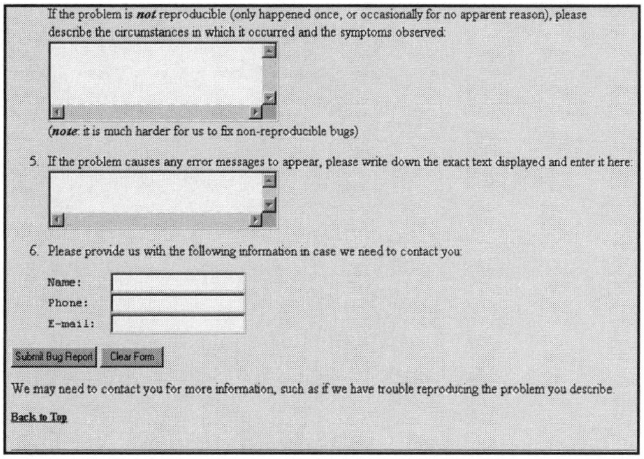

Figure 3.5.
The bottom portion of the Bug Report Form.

> If the problem is *not* reproducible (only happened once, or occasionally for no apparent reason), please describe the circumstances in which it occurred and the symptoms observed:
>
> (*note*: it is much harder for us to fix non-reproducible bugs)
>
> 5. If the problem causes any error messages to appear, please write down the exact text displayed and enter it here:
>
> 6. Please provide us with the following information in case we need to contact you:
>
> Name:
> Phone:
> E-mail:
>
> Submit Bug Report   Clear Form
>
> We may need to contact you for more information, such as if we have trouble reproducing the problem you describe.
>
> Back to Top

NOTE: To use any of the forms included in these discussion groups on your site, you must have the FrontPage Server Extensions on your target server or use a custom CGI script. For more information on these topics, refer to Chapter 20, "Runtime Bots: The Heartbeat of FrontPage Forms."

Beneath the Bug Report Form is a section where you can post known problems with software. Figure 3.6 shows an example. When the bugs mentioned on this page are fixed, you should provide a link to the Download page so that your customers can update their software.

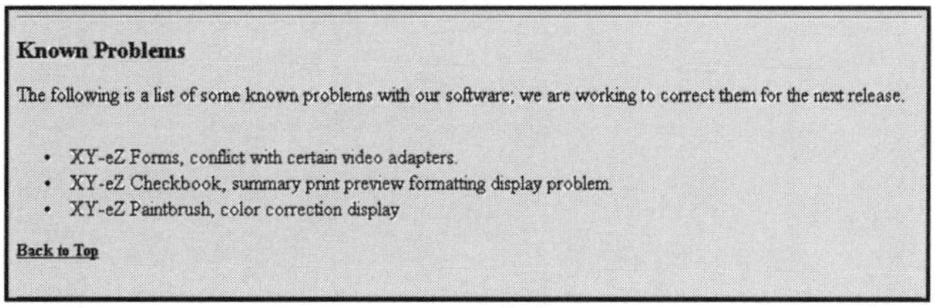

Figure 3.6.
A list of known problems with your software appears on the page.

> **Known Problems**
>
> The following is a list of some known problems with our software; we are working to correct them for the next release.
>
> - XY-eZ Forms, conflict with certain video adapters.
> - XY-eZ Checkbook, summary print preview formatting display problem.
> - XY-eZ Paintbrush, color correction display
>
> Back to Top

Bug reports submitted with the Customer Support Bugs page are placed in the Bug Reports from Customers page (`buglist.htm`). Initially, this page is blank, as in Figure 3.7. As customers report software bugs, the content automatically changes.

Figure 3.7.
Bug reports are automatically inserted into the Bug Reports from Customers page.

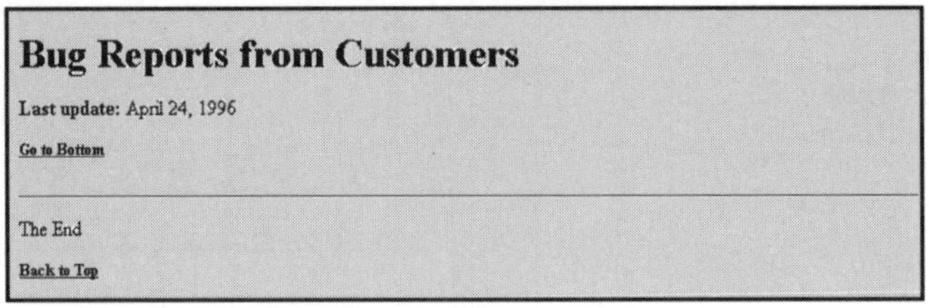

Bug Reports from Customers

Last update: April 24, 1996

Go to Bottom

_____

The End

Back to Top

The Download page (`download.htm`), shown in Figures 3.8 and 3.9, informs the customer of files available for download. The contents area provides links to the files mentioned on the page. Customers can download the files from this page. Beneath the download area is a description of the file formats used.

Figure 3.8.
The top portion of the Download page lists and describes the files available for download.

DOWNLOAD

This page contains links to files we are making available for FTP download. Click on the appropriate link under the *Formats* section of a file's description to begin downloading.

A definition of the file formats is available at the bottom of this page. All file sizes are approximate.

Contents

- XY-eZ Forms Maintenance Update 1.1b
- XY-eZ Checkbook Maintenance Update 1.1e
- XY-eZ Paintbrush Maintenance Update 1.2a

XY-eZ Forms Maintenance Update 1.1b (xyfrm11b.zip or xyfrm11b.tar.Z)

Corrects conflicts with S3 video adapters.

Formats: .zip (169 k), .tar.Z (327 k).
Last updated: April 23, 1996

XY-eZ Checkbook Maintenance Update 1.1e (xychk11e.zip or xychk11e.tar.Z)

Corrects summary print preview formatting problem.

Formats: .zip (384 k), .tar.Z (492 k).
Last updated: April 9, 1996.

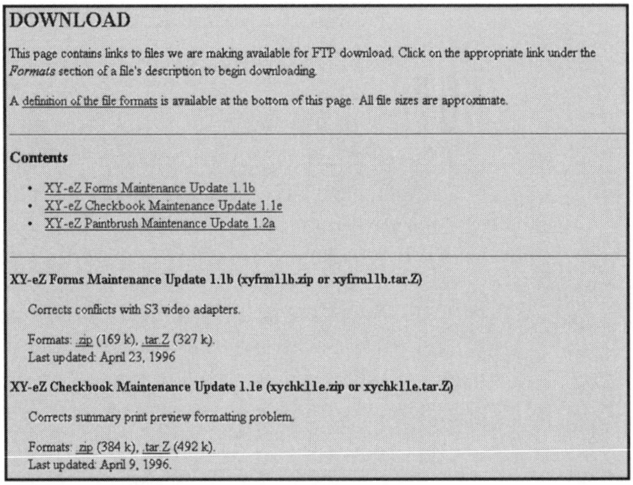

Figure 3.9.
The bottom portion of the Download page describes the file formats available for download.

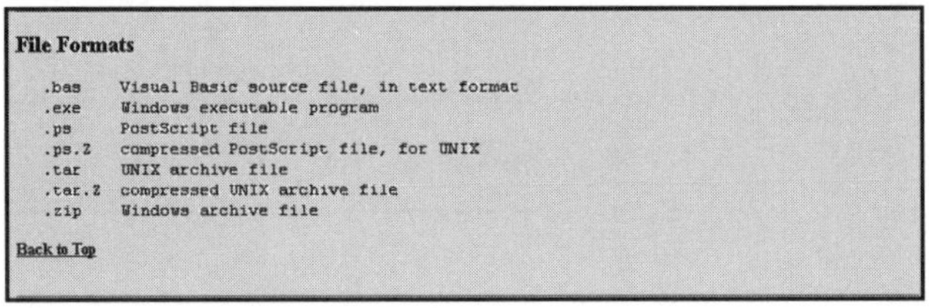

File Formats

```
.bas    Visual Basic source file, in text format
.exe    Windows executable program
.ps     PostScript file
.ps.Z   compressed PostScript file, for UNIX
.tar    UNIX archive file
.tar.Z  compressed UNIX archive file
.zip    Windows archive file
```

Back to Top

The Frequently Asked Questions page is similar to the one shown in Chapter 5, "Lots of Pages—The Template Way."

The Frequently Asked Questions page (`faq.htm`) provides answers to the questions that the company's technical support staff is most often asked. The page includes hyperlinks and bookmarks.

The Suggestions page (`suggest.htm`), shown in Figure 3.10, enables customers to offer ideas for enhancing products or improving services. The results obtained from this form are placed on the Suggestions from Customers page (`feedback.htm`). Changes are updated automatically for you.

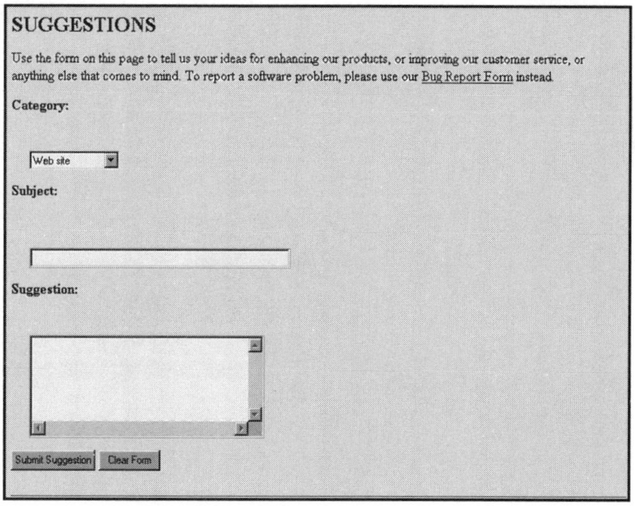

Figure 3.10.
The Suggestions page enables customers to suggest improvements for your products.

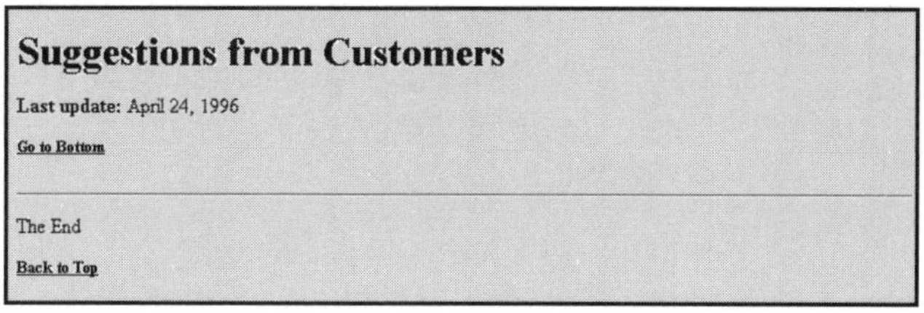

SUGGESTIONS

Use the form on this page to tell us your ideas for enhancing our products, or improving our customer service, or anything else that comes to mind. To report a software problem, please use our Bug Report Form instead.

Category:

[Web site ▼]

Subject:

[   ]

Suggestion:

[   ]

[Submit Suggestion] [Clear Form]

Figure 3.11.
The Suggestions from Customers page updates the suggestions received from customers and places them on the page automatically.

Suggestions from Customers

Last update: April 24, 1996

Go to Bottom

The End

Back to Top

You learn how to create your own Search page in Chapter 22, "Real-Life Examples."

The Search page (`search.htm`) has a text search engine for the Customer Support Web. Visitors can search for a word or phrase on your site. The results appear with links to the appropriate pages.

The Tech Note page (`tn-001.htm`), shown in Figures 3.12 and 3.13, provides information on how to perform a process or resolve a problem with software. It begins with a summary of the tech note, and then it outlines the procedure. A sample screen shot is included on the page as a placeholder.

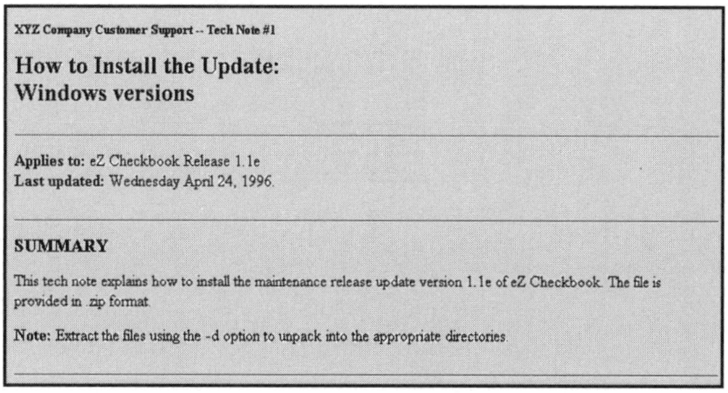

Figure 3.12.
The top portion of the Tech Note page mentions the software to which the note applies and summarizes what the tech note is for.

XYZ Company Customer Support -- Tech Note #1

How to Install the Update: Windows versions

Applies to: eZ Checkbook Release 1.1e
Last updated: Wednesday April 24, 1996.

SUMMARY

This tech note explains how to install the maintenance release update version 1.1e of eZ Checkbook. The file is provided in .zip format.

Note: Extract the files using the -d option to unpack into the appropriate directories.

Figure 3.13.

The lower portion of the Tech Note page outlines the procedure for completing a process.

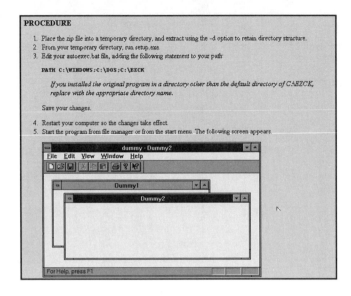

You learn how to create your own What's New page in Chapter 17, "Real-Life Examples."

The What's New page (`whatsnew.htm`) provides an up-to-date listing of what is new on the Customer Support Web. As you make changes to the site, inform visitors of them on this page.

Figure 3.14 shows the Included Page Header (`header.htm`) and the Included Page Footer (`footer.htm`), which appear on all the pages. The header provides links to all the main pages in the site, which ensures consistency and easy navigation. The footer contains trademark information and a link to the Webmaster's e-mail address. Copyright information and the date when the page was last modified also appear in the footer.

Figure 3.14.

The Included Page Header and the Included Page Footer appear on all the pages.

In Chapter 6, you create a Web site that contains two discussions—one public and one private. The pages involved in the discussions are basically the same and are discussed in more detail in that chapter.

The Discussion

The Customer Support Web template generates several discussion pages. They are described in Table 3.1.

Table 3.1. Discussion pages generated by the Customer Support Web template.

Page Name	Page Filename	Description
Discussion	discuss.htm	Entry page for the discussion
Submission Form	cusupost.htm	Used for posting articles in the discussion
Confirmation Form	cusucfrm.htm	Confirms that a visitor's article has been received in the discussion
Search Form	cususrch.htm	Enables a visitor to search through posted articles for words or phrases
TOC	cusutoc.htm	Provides a table of contents for all the articles posted in the discussion; generated automatically
Included Header	cusuhead.htm	The header that appears on all pages; provides links to various pages in the discussion
Included Footer	cusufoot.htm	Puts the date when the page was last updated at the bottom of the page
Included Article Header	cusuahdr.htm	The header that appears on all the discussion articles; provides navigation links to the articles in the discussion and links for posting or replying to articles
Included Article Footer	cusuaftr.htm	Places the date when an article was submitted at the bottom of the page

Customer Support Web Images

The FrontPage Explorer created a subdirectory—`images`—beneath the Web's root directory. It is where you store any images that you import into your Web. It includes two graphics:

❑ The Under Construction icon (`undercon.gif`), which you place on the pages that are not yet completed

❑ A sample screen shot (`scrnshot.gif`), which appears on the Tech Note page and should be replaced with an appropriate graphic of your own

The Web templates give you great ideas for constructing and arranging your own site.

Project Coordination on the Web

The Project Web template creates a Web site that enables a group of individuals who are working on projects to organize their tasks. The Project Web features two discussion groups. It also discusses the members working on the project, milestones, and tasks. It is designed to be a public web, but you can modify it to coordinate internal projects. For that, you need to create a protected Web, which you learn to do in Chapter 6.

Use the File I New Web command in the FrontPage Explorer to create a Project Web. After you complete steps outlined in the "Creating a Web with a Template" task, the FrontPage Explorer transfers several files from the `Program Files\Microsoft FrontPage\Webs\Project.tem` directory, which was created during installation. The Project Web appears in the FrontPage Explorer's summary view, as shown in Figure 3.15.

Figure 3.15.

The Project Web, shown here in the FrontPage Explorer's summary view, contains pages for organizing and discussing projects on the Web.

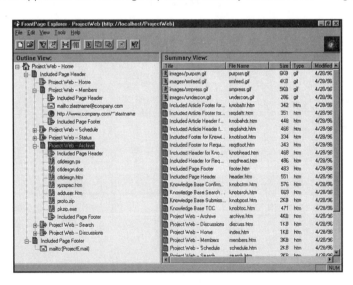

On the Surface

The main section of the Project Web contains links to the main pages in the Project Web. These pages include archives of files, links to the two discussions on the site, project schedules and status pages, and a search form.

Figure 3.16 shows the home page for the Project Web (`index.htm`). It highlights what is new on the site.

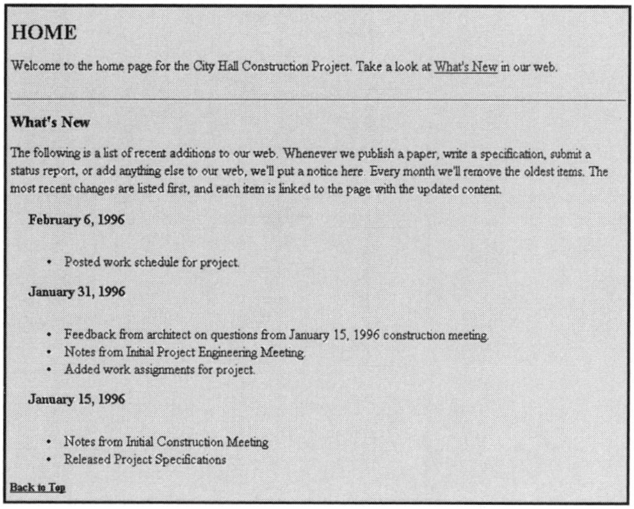

HOME

Welcome to the home page for the City Hall Construction Project. Take a look at What's New in our web.

What's New

The following is a list of recent additions to our web. Whenever we publish a paper, write a specification, submit a status report, or add anything else to our web, we'll put a notice here. Every month we'll remove the oldest items. The most recent changes are listed first, and each item is linked to the page with the updated content.

February 6, 1996

- Posted work schedule for project.

January 31, 1996

- Feedback from architect on questions from January 15, 1996 construction meeting.
- Notes from Initial Project Engineering Meeting.
- Added work assignments for project.

January 15, 1996

- Notes from Initial Construction Meeting
- Released Project Specifications

Back to Top

Figure 3.16.
The home page lists the most recent additions to the site.

The Archive page (`archive.htm`), shown in Figures 3.17 through 3.19, provides links to downloadable files in the Project Web.

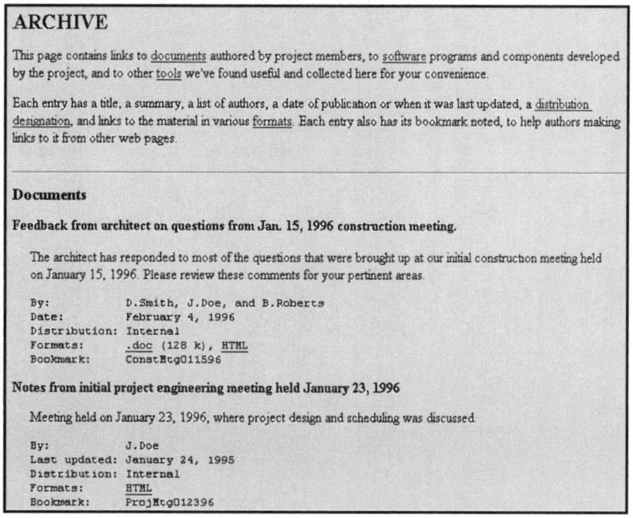

ARCHIVE

This page contains links to documents authored by project members, to software programs and components developed by the project, and to other tools we've found useful and collected here for your convenience.

Each entry has a title, a summary, a list of authors, a date of publication or when it was last updated, a distribution designation, and links to the material in various formats. Each entry also has its bookmark noted, to help authors making links to it from other web pages.

Documents

Feedback from architect on questions from Jan. 15, 1996 construction meeting.

The architect has responded to most of the questions that were brought up at our initial construction meeting held on January 15, 1996. Please review these comments for your pertinent areas.

```
By:           D.Smith, J.Doe, and B.Roberts
Date:         February 4, 1996
Distribution: Internal
Formats:      .doc (128 k), HTML
Bookmark:     ConstMtg011596
```

Notes from initial project engineering meeting held January 23, 1996

Meeting held on January 23, 1996, where project design and scheduling was discussed.

```
By:           J.Doe
Last updated: January 24, 1995
Distribution: Internal
Formats:      HTML
Bookmark:     ProjMtg012396
```

Figure 3.17.
The top portion of the Archive page contains an introduction and describes the documents that are included on the site.

Figure 3.18.
The middle portion of the Archive page lists tools that can be used to extract the archived files and explains how the files are classified.

```
Tools
PKZIP

    File compression and decompression utilities for creating archives under Windows.

    By:           PKWare
    Date:         March 17, 1995
    Distribution: External, Shareware
    Formats:      .exe (725 k)
    Bookmark:     PKZIP

Back to Top


Distribution Designations

Internal
    May only be viewed by people inside the company.
External
    May be viewed by people outside the company.
Published
    Has already appeared in an external publication.

Back to Top
```

Figure 3.19.
The bottom portion of the Archive page describes the document formats in the archives.

```
Document Format Definitions

    HTML    web page (HyperText Markup Language)
    .ps     PostScript
    .doc    Microsoft Word
    .rtf    Rich Text
    .zip    archive file for Windows
    .tar    archive file for UNIX

Back to Top
```

The Discussions page (`discuss.htm`), shown in Figure 3.20, provides links to the Knowledge Base and Requirements discussion groups.

Figure 3.20.
The Discussions page provides links to the Knowledge Base and Requirements discussion groups.

```
DISCUSSIONS

This page contains links to all of the internal discussions for this project. This discussion is maintained on a separate
protected web for internal project discussions and notes.

Requirements Discussion

    We use this discussion to record notes from architectural meetings, construction meetings and engineering
    progress meetings.

Knowledge Base

    We use this discussion to record general questions and answers that crop up in the course of working on our
    project. Appropriate topics include questions relating to installation, coordination with other contractors, and
    anything else that people in the project or interested in similar areas would find generally useful
```

The Members page (`members.htm`), shown in Figure 3.21, contains information on the members of a project team. It lists the members alphabetically and has links to each one's area on the page. The page provides each member's title, job description, and location, as well as links to his e-mail address and home page.

Figure 3.21.

The Members page highlights the people working on a project.

MEMBERS

This page contains contact information for all the members of Project. From here you can send e-mail to project members, or visit their personal home pages.

Alphabetical listing, by last name:

- Doe, John
- Roberts, Bob
- Smith, Douglas

 John Doe, Construction Manager.

Construction Manager
Home Office, Bigcity
Mail Stop 123
Extension 4437
jdoe@bccco.com
http://www.bccco.com/~jdoe

Back to Top

The Schedule page (`schedule.htm`), shown in Figures 3.22 and 3.23, lists weekly schedules, upcoming events, and key milestones for the project.

Figure 3.22.

The top portion of the Schedule page tells what is being worked on and lists upcoming meetings and events.

SCHEDULE

This page contains a list of scheduled project events, and key milestones and deliverables.

In addition, we maintain the following prioritized lists of what we're working on this week, and what we plan to do next week:

This week

1. First floor, west wing, insulation
2. Basement level, painting
3. First floor, east wing, drywalling and painting

Next week

1. First floor, west wing, drywalling and painting
2. Parking lot pavement.

Back to Top

Events

Monday 4/22/96, 1:30 pm

Monthly project review.
Location: main conference room.

Friday 4/26/96, 10:00 am

Project walkthrough with architect.

Back to Top

Figure 3.23.

The bottom portion of the Schedule page highlights milestones and deliverables.

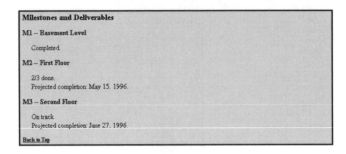

The Search page (`search.htm`) enables visitors to search through your site for text.

The Status page (`status.htm`), shown in Figure 3.24, provides links to status reports stored on your site. Status reports appear monthly, quarterly, and yearly.

Figure 3.24.

The Status page provides links to status reports stored on your site.

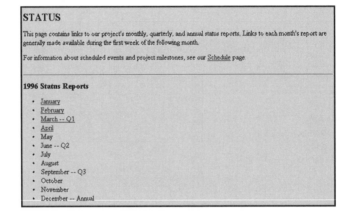

Figure 3.25 shows the Included Page Header (`header.htm`) and the Included Page Footer (`footer.htm`), which appear on all the pages. The header provides links to all the main pages in the site. The footer contains copyright information, the Webmaster's address, and the date when the page was last updated.

Figure 3.25.

The Included Page Header and the Included Page Footer appear on every page.

City Hall Construction Project Web

[Home | Members | Schedule | Status | Archive | Search | Discussions]

Copyright 1996, Big City Construction Company.
For problems or questions regarding this web contact webmaster@bccco.com.
Last updated: April 26, 1996.

The Knowledge Base

The Knowledge Base discussion group is used to record comments and questions that occur as people work on a project. The contents of its pages are similar to those in the Customer Support discussion group, as well as the discussion groups that you create in Chapter 6.

The Table of Contents page (knobtoc.htm) includes a table of contents for the articles submitted to the Knowledge Base discussion. The table of contents is generated in a file called tocproto.htm, which is placed in the _knobas subdirectory in the Project Web.

The Submission Form (knobpost.htm) enables visitors to post messages to the discussion.

The Confirmation Form (knobcfrm.htm) sends a confirmation message to visitors when they submit articles to the discussion.

The Search Form (knobsrch.htm) has a search engine that enables visitors to search the text of the articles contained in the discussion.

The Included Header (knobhead.htm) and the Included Footer (knobfoot.htm) appear on all the pages in the discussion. The header includes links to the Discussion page, the Table of Contents page, the Search Form, and the Submission Form. The footer places the date when the page was most recently updated on the bottom of the page.

The Included Article Header (knobahdr.htm) and the Included Article Footer (knobaftr.htm) are placed on all the articles in the discussion. It includes links to the Discussion page, the Table of Contents page, and the Search Form. It provides a link that enables visitors to reply to articles. The footer places the date when the article was submitted on the bottom of the page.

Project Requirements

The Requirements discussion group is used to discuss which features should be included in software products. You can customize this discussion to suit our own needs. Table 3.2 lists the pages and their URLs. They serve the same functions as in the Knowledge Base discussion. The only difference is that the table of contents for the Requirements discussion is generated in a file called tocproto.htm, which is placed in the _reqdis subdirectory in the Project Web.

Table 3.2. Pages in the Requirements discussion group.

Page Name	Page Filename
TOC	reqdtoc.htm
Submission Form	reqdpost.htm
Confirmation Form	reqdcfrm.htm
Search Form	reqdsrch.htm
Included Header	reqdhead.htm
Included Footer	reqdfoot.htm
Included Article Header	reqdahdr.htm
Included Article Footer	reqdaftr.htm

Project Web Images

The FrontPage Explorer created a subdirectory—images—beneath the web's root directory. It is where you store any images that you import into your web. It includes four graphics:

❑ The Under Construction icon (undercon.gif), which you place on the pages that are not yet completed

❑ Three small graphics (purpsm.gif, smfeed.gif, and smpress.gif), which appear on the Members page as placeholders and should be replaced with photographs of the project members

Creating a Discussion with the Discussion Web Wizard

Frames divide a single page into multiple screens that display their own content. For more information on frames, refer to Chapter 14, "Frames—Pages with Split Personalities."

You can add discussion webs to your other Webs by using the Discussion Web wizard. It enables you to customize your discussion Web before the pages are created. You can link a style sheet to your discussion pages. This, for example, enables you to use colors other than the standard World Wide Web gray. You can also place the discussion articles in frames or create a discussion on a protected web.

To create a discussion web:

1. Choose File I New Web. The New Web dialog box appears.

2. In the New Web dialog box, highlight Discussion Web Wizard.

3. Click OK. The New Web from Wizard dialog box appears.

4. In the Web Server field, enter the name of the server on which this web is created.

5. In the Web Name field, enter the name of the web. Click OK.

Using the Discussion Web Wizard

Like the Personal Web wizard, discussed in Chapter 2, "Let's Get Personal," the Discussion Web wizard guides you through the process of creating a discussion web. After you complete the initial steps outlined in the previous task, the Discussion Web wizard's introductory screen appears.

The Introductory Screen

The introductory screen of the Discussion Web wizard contains text that tells you what you are about to create. A progress bar appears beneath the picture on the left side of the dialog box. This progress bar shows you how far along you are in the process.

You can interrupt the wizard at any time. You can

❏ Click the Cancel button to exit the wizard without creating the web. The FrontPage Explorer asks whether you want to remove the empty web that was created when you began the process.

❏ Click the Back button to review or change choices that you made in previous steps.

❏ Click the Finish button to create the web with the pages you have selected so far.

Click Next to continue setting up the discussion web.

Choosing Your Pages

The second screen of the Discussion Web wizard asks what types of pages you want to include in the discussion web. After you make all your selections, click Next.

The Submission Form is included automatically. This page is named `xxxxpost.htm`, where `xxxx` is a four-letter designation assigned to your files based on the name that you give to the discussion web. It serves the same function as the submission forms already mentioned in this chapter.

The Table of Contents page is named `xxxxtoc.htm`. If you include this page in your web, a table of contents for the articles in the discussion is generated as they are submitted. The wizard suggests that you include this page.

If you include the Search Form, a file named *xxxx*srch.htm is created in your web.

If you sort discussion Web articles into threads, they are arranged by subject. All the replies to an article follow the original posting.

If you include the Confirmation Form, visitors receive a confirmation message when they submit articles to the discussion. This file is named *xxxx*cfrm.htm.

Every Discussion Needs a Name

The third screen of the Discussion Web wizard asks you to give the discussion a descriptive title. This title appears on all the pages.

Based on the title you enter, this screen displays the name of the directory in which the articles are stored. For example, if you call the discussion "Support Discussion," the subdirectory is named _supdis. This title is also used to assign the filenames. Therefore, the names of all the files in the discussion begin with supd.

Click Next to continue.

Selecting Article Headings

The fourth screen of the Discussion Web wizard asks you to choose a set of input fields for the Submission Form. The options are

- ❏ *Subject, Comments.* If you choose this option, the Submission Form includes a textbox in which the visitor enters the subject of the article and a scrolling textbox for the body of the message.
- ❏ *Subject, Category, Comments.* In addition to the subject and comments, the visitor can specify a category for the article. Categories are listed in a drop-down menu.
- ❏ *Subject, Product, Comments.* In addition to the subject and comments, the site visitor can specify a product to discuss in the article. Products are listed in a drop-down menu.

Click Next to continue.

Open or Registered

Chapter 23, "Web Maintenance and Administration," discusses using Registration bots in protected webs in more detail.

The fifth screen of the Discussion web wizard asks whether the discussion will take place on a protected web. Use a protected web if you want only registered users to post articles; a Web Self-Registration Form appears after the discussion web is generated on your site. Create a public web if you want anyone to post articles.

NOTE: With FrontPage's Personal Web Server, you cannot mix protected areas and public areas on the same Web site. If you want to create a protected discussion, you must create a separate web. Refer to Chapter 6 for complete instructions.

Sorting the Articles

The sixth screen of the Discussion Web wizard asks how the table of contents should sort the list of posted articles. Sort from oldest to newest if you want to list the articles in chronological order; this is the default selection. Sort from newest to oldest if you want the most recent postings to appear at the top of the table of contents. Click Next to continue.

Watch That Home Page

The seventh screen of the Discussion Web wizard asks whether you want the Table of Contents page for the discussion to be the home page of the web. Choose No if you are adding this web to an existing web or if there is another home page in your web. The Table of Contents page is named *xxxx*toc.htm.

Choose Yes if you do not intend to add any other web types to this discussion web. The Table of Contents page is named index.htm and is the home page in the web. The wizard reminds you that if you choose Yes, any existing file in the web named index.htm will be overwritten. You should answer No unless you are certain there will not be any additional web content or another home page in the web.

Click Next to continue.

Deciding What the Search Form Reports

The eighth screen of the Discussion Web wizard asks what information the Search Form should report for matching documents. The options are

- ❏ *Subject.* The results report only the subject of the article.
- ❏ *Subject and Size.* The results report the subject of the article and its size in kilobytes.
- ❏ *Subject, Size, and Date.* The results report the subject of the article, its size in kilobytes, and the date it was submitted.

❏ *Subject, Size, Date, and Score.* In addition to the article's subject, size, and date of posting, the results report the degree of relevance to the term or terms used in the Search Form.

Click Next to continue.

Setting Your Style

In the ninth screen of the Discussion Web wizard, you choose the color scheme for your pages. The choices that you make here are saved to your web in the Web Colors file. You base the style of your other pages on this page.

The steps are

1. To use the standard World Wide Web background and text and link colors, choose the Default radio button. Click Next to return to the wizard.

2. To assign custom colors, choose the Custom Radio Button.

3. To change the background texture, click the arrow in the drop-down menu box. A list of several choices appears. A preview of the texture appears in the preview window as you highlight each selection. Click the selection again to choose it.

4. If you want a solid background, choose None for a pattern. The Color Background option activates.

5. To change the background color, click the color square to the right of the background color heading. The Windows Color dialog box appears.

6. After you select the background color, click OK to return to the wizard.

7. To change the text colors, follow the same procedure as you did for choosing the background color. As you select your colors, they update in the preview screen. To view the active link color that you select, click and hold either link in the preview window. Release the mouse button when you are done. Click Next to continue with the wizard.

Choosing Frame Options

For more information on what frames are and what they do, refer to Chapter 14.

In the tenth screen of the Discussion Web wizard, you choose the frame options for the discussion. Frames are a relatively new addition to Web page development, and not all browsers support them. FrontPage also provides alternative choices in this screen. The frame options are

❏ *No frames.* Choose this option if you do not want your discussion articles to be displayed in frames.

❏ *Dual interface.* This is the default choice, and the best one to select if you want to take advantage of frames. Your articles are displayed in frames if the browser is frame-compatible; alternative pages appear if the browser is not.

❏ *Contents above current article.* This option places the table of contents for the discussion above the articles. When the visitor selects an article from the table of contents, it appears in the frame below the contents. No alternative pages are generated with this option.

❏ *Contents beside current article.* This option places the table of contents for the discussion on the left side of the page. When the visitor selects an article from the table of contents, it appears in the right portion of the screen. No alternative pages are generated with this option.

Click Next to continue.

That's It, You're Done!

The final screen of the Discussion Web wizard notifies you that you have answered all the questions. It reminds you of any links that you have to create on your home page. You might want to add these comments to your To Do list.

Click the Finish button to create the Web and to upload the files that you selected when you stepped through the Discussion Web wizard. If you installed FrontPage using the default settings, the files are copied from the `Program Files\Microsoft FrontPage\Webs\Vtidisc.wiz` directory on your hard drive. The discussion Web will appear in the FrontPage Explorer's outline view.

What You Get

Figure 3.26 shows the discussion Web in the FrontPage Explorer's summary view.

In addition to the files mentioned in the "Choosing Your Pages" section, the Discussion Web wizard creates four pages. They are

❏ The Included Header (*xxxx*`head.htm`) and the Included Footer (*xxxx*`foot.htm`), which are placed on the discussion Web's main pages

❏ The Included Article Header (*xxxx*`ahdr.htm`) and the Included Article Footer (*xxxx*`aftr.htm`), which are placed on the discussion articles

The pages in the discussion Web are linked together if you choose the Dual Interface option.

Figure 3.26.

The pages created with the Discussion Web wizard, shown here in summary view.

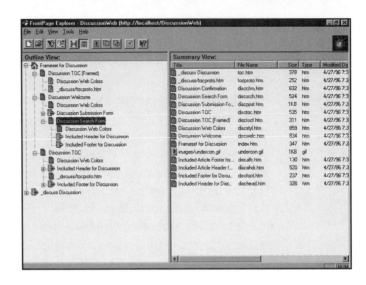

Workshop Wrap-Up

Thanks to the Internet, communicating with others will never be the same. Thanks to FrontPage's discussion templates and wizards, you can easily design custom discussion groups on your own Web site.

Chapter Summary

In this chapter, you learned how to create three different types of Web sites that contain discussion groups. Now that the page templates are there and linked for you, the fun really begins. Editing your pages is simple once you have the basic design of the Web down.

Next Steps

In the next chapter, you create a corporate presence on the Web using the Corporate Presence Web wizard. If you want to continue with what you learned in this chapter, check out the following chapters:

- ❏ Refer to Chapter 5, "Lots of Pages—The Template Way," to add other pages to your site.
- ❏ Refer to Chapter 9, "Composing and Editing Page Content," to modify the content on the page templates.

❏ Refer to Chapter 15, "Automating Pages with Bots," to use the simpler FrontPage Web bots, and Chapter 20, "Runtime Bots: The Heartbeat of FrontPage Forms," to use the bots used in the forms in this Web.

❏ Refer to Chapter 18, "Adding Interactivity—Forms the Easy Way," to add additional form fields and customized forms to your site.

❏ Refer to Chapter 23, "Web Maintenance and Administration," for information on setting up access permissions and proxy servers for your site.

Q&A

Q: Can I add other fields to the forms included in a discussion web?

A: Yes. Chapter 19, "Fields—The Building Blocks of Forms," explains how.

Q: Can I test the protected webs on my local computer before I put them on the Web?

A: Yes. You can open any web from your favorite browser and test it on your local computer as if it were the Web. First make sure that your Web server is running. Then enter a URL in your favorite browser to call in to the protected web.

Suppose, for example, that your server name is `localhost` and that your Web name is called `ProtectedDiscussion`. In your browser, you would specify a URL as follows:

```
http://localhost/ProtectedDiscussion
```

At this point, you are prompted to enter a user name and a password. Enter the name and password as it appears in the Web permissions created for you as the administrator or author. If you enter an incorrect password, a message appears stating that the authorization failed and that you will not gain access to the protected web.

CHAPTER

FOUR

If You Mean Business

Business is a growing part of the Web, and it is bound to get even bigger. Exciting developments down the road will make the Internet boom with activity. Now that the Internet is open to everyone and is coming alive with graphics and multimedia, more and more companies are jumping on the bandwagon—and doing it with style and purpose.

Think back to the days when a growing company had to design product brochures and pay for the expense of printing thousands of copies to distribute to potential customers. On top of the printing costs, the postage ate away at the budget. The Internet has changed all that. Now you can economically let everyone know that you are out there. You are telling not just your local community about yourself, but the world. There is beauty in that.

Unfortunately, the beauty is also a beast. Because of this vast accessibility, there is much competition. Therefore, you need to make the best impression that you can. With FrontPage's Corporate Presence wizard, you get off to a rapid running start. If you choose all the options in the wizard, you can generate fifteen pages, including links, in five minutes. Then all you have to do is edit the content and fill in the blanks.

In this chapter, you

- Use the Corporate Presence wizard to create a professional appearance on the Web
- Learn about some of the bots that you use to design pages
- Choose custom background colors and images and select custom text and link colors for your pages
- Learn about the To Do List
- Learn about the pages and images that the Corporate Presence wizard places in your web

Tasks in this chapter:

- Creating a Web with a Wizard
- Choosing Your Home Page Topics
- Choosing Your What's New Page Options
- Choosing More Options for Products and Services
- Choosing Feedback Page Options
- Storing Request Information
- Choosing Table of Contents Page Options
- Choosing Page Header and Footer Options
- Choosing Your Graphics Style

Preparing Your Information

For more information about substitution bots, see Chapter 15, "Automating Pages with Bots."

The Corporate Presence wizard does not do all the work for you. You might want to get the following information ready before you start the wizard. You can edit it afterward, but it is much easier to do everything in one step. Take advantage of what the wizard does for you automatically. The following information is inserted into several Corporate Presence Web pages through the use of *substitution bots*. They take information variables that you enter as you design your web and place them on your page in designated fields.

- ❏ Full name of the company
- ❏ Street address
- ❏ Telephone number
- ❏ Fax number
- ❏ Webmaster's e-mail address
- ❏ Contact person's e-mail address

Think about the contact information that you place on your pages, especially the telephone and fax numbers. Start with only e-mail addresses, and add more contact information as necessary. Your receptionist will thank you.

Creating a Web with a Wizard

If you look up the word *wizard* in the dictionary, you see that it means a magician or a conjurer. The wizards in FrontPage perform magic, and they conjure up pages that might have otherwise taken you hours to produce. Though the pages are basic, you can customize your pages afterward. When you are pressed for time, though, wizards are the way to go.

You are probably already familiar with wizards. Many software programs use them. They make a tedious task simple by asking you questions. Based on your answers, different option screens appear, and you choose what you want.

This chapter shows a Web site for a growing interior design firm, ACME Interiors. Its pages include all the available options. With this site as guide, you can start using the Corporate Presence wizard. The steps are

1. Choose File I New Web. The New Web dialog box appears.
2. In the New Web dialog box, highlight the Corporate Presence wizard. Click OK or press Enter to continue. The New Web from Wizard dialog box appears.

3. In the Web Server field, enter `localhost` or the name of the server on which you develop webs.

4. In the Web Name field, assign a name for the web. For example, enter `ACMEInteriors`. Click OK.

5. If necessary, enter your name and password in the Name and Password Required dialog box, and click OK. The introductory screen for the Corporate Presence wizard appears.

Corporate Presence the Easy Way

The first screen of the Corporate Presence wizard contains some brief introductory text. It tells you that the wizard will ask you a series of questions. Wizards are good at that; it is their job.

Beneath the picture of the open door at the left of the screen, there is a status bar. The dots in the bar tell you how far along you are.

There are buttons on the bottom of the wizard screen. Here is how you use them:

❏ *Help.* Click Help to get help with the Corporate Presence Wizard. Help mainly tells you how to replace the logo image.

❏ *Cancel.* Click Cancel at any time to exit the wizard. When you start the wizard, it initially creates an empty web until you save pages to it. You are asked whether you want to delete it. Most likely, you will answer yes.

❏ *Back.* Click Back if you want to review or change what you have already done.

❏ *Next.* Click Next to continue to the next screen.

❏ *Finish.* Click Finish from any of the wizard screens to tell the wizard to create pages with the options that you have selected so far.

 # Choosing Your Pages

Click Next now. In the second screen of the Corporate Presence Wizard, you choose the types of pages to include in your Web site. The options are

❏ Home page

❏ What's New

❏ Products and services

❏ Table of contents

❏ Feedback form

❏ Search form

For more information on Search bots, see Chapter 20, "Runtime Bots: The Heartbeat of FrontPage Forms."

A home page is required. If you select a search form, a text search page named `search.htm` is created at your site. Figure 4.1 shows an example. It enables visitors to your site to search through it for words or phrases. The text search page uses a Search bot, which places a search form with a textbox and two pushbuttons on your page.

Figure 4.1.
The text search page allows visitors to search for words or phrases in your Web pages.

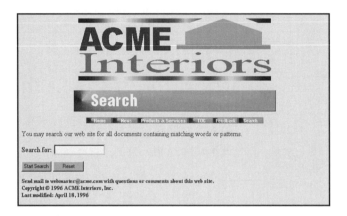

For more information on using the FrontPage Server Extensions on a remote server, refer to Chapter 24, "Working with the FrontPage Servers."

NOTE: The Search bot is a form handler. To use any of the forms that FrontPage generates, you need the FrontPage Server Extensions installed on your target server. If this is not possible, you can process the form with a custom CGI script.

After you make your selections, click Next to continue.

TASK Choosing Your Home Page Topics

The third screen of the Corporate Presence wizard asks what topics you want to include on your home page. The home page is, appropriately, the first page in your web. This is a page that should get people's attention. Tell them who you are and what you do.

Look at the examples in Figures 4.2 through 4.4. They show how a home page appears for a large interior decorating company. They show all the options that you can choose.

Annotation bots let you mark up your pages with reminders of things you need to get done. For more information, see Chapter 15, "Automating Pages with Bots."

❏ *Introduction.* The Introduction section appears immediately beneath the navigation bar in Figure 4.2. An Annotation bot appears on the page to suggest content for this section.

❏ *Mission statement.* The Our Mission section appears beneath the introduction in Figure 4.2. An Annotation bot suggests content for this section.

❏ *Company profile.* The Company Profile section, shown in Figure 4.3, provides an area where you can tell a bit about your company and what you do. An Annotation bot suggests content for this section.

❏ *Contact information.* The Contact Information section, shown in Figure 4.4, is placed on the page here with Substitution bots. An Annotation bot suggests content for this section.

Figure 4.2.

The upper portion of the home page contains the company's logo, a page title graphic, a navigation bar, the Introduction section, and the Our Mission section.

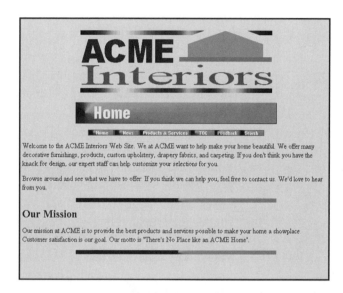

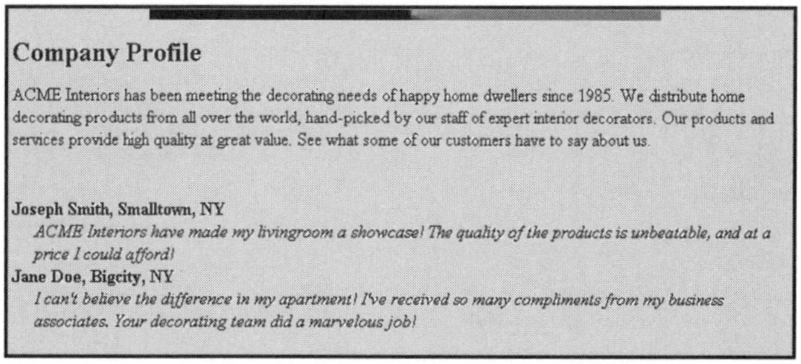

Figure 4.3.

The middle portion of the home page contains the Company Profile section.

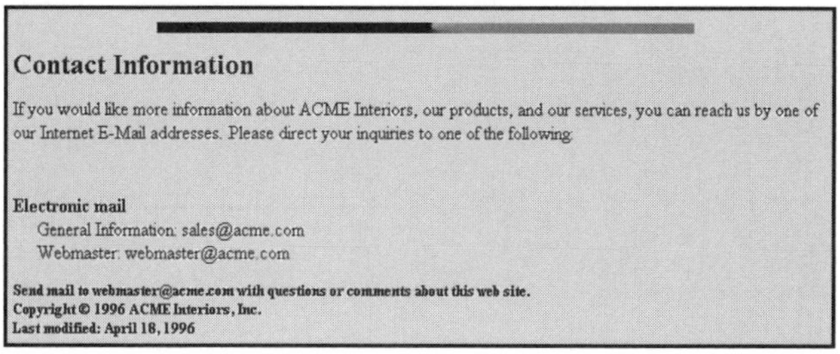

Figure 4.4.

The lower portion of the home page contains the Contact Information section and the footer.

After you make your selections, click Next to continue.

Choosing Your What's New Page Options

If you elect to include a What's New Page in your Web site, you select options for it in the fourth screen. Figures 4.5 and 4.6 show the completed What's New page for the interior decorating company. The options for this page are

❑ *Web changes.* When you choose the Web Changes option, shown in Figure 4.5, Annotation bots guide you through the information you should include. Links to a press release and a product data sheet are placed in this section for you.

❑ *Press releases.* When you choose the Press Releases option, shown in Figure 4.6, three Press Release pages are generated. Links to them appear on the What's New page. Figure 4.7 and 4.8 show a typical Press Release page. It provides announcements of important news about the company, as well as contact information.

❑ *Articles and reviews.* When you choose the Articles and Reviews option, a section titled Recent Media Coverage of Company Name appears on the What's New page. This section, shown in Figure 4.6, features a list of articles in which the interior decorating company is publicized. An Annotation bot gives instructions on what to change.

Figure 4.5.
The upper section of the What's New page includes the company's logo, a page header graphic, a navigation bar, and a Web Changes section.

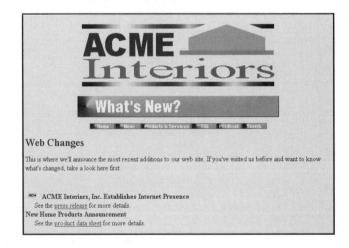

Figure 4.6.

The lower portion of the What's New page includes press releases, recent media coverage, and footer information.

Press Releases

These are the press releases we've issued over the last year. You may want to search for topics by keyword.

- April 16, 1996 -- ACME Interiors Goes National
- March 4, 1996 -- ACME Interiors Receives Award for Interior Design
- December 12, 1995 -- ACME Interiors Announces New Headquarters

Recent Media Coverage of ACME Interiors, Inc.

Articles about ACME Interiors appear in the following publications:

- *Putting It All Together*, **Home Decorating Weekly**, January 14, 1996
- *Best of the Best in Home Decorating*, **Home Decorating Weekly**, October 21, 1995
- *ACME Interiors Shows the Way*, **Bigcity News**, September 4, 1995

Send mail to webmaster@acme.com with questions or comments about this web site.
Copyright © 1996 ACME Interiors, Inc.
Last modified: April 18, 1996

Figure 4.7.

The upper portion of the Press Release page contains the company logo, the page title, and a navigation bar.

ACME Interiors

Press Release 1

Home | News | Products & Services | TBC | Feedback | Search

FOR IMMEDIATE RELEASE

Figure 4.8.

The lower portion of the Press Release page contains the press release, contact information, and footer information.

ACME Interiors Goes National

Plans for Outlet Stores Announced

April 17, 1996-- ACME Interiors, the largest home decorating firm in Anycity, NY, today announced plans to open chain outlet stores in several major cities throughout the country.

"Business is booming since we advertised our company on the Internet", says company president Jack Smith. "We have received tremendous interest from many areas in the country and see a demand for our type of services."

ACME Interiors specializes in high quality decorating products at a reasonable cost to its customers. Additionally, the company plans to have a staff of expert interior decorators in each of the outlet stores.

For More Information Contact:

ACME Interiors, Inc.
Internet: sales@acme.com

Send mail to webmaster@acme.com with questions or comments about this web site.
Copyright © 1996 ACME Interiors, Inc.
Last modified: April 18, 1996

After you make your selections, click Next to continue.

Choosing Products and Services Page Options

If you elect to include a Products and Services page in your site, you choose options for it on two screens. The first screen asks how many of each type of page you want to create.

In the Products field, enter the number of product data sheets that you want. If you enter 0, no product pages are created, and the Products and Services page is instead titled *Company Name* Services Page. Five product data sheets are created for the interior design company.

In the Services field, enter the number of service description pages that you want. If you enter 0, no service pages are created, and the Products and Services page is instead titled *Company Name* Products Page. Three service description pages are created for the interior design company.

When the Products and Services page is created, it provides links to all the product data sheets and service description pages in your Web site. Annotation bots guide you through what needs to be changed or included on this page.

Figures 4.9 and 4.10 show an example of a completed Products and Services page. In the upper portion, shown in Figure 4.9, you see a brief description of the products that the interior design company offers and links to the five pages specified in the wizard screen. In the lower portion of the page, shown in Figure 4.10, you see a brief description of the services that the company offers and links to the three service description pages. The footer appears at the bottom of the page.

Figure 4.9.

The upper portion of the Products and Services page contains the company's logo, a title graphic, a navigation bar, and links to the products pages.

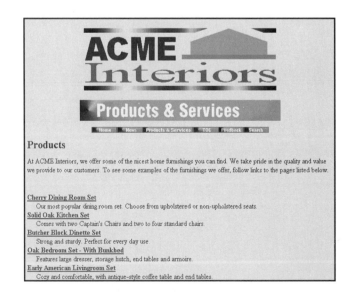

Figure 4.10.

The lower portion of the Products and Services page contains links to the service pages and footer information.

Services

If you don't have the knack for coordinating your home decorating, contact one of our staff to assist you. We offer assistance in several areas:

In-House Consultation
   A member of our interior decorating team can review your design requirements in your home.
Painting and Decorating Services
   Painting and wallpapering specialists will get the job done right, with customer satisfaction as the desired result.
Carpet Installation
   The carpets you choose will be installed as part of the purchase price.

Send mail to webmaster@acme.com with questions or comments about this web site.
Copyright © 1996 ACME Interiors, Inc.
Last modified: April 18, 1996

TIP: If you need to customize your product data sheets and service description pages beyond what the templates offer, create one page. Make your general changes, and then save the page as a template. This saves you the bother of making all the changes on each product page.

After you make your selections, click Next to continue.

Choosing More Options for Products and Services

Based on your selections from the previous screen, you select the information that you want to include on your product data sheets and service description pages in this screen. Different options appear for the product data sheets and the service description pages.

Product data sheets tell visitors to your site about the various products that your company offers. In Figures 4.11 through 4.13, the interior design company advertises one of its furnishings. A section is provided on the page to describe the key benefits of the product. Each product sheet can include

- ❏ *A product image.* You can place a product image and a caption on each page, as in Figure 4.11. A temporary graphic is initially included on the page; an Annotation bot reminds you to replace it. The key benefits of the product, shown in Figure 4.12, are highlighted in a bulleted list.

You use a Save Results bot as a form handler for general types of forms. For more information, see Chapter 20.

- ❏ *Pricing information.* The description of the product, its SKU number, and its price appear on the page in a formatted paragraph, as in Figure 4.12.

- ❏ *An information request form.* You can place a form that uses a Save Results bot on the page. The form, shown in Figure 4.13, enables visitors to your site to request information about the product or service directly from the Web page.

Figure 4.11.

The upper portion of the product data sheet contains a company logo, header graphic, and a photo and description of the product.

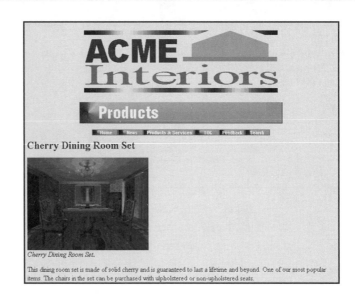

Figure 4.12.

The middle portion of the product data sheet contains the key benefits of the product and pricing information.

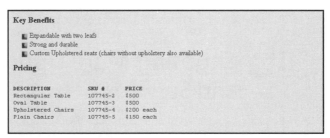

Figure 4.13.

The lower portion of the product data sheet contains an information request form and footer information.

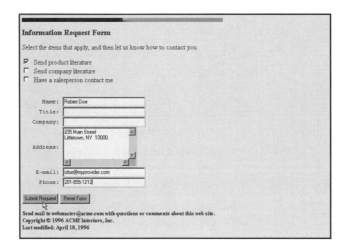

When users submit an information request form to your site, they receive a confirmation page. This confirmation page, shown in Figure 4.14, acknowledges that their request was received at your site. This information is stored in Web page format (`inforeq.htm`) in the `_private` subdirectory of your web.

Figure 4.14.
When users submit an information request form, they receive a confirmation page.

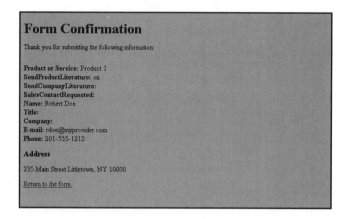

Service description pages tell visitors to your site about the various services and capabilities of your company. A section is provided on the page to describe the key benefits of its products. Figures 4.15 through 4.17 show a service description page at the interior decorating company's site.

Figure 4.15.
The upper portion of the service description page contains the company's logo, a header graphic, a navigation bar, and a description of the service.

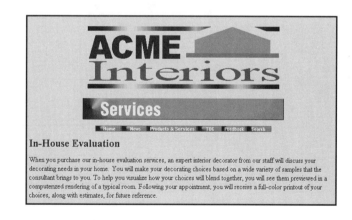

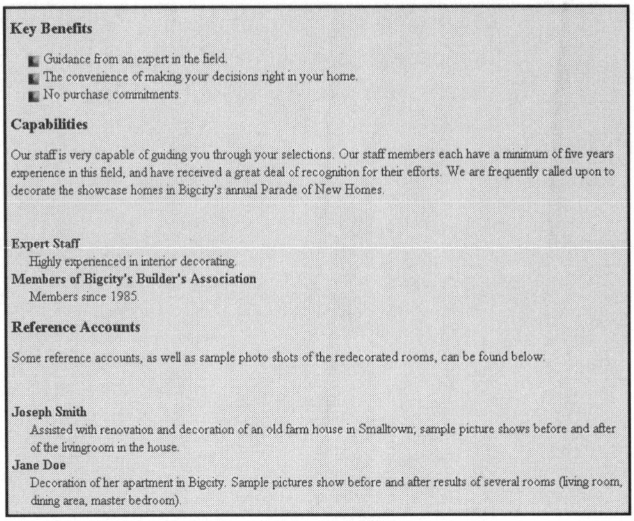

Figure 4.16.
The middle portion of the page describes the key benefits of the service, a capabilities section, and a list of reference accounts.

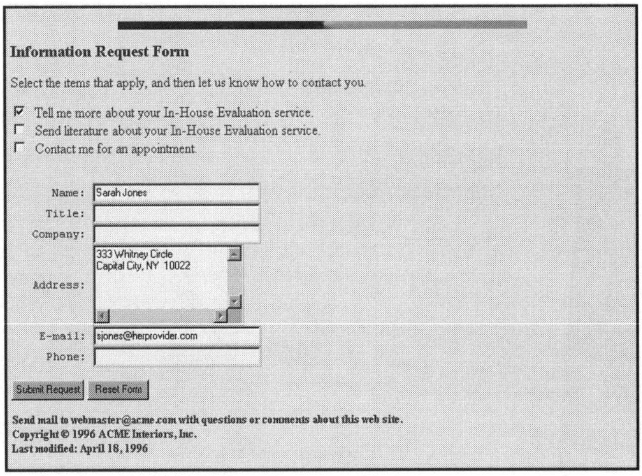

Figure 4.17.
The lower portion of the page contains the information request form and footer information.

You can choose the following options for service description pages:

❏ *A capabilities list.* Capabilities are displayed in a definition list, as in Figure 4.16.

❏ *Reference accounts.* References are displayed in a definition list, as in Figure 4.16.

❏ *An information request form.* The information request form contains the same features as with product data sheets. The service description page's information request form is shown in Figure 4.17. A confirmation form, shown in Figure 4.18, is returned after the form is submitted.

After you make your selections, click Next to continue.

Figure 4.18.

The confirmation page for the service description page's information request form.

Form Confirmation

Thank you for submitting the following information:

Product or Service: Service 1
SendServiceLiterature: on
SendCompanyLiterature:
SalesContactRequested:
Name: Sarah Jones
Title:
Company:
E-mail: sjones@herprovider.com
Phone:

Address

333 Whitney Circle Capital City, NY 10022

Return to the form.

 # Choosing Feedback Page Options

If you elect to include a feedback form on your page, you are asked what you want to collect from visitors when they submit feedback to your site. Figures 4.19 and 4.20 show the feedback form for the interior design company.

Figure 4.19.

The upper portion of the feedback form contains the company's logo, a header graphic, navigation bars, and instructions.

Your opinions are important to us. Please tell us what you think about our web site, company, products, or services. If you provide us with your contact information, we will be able to reach you in case we have any questions.

Figure 4.20.

The lower portion of the feedback form contains the Comments, Category, and Contact Information sections and footer information.

Comments

It looks like you have some very nice prod
We'll have to get together to talk.

Category

Company

Contact Information

Name   Steven Smith
Title   Construction Manager
Company Big Home Constuction Company
Address 4217 Main Street, Bigcity, NY 10022
Telephone
FAX
E-mail   smithy@bighomeco.com

Submit Feedback   Reset Form

Send mail to webmaster@acme.com with questions or comments about this web site.
Copyright © 1996 ACME Interiors, Inc.
Last modified: April 18, 1996

The feedback form enables visitors to your site to send comments to you about your site, company, products, or services. Annotation bots show you where changes are necessary on the page. A Save Results bot for the Comments section uses a scrolling textbox, a drop-down menu, textboxes, and pushbuttons.

When users submit information to your site with the feedback form, a confirmation page is generated. Figure 4.21 shows the confirmation page for the interior design company's feedback form.

Figure 4.21.
The confirmation page for the feedback form.

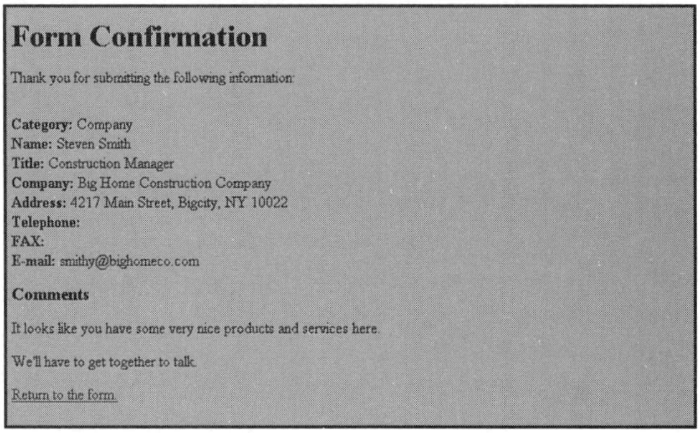

Form Confirmation

Thank you for submitting the following information:

Category: Company
Name: Steven Smith
Title: Construction Manager
Company: Big Home Construction Company
Address: 4217 Main Street, Bigcity, NY 10022
Telephone:
FAX:
E-mail: smithy@bighomeco.com

Comments

It looks like you have some very nice products and services here.

We'll have to get together to talk.

Return to the form.

You can ask for the following information from users. Textboxes appear in the feedback form to hold responses.

- ❏ Full name
- ❏ Job title
- ❏ Company affiliation
- ❏ Mailing address
- ❏ Telephone number
- ❏ Fax number
- ❏ E-mail address

After you make your selections, click Next to continue.

Storing Request Information

If you elect to include information request forms on your product data sheets and service description pages, you are asked how to store the information retrieved from the feedback form. You can choose one of two options:

❏ *Yes, use tab-delimited format.* Choose this option if you plan to use a database program to store the retrieved information. The results are saved in a file named `inforeq.txt`.

❏ *No, use Web page format.* If you choose this option, the information is stored in HTML definition lists on the page. The results are saved in a file named `inforeq.htm`.

Choosing Table of Contents Page Options

If you elect to have a Table of Contents page in your web, a screen asks what options to include in it. Figures 4.22 and 4.23 show the table of contents that is automatically generated by FrontPage for the interior design company's site.

Figure 4.22.
The upper portion of the Table of Contents page contains the company's logo, a header graphic, a navigation bar, and a brief description of the Web site.

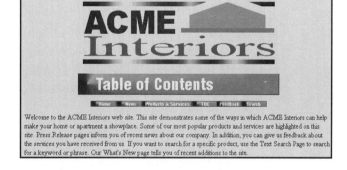

Figure 4.23.
The lower portion of the Table of Contents page contains the table of contents and footer information.

The options for a Table of Contents page are

The Table of Contents bot automatically includes the pages in your Web, beginning with a page that you specify. For more information, see Chapter 15.

❏ *Keep pages list up-to-date automatically.* If you choose this option, a Table of Contents bot is placed on the page.

❏ *Show pages not linked into web.* With this option, you can provide links to any unlinked pages in your site in the table of contents.

❏ *Use Bullets for top-level pages.* The Table of Contents bot inserts a bullet to identify the top-level pages in your web.

NOTE: If you generate the table of contents automatically, be sure to use the File | Page Properties command to change the title of each page. The Table of Contents bot uses the page titles when it generates the contents.

After you make your selections, click Next to continue.

Choosing Page Header and Footer Options

Next, you select what you want to appear at the top and bottom of all your Web pages. The following items can appear at the top of the page:

❏ *A company logo.* A file named `logo.htm` is placed in the web's `_private` subdirectory, which contains a graphic named `logo.gif`. Replace this graphic with your own. The company logo appears on several pages.

❏ *The page title.* If you choose to include page titles, they appear at the top of the page.

❏ *Links to your main Web pages.* Text links or a navigation bar can appear at the top of the page. These links appear on a page named `navbar.htm` in the `_private` directory of your web. If you prefer to have the links appear at the bottom of the page, uncheck this option.

The following items can appear at the bottom of the page:

❏ *Links to your main Web pages.* Text links or a navigation bar can appear at the bottom of the page. These links appear on a page named `navbar.htm` in the `_private` directory of your web. If you prefer to have the links appear at the top of the page, uncheck this option.

❏ *The e-mail address of your Webmaster.* This information is included in the footer by using a Substitution bot.

Timestamp bots place the date when a page was last updated—automatically or manually—on it. For more information, see Chapter 15.

❏ *A copyright notice.* If you choose this option, the line Copyright © Company Name appears in the footers of all the pages. The company name is included by using a Substitution bot.

❏ The d*ate when the page was last modified.* If you choose this option, a Timestamp bot is placed in the footer. It updates the footer with the date when the page was last modified.

After you make your selections, click Next to continue.

 # Choosing Your Graphics Style

You are asked what type of graphics should appear on your page. A preview of each style appears in the wizard screen when you press its radio button. The options are

❏ Plain—no graphics

❏ Conservative

❏ Flashy

❏ Cool

The Plain—No Graphics option produces text-only pages.

 # Choosing Style Sheet Options

You can customize the colors for the background and text using the screen shown in Figure 4.24. The choices that you make here are saved to your web in a file titled Web Colors (filename _private/style.htm). You can base the style of other pages on this one. This is a great improvement added to FrontPage 1.1.

Figure 4.24.
The Corporate Presence wizard has a built-in style page generator.

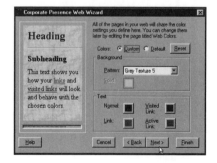

The steps are

1. If you want to use the standard World Wide Web gray background and text and link colors, choose the Default radio button. You do not need to select anything more. Click the Next button to continue your web selections.

2. To assign custom colors, choose the Custom radio button.

3. To change the background texture, click the arrow in the drop-down menu box. A list of several choices appears. The preview windows shows each texture as you highlight the selections. Click a selection again to choose it.

4. If you want a solid background, choose None for a pattern. The Background Color option activates.

5. To change the background color, click the color square to the right of the Background Color heading. The Color dialog box appears.

TIP: Give your site visitors' eyes a break. If you want to use white for the background, soften it with a hint of color. High contrast, such as black text on a white background, tires the eyes. To choose a custom color, click the Define Custom Colors button in the Color dialog box. Add the color to the Custom Colors section.

6. Click OK to return to the wizard screen.

7. The procedure for changing the text colors is the same. As you select colors, they update in the preview screen. To view the Active Link color that you select, click and hold a link in the preview window. Release the mouse button when you are done.

8. Click Next to continue with the wizard.

Choosing the Under Construction Graphic

The wizard asks whether you want to tell visitors to your site that it is under construction. If you indicate yes, an Under Construction icon is included on your pages. The only catch is that you must remember to remove it when you are done building the page.

After you make your selection, click Next to continue.

Entering Your Company Location

Now you enter the location information that you gathered at the beginning of this chapter. This information is included in various locations on your pages through the use of Substitution bots.

The figures in this chapter show the following location information:

```
Full name of company: ACME Interiors, Inc.
One word version of name: ACME
Street address: 123 Busy Street, Anycity, NY 00000
```

After you enter your information, click Next to continue.

Entering Your Company Contact Information

Next, you enter the contact information. This information is included in various locations on your pages through the use of Substitution bots.

Enter the following information:

Telephone number: 313-555-1212
Fax number: 313-555-1212
Webmaster's E-mail address: webmaster@www.provider.com
E-mail for general information: sales@acmecorp.com

After you enter your information, click Next to continue.

What's To Do?

You can display the To Do list at any time from the FrontPage Explorer or from the FrontPage Editor. Simply select Tools | Show To Do List from either application. For more information on To Do lists, see Chapter 7, "What to Do?"

The final screen of the Corporate Presence wizard asks whether you want to view the To Do list after the web is created. If you do not want to view the list, uncheck the option.

To create the Web site with the choices that you made in the wizard, click the Finish button. The FrontPage Explorer generates files based on your decisions, and your Web site appears.

Figure 4.25 shows the To Do List created with the Corporate Presence wizard. You no doubt will want to add more tasks after you review the pages.

Figure 4.25.
The Corporate Presence wizard places some tasks in your To Do list automatically.

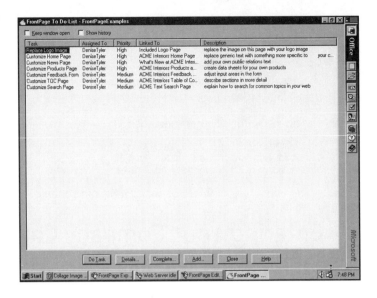

Look at What You Get

Figure 4.26 shows the Corporate Presence Web pages displayed in the FrontPage Explorer's Link View. The cursor indicates the icon in the toolbar that you click to select this view.

Figure 4.26.
The Corporate Presence Web pages shown in the FrontPage Explorer's Link View.

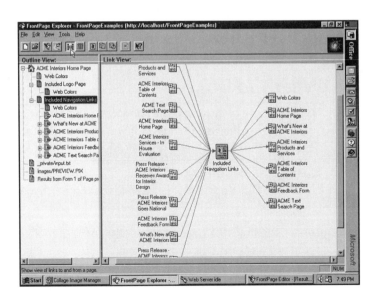

The pages and graphics are displayed in the FrontPage Explorer's Summary View. The cursor indicates the icon that you click to display your webs in this view. Summary View is handy when you are working with large webs because you can sort the content into categories.

Table 4.1 describes all the pages created with the Corporate Presence wizard. Table 4.2 describes all the graphics included in the `images` subdirectory of your corporate-presence web.

Table 4.1. Files created with the Corporate Presence wizard.

Filename	Description
index.htm	Home page
feedback.htm	Feedback Form page
news.htm	What's New page
pr01.htm	Press Release page 1
pr02.htm	Press Release page 2
pr03.htm	Press Release page 3
prod##.htm	Product data sheet pages
products.htm	Products and Services Page
search.htm	Text search page
serv##.htm	Service description pages
toc.htm	Table of Contents page
_private/inforeq.htm	Results from Form 1 of Prod01 or Serv01
_private/logo.htm	Included Logo page
_private/navbar.htm	Included navigation links
_private/style.htm	Web colors

Table 4.2. Graphics created with the Corporate Presence wizard.

Filename	Description
bfeed.gif	Navigation bar button, Feedback Form page
bhome.gif	Navigation bar button, home page
bnews.gif	Navigation bar button, What's New page
bprdsrv.gif	Navigation bar button, Products and Services page
bsrch.gif	Navigation bar button, Search page
btoc.gif	Navigation bar button, Table of Contents page

continues

Table 4.2. continued

Filename	Description
bullet.gif	Bullets used for service description
div.gif	Horizontal bar dividers
hfeed.gif	Header graphic, Feedback Form page
hhome.gif	Header graphic, home page
hnews.gif	Header graphic, What's New page
hprdsrv.gif	Header graphic, Products and Services page
hprods.gif	Header graphic, product data sheets
hservs.gif	Header graphic, service descriptions page
hsrch.gif	Header graphic, Search page
htoc.gif	Header graphic, Table of Contents page
logo.gif	Company logo
prodimg.gif	Product image for the product data sheet
smallnew.gif	New! graphic for the What's New page
undercon.gif	Under Construction icon
texture.jpg	Background texture image that you choose

Just think—you did all this in a matter of minutes. It is definitely worthwhile to start with the Corporate Presence wizard.

Workshop Wrap-Up

Wizards are like magic. In a matter of minutes, you created fifteen pages, complete with link and graphic placeholders. This is especially impressive considering how long it would have taken you to accomplish all this using other methods.

Chapter Summary

In this chapter, you stepped through the Corporate Presence wizard to create a corporate presence on the Web. The pages described your company and the products and services you have to offer. The wizard also generated pages that allowed visitors to interact with you from your Web site, through feedback or information requests. You learned how to customize your corporate presence site by choosing several different options available in the wizard. The pages you created were linked for you automatically by the wizard.

Next Steps

To continue with the pages that you created with the Corporate Presence wizard:

- ❏ See Chapter 5, "Lots of Pages—The Template Way," to add other page templates to your web.
- ❏ See Chapter 9, "Composing and Editing Page Content," for instructions on how to add and edit content to your corporate-presence web.
- ❏ See Chapter 11, "Sprucing Up Your Pages," to learn about using images and enhancing the appearance of your Web pages.
- ❏ See Chapter 15, "Automating Pages with Bots," to learn how to use the simpler FrontPage Web bots. See Chapter 20, "Runtime Bots: The Heartbeat of FrontPage Forms," to learn about the bots used in the forms in this Web.

Q&A

Q: My remote server requires that I use a home page with a name other than `index.htm`. Do I have to correct links on many pages if I rename my home page?

A: In the corporate-presence web, all the links to the home page appear in the Included Navigation Links page. An Include bot places this navigation bar on several pages, which is why the pages have links to the home page.

Include bots place the contents of another file in a page. Use them for content that appears on several pages. That way, you need to change only one file. For more information, see Chapter 15.

If your home page must be named something different when it is on your Web site, highlight the page title in any view of the FrontPage Explorer. Choose Edit | Properties, or use the Alt+Enter shortcut. In the Properties dialog box, type the new page name, and click the Apply button. The Confirm Updating Links dialog box asks whether you want to update the links that reference this page. Choose Yes.

Q: Do I have to keep my files in the directories that were made when the Web was created?

See Chapter 23, "Web Maintenance and Administration," to learn how to configure FrontPage to use a different home page name.

A: No. New features in FrontPage 1.1 enable you to move files to different directories in your Web and to correct any broken links as you do so. You can edit the page properties and include a subdirectory name before the page name. If the subdirectory does not exist in your Web, it is created.

Q: What are all those other directories and files included in the Web that I just created? It looks as though FrontPage created copies of all my files in other directories.

For further information on this point, see Chapter 24.

A: Those additional directories include the FrontPage Server Extensions, where applicable, and information used by the server administrator. If you use some of FrontPage's advanced features—including some of the bots—you must keep all those directories and files in your Web. The HTM files in the extra directories contain information for the FrontPage Server Extensions.

Q: I cannot see the purple text of the Annotation bots when I open my pages in another browser. Why?

A: The Annotation bots are designed for just that reason. They enable you to put notes on a page to remind you of what needs to be done on it and where. You can view the Annotation bot text from within the FrontPage Editor, but it does not appear in other browsers, such as the Internet Explorer or Netscape. Likewise, if you place an Annotation bot on a page to remind yourself of something, you should add the item to the To Do list at the same time. This helps you keep track of things much more easily.

Q: Where do the Substitution bots get the company information?

A: The Corporate Presence wizard places the company information that you entered into the Web settings. You can find it if you select Tools | Web Settings and then choose the Parameters tab of the Web Settings dialog box.

Q: The responses from all my product data sheets and service description pages are going to one file, `inforeq.htm`, on my web. Can I separate the responses into different files?

A: When you initially create your web, all information request forms on the products and services pages store the retrieved information in the `inforeq.htm` file. If you want to create individual retrieval files for each page, for example, you need to edit the Save Results bot on each product and service page to point to another file. Simply copy the `inforeq.htm` file and save it under different names. You also need to edit the Save Results Bot properties of the products and services pages to point to the correct results file, as outlined in Chapter 20.

Q: How do I replace the logo image in the corporate-presence web?

A: If your logo is saved in GIF format, use the File | Import command to add the image to the web. The Add File button invokes the Add File to Import List dialog box. Add the image to the Import File to Web list, and use the Edit URL button to rename it to

```
images/logo.gif
```

Click the Import Now button. The old logo image is replaced.

If your logo image is saved in a format other than GIF, open the web's Included Logo page (`logo.htm`) in the FrontPage Editor. Use the Insert | Image command to add your logo to your page. This enables you to import a wide variety of graphic types. These procedures are explained in more detail in Chapter 11, "Sprucing Up Your Pages."

FIVE

Lots of Pages— The Template Way

In this chapter, you

- ❏ Add pages to an existing web
- ❏ Create a new page based on a FrontPage template
- ❏ Review the content of the FrontPage templates
- ❏ Save pages to your currently opened web
- ❏ Save your own pages as templates

Tasks in this chapter:

- ❏ Opening an Existing Web
- ❏ Creating a New Page
- ❏ Linking to a New Page Based on a Template
- ❏ Saving Pages to the Web
- ❏ Creating Templates of Your Own

Are you someone who likes to get things done quickly and efficiently? I am. Sometimes my creativity is blocked, while other times I just want to get the groundwork done in a hurry so that I can get to the fun part of dressing up the pages. That is what I enjoy the most.

If you are pressed for time or short on ideas for pages, FrontPage has a bountiful supply of templates from which you can choose. Although most of the pages are designed for business purposes, they give you a basic structure to work from. You can modify the content in any way you choose. There are some good ideas in these templates. They can help get those creative cells working in your brain.

Opening an Existing Web

You cannot get all your work done in one day. Most likely, when you create new pages, you save them to a web that already exists on your computer. It is simple to open an existing web to save pages to it.

1. From the FrontPage Explorer, choose File I Open Web. The Open Web dialog box appears.

2. From the drop-down list, choose the server on which your existing web is located.

3. Click the List Webs button. A list of webs on the server appears.

4. Highlight the name of the web that you want to edit or add pages to. Click OK or press Enter to open the web.

NOTE: The Name and Password Required dialog box appears if you have not yet performed a task that requires authorization. Your web opens after you perform these steps.

Creating a New Page

Now that you have a web open, you can add pages to it. Use the FrontPage Editor to create new pages and add them to the web.

To create a new page,

1. From the FrontPage Editor, choose File I New, or use the shortcut Ctrl+N. The New Page dialog box appears.

2. Highlight the type of page that you want to create. Click OK or press Enter. Your page appears in the FrontPage Editor.

NOTE: For purposes of this book, I have divided the templates into two categories. Use the basic templates if you do not have the FrontPage Server Extensions on your target server. The advanced templates use the FrontPage Bots that require the server extensions.

Basic Pages

You can use the basic page templates regardless of whether you have the FrontPage Server Extensions on your target Web server. They use the basic features of FrontPage, as well as the more commonly used FrontPage Web bots. In FrontPage, what you see is what you get. The page templates make great Web pages possible.

The Normal template creates a blank page to which you can add your own content. It is the template that you most often use.

The Meeting Agenda template, shown in Figures 5.1 and 5.2, describes the date, time, location, and purpose of a meeting. The topics for discussion and a list of attendees also appear on the page. Footer information shows when the page was most recently updated.

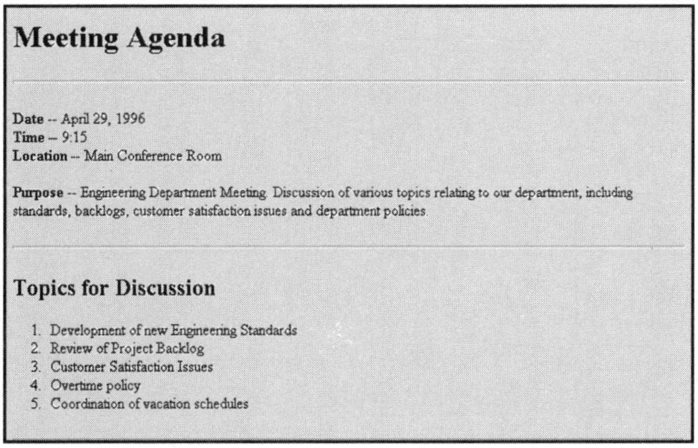

Figure 5.1.

The upper portion of the Meeting Agenda page gives details of the meeting and topics for discussion.

Meeting Agenda

Date -- April 29, 1996
Time -- 9:15
Location -- Main Conference Room

Purpose -- Engineering Department Meeting. Discussion of various topics relating to our department, including standards, backlogs, customer satisfaction issues and department policies

Topics for Discussion

1. Development of new Engineering Standards
2. Review of Project Backlog
3. Customer Satisfaction Issues
4. Overtime policy
5. Coordination of vacation schedules

Figure 5.2.

The lower portion of the Meeting Agenda page lists the attendees.

Attendees

- All Engineering Department Members
- Jack Smith
- Jane Thomas
- Bill Rogers

For questions or comments concerning this page, contact sbinkley@www.provider.com.
Revised: April 24, 1996.

The Bibliography template, shown in Figure 5.3, provides a list of publications. For each publication, you see the author's last name and first initial, its title, the city and state where it was published, and the name of publisher.

Figure 5.3.
Use the Bibliography page when you want to display a list of references for a topic.

Bibliography

Thomas, B., 1992. *Creating Graphics for the Internet*. Los Angeles, CA. The Publisher.

Doe, N. 1993. *How to Design Graphics for the Internet*. New York, NY. Another Publisher.

Smith, F. 1995. *Web Pages the Easy Way*. Midwest City, IL. Computer Book Publisher.

Revised: April 24, 1996.

The Directory of Press Releases template, shown in Figure 5.4, helps you organize press release pages by date and title. The most recent entries appear at the top. You need to add links to the press release pages that appear on your site.

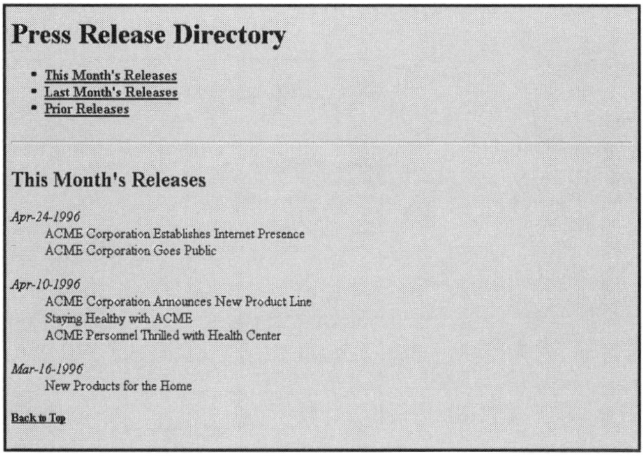

Figure 5.4.
The Directory of Press Releases page template enables you to organize press releases by date and title.

Press Release Directory

- **This Month's Releases**
- **Last Month's Releases**
- **Prior Releases**

This Month's Releases

Apr-24-1996
    ACME Corporation Establishes Internet Presence
    ACME Corporation Goes Public

Apr-10-1996
    ACME Corporation Announces New Product Line
    Staying Healthy with ACME
    ACME Personnel Thrilled with Health Center

Mar-16-1996
    New Products for the Home

Back to Top

TIP: Use a Scheduled Image bot to add a calendar graphic to Press Release Directory pages. The Scheduled Image bot allows you to specify a start and end date within which an image appears on a page.

You add an employee directory to a project in Chapter 6, "Real-Life Examples."

The Employee Directory template provides an alphabetical list of the employees in your company. The section for each employee contains his or her photograph, his or her title, current projects, office location, mail stop, telephone number and extension, e-mail address, and a link to his or her home page.

TIP: If your company contains more than a few employees, you might want to split this page into several pages—such as by department or by letter of the alphabet—and provide links to them on a master page. You might also want to add a Search bot to search for employee names if your workforce is very large.

The Frequently Asked Questions template, shown in Figure 5.5, provides a numbered table of contents of the questions that appear on the page. It uses bookmarks and links to jump to each question and answer that appear on the page.

Figure 5.5.

The Frequently Asked Questions page provides a numbered table of contents and bookmarks.

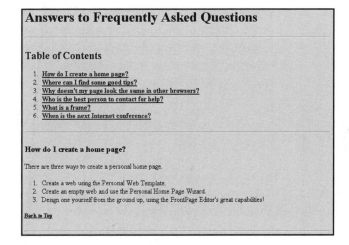

The Glossary of Terms template, shown in Figure 5.6, contains definitions for the terms used in a given subject. Each section name is designated by a letter of the alphabet. You create new entries in alphabetical order inside the appropriate section.

Figure 5.6.

The Glossary of Terms page provides an alphabetical list of terms and definitions.

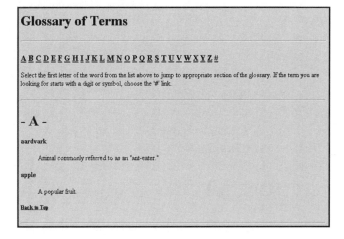

You design a hot list in Chapter 12, "Real-Life Examples."

The Hot List template provides links to other sites on the Web for a given subject. A manually generated table of contents, containing five categories, appears at the top of the page. Each category contains five sites.

The HyperDocument page is one section of a large hyperlinked manual or report. It is used in conjunction with a home page and a table of contents. You replace the gray buttons on the page with icons that are appropriate for the content of the section.

The Lecture Abstract template, shown in Figure 5.7, announces an upcoming lecture, talk, or meeting. The title of the lecture appears at the top of the page. The name of the speaker, his or her role and organization, and the date of the lecture follow. You add an abstract of the lecture and the topics covered in the appropriate fields. A biography of the speaker appears at the bottom of the page. There is also a link to a page that lists other seminars or workshops.

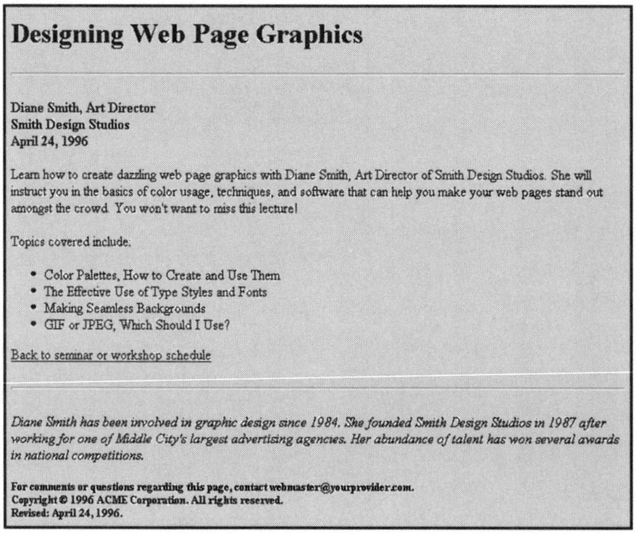

Figure 5.7.
Use the Lecture Abstract template to announce an upcoming lecture.

Designing Web Page Graphics

Diane Smith, Art Director
Smith Design Studios
April 24, 1996

Learn how to create dazzling web page graphics with Diane Smith, Art Director of Smith Design Studios. She will instruct you in the basics of color usage, techniques, and software that can help you make your web pages stand out amongst the crowd. You won't want to miss this lecture!

Topics covered include:

- Color Palettes, How to Create and Use Them
- The Effective Use of Type Styles and Fonts
- Making Seamless Backgrounds
- GIF or JPEG, Which Should I Use?

Back to seminar or workshop schedule

Diane Smith has been involved in graphic design since 1984. She founded Smith Design Studios in 1987 after working for one of Middle City's largest advertising agencies. Her abundance of talent has won several awards in national competitions.

For comments or questions regarding this page, contact webmaster@yourprovider.com.
Copyright © 1996 ACME Corporation. All rights reserved.
Revised: April 24, 1996.

TIP: Design a lecture abstract when you book a lecture, and use a Scheduled Include bot to place the page on your site two weeks before the lecture. Then have the Scheduled Include bot remove the page from your site after the lecture has occurred.

The Office Directory template, shown in Figures 5.8 and 5.9, is useful if your company has many offices scattered throughout the United States, Canada, and other countries. Every state appears on this page, as well as every Canadian province and several foreign countries. Delete the ones that do not apply. The page also includes a link to an example of how office information is displayed, as shown in Figure 5.9.

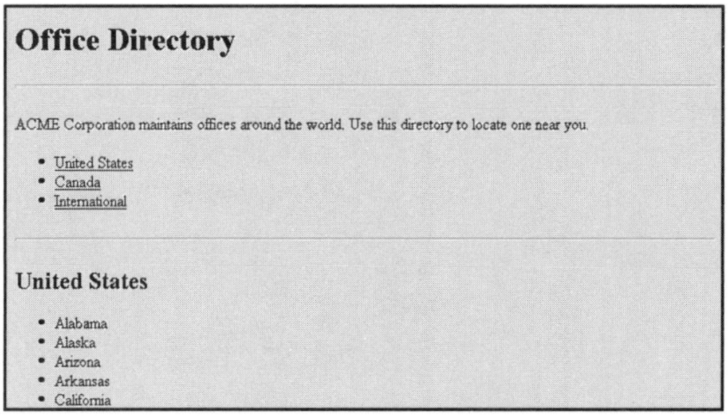

Figure 5.8.

The top portion of the Office Directory template provides a bulleted list of every state, every Canadian province, and several foreign countries.

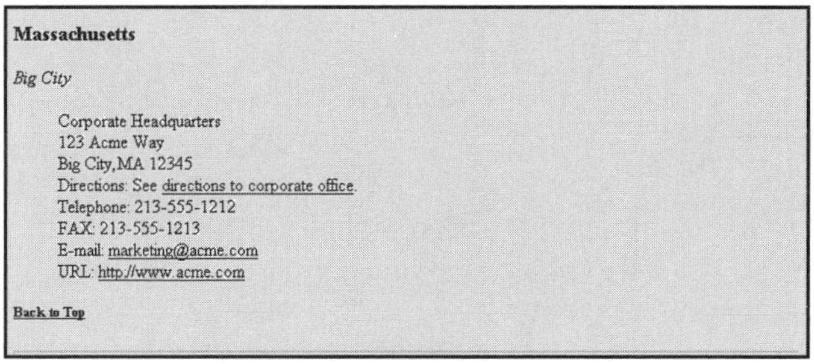

Office Directory

ACME Corporation maintains offices around the world. Use this directory to locate one near you.

- United States
- Canada
- International

United States

- Alabama
- Alaska
- Arizona
- Arkansas
- California

Figure 5.9.

You can enter location information for each office.

Massachusetts

Big City

Corporate Headquarters
123 Acme Way
Big City, MA 12345
Directions: See directions to corporate office.
Telephone: 213-555-1212
FAX: 213-555-1213
E-mail: marketing@acme.com
URL: http://www.acme.com

Back to Top

The Press Release template is similar to the press release that appears in Chapter 4, "If You Mean Business."

The Press Release template is used along with the Directory of Press Releases template. A title and subtitle of the press release starts off the form, and the date and announcement follow. Company contact information appears at the bottom of the page.

TIP: Develop your press releases ahead of time, and use a Scheduled Include bot to release them to your site on the right day.

The Product Description template is an enhanced version of the product data sheet discussed in Chapter 4.

The Product Description template contains a summary of a product. It describes key features of product, lists its benefits, and shows product specifications. You can also include an image of the product.

The Seminar Schedule template, shown in Figure 5.10, presents a conference schedule. Bookmarks and links provide navigation throughout the form. Each session includes the title of the lecture and the speaker's name, role, and organization.

TIP: The Scheduled Image and Scheduled Include bots can make your seminar schedule update itself dynamically and automatically.

Figure 5.10.
A Seminar Schedule page describes ongoing seminars.

Seminar Schedule

The seminar will be divided into the following tracks or sessions:

- Gardening for Your Family
- Landscape Design
- Decorating Your Home with Flowers

Gardening for Your Family

April 21, 1996

Planning Your Garden
    Sarah Williams, Consultant, Smalltown Garden Center

When to Plant Your Vegetables
    Robert Jackson, Specialist, Jackson's Seed Company

Harvest Time
    Sarah Williams, Consultant, Smalltown Garden Center

Back to Top

The Software Data Sheet template, shown in Figures 5.11 through 5.14, includes a graphic or screen shot of a software product; its key benefits and features; a section for system requirements, pricing, and availability; and company contact information.

Figure 5.11.
The top portion of the Software Data Sheet page provides a graphic of the software.

Sammy's Graphic Bonanza (tm)

Great Clip Art for All Your Needs!

You develop your own cards, brochures and web pages by combining original clip art.

You design a table of contents in Chapter 12.

The Table of Contents template uses a Table of Contents bot to automatically generate a table of contents for your Web site. It is ideal for sites that contain many pages.

You design a What's New page in Chapter 12.

The What's New template adds a What's New page to your site. This page is similar to the page created with the Corporate Presence Web, discussed in Chapter 4, "If You Mean Business." You manually develop a list of major changes to your web and place the most recent changes at the top of the list.

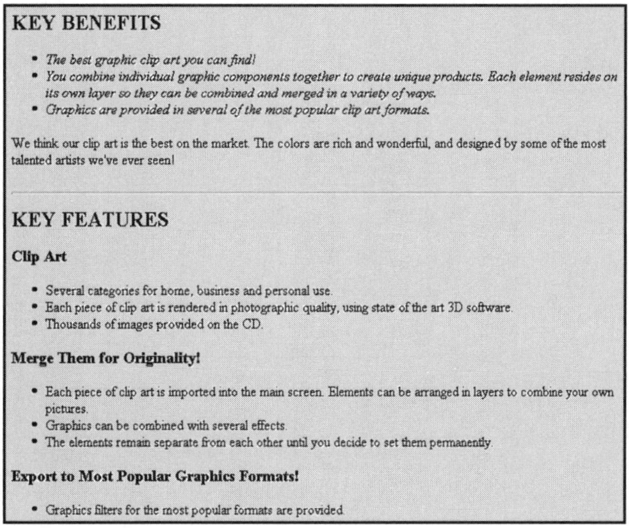

Figure 5.12.

The second portion describes key benefits and features of the software.

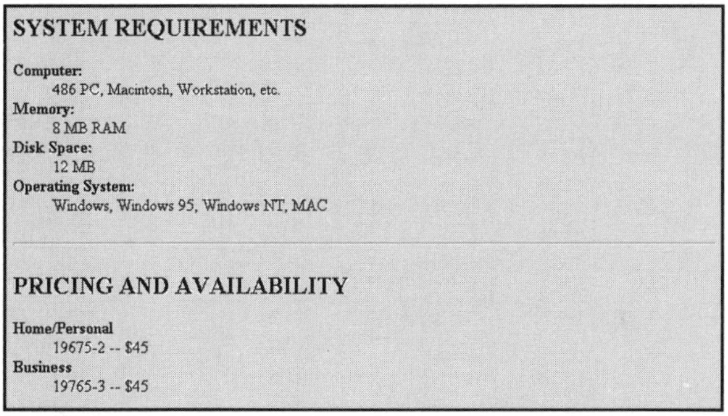

KEY BENEFITS

- *The best graphic clip art you can find!*
- *You combine individual graphic components together to create unique products. Each element resides on its own layer so they can be combined and merged in a variety of ways.*
- *Graphics are provided in several of the most popular clip art formats.*

We think our clip art is the best on the market. The colors are rich and wonderful, and designed by some of the most talented artists we've ever seen!

KEY FEATURES

Clip Art

- Several categories for home, business and personal use.
- Each piece of clip art is rendered in photographic quality, using state of the art 3D software.
- Thousands of images provided on the CD.

Merge Them for Originality!

- Each piece of clip art is imported into the main screen. Elements can be arranged in layers to combine your own pictures.
- Graphics can be combined with several effects.
- The elements remain separate from each other until you decide to set them permanently.

Export to Most Popular Graphics Formats!

- Graphics filters for the most popular formats are provided.

Figure 5.13.

The third portion provides information on requirement information, pricing, and availability.

SYSTEM REQUIREMENTS

Computer:
  486 PC, Macintosh, Workstation, etc.
Memory:
  8 MB RAM
Disk Space:
  12 MB
Operating System:
  Windows, Windows 95, Windows NT, MAC

PRICING AND AVAILABILITY

Home/Personal
  19675-2 -- $45
Business
  19765-3 -- $45

Figure 5.14.

The bottom portion provides contact, copyright, and trademark information.

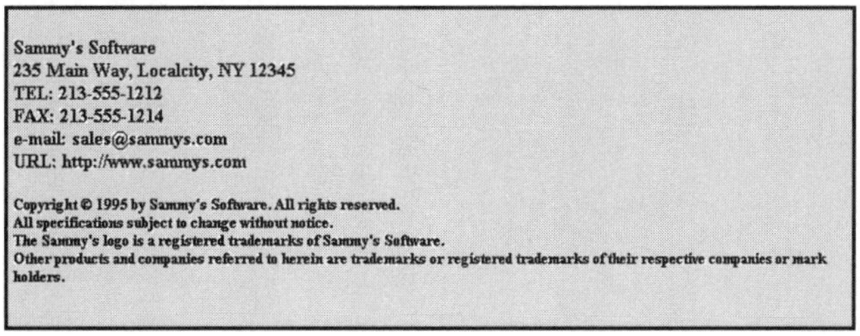

Sammy's Software
235 Main Way, Localcity, NY 12345
TEL: 213-555-1212
FAX: 213-555-1214
e-mail: sales@sammys.com
URL: http://www.sammys.com

Copyright © 1995 by Sammy's Software. All rights reserved.
All specifications subject to change without notice.
The Sammy's logo is a registered trademarks of Sammy's Software.
Other products and companies referred to herein are trademarks or registered trademarks of their respective companies or mark holders.

Figure 5.15.
The key features of a page template.

Name of Form	Links		Lists			Other		
	Bookmarks	Links	Bulleted	Definition	Numbered	Horiz Lines	Images	Mailto
Normal Page								
Bibliography Page	✔					✔		
Confirmation Form						✔		
Directory of Press Releases	✔		✔	✔		✔		
Employee Directory	✔	✔	✔			✔	✔	✔
Employment Opportunities	✔		✔		✔	✔	✔	
Feedback Form				✔		✔		
Frequently Asked Questions	✔				✔	✔		
Glossary of Terms	✔			✔		✔		
Guest Book						✔		
Hot List	✔		✔			✔		
Hyper Document Page	✔	✔				✔	✔	
Lecture Abstract		✔	✔			✔		
Office Directory	✔	✔	✔	✔		✔		✔
Press Release						✔		
Product Description	✔		✔	✔		✔		
Product or Event Registration						✔		
Search Page	✔			✔		✔		
Seminar Schedule	✔		✔	✔		✔		
Software Data Sheet			✔	✔		✔	✔	
Survey Form	✔		✔		✔	✔		
Table of Contents						✔		
User Registration				✔		✔		
What's New				✔		✔		

The Features Behind the Pages

Figure 5.15 summarizes the key features of each basic page template. Figure 5.16 summarizes the basic bots used in each page template.

Figure 5.16.

The basic bots in a page template.

Name of Form	Annotation	Include	Sched Image	Sched Include	Substitution	Timestamp	Table of Contents
Normal Page							
Bibliography Page	✔					✔	
Confirmation Form	✔					✔	
Directory of Press Releases	✔					✔	
Employee Directory	✔					✔	
Employment Opportunities	✔					✔	
Feedback Form	✔					✔	
Frequently Asked Questions	✔					✔	
Glossary of Terms	✔					✔	
Guest Book	✔	✔					
Hot List	✔					✔	
Hyper Document Page	✔					✔	
Lecture Abstract	✔					✔	
Office Directory	✔					✔	
Press Release	✔						
Product Description	✔						
Product or Event Registration	✔					✔	
Search Page	✔					✔	
Seminar Schedule	✔					✔	
Software Data Sheet	✔						
Survey Form	✔					✔	
Table of Contents	✔					✔	✔
User Registration	✔					✔	
What's New						✔	

Advanced Pages

Refer to Chapter 20, "Runtime Bots: The Heartbeat of FrontPage Forms" for information on assigning a CGI script to a form. Refer to Chapter 24, "Working with the FrontPage Servers," for information on the server extensions.

Some templates use the advanced bots as form handlers. These advanced bots require that the FrontPage Server Extensions exist on your target web server. Alternatively, you can specify a custom CGI script to handle the forms on the pages.

Pages generated with the FrontPage page templates look as though they took hours on your part. No one has to know that you generated them in a matter of minutes.

The confirmation form is similar to the form created in the discussion webs in Chapter 3, "Can We Talk?" and Chapter 6.

The Confirmation Form template acknowledges receipt of responses from visitors to your site when they submit forms with a Discussion, Save Results, or Registration bot. It uses Confirmation Field bots to include information on the form automatically.

The Feedback Form template enables visitors to your site to submit comments, complaints, and suggestions about your company or Web site. It has fields for visitors to enter contact information.

You create a guest book page in Chapter 22.

The Guest Book template provides a page where visitors to your site can add comments about it. Their comments appear in a log at the bottom of the page for others to see.

The Employment Opportunities template notifies others of available jobs at your company. The form begins with a bulleted list of available positions and bookmarked links to appropriate sections on the page. (See Figure 5.17.) Each position contains a job description, applicant requirements, and contact information. (See Figure 5.18.)

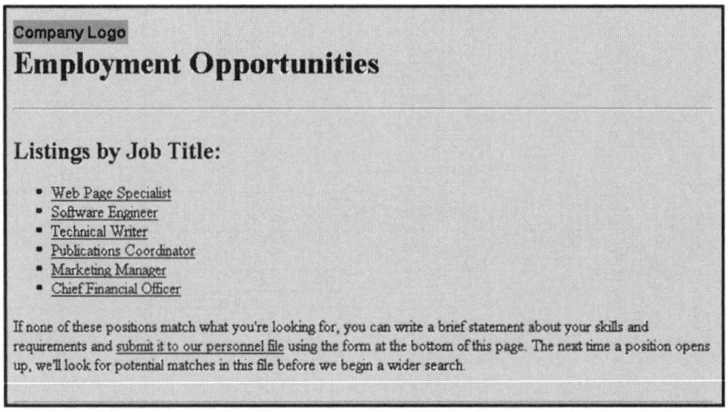

Figure 5.17.
A list of available positions appears at the top of the Employment Opportunities page.

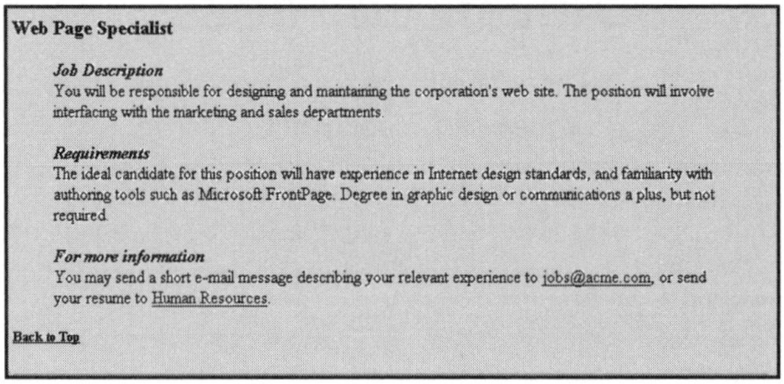

Figure 5.18.
Each position is described.

A General Inquiries section follows the list of openings. (See Figure 5.19.) It notifies visitors whom to contact if they want further information on the openings in your company.

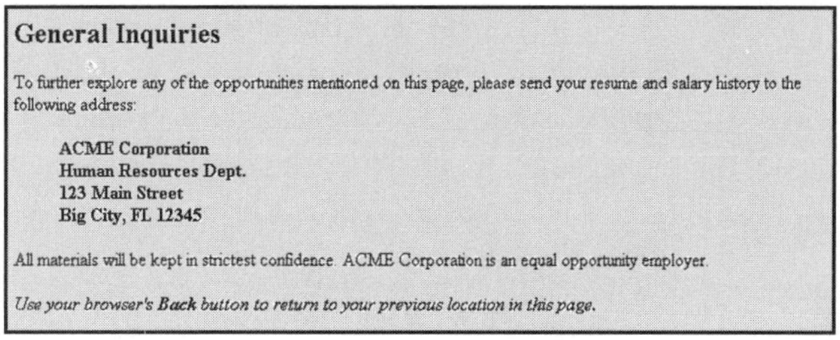

Figure 5.19.

Contact information for general inquiries.

General Inquiries

To further explore any of the opportunities mentioned on this page, please send your resume and salary history to the following address:

ACME Corporation
Human Resources Dept.
123 Main Street
Big City, FL 12345

All materials will be kept in strictest confidence. ACME Corporation is an equal opportunity employer.

*Use your browser's **Back** button to return to your previous location in this page.*

The Personnel File section on the page asks potential applicants about their current responsibilities and relevant experience. (See Figure 5.20.) Contact information is also entered in this form. (See Figure 5.21.)

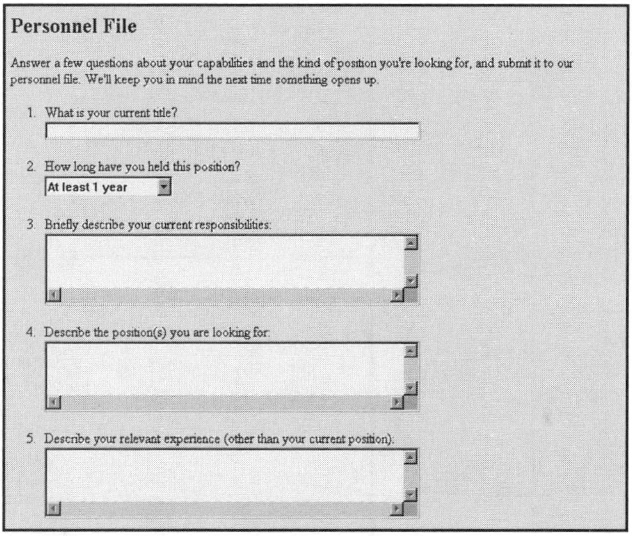

Figure 5.20.

The Personnel File section of the page asks potential applicants about their current responsibilities and other relevant experience.

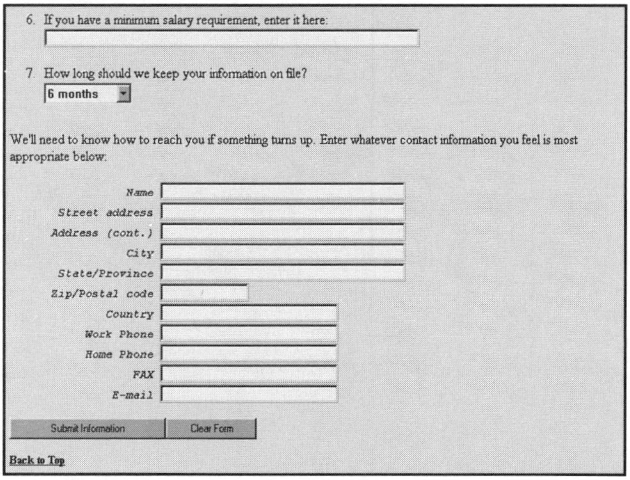

Personnel File

Answer a few questions about your capabilities and the kind of position you're looking for, and submit it to our personnel file. We'll keep you in mind the next time something opens up.

1. What is your current title?

2. How long have you held this position?
   At least 1 year

3. Briefly describe your current responsibilities:

4. Describe the position(s) you are looking for:

5. Describe your relevant experience (other than your current position):

Figure 5.21.

Contact information is entered in the lower portion of the page.

6. If you have a minimum salary requirement, enter it here:

7. How long should we keep your information on file?
   6 months

We'll need to know how to reach you if something turns up. Enter whatever contact information you feel is most appropriate below:

Name
Street address
Address (cont.)
City
State/Province
Zip/Postal code
Country
Work Phone
Home Phone
FAX
E-mail

Submit Information   Clear Form

Back to Top

The Registration template enables visitors to your site to register a product serial number or to register for an event, as shown in Figures 5.22 and 5.23. Users enter personal information in various fields on the form. A check list provides multiple options from which they can select. The form also contains fields for the registration or serial number of a product.

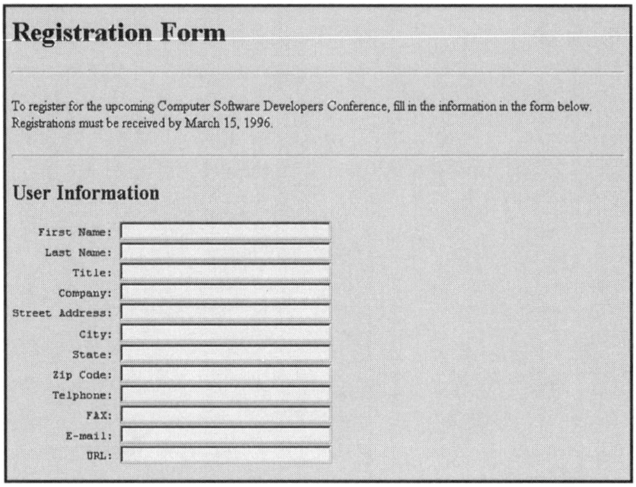

Figure 5.22.

Contact information is entered in the upper portion of the Registra- tion page.

Registration Form

To register for the upcoming Computer Software Developers Conference, fill in the information in the form below. Registrations must be received by March 15, 1996.

User Information

First Name:	
Last Name:	
Title:	
Company:	
Street Address:	
City:	
State:	
Zip Code:	
Telphone:	
FAX:	
E-mail:	
URL:	

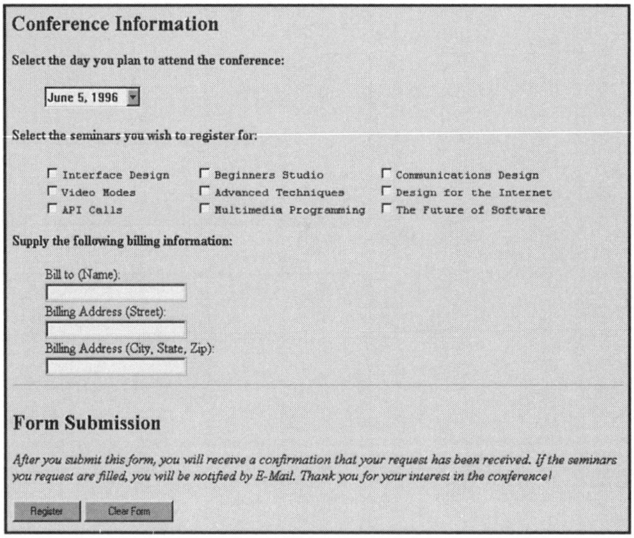

Figure 5.23.

You can modify the lower portion of the Registration page to enable visitors to your site to register for an event.

Conference Information

Select the day you plan to attend the conference:

June 5, 1996 ▾

Select the seminars you wish to register for:

☐ Interface Design   ☐ Beginners Studio   ☐ Communications Design
☐ Video Modes   ☐ Advanced Techniques   ☐ Design for the Internet
☐ API Calls   ☐ Multimedia Programming ☐ The Future of Software

Supply the following billing information:

Bill to (Name):

Billing Address (Street):

Billing Address (City, State, Zip):

Form Submission

After you submit this form, you will receive a confirmation that your request has been received. If the seminars you request are filled, you will be notified by E-Mail. Thank you for your interest in the conference!

[Register]   [Clear Form]

The User Registration template creates a more complete and thorough version of the registration form discussed in Chapter 6. You might want to replace that form with this one. Edit the content to suit your purposes.

The User Registration template is similar to the Registration form, but it contains more fields for the user to enter information. The introductory text explains the benefits of signing up for a registered web or discussion.

The Search Page template places a search engine on your site. Examples of how to search for text appear at the bottom of the page.

The Survey Form template enables you to collect information on any topic. The form provides areas for questions, along with several types of response fields. You can cut, paste, and edit the fields easily.

You build a search page in Chapter 22.

The Features Behind the Pages

Figure 5.24 shows the advanced form bots that are used in the page templates. Figure 5.25 shows the form fields that are included on them.

Figure 5.24.
The advanced form bots in page templates.

Name of Form	Confirmation	Discussion	Registration	Save Results	Search
Confirmation Form	✔				
Employment Opportunities					✔
Feedback Form					✔
Guest Book					✔
Product or Event Registration					✔
Search Page					
Survey Form					✔
User Registration				✔	

Figure 5.25.
Form fields.

Name of Form	Checkboxes	Drop-Down Menus	Pushbuttons	Radio Buttons	Scrolling Text Boxes	Text Boxes
Confirmation Form						
Employment Opportunities		✔	✔		✔	✔
Feedback Form	✔	✔	✔	✔	✔	✔
Guest Book			✔		✔	
Product or Event Registration	✔	✔	✔			✔
Search Page			✔			✔
Survey Form	✔	✔	✔	✔	✔	✔
User Registration			✔			✔

Linking to a New Page Based on a Template

You can create a new page and a link on an existing page at the same time. When you create a new page in this manner, you can base the new page on one of the templates discussed in this chapter.

1. On the originating page, highlight the text that you want the user to click to activate the link.

2. Choose the Edit l Link command, or click the Create or Edit Link button on the FrontPage menu bar. The Create Link dialog box appears.

3. Click the New Page tab. Assign a title for the page, and enter its URL in the designated fields.

4. By default, you edit the new page immediately. If you want to add the page to the To Do List, check the Add Page to To Do List radio button. Click OK. The New Page dialog box appears.

5. Select the template on which to base the new page. Choose OK. The page is added to the current web.

Saving Pages to the Web

After you create or edit your pages, you save them to your FrontPage web.

1. From the FrontPage Editor, choose File l Save. The Save to Web As dialog box appears.

2. Enter the title and URL that you want to assign to the new page. Click OK or press Enter to save the file to the current web.

Creating Templates of Your Own

If the templates that FrontPage provides are not sufficient, you can always make your own. Suppose, for example, that you created a great page that want to use as a template for others. With FrontPage, it is easy to make your own templates.

1. After your page is complete, choose File l Save. The Save As dialog box appears.

2. Enter a title for the template. The title you enter appears in the New Page dialog box when you base a new page on this template. Enter the following title:

```
Killer Home Page Template
```

3. Enter a name for the template. This name is used for the template folder and the filename. Don't add an extension here. Enter the following name:

`kllrhmpg`

The template directory is named `kllrhmpg.tem`, and the page template is named `kllrhmpg.htm`.

4. Enter a description for the template. When you create a new page based on the template, this description appears at the bottom of the New Page dialog box. Enter the following description:

`Creates a killer home page with multi-colored text, built-in sound, and animation.`

5. Click OK to save the page as a template.

A new directory is created in the `/Microsoft FrontPage/Pages` subdirectory. Now whenever you create a new page, this template is listed in the New Page dialog box.

Workshop Wrap-Up

This chapter wraps up the built-in templates and wizards provided with FrontPage. Much work and thought has gone into these pages. The webs and pages generated with FrontPage can save you a great deal of time.

Chapter Summary

In this chapter, you learned how to open an existing web and how to add to it pages based on the FrontPage page templates. You reviewed the features of each page template. You learned how to save new pages to your web and how to create your own templates of your own.

Next Steps

In the next chapter, you will create a corporate web site that combines some of FrontPage's wizards and templates. You also learn how to set up the registration form for a protected web.

To learn how to edit the pages covered in this chapter, check out the following chapters:

❏ To add or edit bookmarks and links, see Chapter 8, "Getting from Here to There."

❏ To create and edit the various types of lists, see Chapter 10, "Organizing Information with Lists."

❏ To work with images and other enhancements, see Chapter 11, "Sprucing Up Your Pages."

❏ To add or edit the basic bots into your pages, see Chapter 15, "Automating Pages with Bots."

❏ To edit the form fields included in these pages, see Chapter 19, "Fields—The Building Blocks of Forms." Chapter 20, "Runtime Bots: The Heartbeat of FrontPage Forms," shows you how to edit the properties of the form bots used in this chapter.

Q&A

Q: I have some existing content on the Web, and I want to add some pages there. I don't really want to create a FrontPage web on that site. Can I create my pages in FrontPage and ftp them to the site?

A: Yes, you can use the FrontPage Editor as you would any other editor to design your pages. However, if you plan to put your pages on a site that does not have the server extensions, make sure that your pages do not use any of the bots that work at browse time—such as those mentioned in Chapter 20.

Q: I have several products—employees, services, and so on—that I want to create pages for. I want to create the pages all at once and individualize them later. Is there an easy way to do this?

A: Create your first page as you normally would. Include all the general information that is common to all the pages.

There are a couple of ways to make the additional copies after this. The first way is to save the page as a template, after which it appears in the New Page dialog box when you create a new page. You learn how to create a template in Chapter 12.

You can also use another approach. You can save the first page into your open web with the File I Save command. For each subsequent page, use the File I Page Properties command in the Editor to change the title and the URL of the new page. Then use the File I Save As command to place the new copy into your open web. After you create all your pages, you can edit them individually as necessary.

Q: Can I save pages to locations on my hard drive other than the currently opened web?

A: Yes. If you choose the File I Save or File I Save As command, you can click the Save To File button located in the lower-right corner of the dialog box. The Save As dialog box appears. Locate the directory or folder to which you want to save your page, and press OK to save the page. If any images are included in the page, you can save them in the same directory or folder, or you can choose another one.

SIX

Real-Life Examples

In the previous chapters, you learned how to use FrontPage's templates to develop Web sites quickly and easily. What if you want to create your own Web site, using many of the pages that the templates and wizards provide? In FrontPage, it is easy to add the contents of one of the Web templates to another. It is just a matter of enabling a checkbox.

The Scenario

In this chapter, you create a Web site that has the following features:

- ❏ A general corporate presence section with a home page that introduces your company
- ❏ Pages that demonstrate the products your company has to offer
- ❏ Navigation links that enable customers to jump to the main pages in the Web quickly and easily
- ❏ A survey form for asking customers what they think of your company and its products
- ❏ A distinctive appearance with graphics and custom colors

❏ A public discussion area where customers can communicate with your company on a variety of topics

❏ A private discussion area where employees can discuss internal topics

❏ Company-sponsored personal home pages for employees, which are linked to an employee directory that is organized by department

Sounds like a tall order, right? Not with FrontPage. It makes combining Web templates and pages easy.

 # Building the Presence

In Chapter 4, "If You Mean Business," you learned how to develop a site using the Corporate Presence wizard. This project does not use everything that the Corporate Presence Web has to offer, but some pages fit the bill well. Use the Corporate Presence wizard to generate some of the pages in the Web. The steps are

1. Choose File I New Web. The New Web dialog box appears.

2. In the New Web dialog box, highlight Corporate Presence Wizard. Click OK to continue. The New Web from Wizard dialog box appears.

3. In the Web Server field, choose your server from the drop-down menu if it does not already appear in the designated field.

4. In the Web Name field, assign a name for the Web. Enter

   `AcmeCorp`

5. Click OK to create the pages in the Corporate Presence Web.

You've Been Here Before

At this point, the introductory screen of the Corporate Presence wizard appears. Click Next to choose the pages that you want to include.

Products

The second screen in the wizard asks what types of pages you want to include in your Web site. The only pages required are the home page—which is automatically included—and the products page. Therefore, choose the Products and Services option, and click Next to continue.

The Initial Impression

Refer to Chapter 4, "If You Mean Business," for a closer look at the Corporate Presence home page.

In the third screen of the Corporate Presence wizard, you choose the options that you want to include in your home page. This time, don't include a mission statement, but choose these options:

❑ Introduction

❑ Company Profile

❑ Contact Information

Figure 6.1 shows an example of the home page. After you make your selections, click Next to continue.

Figure 6.1.

The home page is the entry page in your Web site.

Remember? Only Products

In the fourth screen of the Corporate Presence wizard, you choose how many products and services pages to include in the site. For the time being, create one product page. After you customize the initial page, you can save it as a template and use it for additional pages. Service pages are not necessary for this Web site. Enter 1 for products and 0 for services.

Refer to the Products and Services page in Chapter 4 for more information on this page.

When you specify only products pages, the FrontPage Explorer creates a products page, as in Figure 6.2. After you make your selections, click Next to continue.

Figure 6.2.
The products page provides links to all the product data sheets in your site.

Refer to Chapter 4 for a closer look at product data sheets.

What Should You Tell Them?

The fifth screen in the wizard asks what type of information you want to include in your product data sheets, shown in Figure 6.3. The options for the service description pages are grayed out because you elected not to create them. For the products page, choose the following options:

- ❑ Product image
- ❑ Information request form

After you make your selections, click Next to continue.

Figure 6.3.
The product data sheet provides information about the products that you offer.

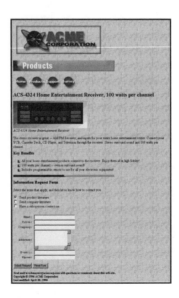

Top and Bottom

Refer to Chapter 4 for a closer look at headers and footers for the Corporate Presence Web pages.

In the sixth screen of the wizard, you choose what you want in the header and the footer of the pages. For the header information, select

❑ Your company's logo

❑ Page title

❑ Links to your main Web pages

At the bottom of the form, you want to include a copyright notice and the date when the page was most recently modified. You also want to include your e-mail address. For the footer information, select

❑ E-mail address of your Webmaster

❑ Copyright notice

❑ Date page was last modified

After you make your selections, click Next to continue.

Setting the Style

The seventh screen of the wizard asks what type of graphic style you want for your pages. Select the style that you want, and click Next to continue.

Setting More Style

In the eighth screen of the wizard, you choose the color scheme for your pages. All the pages in the Web use this color scheme. The steps are

1. In the Colors section, choose the Custom radio button.

2. For the background texture, choose Gray Texture 5 from the drop-down menu.

3. For the normal text color, click the color square and choose the seventh color in the fifth row in the Color dialog box (very dark purple). Click OK to return to the wizard.

4. For the visited link color, click the color square and choose the seventh color in the third row in the Color dialog box (deep burgundy). Click OK to return to the wizard.

5. For the link color, click the color square and choose the sixth color in the second row in the Color dialog box (deep aqua). Click OK to return to the wizard.

6. For the active link color, click the color square and choose the last color in the third row in the Color dialog box (deep rose). Click OK to return to the wizard.

7. Click Next to continue with the Discussion Web wizard.

TIP: You can change color selections later. Edit the page properties of the Web Colors page in the Corporate Presence Web by using the File | Page Properties command. The other pages in your Web update with the new choices automatically.

Putting on the Hard Hat

The eighth screen in the wizard asks whether you want to include the Under Construction icon in your pages. This is your choice. Click Next to continue.

Where Your Company Is

In the ninth screen in the wizard, you enter the company information and a name for the Web. Enter the following information:

❏ Full name of company: ACME Corporation

❏ One word version of name: ACMECORP

❏ Street address: 123 Busy Street, Anycity, NY 00001

After you enter your information, click Next to continue.

The Number You Have Dialed

In the tenth screen, you enter company contact information. Enter the following information:

❏ Telephone number: 313-555-1212

❏ Fax number: 313-555-1213

❏ Webmaster's e-mail address: Webmaster@acmecorp.com

❏ E-mail address for general information: marketing@acmecorp.com

After you enter your information, click Next to continue.

Creating the Web

The final screen in the wizard asks whether you want to view the To Do list after the Web is created. You do not want to view it at this time because you have more pages to add, so uncheck the option. To create the Web site, click the Finish button. Your Web site appears in the Explorer window. Figure 6.4 shows an expanded view of the links in Summary View.

Figure 6.4.
Your Corporate Presence pages appear in the Explorer window.

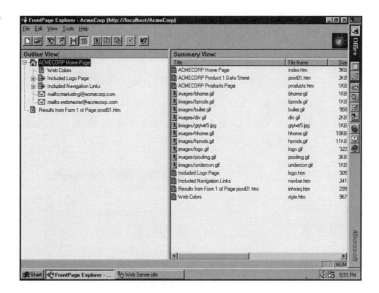

Reviewing the Web

Based on the options that you chose, your Web site has seven pages. They are described in Table 6.1.

Table 6.1. The ACME Corp Corporate Presence web.

Filename (URL)	Description
index.htm	ACME Corp home page
prod01.htm	ACME Corp product 1 data sheet
products.htm	ACME Corp products page
_private/inforeq.htm	Results from Form 1 of the prod01.htm page
_private/navbar.htm	Included navigation links
_private/logo.htm	Included logo page
_private/style.htm	Web colors

Now that you have completed the Corporate Presence portion of your web, you can create the public discusqèœn group.

Adding One Web to Another

You want to add a Customer Support discussion area to your Web site. You could use the Customer Support Web template, which is discussed in Chapter 3, "Can We Talk?" However, you can also use the Discussion Web wizard. It enables you to customize your Discussion web.

To add the Discussion Web wizard pages to your current Web:

1. Choose File I New Web. The New Web dialog box appears.

2. Highlight the Discussion Web wizard.

3. Check the Add to the current Web checkbox, which appears beneath the Web option list, as shown in Figure 6.5.

Figure 6.5.

Check the Add to the current Web checkbox to add the Discussion Web to your existing Web site.

4. Choose OK to continue creating your Discussion Web.

5. The introductory screen in the Discussion Web Wizard now appears on your screen. Click Next to continue.

Pulling Out the Stops

You want a full-featured discussion web in your site. It should have a table of contents for the articles, a search form, threaded replies, and a confirmation page. Constructing everything is an easy task. In the second screen of the Discussion Web wizard, select all the options. Click Next to continue.

Your Discussion Needs a Name

In the third screen in the Discussion Web wizard, you assign a descriptive title for the discussion. This title appears in the main pages of your discussion web. Enter the following name:

```
ACME Corp Customer Support Discussion
```

Based on this name, the wizard informs you that the articles in this discussion will be stored in the _accsd directory or folder. In addition, the files generated by this discussion will be prefixed with accs. Click Next to continue.

Custom Fields Are Required

In the fourth screen in the wizard, you choose a set of input fields for the submission form. Choose the Subject, Category, Comments option, and click Next to continue.

Let Everyone In

In the fifth screen in the wizard, you choose whether the discussion takes place on a protected web. This part of the web is public, so select the Anyone Can Post Articles option. Click Next to continue.

Sorting Your Articles

In the sixth screen in the wizard, you choose how the table of contents sorts the list of posted articles. Select the default option, which is to sort from oldest to newest. Click Next to continue.

Watch That Home Page

The seventh screen in the wizard asks whether you want the Table of Contents page for the discussion to be the home page in the web. The web already has a home page, so you should choose no. Click Next to continue.

The Report

In the eighth screen in the wizard, you choose the information that the search form reports for matching documents. Select the Subject, Size, Date option. Click Next to continue.

Choose Your Style

In the ninth screen in the wizard, you choose colors for the pages. For the sake of consistency, you should select the same colors as you did for the corporate presence web. The steps are

1. In the Colors section, choose the Custom radio button.
2. For the background texture, choose Gray Texture 5 from the drop-down list.

3. For the normal text color, click the color square and choose the seventh color in the fifth row in the Color dialog box (very dark purple).

4. For the visited link color, click the color square and choose the seventh color in the third row in the Color dialog box (deep burgundy).

5. For the link color, click the color square and choose the sixth color in the second row in the Color dialog box (deep aqua).

6. For the Active Link color, click on the color square and choose the last color in the third row (deep rose).

7. Click Next to continue.

TIP: You can change the page properties of the Discussion pages to use the Corporate Presence Web colors page as an alternative.

Select Your Frame Options

In the tenth screen in the wizard, you choose how the articles should be displayed in the discussion. Select the Dual Interface option. This means that the articles are displayed in frames if the browser supports them or in regular pages if the browser does not. Click Next to continue.

You Are Done

The final screen in the wizard notifies you that you have answered all the questions. It tells you that there are two main screens in the discussion:

❏ A frame set for the ACME Corp Customer Support discussion
❏ An ACME Corp Customer Support discussion submission form

NOTE: You need to provide a link to the frame set for the ACME Corp Customer Support discussion. In the figures in this chapter, a link is added to the included navigation links page.

Click Finish to create the web. You are asked whether you want to replace the existing `grytxtr5.jpg` file. Answer no. The wizard then uploads files based on the template in the `Program Files\Microsoft Frontpage\Webs\Vtidisc.wiz` directory on your hard drive.

What Has Been Added

The Discussion Web appears in the Outline View of the FrontPage Explorer. Figure 6.6 shows the Web added to the pages that you created with the Corporate Presence wizard. Fourteen additional pages are added to your Web site. They are described in Table 6.2.

Figure 6.6.

The new pages appear in the FrontPage Explorer.

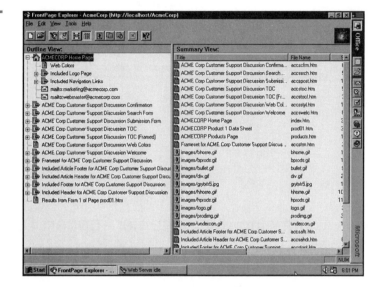

Table 6.2. Customer Support discussion pages that are added to the web.

Filename (URL)	Page Title
accsfrm.htm	Frameset for ACME Corp Customer Support Discussion
accstoc.htm	ACME Corp Customer Support Discussion TOC
accstocf.htm	ACME Corp Customer Support Discussion TOC (Framed)
accswelc.htm	ACME Corp Customer Support Discussion Welcome
accscfrm.htm	ACME Corp Customer Support Discussion Confirmation
accssrch.htm	ACME Corp Customer Support Discussion Search Form
accspost.htm	ACME Corp Customer Support Discussion Submission Form
accsaftr.htm	Included Article Footer for ACME Corp Customer Support Discussion
accsahdr.htm	Included Article Header for ACME Corp Customer Support Discussion

continued

Table 6.2. continued

Filename (URL)	Page Title
accsfoot.htm	Included Footer for ACME Corp Customer Support Discussion
accshead.htm	Included Header for ACME Corp Customer Support Discussion
accsstyl.htm	ACME Corp Customer Support Discussion Web Colors
_accsd/toc.htm	_accsd Discussion
_accsd/tocproto.htm	_accsd/tocproto.htm

TIP:

To view the files in the hidden directories in your web, use the Tools | Web Settings command. Click the Advanced tab in the Web Settings dialog box. Under Options, check Show documents in hidden directories.

Examining the Customer Support Discussion Pages

Now take a closer look at the pages that the Discussion Web wizard generates. The home page of the discussion is the frame set for the Customer Support discussion. If your browser supports frames, Figure 6.7 shows how the frame set looks. The contents are displayed in a frame at the top of the page, and the Welcome section with the discussion articles is displayed at the bottom of the page.

Figure 6.7.
The first page of the Customer Support Discussion displayed in frames.

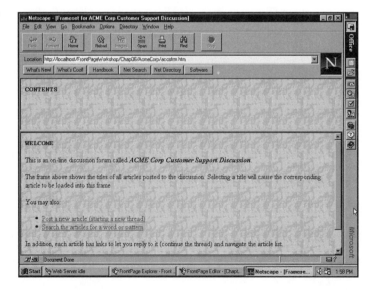

If your browser does not support frames, the table of contents shown in Figure 6.8 appears. This is the page titled Customer Support Discussion TOC.

Figure 6.8.

This version of The Table Of Contents page appears if the browser does not support frames.

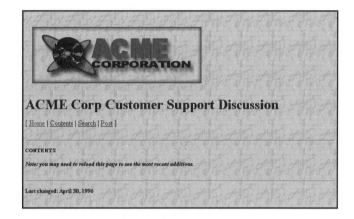

The Customer Support Discussion TOC (framed) page is shown in Figure 6.9. It is included in the frame set shown in Figure 6.7.

Figure 6.9.

This version of the Table Of Contents page appears within the frame set.

The Customer Support Discussion Welcome page, shown in Figure 6.10, is also included in the frame set. If your browser does not support frames, however, it appears as shown in Figure 6.10. The Welcome page tells visitors to your site how to use the discussion and submit articles.

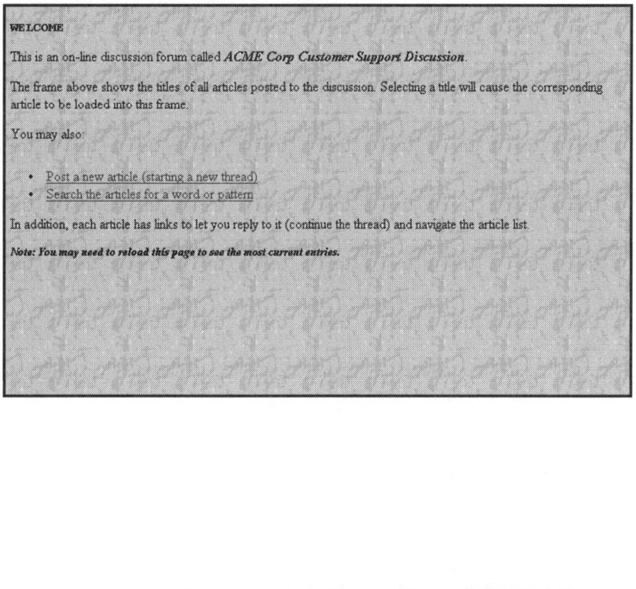

Figure 6.10.

The Welcome page provides instructions on how to use the discussion.

When a visitor submits an article to the discussion, he receives a confirmation message. The Customer Support Discussion Confirmation page, shown in Figure 6.11, includes the title of the article submitted. It instructs the visitor to return to the table of contents to see the article in the list.

Figure 6.11.
When site visitors submit articles, the Confirmation page provides an acknowledgment.

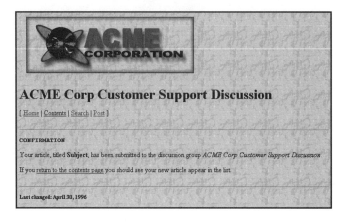

You build your own search page in Chapter 22, "Real-Life Examples."

Site visitors can also search through the articles in the discussion for a word or phrase by using the Customer Support Discussion search form. This form, shown in Figure 6.12, includes a basic search engine. You might want to add examples of how to search for text.

Figure 6.12.
Site visitors can search for a word or phrase within the articles with the Search page.

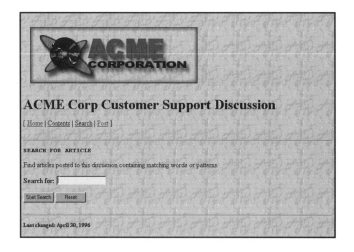

A site visitor submits an article to the discussion with the Customer Support Discussion Submission page, shown in Figure 6.13. He enters the subject of the message, selects a category from a drop-down list box, and enters the body of the article in the Comments field. When the visitor clicks the Post Article button, the article is submitted to the discussion.

Figure 6.13.

Site visitors use the Discussion submission page to post articles to the discussion.

ACME Corp Customer Support Discussion

[Home | Contents | Search | Post]

POST ARTICLE

Subject:

Category:
Products

From:

Comments:

Post Article   Reset Form

Last changed: April 30, 1996

The included article header for the Customer Support discussion, shown in Figure 6.14, contains links to the home page, the discussion's Table of Contents page, the discussion search form, and the discussion submission form. In addition, visitors can post replies to messages, navigate to the previous and next messages in the thread, and go to the first article in the discussion. This header appears on the articles in the discussion. The included article footer for the Customer Support Discussion contains no information. You can add content to it if you want.

Figure 6.14.

This header appears on all discussion articles. The footer is blank.

ACME Corp Customer Support Discussion

[Home | Contents | Search | Post | Reply | Next | Previous | Up]

Figure 6.15 shows the included header and the included footer for the Customer Support discussion. They both appear on the main pages in the discussion. The included header contains links to the home page, the discussion's Table of Contents page, the discussion search form, and the discussion submission form. The included footer contains the date when the page was last updated.

Figure 6.15.

This header and footer appear on all the main pages in the discussion.

ACME Corp Customer Support Discussion

[Home | Contents | Search | Post]

Last changed: April 29, 1996

Figure 6.16 shows the table of contents for the discussion. Initially, this page contains a heading that displays the directory name for the discussion. You may want to edit this to be more descriptive of the discussion you created. As users submit articles to the discussion, the subject of the article is placed in the table of contents page.

Figure 6.16.
The table of contents updates automatically as articles are submitted.

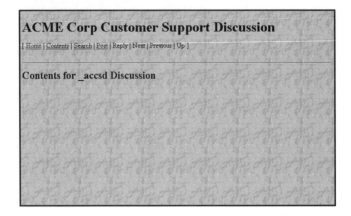

Adding a Survey Page

Now use the Survey Form template to add a customer survey form to the site. The steps are

1. From the FrontPage Editor, choose File I New. The New Page dialog box appears.

2. From the New Page dialog box, highlight the Survey Form option. Click OK. The page appears in the FrontPage Editor.

3. To set the Web colors for the page, choose File I Page Properties. The Page Properties dialog box appears.

4. Change the title of the page to ACME Corp Customer Survey.

5. Under Customize Appearance, check the Get Background and Colors from Page option.

6. Click the Browse button. The Current Web dialog box appears.

7. Highlight Web Colors, the last file in the list, and click OK. The new color scheme is added to the page. The Page Properties dialog box appears.

8. Click OK. The new colors appear in the page.

9. Change the URL of the page to custsurv.htm.

10. Click OK to save the file to the web.

The upper portion of the survey form, shown in Figure 6.17, contains the purpose for the form, and a table of contents of the sections on the page. The visitor jumps to the appropriate section by clicking its link. Following the contents are brief instructions of how to complete the survey.

Figure 6.17.

The upper portion of the survey form contains a description of the form and the page's table of contents.

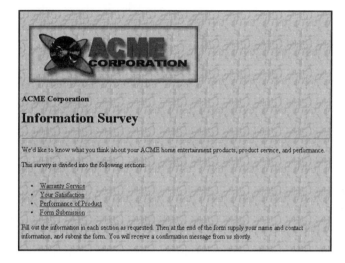

In each section in the survey form, you ask a series of questions, as in Figure 6.18. You can modify the form to suit any purpose.

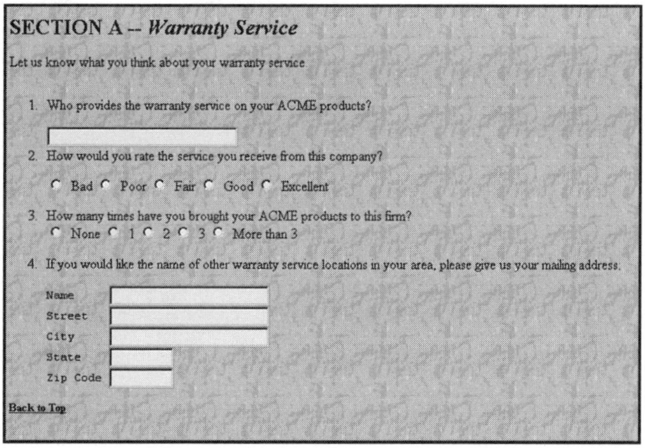

Figure 6.18.

Each section of the page has questions that relate to its heading.

After the visitor completes the survey, he submits it to your site by using the Form Submission area, shown in Figure 6.19. A footer is included in the lower part of the page.

Figure 6.19.

The lower portion of the page contains the submission area and footer information.

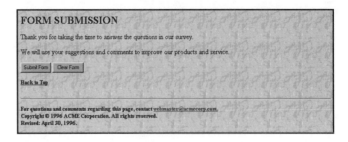

Creating the Private Web

You want to add a private discussion to your web so that employees can coordinate projects, exchange messages, or keep in contact with colleagues who are frequently on the road. You cannot add the private discussion to the current web, though. To restrict a Web with FrontPage's Personal Web Server, you must include a special Web registration form in your FrontPage root web. This registration form requires that an entire Web site be classified as restricted; you cannot mix public and private areas within a single Web site with the Personal Web Server. The way to get around this is to create a new Web site for the private section and to provide links between the public and private webs.

Building a Private Discussion

Creating the Private Employee discussion is easy because the choices that you made when you created the Customer Support discussion will be the default values when you step through the Discussion Web wizard again. Return to the FrontPage Explorer to create a new Web for the private employee discussion. The steps are

1. Choose File I New Web. The New Web dialog box appears.

2. In the New Web dialog box, highlight Discussion Web Wizard. Click OK to continue. The New Web from Wizard dialog box appears.

3. In the Web Server field, choose your server from the drop-down menu if it does not already appear in the designated field.

4. Verify that the Add to the Current Web checkbox is unchecked; it should be unchecked by default. Click OK to continue.

5. In the Web Name field, assign a name for the web. Enter ACMECorpEmp. Click OK to return to the New Web dialog box.

6. When the introductory screen in the Discussion Web wizard appears, click Next.

7. In the second screen in the wizard, verify that all the options (Table of Contents, Search Form, Threaded Replies, and Confirmation Page) are checked. Click Next to continue.

8. In the third screen, enter the following descriptive title for the discussion:

   `ACME Corp Employee Discussion`

   You are informed that the discussion articles will appear in the `_aced` directory or folder. In addition, your filenames will contain the prefix `aced`. Click Next to continue.

9. In the fourth screen, verify that the Subject, Category and Comments option is still selected for the article input fields. Click Next to continue.

10. The fifth screen asks whether the discussion will take place in a protected Web. Choose the Yes, Only Registered Users Can Post Articles option.

11. In the sixth screen, verify that the article sorting option is set to Oldest to Newest. Click Next to continue.

12. Because this web also has an employee directory, you must create a custom page or another home page that provides links to it and the discussion. In the seventh screen, verify that you do not want the Table of Contents page to be the home page of the web. Click Next to continue.

13. In the eighth screen, verify that the search form reporting option is set to Subject, Size, and Date. Click Next to continue.

14. In the ninth screen, the color selections that you chose earlier should still be selected. Click Next to continue.

15. In the tenth screen, verify that the article display option is set to Dual Interface. Click Next to continue.

16. The final screen tells you that the main pages are the frame set for the ACME Corp Employee Discussion and the ACME Corp Employee Discussion Submission Form. Click Finish to generate the new Web pages.

Registering the Web

You learn how to use and configure Registration bots in Chapter 20, "Runtime Bots: The Heartbeat of FrontPage Forms."

Before the pages appear in the FrontPage Explorer, the FrontPage Editor opens. Then you see the Web Self-Registration form, shown in Figure 6.20. This form uses a Registration bot, which asks visitors to your site for their name and password before they can enter the protected discussion.

The Web Self-Registration form contains instructions for you. First, you change the permissions for the web. Next, you open the root web. Finally, you save the registration form to the root web.

Figure 6.20.
You need to put the Web Self-Registration form in your server's root web.

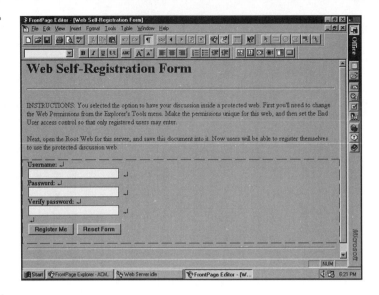

 Setting the Web Permissions

To change the permissions for a protected discussion web:

1. Return to the FrontPage Explorer. Choose Tools I Permissions. The Web Permissions dialog box appears.

2. The Settings tab should be selected by default. Choose the Use Unique Permissions for This Web option. Then click the Apply button.

To add new users to your protected web, refer to the instructions in Chapter 23, "Web Maintenance and Administration."

3. Click the End Users tab. Choose the Registered Users Only radio button. Then click the Apply button.

4. Click OK to exit the Web Permissions dialog box and apply the new settings to the web.

 Opening the Root Web

Now you need to open the root web of your server so that you can save the registration form to it. To open the root web on your server,

1. From the FrontPage Explorer, choose File I Open Web. The Open Web dialog box appears.

2. Choose the server on which you created the discussion web. To view the list of webs on the server, click the List Webs button.

3. From the Web list, highlight <Root Web>. Click OK. The root web opens in the FrontPage Explorer.

Saving the Registration Form to the Root Web

To save the Web Self-Registration Form into the root web:

1. Return to the FrontPage Editor. The Web Self-Registration Form is still there.

2. Choose File | Save. The Save As dialog box appears. Change the page title to `ACME Employee Discussion Registration Form`. Change the page URL to `acedreg.htm`.

3. Click OK to save the file to your root web.

Viewing the Result

Reopen the ACMECorpEmp Web with the FrontPage Explorer's File | Open Web command. The Discussion Web appears in the Outline View of the FrontPage Explorer. Figure 6.21 shows the fourteen pages that are added to the private Web site. Their content is identical to that of the pages in the Customer Support discussion. The page titles and their URLs are listed in Table 6.3.

Figure 6.21.

The pages in the Employee discussion are added to your web.

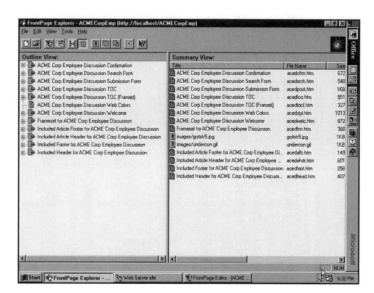

Table 6.3. Employee discussion pages that are added to the Web.

Filename (URL)	Page Title
acedfrm.htm	Frameset for ACME Corp Employee Discussion
acedtoc.htm	ACME Corp Employee Discussion TOC
acedtocf.htm	ACME Corp Employee Discussion TOC (Framed)
acedwelc.htm	ACME Corp Employee Discussion Welcome
acedcfrm.htm	ACME Corp Employee Discussion Confirmation
acedsrch.htm	ACME Corp Employee Discussion Search Form
acedpost.htm	ACME Corp Employee Discussion Submission Form
acedaftr.htm	Included Article Footer for ACME Corp Employee Discussion
acedahdr.htm	Included Article Header for ACME Corp Employee Discussion
acedfoot.htm	Included Footer for ACME Corp Employee Discussion
acedhead.htm	Included Header for ACME Corp Employee Discussion
acedstyl.htm	ACME Corp Employee Discussion Web Colors
_aced/toc.htm	_aced Discussion
_aced/tocproto.htm	_aced/tocproto.htm

Adding the Employee Directory

You want to add an employee directory in this Web site. Links to the employees' home pages appear on this page. The steps are

1. From the FrontPage Editor, choose File | New. The New Page dialog box appears.
2. In the New Page dialog box, highlight the Employee Directory page. Click OK.
3. To set the Web colors for the page, choose File | Page Properties. The Page Properties dialog box appears.
4. Under Customize Appearance, check the Get Background and Colors from Page option.
5. Type `acedstyl.htm`, or use the Browse button to select ACME Corp Employee Discussion Web Colors from the Current Web dialog box.
6. Change the title of the page to `ACME Corp Employee Directory`.
7. Click OK. The Name and Password Required dialog box appears. It tells you that you need end user permission for the AcmeCorpEmp web.

8. You have rights to the web as an administrator. Enter your name and password. Then click OK to update the page properties.

9. Choose File I Save to save the page to the web. The Save As dialog box appears.

10. Change the page URL to `acempdir.htm`. Click OK to save the page.

11. When you are asked whether you want to save the graphics to the web, check Yes to All. The new page is saved to the web.

Now you can return to the FrontPage Explorer. The new page is added to your web. If you do not see all your pages listed in the Outline View of the FrontPage Explorer, use the View I Refresh command to update the display.

Figures 6.22 and 6.23 show the employee directory. The upper portion provides links to the employees listed on the page. For each employee, a picture, title and department information, and contact information appear. Links to the employee's home page and e-mail address are also provided.

Figure 6.22.

The upper portion of the employee directory contains links to all the employees listed on the page.

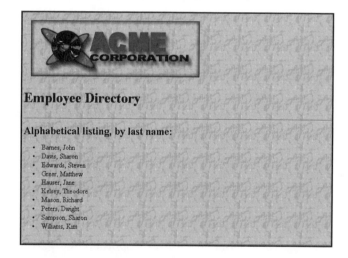

Figure 6.23.

The employee sections on the page include departmental and contact information.

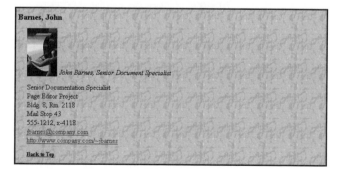

Workshop Wrap-Up

Creating large Web sites is no longer tedious. Combining webs and pages with FrontPage makes the job a snap. You can add pages to your webs to your heart's content. As your page library grows, the job gets even easier.

Chapter Summary

In this chapter, you learned how to combine pages from FrontPage's Web and page templates into a single Web site. You also learned how to register a protected web. You can add pages easily with FrontPage. With templates and wizards, designing webs is a piece of cake.

Next Steps

In the next chapter, you examine your pages more closely and decide what to add to your To Do List. You learn how to add tasks and how to mark them as complete when the pages are finished. You will soon learn how to build your own pages from scratch and edit them. You will find that the steps in building your own pages are just as simple.

Q&A

Q: Why is the background image a JPG file?

A: The first reason is to minimize the size of the file. The background appears on all the pages and is downloaded often. Saving the file in JPG format reduces its size and, therefore, decreases the download time. The other reason is that JPG files can contain more than 256 colors. Backgrounds with subtle color differences can be very effective. You can place true-color images in your Web pages if you use JPG file format.

Q: Can a visitor respond to a discussion group article by e-mail?

A: No, all responses to discussion group articles are stored on the Web as consecutively numbered Web pages (`.htm` extension).

Q: Can some visitors be allowed access to some private groups while others are allowed access to other private groups?

A: Yes, each private discussion can be configured to allow as many visitors as you like. A single user can also be granted permission to access more than one Web by entering his or her name and password in each Web's Permissions dialog box. Refer to Chapter 23 to learn how to assign permissions for an end user to gain access to your private webs.

CHAPTER

SEVEN

What to Do?

"I've got sticky notes all over my monitor! Aaagh!"

Sound familiar? As the number of pages in your web grows, you will discover that it is hard to keep track of which pages you need to add or revise—especially if your web has many pages or if multiple people are working on them at once. It also adds to the confusion if you lose track of who is doing what and what needs to be done.

Don't get me wrong. Sticky notes are one of the greatest inventions to come around in a long time, and I use them a lot. I use them less now, though, since I use FrontPage to design my Web site. I use the To Do list to keep track of things for me. I can see through to my monitor screen again.

What To Do Lists Do

Think of your To Do list as the personal information manager of Web development. You use the To Do list to track what needs to be done on a Web site or on a particular page. If you are developing a site in which multiple authors will work on the same web, you can learn quickly what tasks you are responsible for. You can use the To Do list to remind yourself of whom you need to consult about your pages, attach notes to other authors about what they need to do on the page, and so on. Essentially, anything you put on a sticky note can be added to your To Do list. You can get those sticky notes off your monitor and into the computer where they belong!

In this chapter, you

- ❏ Manually add items to the To Do list from the FrontPage Explorer and the FrontPage Editor
- ❏ Learn the best way to add items to the To Do list
- ❏ Add tasks to the To Do list when you create a link to a new page
- ❏ Add tasks to the To Do list when you verify internal and external links
- ❏ Sort tasks by category
- ❏ Complete and delete tasks from the To Do list

Tasks in this chapter:

- ❏ Adding Tasks to Your To Do List
- ❏ Showing the To Do List
- ❏ Adding Task Details or Modifying Tasks
- ❏ Completing Tasks

Suppose, for example, that three people work on a Web site. The administrator develops the overall content. Another author does the artwork. The third author adds special HTML code or enhanced features to the pages. The To Do list helps you coordinate what these folks have to do.

What Are To Do Tasks?

Tasks are items that need to be completed on a page. Each task has a name, a responsible person, and a description. You can make the task as simple or as detailed as you like. For example, if you are working on your own, you can enter a task like Complete survey page. Because you are responsible for the entire job, you know what you have to do.

When you coordinate with others on a page, though, you might have an idea that falls outside your normal area of expertise. It is better to assign that task to someone else who can handle it better. You can attach the task to the page—along with a description of your idea—and assign it to another author.

Don't Let the List Manage You

When you add tasks to your To Do list, keep the list as compact as possible. For example, if five items on a page need to be completed and you are responsible for three of them, bundle those three tasks into one description. You can always edit the description after you complete one of the tasks. Otherwise, you can imagine how big a To Do list can get if you enter five tasks for each of 100 pages. In that case, the To Do list would be managing you. Remember: The To Do List is there to save you time—not to create more work.

As a general rule, if an item depends on the actions of another individual—even, perhaps, a customer—it is a good idea to add a task for it.

 ## Adding Tasks to Your To Do List

There are several ways to add tasks to a To Do list. Some wizards, such as the Corporate Presence wizard, add them automatically. In other cases, you add tasks manually after you examine the pages to see what needs to be worked on.

You can add a task to a To Do list in several ways:

- ❑ You can add a task manually from the FrontPage Explorer or from the FrontPage Editor.
- ❑ You can add a task automatically when you create a link to a new page.
- ❑ You can add a task automatically when you verify broken links in your web.

Adding Tasks Manually

You use the FrontPage Explorer to add a task to any page, graphics image, or other type of file in the current web.

1. Open the web in the FrontPage Explorer.

2. Highlight the page, image, or file to which you want to attach a task. It is easiest to do this in the FrontPage Explorer's Outline View or Summary View. Figure 7.1 shows a task being added for an image in the web.

Figure 7.1.

Highlight the Web page, image, or other file to which you want to attach a task.

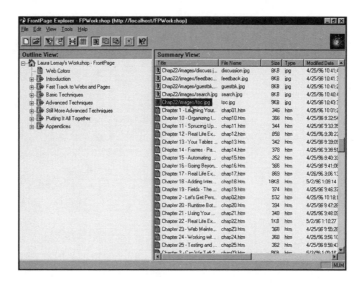

3. Choose Edit | Add To Do Task, or click the Add To Do Task button on the toolbar. The Add To Do Task dialog box appears. (See Figure 7.2.)

Figure 7.2.

Complete the task for the file in the Add To Do Task dialog box.

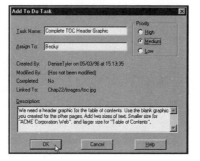

You use the FrontPage Editor to add a task to the currently opened page.

NOTE: You cannot add a task for an image or other type of file from the FrontPage Editor.

1. Open the page to which you want to attach a task.
2. Choose Edit I Add To Do Task. The Add To Do Task dialog box appears. Figure 7.3 shows an example of a task being added to a page.

Figure 7.3.

A task can be assigned to the currently opened page in the FrontPage Editor.

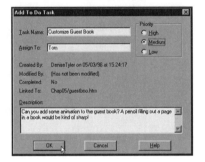

NOTE: The page to which you add a To Do task must exist in the currently opened web. There might be a case in which you open a page from one web and do not save or close it before you open another web. When you return to that page in the FrontPage Editor and try to add a task to it, you get an `Unable to Open To Do List` message. To resolve this problem, open the web from which you opened the page and add the task again.

If you add a task to a page that has not yet been saved to the web, you are prompted to save the page to the web before you add the To Do task. Choose Yes to save the page to the web, and add the task. Choose No if the web to which you want to save the page is not currently open. Open the web, save the page to it, and then add your To Do task.

Sometimes, you might have tasks that are of a general nature or that might apply to more than one page. In a case like this, you can add a task from the To Do List itself. Tasks added this way do not attach to a particular page.

To add tasks of a general nature, use the Add Task button in the To Do List dialog box. The Add To Do Task dialog box appears, as shown in Figure 7.4.

Figure 7.4.
You can enter tasks that are not linked to any page or file in your web.

The Add To Do Task dialog box enables you to assign a name for the task, assign an author, prioritize the task, and describe what is to be completed on the page. To add this information:

1. Open the Add To Do Task dialog box using one of the procedures described earlier.

2. Assign a name for the task in the Task Name field.

3. Type the name of the author to which the task is assigned in the Assign To field.

4. Enter a description for the task. The description can contain as much information as you see fit.

5. Assign a priority to the task. Anything that relates to completing the text content of the page is a high priority. Medium priority might involve fixing broken URLs, revising content, or running a spell check. Adding extra elements that merely enhance the appearance of the page are low priority.

6. Choose OK. The task is added to the To Do List.

Adding Tasks When Creating Links to New Pages

In Chapter 8, "Getting from Here to There," you learn how to create a link to a new page. You can add this new page to the To Do list rather than edit it immediately. You do this with the New Page tab of the Create Link dialog box. From this dialog box, click the Add New Page to To Do List button. (See Figure 7.5.)

Figure 7.5.
You can add a task automatically to the To Do list when you create a link to a new page.

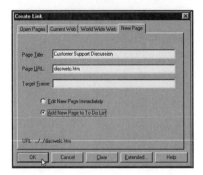

Figure 7.6 shows an example of a task that has been added from the Create Link dialog box. You can edit the details of the task.

Figure 7.6.
This task was added from the Create Link dialog box. Tasks added while you verify links are also shown here.

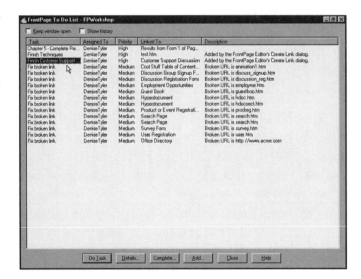

Adding Tasks When Verifying Links

In Chapter 25, "Testing and Publishing Your Web," you learn how to verify internal and external links before you publish your web. You can add broken links to the To Do List with the Add Task button in the Verify Links dialog box. (See Figure 7.7.) You can add tasks to either internal or external links in this manner.

Figure 7.7.
You can add a task automatically when you verify the links in your web.

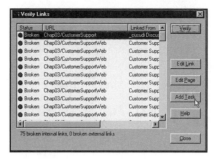

 # Showing the To Do List

Once tasks are added to the To Do list, you can use it to keep track of what has been done or who is assigned to a particular task. You must have an open web to use the To Do List. When a web is open, you can show the To Do List from the FrontPage Explorer or the FrontPage Editor. In either case, you use one of the following two procedures:

❏ Use the Tools I Show To Do List command. The number of outstanding tasks is displayed beside the menu command.

❏ Use the Show To Do List icon on the toolbar.

Either procedure opens the To Do List dialog box. (See Figure 7.8.)

Figure 7.8.
The To Do list helps you keep track of what you need to complete on your pages.

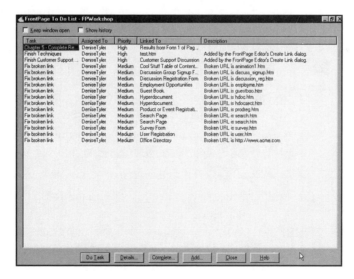

Two checkboxes appear at the top of the To Do List dialog box. Check the Keep Window Open box if you want to keep the To Do list open while you complete tasks. If you do not choose this option, the To Do list closes when the page associated with a particular task is opened. Check the Show History box if you want to view both completed and incomplete tasks.

The To Do List arranges tasks in columns. You can sort the tasks by category by clicking the appropriate column heading. The categories are

- ❏ **Task:** This is the name of the task. By default, tasks are listed in the order in which they were entered.

Refer to Chapter 23, "Web Maintenance and Administration," for instructions on how to add additional authors to your Web site.

- ❏ **Assigned To**: This column shows the author who is responsible for completing the task. Of course, if you are working alone, there is only one author—you.

- ❏ **Priority**: This column sorts tasks by priority. High-priority tasks appear at the top of the list, followed by medium-priority and low-priority tasks.

- ❏ **Completed**: This column appears only if the Show History box is checked. It sorts tasks by the date when they were completed.

- ❏ **Linked To**: If multiple tasks are assigned to a page, you can sort the To Do list to display them conjointly. This column shows the title of a page, the URL of a page, or a graphics file.

- ❏ **Description**: You can also sort tasks by their descriptions. A description is entered when you add tasks manually. Some descriptions are entered by wizards, such as the Corporate Presence wizard. Task descriptions are also entered when you verify links. You can edit the descriptions at any time.

Five buttons appear at the bottom of the To Do List dialog box. They are

To learn how to associate graphic files with the editor of your choice, refer to Chapter 16, "Going Beyond the FrontPage Editor."

- ❏ **Do Task**: When you click this button, the page or graphics file associated with the task is opened in the FrontPage Editor or the graphics editor.

- ❏ **Details**: Click this button to edit the name of the task, assign a new author for it, revise its priority, or edit its description.

- ❏ **Complete**: Click this button to mark a task as complete.

- ❏ **Add:** Click this button to add a task to the To Do List.

NOTE: When you add a task from the To Do list dialog box, it does not get linked to a page. You can use this feature to enter general tasks that are applicable to multiple pages or to add general reminders.

❑ **Close**: Click this button to close the To Do List. You need to click it only if you enabled the Keep Window Open option.

Adding Task Details or Modifying Tasks

Task details are the elements that make up a task: its name, the person assigned to it, and its description. Sometimes, you need to modify a task, especially if it was added automatically by a wizard or through the Create Link or Verify Links dialog boxes. To modify a task:

1. Click the Details button in the To Do List dialog box. The Task Details dialog box appears. It contains the same information as in the Add To Do Task dialog boxes shown in Figures 7.2 through 7.4.

2. Revise the details as necessary. You can change the name of the task name, the person assigned to it, or its description.

3. Click OK to revise the task. Click Cancel to close the dialog box without revising the task.

Completing Tasks

To complete a task, it is best to open the page from the To Do list itself. It is much easier to keep track of the tasks this way. This is a good habit to get into if many authors work on the same web. The To Do List tracks who is assigned to a page or a task.

To open a page from the To Do list:

Refer to Chapter 16 to learn how to configure editors for images or other types of files.

1. Click the Do Task button in the To Do List dialog box. The page, graphic, or file opens in its respective editor.

2. Revise the page or other file as indicated by the task.

3. Choose File I Save to save the page to the web. You are asked whether you want to mark the task as complete. Choose Yes to complete the task or No to keep the task in the To Do list.

What if you forgot to open the page from the To Do List and completed what you were supposed to do? What if you mistakenly added a task to the wrong page? You can use the Complete Task button in the To Do list to remedy either situation.

1. Click the Complete button in the To Do List dialog box. The Complete Task dialog box appears. (See Figure 7.9.)

Figure 7.9.

Use the Complete Task dialog box to mark a task as completed or to delete it from the To Do list.

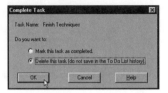

2. At this point, you have one of two options. You can mark the task as completed and place it in the To Do List history. To view the task again, check the Show History option in the To Do List dialog box. On the other hand, you can delete the task, which removes it from the To Do list. It is not saved in the history list, so be sure you want to delete it.

3. Click OK to exit the Complete Task dialog box. The task no longer appears in the To Do list.

Closing the To Do List

Normally, when you choose a task from the To Do list, it automatically closes. If you kept the To Do list open while you worked, however, you can close it by clicking the Close button in the To Do List dialog box.

Printing the To Do List

There is no Print button in the To Do List dialog box. To print your list, you need to use a roundabout method. The items in your To Do list exist in a Web file in the `_vti_pvt` directory on your server. Suppose, for example, that you installed your FrontPage Web content to a directory called `D:\FrontPage Webs\Content`. The web is named PersonalWeb. The To Do List HTM file, then, appears in the `D:\FrontPage Webs\Content\PersonalWeb\_vti_pvt\_x_todo.htm` directory.

If you want to print the To Do list from the FrontPage Editor, you can open the file from the currently opened web by following these steps:

1. Choose File | Open File.

2. Navigate to the directory that contains the file. Highlight the `_x_todo.htm` file, and choose Open.

3. The page appears in the FrontPage Editor, as shown in Figure 7.10. Choose File | Print to print out the To Do List.

Figure 7.10.

The To Do list appears in a Web document in one of the hidden directories in your web.

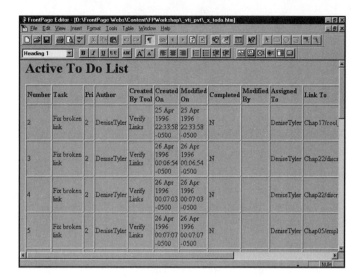

Workshop Wrap-Up

To Do lists help make Web development much easier. Your desk will be clear of note paper, and you will be able to see your monitor. Keep in mind, though, that you are in charge of your To Do list—not the other way around. Keep things as basic as you can while still getting your intent across. You are sure to find To Do lists excellent management tools.

Chapter Summary

In this chapter, you learned how and when to add tasks to a To Do list several ways. Whether you add tasks manually or automatically, you can keep track of your Web projects much better with a To Do list.

Next Steps

In the following chapters in this book, you learn how to create basic pages. You will progress from basic concepts, such as entering text on your pages, to organizing information in lists and adding images.

- ❏ In Chapter 8, "Getting from Here to There," you learn how to create and edit links and bookmarks.
- ❏ In Chapter 9, "Composing and Editing Page Content," you learn the basics of entering paragraphs, text styles, headings, and other types of text effects in your pages.

❏ In Chapter 10, "Organizing Information with Lists," you learn about the different kinds of lists that you can use for organizing information. You also learn how to add enhanced features to lists.

❏ In Chapter 11, "Sprucing Up Your Pages," you learn how to add images to your pages, including images for page navigation.

❏ In Chapter 12, "Real-Life Examples," you bring all these techniques together and design some pages of your own. You complete a home page, favorite links pages, and a navigation bar.

Q&A

Q: If I mark a task as completed or delete it by mistake, is there any way to get it back in the To Do List?

A: No. You must enter the task again if you want it to reappear as an unfinished task.

Q: When an author logs into a web, is there an easy way to tell how many tasks he has to complete in that web?

A: Yes. There can be many tasks in the To Do list. The easiest way to find the tasks assigned to a particular author is to sort the list by the Assigned To field. This groups all the tasks assigned to an author together.

Q: In the examples in this chapter, three authors are assigned to the web. What if one author quits? Can the other authors complete his tasks?

A: Yes. An author can modify, complete, or delete a task assigned to another author. The procedures are the same as discussed in this chapter.

Q: I want to assign a task to another author, but I do not know who the other authors are. How can I get this information?

A: The web administrator assigns the authors for the web. Unfortunately, the only way to view the authors assigned to the web is by using the Tools I Permissions command, which only an administrator can use. To remedy this, the administrator can add a general task to the To Do list by using the Add Task button in the To Do list dialog box. He might create a task like this:

```
Task: Authors assigned to this web.
Assigned to: The administrator's name.
Priority: High (keeps it at the top of the list).
Linked to: (It won't be linked to any page).
Description: The authors assigned to this Web are Becky, Sam, and Tom.
```

EIGHT

Getting from Here to There

The first time I went on the Internet, what I thought would only be a one-hour browsing session lasted four hours. I began by looking for information on graphic development. I did a Web search for related pages. The search returned thousands of pages, so I picked one that sounded promising. Once I got to the site, I went deeper into areas that were more relevant to the topics in which I was interested. Each site led me to another. It was like having a huge library in my living room.

Links and bookmarks are what give Web pages this level of interactivity. Without them, you cannot easily enable people to see what it is on your site or to find other sites with similar information. With links and bookmarks, a user can simply click a mouse on text or a graphic to navigate to all types of pages, download files, find newsgroups, and send e-mail.

In this chapter, you

- ❏ Get some pointers on planning your Web site
- ❏ Create bookmarks on your pages and navigate to specific places on them
- ❏ Create links to Web pages, files, and other Web protocols
- ❏ Use images as links and designate specific areas in an image for navigating to other pages
- ❏ Use the FrontPage Editor to follow links

Tasks in this chapter:

- ❏ Creating Bookmarks
- ❏ Creating Image Links
- ❏ Specifying Alternative Text Representations
- ❏ Creating Clickable Images
- ❏ Highlighting Hotspots
- ❏ Selecting, Moving, Resizing, and Deleting Hotspots
- ❏ Linking to Open Pages
- ❏ Linking to Other Pages in Your Current Web
- ❏ Linking to the World Wide Web
- ❏ Following Links

Planning Your Web Site

There is no doubt about it—it takes some planning to create a good Web site. Before you start designing your pages, think about what you want to accomplish with your site and how the content should be organized. Most Web sites focus on one or more topics of interest. Each topic is organized in a group of pages that make up one section of a web. If you are working on a personal Web site, what do you want to focus on?

That is an important question. It is one of the first obstacles that you have to face. Once you hear that you have 1, 5, or even 25 megabytes of space to store pages on your server, you are in a quandary over what to fill them with. Your home page typically welcomes people to your site and explains what it is about, but you can use it as a gateway to much else. If you cannot think of anything more than filling your site with pictures of your kids and pets, here are some ideas:

❏ Focus on specific personal interests. These include hobbies, music and art preferences, favorite television shows, things you collect, or photographs of the secret chambers in the Great Pyramid from a trip you took in 1992. If you are interested in these topics, other people probably are as well. You might want to point visitors to other areas on the Web that discuss the same things.

❏ Talk about your expertise in certain areas. Do a search to see what the hottest topics on the Web are. If you can think of something you like that relates to any of those topics, you can have many visitors. Likewise, if you are an expert at something novel, such as building a remote-controlled, robotic combination vacuum cleaner and mop, people might want to hear about it, too.

❏ Show off your creative talents. If you sculpt, build custom sailboats, make cakes and candies, do landscaping, or plant great gardens, take photographs of your accomplishments and put them on the Web.

TIP: If you do not have a scanner or access to one, but do have a CD-ROM drive, ask your photo shop to put your photographs on a photo CD. Many shareware and commercial graphics programs support the Photo-CD format.

❏ Publish your works. Put samples of your poetry or a small novella on the Web. Share MIDI or WAV files of the music that you write with visitors to your site.

TIP: MIDI files, which contain note and instrument data for MIDI-compatible instruments and sound cards, are generally much smaller than WAV files. The disadvantage to using MIDI files is that they can sound quite different, depending on the instrument or sound card that the user has.

WAV files are digital recordings of sound or music. The advantage to using them is that the file will sound the same from system to system. However, file sizes can become quite large. Many sound-editing programs offer ways to compress WAV files without too much loss in quality.

You learn how to attach a background sound to your pages in Chapter 21, "Using Your Own HTML Code."

Once you have the basic idea for your Web site, think about how you want to organize the information. Make it easy for visitors to find their way around your site.

Figure 8.1 shows an example of an initial idea. The home page is linked to two main areas, which contain pages that discuss the person's areas of interest—white water rafting and myths and mysteries. It is a good idea to provide navigation links on each page so that users can return to other pages easily. For example, all the pages on white water rafting should include links back to the main page of the section, which in turn should contain a link back to the home page. Likewise, there should be links to navigate between the pages on rafting.

Figure 8.1.

Plan your information before you start building your Web site.

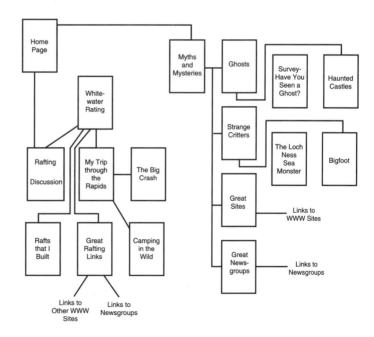

Compare this to the hierarchical linking diagram shown in Figure 8.2. A structure like it might be good for an online book. The lack of links to other sections, however, means that users can quickly get lost, especially if the navigation is several levels deep. Provide a means for users to get around so that they do not have to backtrack through several levels to get to other areas of interest. The home page should provide links to the sections in the book—that is, the second level. Every second-level page should contain navigational links to the home page, the other second-level pages, and each of its third-level pages. Links to the preceding chapter should appear at the beginning of each chapter, and links to the following chapter should appear at the end of each chapter—just where people are most likely to need them.

Figure 8.2.
Hierarchical linking is good to use for online books.

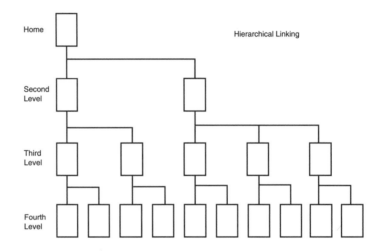

Bookmarks: Navigating Within Pages

Links and bookmarks are traditionally called *anchors* in the Web world, which is why they have an A tag. Bookmarks differ from links in that they mark a specific spot on a page. Just as bookmarks serve as placeholders when you read a book, they perform basically the same function on a Web page.

Creating Bookmarks

A page that contains bookmarks typically has a small table of contents at the top, which links the user to bookmarked headings on the page. At the end of the bookmark's section, another link takes the user back to a bookmark located at the top of the page or at the table of contents.

To create a bookmark on your page:

1. From the FrontPage Editor, select the text that you want to use as a book-mark. Usually, this is a section heading.

2. Choose Edit | Bookmark. The Bookmark dialog box appears. (See Figure 8.3.)

Figure 8.3.

You create a new bookmark with the Bookmark dialog box.

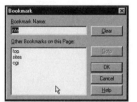

3. By default, the text that you select for the bookmark appears in the Book-mark Name field. Though FrontPage allows you to create bookmark names that contain spaces, some browsers will not recognize them, and the bookmarks may not work properly. It is a good idea to keep bookmarks fairly short because it saves typing when linking to them from another page in the Web. A list of other bookmarks on the page appears beneath the bookmark name. Each bookmark on the page must have a unique name.

4. Click OK to close the Bookmark dialog box. The bookmark text on the page becomes underlined with a dotted line.

 # Visiting Bookmarks

You can visit a bookmark on your page without creating a link to it. The steps are

1. Select any text on the page, and choose Edit | Bookmark. The Bookmark dialog box appears.

2. In the Other Bookmarks on this Page field, select the bookmark that you want to visit.

3. Click Goto. The FrontPage Editor scrolls to the bookmark.

4. Click OK or Cancel to close the Bookmark dialog box.

You also can visit a bookmark on another page. Suppose, for example, that you have the page `oriental.htm`, which is named "Cooking Great Chinese Food." On it is a section called "Picking Fresh Vegetables" with the bookmark `freshveggies`. When you create a link to this bookmark, the URL looks like

```
oriental.htm#freshveggies
```

You do not have to select the text, as in Figure 8.4. The figure emphasizes the relationship between the link to the bookmark and the bookmark itself.

Figure 8.4 shows how to visit the bookmark from the page that links to it. The steps are

1. Place the pointer anywhere within the text that the user clicks to go to the page or bookmark. The originating page is shown in the top portion of Figure 8.4.

Figure 8.4.

When you visit a bookmark on a different page, FrontPage opens it and scrolls to its bookmark.

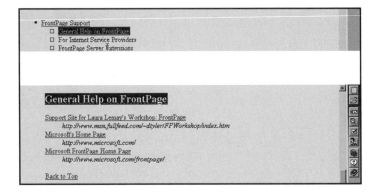

2. Choose Tools I Follow Link, or click the Follow Link button. The FrontPage Editor opens the other page and scrolls to the bookmark that you want to visit on the page. This is the portion of the page shown in the bottom portion of Figure 8.4.

 # Deleting Bookmarks

Deleting a bookmark is easy. The steps are

1. Place the mouse pointer anywhere within the text of the bookmark.

2. To delete the bookmark without deleting the associated text on the page, select Edit I Unlink. The bookmark is removed, but its heading text remains.

   To delete the bookmark as well as its associated text, select Edit I Bookmark and click Clear in Bookmark dialog box.

TIP: An even quicker way to delete a bookmark or any other page element is to use the Delete key.

Links: Reaching Outward

It is convenient to be able to jump to different locations on a page, but that is not what the Web is all about. The Web is about reaching outward. To accomplish this, you provide links on your pages. Links can take users to other pages in your web, to pages in other people's webs, to newsgroups, and to other types of Internet protocols. You can even put a link on your page to get e-mail delivered to your mailbox. You can create three basic types of links:

❏ Text links

❏ Image links

❏ Clickable image links (image maps)

Text Links

Whenever you see blue underlined text on a page, you know that it will take you somewhere else. For that reason, it is redundant to say "Click here." Instead, make your links descriptive. Figure 8.4 shows examples of text links.

Creating Text Links from the FrontPage Explorer

You can use the FrontPage Explorer to create a text link from the page that is currently opened in the FrontPage Editor to another page in the current web. As Figure 8.5 shows, creating a link this way involves only three easy steps. They are

1. From any view in the FrontPage Explorer, highlight the destination page— the page to which you want to link—as in part 1 of Figure 8.5.

2. Left-click and drag the page from the FrontPage Explorer to an open page in the FrontPage Editor. The mouse pointer becomes a link pointer, as in part 2 of Figure 8.5.

3. Move the link pointer to the line where you want to create the link, and release the left mouse button. A text link to the destination page appears on the opened page in the FrontPage Editor. The title of the page appears in the text link, as in part 3 of Figure 8.5.

Figure 8.5.
Creating a text link from the FrontPage Explorer.

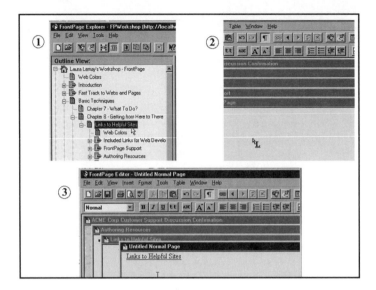

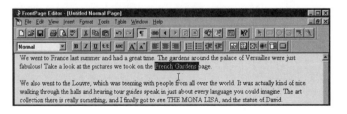

TASK

Creating Text Links from the FrontPage Editor

You use the FrontPage Editor to create a text link to another page that is opened in the Editor. The steps are

1. In the FrontPage Editor, open the page from which you want to originate the link.

2. Select the text that you want the user to click to activate the link, as in Figure 8.6.

3. Select Edit I Link, or click the Create or Edit Link button on the toolbar. The Edit Link dialog box appears.

4. Create a link using one of the methods discussed in "Where You Can Link," later in this chapter. You can create links to an opened page, a page in your current web, a page in the World Wide Web, or to a new page.

Figure 8.6.
Creating a text link from the FrontPage Editor.

Image Links

Image links are commonly used as navigational buttons and navigation bars, but images can be used for links in all sorts of ways. For example, you can provide a thumbnail of a picture, which users can click to download it or display it in a larger view.

Creating Image Links

Creating image links is just as simple as creating text links. The steps are

1. Insert an image on the page.
2. Click the image to select it. It becomes surrounded by a selection bounding box, as in Figure 8.7.

Figure 8.7.
Select an image and click the Create or Edit Link button to create an image link.

Refer to Chapter 11, "Sprucing Up Your Pages," to learn how to insert images into your pages.

3. Use the Edit I Link command, or click the Create or Edit Link button on the FrontPage Editor toolbar. The Edit Link dialog box opens.
4. Complete the information in the Edit Link dialog box.

Specifying Alternative Text Representations

Sometimes, the people who visit your Web site are not using browsers that can display images. These browsers are becoming increasingly rare, but other browsers provide the option to turn image display off. Many people choose not to download images because of the time involved. This is not a problem when images are placed on a page just to be seen. When they serve a function, however, you must provide an alternative for people who do not want to download all that artwork.

❑ *Provide a text version of the image link or links elsewhere on the page.* This option might be your only choice if the graphic is a clickable image that contains multiple links.

❑ *Specify an alternative representation, which displays text in place of the graphic on the page.* This option is a good choice if you use a navigation bar similar to the one used in the Corporate Presence wizard, in which a series of individual images are placed one after another to make up the navigation bar.

By default, FrontPage creates image maps that are used with the FrontPage Server Extensions. Refer to Chapter 23, "Web Maintenance and Administration," to learn how to assign a different image map handler.

To specify an alternative text representation:

1. Click the image to select it.

2. Choose Edit I Properties, or right-click and choose Properties from the pop-up menu. The Image Properties dialog box appears.

3. In the Alternative Representations I Text field, specify the text that you want to display as an alternative to the graphic. If it is an alternative for a navigation bar, in which a series of images are placed one after another, enter a brief description of the link. For example, to link to a table of contents, enter Contents or TOC.

4. Choose OK to exit the Image Properties dialog box.

Clickable Image Links

Clickable images, also known as *image maps,* are graphics that contain hotspots. The hotspots provide links to different pages from within the same image. They are useful and enable you to add creativity to the links on your pages. Figure 8.8 shows a graphic that contains one rectangular and several polygonal hotspots.

Figure 8.8.
Clickable images can contain links to several different pages on the Web.

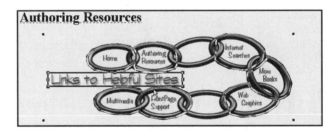

 ## Creating Clickable Images

You can turn any graphic on your page into a clickable image. Simply select the image, create a hotspot or hotspots on it, and assign a link to the hotspot. The steps are

1. Click the image in which you want to add a hotspot. The Image toolbar activates.

2. Select the type of hotspot that you want to create from the Image toolbar.

    Circular hotspots. Click the Circle icon and move the cursor inside the image. The cursor becomes a pencil. Position the pencil at the center point of the circular hotspot, and left-click to set the center of the circle. Drag the circle until it surrounds the hotspot area, and release the mouse button.

    Rectangular hotspots. Click the Rectangle icon and position the mouse pointer at the first corner of the rectangle. Left-click and drag to the diagonally opposite corner of the rectangle. Release the left mouse button to complete the hotspot.

Polygonal hotspots. Click the Polygon button, and position the pointer at the starting point of the polygon. Click to set the first point. Drag the mouse pointer to the end of the first segment, and click again. Continue around the hotspot area in this manner. To end the polygonal hotspot, click the mouse at the originating point of the hotspot. Alternatively, double-click the next-to-the-last segment; when you do this, FrontPage connects the next-to-the-last point to the origin point with a straight line.

3. After you release the mouse button, the Edit Link dialog box appears.

4. Complete the information in the Edit Link dialog box.

 # Highlighting Hotspots

When you edit the shapes of your hotspots so that they do not overlap too much, it is sometimes hard to see their outlines on dark backgrounds. Use the Highlight Hotspots command to find hotspots easier. The steps are

1. Click the image to activate the Image toolbar.

2. Click the Highlight Hotspots button, which is the next-to-the-last button on the Image toolbar. The image disappears, and you can see the hotspot areas, as in Figure 8.9.

Figure 8.9.
Use the Highlight Hotspots button to view hotspots easily.

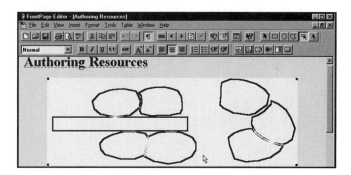

 # Selecting, Moving, Resizing, and Deleting Hotspots

You need to select a hotspot to move, resize, or delete it. To select a hotspot:

1. Click the image where the hotspot appears.

2. Select the hotspot by clicking it. It becomes surrounded by a bounding box with sizing handles at each of the corners.

To move a hotspot:

1. Select the hotspot.
2. Left-click and drag the hotspot to a new location; use the Escape key to return the hotspot to its original position. Alternatively, use the up, down, left, and right arrow keys to move the hotspot to a new location.

To resize a hotspot:

1. Select the hotspot.
2. Click and drag any of the Resizing handles or Resizing points in the hotspot. They are designated by small squares.

To delete a hotspot:

1. Select the hotspot.
2. Use the Edit | Clear command, or press the Del key.

Where You Can Link

You now know how to create a link. All the methods described so far open the Edit Link dialog box. This dialog box enables you to link to

❑ Pages that you have opened in the FrontPage Editor

❑ Pages in your current web

❑ Pages or files on the World Wide Web

❑ New pages that you have yet to create

Linking to Open Pages

Choose the Open Pages tab, shown in Figure 8.10, to create a link to another page that is opened in the FrontPage Editor. The steps are

You also have the option to enter a target frame for the link. Refer to Chapter 14, "Frames—Pages with Split Personalities," for more information on target frames.

1. Select the page to which you want to link from the list that appears in the dialog box.

2. If you are linking to a bookmark on the destination page, select the name of the bookmark from the drop-down list. No bookmarks are listed if the destination page has none.

3. Click OK to close the Edit Link dialog box.

Figure 8.10.
Use the Open Pages tab to link to other pages that are opened in the FrontPage Editor.

 TASK

Linking to Other Pages in Your Current Web

Choose the Current Web tab, shown in Figure 8.11, to create a link to any page, graphic, or file that exists in the web that is currently open in the FrontPage Explorer.

Figure 8.11.
Use the Current Web tab to link to other pages in the current web.

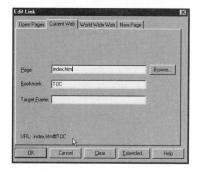

The steps are

1. In the Page field, enter the filename of the page to which you want to link, or click the Browse button to choose from the list of pages in the current web.

2. If you are linking to a bookmark on the destination page, select the name of the bookmark from the drop-down list. No bookmarks are listed if the destination page has none.

3. Click OK to close the Edit Link dialog box.

TASK

Linking to the World Wide Web

You can create links to pages on the World Wide Web, including pages that exist in other webs on your own Personal Web Server. You also can create links to other Web protocols. Table 8.1 describes the protocols to which you can link.

Table 8.1. Web protocols.

Protocol	URL Example	Description
file	`file://localhost/directory/filename.ext`	Specifies a file on your local host.
FTP	`ftp://www.anyserver.com/downloads/program.zip`	File transfer protocol. Used for a file that is accessible across the Internet.
gopher	`gopher://anygopher.tc.university.edu/2`	Gopher protocol. Creates a link to a directory-based protocol.
http	`http://www.anyserver.com/mylink.htm`	Hypertext transfer protocol. Enables Web clients to retrieve information from Web hosts.
http	`http://www.anyserver.com/mylink.htm#graphics`	Creates a link to a bookmark on a page.
mailto	`mailto:myemail@www.myprovider.com`	Creates a link to an e-mail address.
news	`news:alt.example.nosuchgroup`	Retrieves files from a Usenet newsgroup.
Telnet	`telnet:/yourname:password@yourhost:port`	Used for a remote Telnet login session.
WAIS	`wais://yourhost:port/database`	Provides links to database information on Wide Area Information Servers.

Sometimes you need to provide a relative URL. In this case, you use the Other protocol. Suppose, for example, that the source URL is http://www.myserver.com/personal/index.htm and that the target URL is http://www.myserver.com/business/index.htm. The relative URL is ../business/index.htm.

NOTE: Your files might end up on a system that is case-sensitive. This is typical of servers that run on UNIX systems. As a general rule, most Web developers use all lowercase letters when they enter URLs to avoid conflicts with case-sensitivity. In addition to the letters of the alphabet and the numbers 0 through 9, you can use the following symbols:

-, ., +, ', _

Use the World Wide Web tab, shown in Figure 8.12, to create a link to a page, a file, or a protocol on the World Wide Web.

Figure 8.12.
Use the World Wide Web tab to link to pages on the World Wide Web.

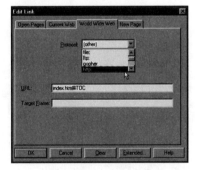

The steps are

1. From the list of protocols, choose the one that applies to the page or protocol to which you are linking.
2. In the URL field, enter the absolute URL of the page or protocol to which you want to link.
3. If you are linking to a bookmark on the destination page, append the bookmark name to the URL, preceded by a pound sign.
4. Click OK to close the Edit Link dialog box.

Linking to a New Page

Choose the New Page tab, shown in Figure 8.13, to create a link to a new page that will be placed in the currently opened web. The steps are

Figure 8.13.
Use the New Page tab to link to pages that do not yet exist in the currently opened web.

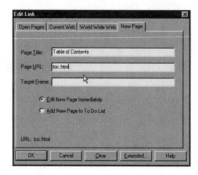

1. Enter a page title for the new page in the Page Title field.
2. The Edit Link dialog box enters a URL for the page automatically, based on the title that you enter. If you want to edit the title, change it in the Page URL field.
3. At this point, you can

    Edit the new page immediately. If you choose this option, the new page opens in the FrontPage Editor. You can add content to it right away.

    Add the new page to To Do list. If you choose this option, the new page is saved to your web, and a task for it is added to the To Do List.

Refer to Chapter 7, "What to Do?" for an example of a task that is added from the Edit Link dialog box.

4. Click OK. The Template or Wizard dialog box appears.
5. Select the template on which you want to base the new page. Choose the Normal template if you want to create page content of your own.
6. Click OK. If you base the new page on one of the page wizards, follow its instructions to complete the page.

Following Links

The FrontPage Editor has built-in browsing capabilities that enable you to follow the links in your webs and the World Wide Web. Although not a high-powered browser, it enables you to test your links as you design them.

To follow a bookmark, a text link, or an image link forward:

1. From the FrontPage Editor, place the mouse pointer anywhere within the text or image hotspot that contains the link, or select any part of the link.

2. Select Tools I Follow Link, or click the Follow Link button on the FrontPage Editor toolbar. If you follow a link to a bookmark, the FrontPage Editor scrolls to the bookmark. If you follow a link to another page, it opens in a new window in the FrontPage Editor.

3. After you follow a bookmark link, a text link, or an image link forward, use the Back button in the FrontPage Editor to return to the page from which you navigated. The originating page reopens at the location of the link that you followed.

Sometimes the server to which you are following a link is unresponsive. You can stop the process by selecting Tools I Stop from the FrontPage Editor or by clicking the Stop button on the FrontPage Editor toolbar.

Changing, Unlinking, and Deleting Links

It is a fact of life on the Web that sites have a tendency to evolve and change. Ten pages quickly become dozens. They are renamed, relocated, deleted, or divided into other pages.

To change the URL of a text link or an image link:

1. Select the link that you want to change. For a text link, place the mouse pointer anywhere within the text that contains the link, or select any part of it. For an image link, select the image or the hotspot within the image that contains the link.

2. Use the Edit I Link command, or click the Create or Edit Link button in the FrontPage Editor toolbar. The Edit Link dialog box appears.

3. Use the Edit Link dialog box to change the URL.

To unlink a link:

1. Select the characters that you want to delete from within the text link.

2. Choose Edit I Unlink. The link is deleted from the text—or the part of the text—that you selected. The text associated with the link remains.

To delete a text link or an image link:

1. Select the link that you want to delete. For a text link, place the mouse pointer within the text associated with the link. For an image link, select the image or hotspot in the image that contains the link.

2. Select Edit I Link, or click the Create or Edit Link button on the toolbar. Then click Clear. Alternatively, you can press the Del key.

Adding Extended Attributes to Links

Chapter 11 explains in more detail what extended attributes are used for. FrontPage supports the most common attributes associated with links, but the capability to add additional attributes that are not supported is available in the Edit Link dialog box.

To add extended attributes to a link:

1. Select the link to which you want to add an extended attribute.

2. Choose Edit I Properties. The Edit Link dialog box appears.

3. Click the Extended button. The Extended Attributes dialog box appears.

4. Click the Add button. The Set Attribute Value dialog box appears.

5. Enter the name of the attribute in the Attribute Name field.

6. To associate a value with the attribute name, check the Specify Value checkbox. Enter the value of the attribute in the Value field.

7. Click OK to close the Set Attribute Value, Extended Attributes, and Edit Link dialog boxes.

Recalculating Links

When multiple authors work on the same web at the same time, you can easily lose track of who has done what. Likewise, when you create webs with wizards or import pages into your web, you sometimes see a red triangle beside the page when you are in the FrontPage Explorer's Outline View. This usually occurs when a page that contains a link is imported to a web before the destination page is imported. Use the Recalculate Links command to update the web display in the FrontPage Explorer. In many cases, this command gets rid of those red triangles.

To update the web display or to create the text index for the Search bot, use the Tools I Recalculate Links command. The FrontPage Explorer refreshes the display of the web in Outline View.

Workshop Wrap-Up

You have learned roughly all there is to know about creating and using links with FrontPage. You are now set to tackle building your Web site from the ground up. Choose a theme, plan the areas that you want to include on your site, and the rest will happen over time. Rome was not built in a day, nor will be your custom pages. Sites constantly evolve and change as new standards are developed for the Internet. The more you become familiar with what is out there and what you can do, the more you can incorporate into your site.

Chapter Summary

In this chapter, you learned how to navigate through your pages and out to other areas of the Internet by using bookmarks and links. You were given suggestions about what to include in your site, and you learned how to link pages together with text, images, and image maps.

Next Steps

In the next chapter, you learn about the basic elements that make up a page—paragraphs, headings, and text styles. You learn when to use them and how to arrange content for the best appearance.

For additional information that relates to the topics discussed in this chapter, check out the following chapters:

- ❏ Refer to Chapter 11, "Sprucing Up Your Pages," to learn how to import images into your web and onto your pages.
- ❏ Refer to Chapter 14, "Frames—Pages with Split Personalities," to learn how to configure target frames.
- ❏ Refer to Chapter 25, "Testing and Publishing Your Web," to learn how to verify links and repair broken links.

Q&A

Q: I am uncertain about when to use relative URLs and how to enter them. Can you help me?

A: A good example of when to use a relative URL is to provide a link to a page that is in another web on your Personal Web Server. It does not fall into the category of pages in your current web, nor does it fall into the category of World Wide Web documents.

Suppose, for example, that you are working on the following page in the current web:

`http://yourservername/MyWeb/funstuff/comics.htm`

From this page, you want to link to a page in another web on your own server, such as

`http://yourservername/Comedy/3stooges.htm`

The common portion of these two webs is `http://yourservername`. To return to the common root, you have to go back two levels from the `comics.htm` page. As in the old days of DOS, you go backward one level by entering two periods (`..`). Therefore, when you create a link from the `comics.htm` page to the `3stooges.htm` page, choose the `Other` protocol in the World Wide Web tab of the Edit Link dialog box. The relative URL will look like

`../../Comedy/3stooges.htm`

Q: Why is it best to use relative URLs?

A: Relative URLs are portable. When you develop your Web site on your local computer and subsequently relocate the pages or rename directories, the relationships between the pages are maintained, and the links will not break. In contrast, when you use absolute or base URLs, you need to edit each URL to reflect the new location. This is a tedious and time-consuming task.

Q: Do all browsers support `mailto:` links?

A: No—if a browser does not support a `mailto:` link, the user receives an error message.

NINE

Composing and Editing Page Content

Now that you are thinking about what you want to put on your site, you probably want to start building your own pages. You should have a fairly good idea of the types of pages you want to put in your web. Roll up your sleeves, because it is time to start building those pages. This chapter starts with the basics: working with headings, paragraphs, and text styles.

In this chapter, you

- ❑ Learn about the basic content elements that are contained on a page
- ❑ Use headings to identify the contents on your page
- ❑ Learn about the basic types of paragraph styles and what they are used for
- ❑ Format text and paragraphs to add style without images
- ❑ Edit your content using the clipboard as a helper
- ❑ Find, replace, and check the spelling of the content on your pages

Tasks in this chapter:

- ❑ Working with a Normal Web
- ❑ Entering Headings on a Page
- ❑ Inserting Headings
- ❑ Inserting Paragraphs
- ❑ Editing Content
- ❑ Spell-Checking Content

Working with a Normal Web

As you read along, you should reproduce the examples in this chapter and the ones that follow. Create a web in which you can practice. When you create a normal web, a single blank page is placed in it. You already know the procedure: Simply specify a normal web in the FrontPage Editor's New Web dialog box.

Building a Page

It is usually best to build pages in several passes. First, plan the content of your pages by putting in the headings. Starting this way gives you a feel for the content that you want to include on a page. It is also easier to create bookmarks when there is not much text in between headings—you have less to scroll through.

After you enter the headings, enter the content beneath each heading. Look at the section and decide what best conveys the information that you want to include. Sometimes, plain text is all that is necessary. Other times, a list or a table might be more effective in getting the message across.

While you enter the content, create the links to the other pages in the same section; create the new pages in the process. Add the pages to your To Do list, and enhance the task descriptions if necessary.

After the basic content is on the pages, develop the navigation links for the section. This gives you the opportunity to take a final look at the pages. Decide which pages belong in the navigation bar and which ones should have the navigation bar included on them. Use the Include Bot to place a text version of the navigation links on the page first. This way, you can make sure that you like how the links flow before you make the graphics. You can even put pages on the Web at this point. At least they will be doing something while you develop the graphics.

After the graphics are done, edit the navigation bar to display the graphics in place of or in addition to the text links. All the pages that contain the new navigation bar are updated automatically because of the Include bot.

Refer to Chapter 15, "Automating Pages with Bots," for more information on how to use the Include bot.

Finally, develop header graphics and footers, using the same basic design throughout each of the pages in a section. Try to give your pages a consistent look and feel. Update the pages to which you added graphics on the remote server—including the pages that have the navigation bar included within them.

Now, take a look at the basic building blocks that you use in your pages—headings and paragraphs.

Using Paragraphs and Headings

A paragraph is a line or a group of contiguous lines that use the same format and are separated in the FrontPage Editor with white space. Once you hit the Enter key at the end of a line, you start a new paragraph. The paragraph is separated by what appears to be an extra space.

TIP: You can use line breaks to start a new line in the same paragraph.

When you format a paragraph, all the text contained in the paragraph changes to that format. You cannot mix paragraph styles in a paragraph. You can, however, mix character styles in a paragraph, which are discussed later in this chapter.

Entering Headings on a Page

You have a blank page in front of you, and you are wondering where to start. First, organize your thoughts by putting headings on your pages. Figure 9.1 shows three levels of headings for a page in the early stages of development. The first heading— the page title—is Heading 1. Four sections are formatted as Heading 2: Picking Your Potato, Making the Gravy, Adding Spices, and What to Top Your Potatoes With. Some sections have additional topics listed beneath them. Those headings are formatted as Heading 3. It is like formatting an outline in a word processor.

Figure 9.1.

Organize your thoughts by placing headings on your page first.

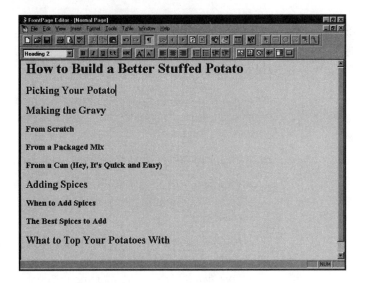

When you create a page based on the Normal template in FrontPage, it opens up in the FrontPage Editor and appears completely blank. If you immediately start typing, the text is entered on the page in normal paragraph format.

A Quick Way to Format a Paragraph or Heading

A quick way to format the first line on your page into a Heading 1 paragraph is to use the style bar, shown in Figure 9.2. Click the arrow in the drop-down menu box, and choose the heading or other paragraph style.

Figure 9.2.
Use the style bar to format text into another commonly used style.

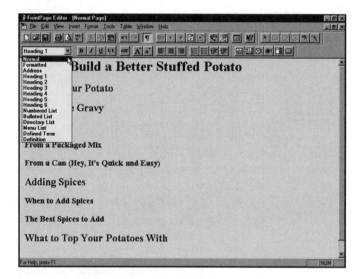

Formatting with the Paragraph Format Dialog Box

You can also use the Format I Paragraph command to insert a paragraph or heading. When you use this command, the Paragraph Format dialog box, shown in Figure 9.3, appears.

From the Paragraph Format dialog box, you can perform these procedures:

❏ *Choose a format for a paragraph.* You can choose normal, formatted, and address paragraphs, along with six levels of headings—Heading 1 through Heading 6.

❏ *Apply an extended attribute to a paragraph.* Simply click the Extended button.

❏ *Specify the paragraph's alignment.* Simply click the Paragraph Alignment drop-down menu to display the list of choices. Left alignment is the default.

You can also choose center or right alignment. Figure 9.4 shows three paragraphs that are left-, center-, and right-aligned.

Figure 9.3.
The Paragraph Format dialog box provides one way to format the paragraphs on a page.

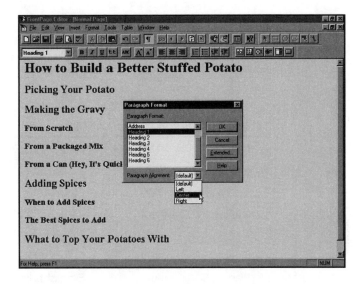

TIP: Use the alignment buttons on the FrontPage Format toolbar to align paragraphs or text quickly.

After you make your paragraph format choices, click OK to return to the FrontPage Editor.

 ## Inserting Headings

After you place a heading on a page, you probably want to press Enter and start typing another line. When you do this, the new line uses the same format as the previous one—including its alignment, color, and character style. In the example here, your second line would appear as a Heading 1. Use the Insert I Heading command to start a new line with a different heading.

1. Position the cursor at the end of the line after which you want to insert the heading.

2. Select the Insert I Heading I 2 (Large) command—or whatever heading you plan to use. The insertion point moves to a new line—actually, a new paragraph—and is formatted to the heading or paragraph style that you select.

Six levels of headings are available in FrontPage. Their font sizes are shown in Table 9.1.

NOTE: Table 9.1 lists the font sizes as they are applied in the FrontPage Editor. Users might have their browsers set to display headings and fonts differently.

Table 9.1. Heading styles—HTML tags and font sizes.

Heading	HTML Tag	Font Size in FrontPage Editor
Heading 1	<H1>	24-point bold
Heading 2	<H2>	18-point bold
Heading 3	<H3>	14-point bold
Heading 4	<H4>	12-point bold
Heading 5	<H5>	10-point bold
Heading 6	<H6>	8-point bold

Inserting Paragraphs

You use some of the same methods discussed earlier to add text content to a page. For example, you can use the style bar or the Format I Paragraph command to format text paragraphs. To insert a new paragraph on your page, use Insert I Paragraph. You can choose from three types of text paragraphs: normal, formatted, and address.

Normal Paragraphs

Normal paragraphs are the meat-and-potatoes paragraph of your Web page. You use them for most of your content.

To insert a normal paragraph on a page:

1. Position the cursor at the end of the line that precedes the paragraph you want to start. In the example shown in Figure 9.4, the insertion point is placed at the end of the first heading.
2. Choose Insert I Paragraph I Normal. FrontPage begins a new paragraph on a new line, putting white space between the paragraphs.

Figure 9.4.

Normal paragraphs are used most commonly in your pages.

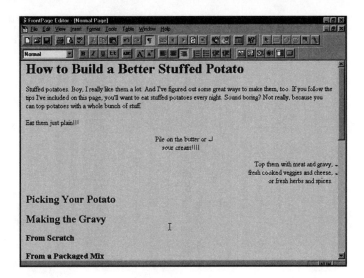

3. Enter the text for the paragraph. You can continue to add paragraphs by pressing the Enter key. A new paragraph begins; it uses the same formatting as the preceding paragraph. The same character styles and formats are used until you position the insertion point on another part of the page.

Formatted Paragraphs

Use formatted paragraphs when you need to provide content in a fixed-width format. You cannot use tabs in HTML pages, but formatted paragraphs enable you to add additional spaces to your text and give the appearance of using tabs. This type of paragraph is good for text-based tables, ASCII art, and code. Figure 9.5 shows three examples of formatted paragraphs. Line breaks split each paragraph into several lines.

To insert a formatted paragraph on a page:

1. Position the cursor at the end of the line that precedes the paragraph you want to start.

2. Choose Insert I Paragraph I Formatted. FrontPage begins a new paragraph on a new line, putting extra space between the paragraphs.

3. Enter the text for the paragraph. The text appears in fixed-width format. Use line breaks to begin new lines within the same paragraph.

Figure 9.5.
Use formatted paragraphs when you need to use fixed-width text.

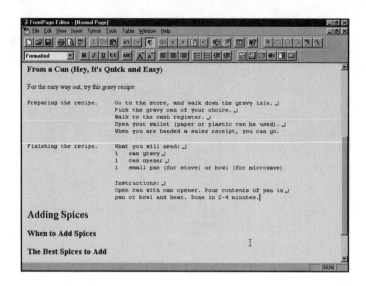

Address Paragraphs

Address paragraphs format text in italics. The traditional use for an address paragraph is to place author information at the beginning or the end of a page. Most commonly, this information is placed at the end of a page, as shown in Figure 9.6.

Figure 9.6.
Use address paragraphs to place author information or other italicized content on a page.

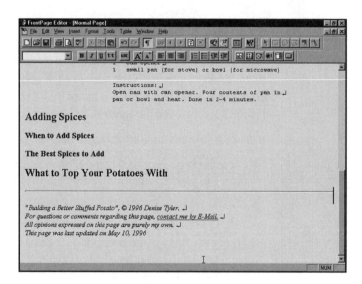

To insert an address paragraph on a page:

1. Position the cursor at the end of the line that precedes the paragraph you want to start.

2. Choose Insert I Paragraph I Address. FrontPage begins a new paragraph on a new line, putting extra space between the paragraphs.

3. Enter the text for the paragraph. The text appears in italic format. Use line breaks to begin new lines within the same paragraph.

Reformatting Paragraphs

You can easily change a paragraph from one format to another. For example, you can change an address paragraph to a heading, a normal paragraph, or a formatted paragraph. In Figure 9.7, the address paragraph has been reformatted to a Heading 5.

Figure 9.7.
You can change the formatting of a paragraph.

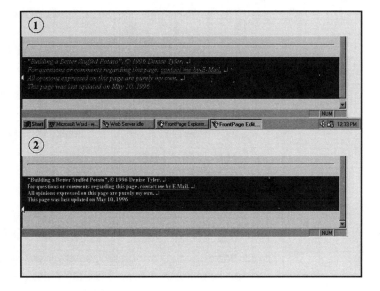

To change a paragraph style:

1. Position the cursor at the far left side of the page. It turns into a selection pointer (an arrow pointing to the right).

2. Double-click to select the paragraph. It appears in inverse video when selected.

3. Choose a new paragraph style from the style bar, or use the Format I Paragraph command to select a style from the Paragraph Format dialog box.

Splitting Paragraphs

To split a paragraph into two or more paragraphs that use the same paragraph style, position the insertion point where you want to split the paragraph. Then press Enter. The paragraph is split at the point you specified, and the parts are separated by white space.

To split a paragraph into two paragraphs while applying a different style for the second paragraph, position the insertion point where you want the paragraph to break. Choose the Insert I Paragraph command, and select a new style. FrontPage splits the current paragraph at the insertion point.

Adding Line Breaks

Chapter 11, "Sprucing Up Your Pages," discusses the other types of line breaks, as well as how to use them with images.

When you press the Enter key to start a new line on a page, it starts a new paragraph and inserts white space after the preceding paragraph. To start a new line of text without starting a new paragraph or adding white space, use line breaks.

TIP: To view where the line breaks are on your page, click the Show/Hide button, which shows and hides paragraph marks. This button is the one with the paragraph mark on it. It is located just to the left of the Create or Edit Link button on the tool bar.

To insert a line break:

1. Choose Insert I Line Break. The Break Properties dialog box appears.
2. Choose Normal Line Break. This forces a line break without clearing images in the left or right margin.
3. Click OK.

Adding Extended Attributes to Paragraphs

You can add extended attributes to paragraphs by clicking the Extended button in the Paragraph Format dialog box. These attributes are added to the HTML code that FrontPage generates for the paragraph.

To add extended attributes to a paragraph:

1. Select the paragraph to which you want to add the attribute.
2. Choose Edit I Properties. The Paragraph Format dialog box appears. Click Extended. The Extended Attributes dialog box appears. Click Add. The Set Attribute Value dialog box appears.
3. In the Name field, enter the name of the attribute.
4. To associate a value with the name, select Specify Value and add the value of the attribute in the Value field. If you select Specify Value but leave the value field empty, FrontPage associates the name with an empty string.
5. Click OK.

Text Styles and When to Use Them

You can format any text on your page to use a different color, alignment, or font size. You can also use several different types of text styles. Table 9.2 describes the various styles and typical uses for them.

NOTE: Text styles are not to be confused with font faces. The FrontPage Editor works with two basic types of text styles—a proportional font (Times Roman) and a fixed-width font (Courier). All of the character styles you choose in FrontPage are based on these two font styles. Refer to Chapter 21, "Using Your Own HTML Code," to learn how to assign different font faces to your Web pages.

Table 9.2. Character styles and HTML tags.

Style	HTML Tag	Typical Use
	Regular Styles	
Strong	`<STRONG>`	Marks a strong emphasis. It is often rendered the same as bold text.
Emphasis	`<EM>`	Emphasizes text. It can be rendered in italics or as underlined text in browsers.
Underline	`<U>`	Underlines text. You can also use the Underline button on the FrontPage Editor tool bar.
Strikethrough	`<STRIKE>`	Renders text with a line drawn through it. It is often used in legal online documents.
Typewriter font	`<TT>`	Renders text in fixed-width format. You can also use the TT button on the FrontPage Editor Format toolbar.
	Special Styles	
Citation	`<CITE>`	Marks a citation from a book or other published source.
Definition	`<DFN>`	Marks a definition. It is usually preceded by a term.
Sample	`<SAMP>`	Renders sample text or special characters.
Blink	`<BLINK>`	Causes selected text to blink on and off. Use it sparingly.

continues

Table 9.2. continued

Style	HTML Tag	Typical Use
	Special Styles	
Code	\<CODE\>	Marks computer source code. It is rendered as fixed-width text in FrontPage Editor, but it is rendered as monospaced text in some browsers.
Variable	\<VAR\>	Marks a variable used in computer code, equations, or similar work. It is usually rendered in italics.
Bold	\<B\>	Renders text as bold. Can use Bold button on the FrontPage Editor tool bar.
Italic	\<I\>	Renders text as italic. You can also use the Italic button on the Frontpage Editor toolbar.
Keyboard	\<KBD\>	Marks instructions that a user enters by keyboard. It is rendered as fixed-width text in FrontPage Editor, but it is rendered as monospaced text in some browsers.

Use the Format I Characters command to apply formatting to the text on a page. You can apply formatting to a single character, a word, a group of words, a sentence, a paragraph, or even the entire page.

1. Select the text you want to format. You can select a contiguous area (multiple lines) by using the Shift key and clicking at the start and the end of the area you want to format.

2. Choose Format I Characters. The Character Styles dialog box appears.

3. Select the style from the Regular Styles or the Special Styles section of the dialog box. The styles are described in Table 9.2.

TIP: You can use the Bold Text, Italic Text, Underline Text, or Typewriter Font buttons on the Format toolbar to change text styles quickly.

4. Select a font size from the Font Size drop-down list. The available sizes are Normal, 1 (8-point), 2 (10-point), 3 (12-point), 4 (14-point), 5 (18-point), 6 (24-point), and 7 (36-point). The default size is 3 (12-point).

TIP: Use the Increase Text Size or Decrease Text Size buttons on the tool bar to change the size of your text quickly. Each time you click the button, the size of the text increases or decreases by one increment.

5. The default text color is that which you chose in the Page Properties dialog box. You can also specify a different text color. Check the box beside Set Color. Click the Choose button to choose a font color from the Color dialog box.

TIP: Use the Text Color button on the tool bar to change the color of your text quickly.

6. Click OK to exit the Character Styles dialog box.

In Figure 9.8, the three aligned paragraphs are selected for formatting. The font size is increased from the default font size—3 (12-point)—to 5 (18-point) by twice using the Increase Text Size button on the tool bar. The Italic button is used to put the text in italics. The Font Color button is used to change the text to blue.

Figure 9.8.

Normal text can be reformatted in interesting ways when you combine different formats.

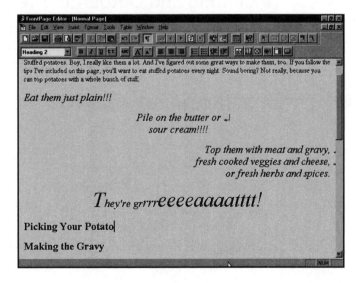

The words They're great shown in Figure 9.8 demonstrate how you can apply character formatting to a portion of a word. The font size is increased a few letters at a time. As you can see, you can use character formatting to achieve interesting effects without relying on graphics.

Special Text Formatting

FrontPage enables you to format text in other ways as well. You can use superscript and subscript text, increase or decrease indentation, and insert special characters. The procedures are quite simple.

Using Superscript and Subscript Text

Use superscript and subscript text to designate footnotes or dropped text. To raise a character or a group of characters above the base line of the text, use superscript text.

1. Select the text you want to change.
2. Choose Format I Characters. The Character Styles dialog box appears.
3. In the Vertical Position field, choose Superscript to raise the text. Click the up arrow or enter a numeric level of superscripting that is one or more levels higher than the text on the base line. Alternatively, choose Subscript to lower the text. Click the down arrow or enter a numeric level of subscripting that is one or more levels lower than the text on the base line.
4. Press OK to exit the Character Styles dialog box.

Indenting and Outdenting Text

You can indent or outdent text to add emphasis to your layout. Use the Increase Indent button to indent the text toward the right. Use the Decrease Indent button to outdent the text toward the left.

Inserting Special Characters

Special characters are items such as trademark, registration, and copyright symbols; accent marks on text; special currency symbols; and common fractions. To insert a special character:

1. Choose Insert I Special Character.
2. Select a character to insert by clicking it. Use the arrow keys to move through the available selections.
3. Click Insert to insert the currently selected character. You can also insert a character by double-clicking it.
4. Click Close to exit the Insert Special Character dialog box.

Editing Content

What if you want to rearrange your content and place some of it on a different page? What if you placed section 3 before section 4 instead of after it? Mistakes sometimes happen, but it is not tough to fix them.

Undoing Mistakes

FrontPage has a multiple-level Undo function. This means that you can undo several steps. Choose Edit I Undo or click the Undo button for each step that you want to undo.

Using the Clipboard as a Helper

If your hot list is so long that you have to scroll to read all of it, you might want to split it up into several pages. To do this, you can cut the text from one page, place it in the clipboard, and paste it into another page.

Likewise, consider all those Back to Top links that you must create on a page after the bookmarked sections. You actually need to create them only once. Make the first link, copy it to the clipboard, and paste the text and its link into all the other sections. The same applies for graphics used as bullets or dividers on your pages. Copy the first one into the clipboard, and paste it somewhere else.

To copy and paste text and images to and from the clipboard:

1. Select the text or image you want to copy.
2. Choose Edit I Copy, or click the Copy button on the tool bar.
3. Place the insertion point where you want to paste the text or image. You can place the insertion point anywhere on the current page or on another page that is opened in the FrontPage Editor.
4. Choose Edit I Paste, or click the Paste button on the toolbar.

Cutting or Deleting Text

There are two ways to delete text. One method places the text into the clipboard for pasting into another location. The other method deletes the text from the page without placing it into the clipboard.

To delete text from a page and place it into the clipboard, use the Edit I Cut command or click the Cut button. To delete text from a page without placing it into the clipboard, choose Edit I Clear or press Del.

You can also delete the character before the insertion point by pressing the Backspace key for each character you want to delete. To delete text after the insertion point, press Del for each character you want to delete.

Removing Formatting

If you change the format of your text—such as if you increase or decrease the font size—you can return the text to the default format. Simply select the text, and press Ctrl+Space. The text returns to the default format for its paragraph style.

Finding and Replacing Text

Suppose that you are writing a page about flowers, and you forget what you wrote about petunias earlier. You need to find exactly what you said about it. To find text:

1. Choose Edit | Find. The Find dialog box appears.
2. Specify the text that you want to place in the Find What field.
3. Choose whether you want to search up or down from the insertion point in the Direction field.
4. Choose Match Whole Word Only to limit the text to words that match only the whole word you specify. Choose Match Case to limit the text to words that match the capitalization of the word you specify.
5. To find the next match, click Find Next.
6. Click Cancel to exit the Find dialog box.

You realize that what you said about petunias actually applies to daffodils. Instead of retyping everything, you can use the Replace command. To replace text:

1. Choose Edit | Replace. The Replace dialog box appears.
2. Specify the text that you want to find.
3. Specify the replacement text in the Replace With field.
4. Click Replace to replace the most recently found text with the replacement text. Click Find Next to find the next occurrence. This enables you to choose which instances of the text you want to change. Click Replace All to replace all instances of the text.
5. Click Cancel to exit the Replace dialog box.

Spell-Checking Content

It is always a good idea to spell-check your pages before they go out to the public. FrontPage has a built-in spell-checker at your disposal. The spell-checker starts at the beginning of the page and checks the spelling of each word. When a spelling error is found, it is displayed in the Not in Dictionary field in the Spelling dialog box. If the spelling resembles a word in the standard dictionary, replacement words are suggested. To use the spell-checker:

1. Choose Tools I Spelling, or click the Check Spelling button.

2. To correct a spelling error, click one of the proposed corrections in the Suggestions field or edit the Change To field. Click Change to change a single instance of the spelling error. Click Change All to change all instances of the spelling error. The error or errors are corrected, and the next spelling error is displayed.

3. The spell-checker might indicate that a word is misspelled when actually it is spelled correctly. If you do not want to place the word in your custom dictionary, you can tell the spell-checker to ignore it. Click Ignore to ignore a single instance of the word. Click Ignore All to ignore all instances of the word. You might want to place words that will be used on other pages in your custom dictionary. Simply click the Add to Custom Dictionary button.

4. Choose Cancel to exit the Spelling dialog box.

Workshop Wrap-Up

Once you have an idea of the information you want to include on your web, entering content into your pages is very simple. Starting with basic headings helps you organize your thoughts. You can use character styles and formatting to add your content. Using different character styles, you can add emphasis to areas on your Web page. After the content is complete, you can use the FrontPage spell-checker to verify that your content is spelled correctly.

Chapter Summary

Your text can be more than simple text. You can use color, change the alignment, increase or decrease the font size, select different formats, and even insert special characters. After your text is placed on a page, you can spell-check it.

Next Steps

❏ To use lists to organize your page content, see Chapter 10, "Organizing Information with Lists."

❏ To create style sheets, specify text and link colors, and add images to your pages, see Chapter 11, "Sprucing Up Your Pages."

❏ To organize text and images in tables, see Chapter 13, "Your Tables Are Ready."

❏ To use the Internet Explorer Extensions to display your documents using Windows fonts, see Chapter 21, "Using Your Own HTML Code."

Q&A

Q: Why do the headings get smaller as the numbers get larger, and the character styles get larger as the numbers get larger?

A: The reason why the headings get smaller as their numbers get larger is because they correspond to hierarchical logic. Typically, your page title is displayed in Heading 1, topics beneath it in Heading 2, topics beneath them in Heading 3, and so on. Text styles increase in size as their designations increase because it is most logical. A small number indicates a small font size; a large number indicates a large font size.

Q: Are there any rules regarding what font size to use following a heading?

A: Not really, except that you might want to use a heading that is at least the same size or larger than the text beneath it. Normal paragraphs use a default font size of 3 (12-point), which means that Heading 1 through Heading 4 look all right with it. If you use smaller headings, such as Heading 5 or Heading 6, you might want to decrease the font size.

Q: Can I change the default size of the font in the FrontPage Editor?

A: No. This setting is not user-definable. You must set the font size or use the Increase Font Size or Decrease Font Size buttons on the tool bar to change the size of your text.

TEN

Organizing Information with Lists

Do you have links to sites that you want to point people to? Have you written a great paper that shows people how to build, install, or complete something? Lists are among the best ways to organize information like this. They help information stand out clearly. There are several different types of lists that you can use in your pages.

List Types and When to Use Them

There are five basic types of lists that you can use in your pages. When you use a list type, FrontPage anticipates how you want the list to be formatted. For numbered lists, FrontPage automatically places numbers at the beginning of the line. Bulleted lists are preceded by bullets. Definition lists start with a term at the beginning of the line and indent the definition.

The five types of lists are

❏ Numbered lists

❏ Bulleted lists

❏ Definition lists

❏ Directory lists

❏ Menu lists

Numbered lists are used to place items in a definite order. They are good for describing steps or procedures. Bulleted lists, on the other hand, are useful when you want to display a list of items that do not necessarily have to be arranged in a logical order.

Definition lists are used for entering a term and its definition, such as in a glossary, or for adding a title and a description in a hot list.

Directory lists and menu lists are used to place short items in a list. Although they are not often used, FrontPage supports them.

 # Creating a Numbered List

Use numbered lists when you want to present an ordered list of items. Top Ten lists are popular on the Web. Obviously, many people like to use numbered lists. I have my own Top Ten list, shown in Figure 10.1.

Figure 10.1.
Use numbered lists when you need to arrange items in a specific order.

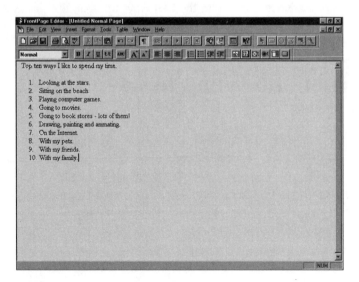

Numbered lists are usually rendered as paragraphs separated by white space and prefixed by numbers. You can prefix them in other ways, though, as you learn in the "Adding Extended Attributes to a Numbered List" task.

To create a numbered list:

1. Start the list. Position the insertion point at the end of the line after which you want the list to start, and choose Insert I List I Numbered. Alternatively, position the insertion point at the beginning of the first line in the list. Then choose Numbered List from the Style Bar, or use the Numbered List button on the toolbar. In either case, FrontPage positions the insertion point at the beginning of the line and enters the first number for you automatically.

2. Enter an item for the list. Press Enter to add additional items. The list numbers increment for you automatically.

3. Press Enter twice or use Ctrl+Enter to complete the list.

Creating a Nested Numbered List

Sometimes you need to create nested lists—that is, multilevel lists—to arrange content. You can use the Insert I List commands or the Increase Indent and Decrease Indent buttons to create a nested list.

1. Position the insertion point at the end of the line which precedes the line you want to indent.

2. Choose Insert I List I Numbered or press the Increase Indent button twice. The insertion point moves to the next line, and it starts a new number sequence (see Figure 10.2).

Figure 10.2.
To create nested numbered lists, use the Insert I List I Numbered command or the Increase Indent and Decrease Indent buttons.

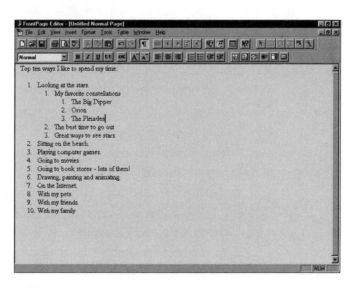

3. Enter your list items until the items in the nested area are complete. Your list items are entered into the same level of the nested list.

4. To return to the original level in the list, position the insertion point at the end of the last indented list item. Click the Decrease Indent button twice. The number increments to the next number within that level.

Adding Extended Attributes to a Numbered List

Look at the numbered list in Figure 10.2. A multilevel list is sometimes arranged with numbers and letters to designate the levels, as in an outline. How can you do that?

In FrontPage, the default is to use numbers in a numbered list, but you can assign other attributes to them. For example, you can specify large letters, small letters, large Roman numerals, or small Roman numerals in a numbered list. To do this, you use extended attributes. Table 10.1 describes the attributes that you can add to a numbered list.

Table 10.1. Numbered list attributes (Netscape).

Name	Value	Description
START	n	Specifies a starting number for the list, with n being a positive integer
TYPE	A	Uses large letters in the list
TYPE	a	Uses small letters in the list
TYPE	I	Uses large Roman numerals in the list
TYPE	i	Uses small Roman numerals in the list

To add extended attributes to a numbered list:

1. Position the insertion point within the first item in the numbered list that you want to change, or select the line.
2. Right-click and choose List Properties from the pop-up menu. The List Properties dialog box appears.
3. Click the Extended button. The Extended Attributes dialog box appears.
4. Click the Add button to add an attribute. The Set Attribute Value dialog box, shown in Figure 10.3, appears.
5. Enter one of the attribute name/value pairs shown in Table 10.1. Where an attribute value is given, check the Specify Value checkbox (checked by default) in the Set Attribute Value dialog box. The information is entered as in Figure 10.3.

Figure 10.3.

You can add letters or Roman numerals to the list instead of numbers through extended attributes.

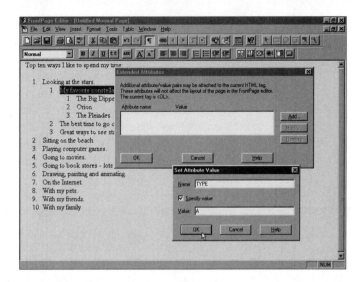

6. Click OK to exit the Set Attribute Value, Extended Attributes, and List Properties dialog boxes.

You might be a little confused at this point, because the FrontPage Editor does not change the appearance of the list. If you use your browser to look at the list, though, you can see the change. For example, I changed the second level of my list to use large letters. Figure 10.4 shows what it looks like in Internet Explorer. Notice that the second and third items in that level of the numbered list are automatically incremented to the next value.

Figure 10.4.

You can view the attributes that you add with some browsers, such as Internet Explorer and Netscape 2.0.

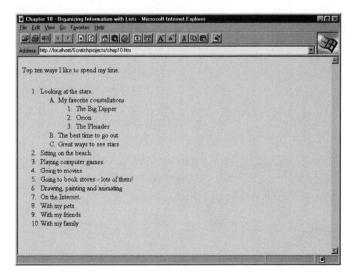

Creating a Bulleted List

When you want to list items but do not have to put them in a specific order, you can use bulleted lists. Many people use bulleted lists to display links to their favorite sites, and there are many other applications for them as well. In most browsers, bulleted lists are displayed as paragraphs separated by white space. Items are preceded by bullets, which are sometimes rendered differently. For example, when the list shown in Figure 10.5 is opened in Netscape, it looks the same as it does in the FrontPage Editor. It uses unfilled and filled squares for the second and third levels. When the same list is displayed in Internet Explorer, however, round bullets are used for all the levels.

Figure 10.5.
Use a bulleted list to create a list of items that do not have to be arranged in a particular order.

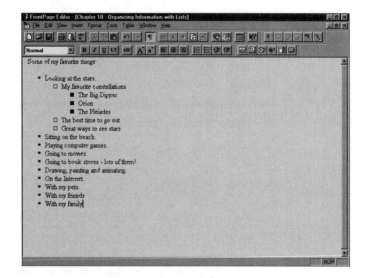

To create a bulleted list:

1. Position the insertion point on the line that precedes the list, and choose Insert | List | Bulleted. Alternatively, position the insertion point on the line where you want to begin the list. Then choose Bulleted List from the style bar, or use the Bulleted List button on the toolbar. In either case, FrontPage inserts a bullet for you.

2. Enter the first item in the list, and press Enter. The insertion point moves to the next line and inserts a new bullet.

3. Type the next list item.

4. Press Enter twice or use Ctrl+Enter to complete the list.

TIP: You can create a nested bullet list using the same procedures outlined in the "Creating a Nested Numbered List" task. Just substitute the bulleted list instead.

Adding Extended Attributes to a Bulleted List

You can change the type of bullet in a bulleted list by using extended attributes. Extended attributes enable you to use discs, circles, or squares for bullets in a bulleted list. Table 10.2 describes the attributes that you can add to a bulleted list. Remember, though, that some browsers display the bullets differently. For example, some browsers render disc bullets as squares, and others render them as circles. Square bullets are usually rendered as filled squares. Circle bullets are rendered as unfilled squares in some browsers.

Table 10.2. Bulleted list attributes (Netscape).

Name	Value	Description
TYPE	DISC	Uses a disc-shaped bullet
TYPE	CIRCLE	Uses a circular bullet
TYPE	SQUARE	Uses a square bullet

The default for a bulleted list is a circular bullet. The default for indented items in a nested bulleted list is a square bullet.

To add extended attributes to a bulleted list:

1. Position the insertion point within the first item in the bulleted list that you want to change, or select the line.
2. Right-click and choose List Properties from the pop-up menu. The List Properties dialog box appears.
3. Click the Extended button in the List Properties dialog box. The Extended Attributes dialog box appears.
4. Click the Add button to add an attribute. The Set Attribute Value dialog box appears.
5. Enter one of the attribute name-value pairs shown in Table 10.2. Where an attribute value is given, check the Specify Value checkbox (checked by default) in the Set Attribute Value dialog box.

6. Click OK to exit the Set Attribute Value, Extended Attributes, and List Properties dialog boxes.

Using a Definition List

Use definition lists to present a term and its definition, such as in a glossary. You also use definition lists to provide a list of items when you want to include a description for each one. Generally, the definition term is aligned with the left margin of the page, and its definition is indented.

Figure 10.6 shows examples of definition lists. The top list is a traditional definition list; the terms and definitions appear single-spaced with no white space between them. The proper way to build a definition list is as follows:

1. Place the insertion point on the line before which you want to start the definition list.

2. Choose Insert I Definition I Term. The insertion point moves to the beginning of the next line.

3. Enter the term. For example:

    `Home Page`

4. Choose Insert I Definition I Definition to place the definition on the next line. The insertion point moves to the next line and is indented by one level.

5. Enter a definition for the term. For example,

    `The page on your web where it all begins.`

6. Repeat steps 2 through 5 to add additional items.

7. Press Enter twice to end the list.

NOTE: When you use the Insert I Definition I Term and Insert I Definition I Definition commands in repeated succession, you should be able to select the entire list by moving your cursor to the far left margin, where it turns into a selection pointer. Double-click in a white space area—not on a term or a definition—to select the entire list.

In the bottom list shown in Figure 10.6, definition list commands create a hot list, but additional white space is added between the items. Each term and definition is actually a single definition list in itself. You can create a similar hot list, without typing any URLs.

1. Open the FrontPage Editor and create a page on which your links will appear.

2. Open your browser to navigate through the Web while you edit your pages.

TIP: You also can use the FrontPage Editor to navigate through the Web by using the Follow Link command or button. In this case, though, it is easier to keep the Editor open to the page you are editing. It makes cutting and pasting easier.

3. When you navigate to a page that you like, return to the page that you are editing and use Insert I Definition I Term to enter the page title as a term.

4. Choose Insert I Definition I Definition, or press Enter and choose Definition from the Style Bar.

5. Highlight the page URL that appears in your navigator. (This is the Address field in Internet Explorer or the Location field in Netscape 2.0.) Press Ctrl+C to copy the URL to your clipboard.

6. Paste the URL into the definition line on your page in the FrontPage Editor.

7. Press Enter to add more description for this page if you like.

8. Select the term line and create a link to the World Wide Web. Paste the URL from your clipboard into the Edit Link dialog box.

9. To create the term and definition for the next pages, position the insertion point at the end of the last line in the present definition.

10. Press the Decrease Indent button twice, and choose Defined Term from the style bar. Extra space appears between your terms and definitions, as in Figure 10.6.

In Figure 10.6, some text formatting has been added. Bold format is used for the page titles, and italic format is used for the URL in the page's definition.

Figure 10.6.
Text formatting added.

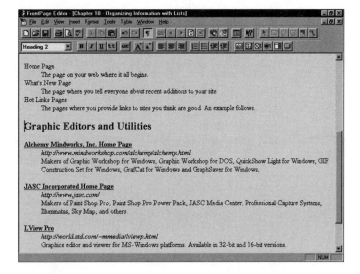

Creating Directory and Menu Lists

FrontPage supports two more types of lists: directory lists and menu lists. They were intended for programmers and are not used very often any more. Many browsers do not support them well. Directory lists were typically used to list the contents of a directory. Similarly, menu lists were used to display the contents of a menu or short items of twenty characters or less.

> **NOTE:** Some browsers do not recognize directory or menu lists. It is safer to use a bulleted list or numbered list instead. In the FrontPage Editor, directory and menu lists appear like bulleted lists. Some browsers, however, do not display bullets for these lists.

To create a directory or menu list:

1. Place the insertion point at the end of the line after which you want to create the list.
2. Choose Insert | List | Directory or Insert | List | Menu.
3. Enter a list item.
4. Press Enter to add additional items.
5. Press Enter twice to end the list.

Editing Lists

You can easily change one type of list to another, insert new items in a list, or delete list items all together.

Changing the List Type

If you change your mind about how you want to present your lists, you can change the list type easily. Numbered lists convert to bulleted lists with no problem. When you change from any other type of list to a definition list, though, all the list items become formatted as definitions—not as terms. You need to format the terms individually. If you reformat a nested list, the levels are retained when you reformat them. In some cases, you might need to reformat the inner levels first and work your way back to the first level.

To change the list type:

1. Select the list whose type you want to change.
2. Choose Edit | Properties, or right-click to open the List Properties dialog box.
3. Select the new format for the list in the List Format field. Click OK.

Deleting Lists or List Items

To delete a list or a list item from a page:

1. Select the list or list item that you want to delete. To select a list, move the pointer to the selection bar next to the list and double-click; the entire list is selected. To select a list item, place the pointer over the number or bullet of the item and double-click; the item is selected.
2. Choose Edit | Clear, or press the Delete key.

NOTE: If you are unable to select an entire definition list, it may have been set up incorrectly. Refer to the Q&A section in this chapter for further information.

Inserting List Items

To insert list items, just place the insertion point where you want to insert the new item and press Enter. A new number, bullet, or term is started for you. Enter the new list item as you normally would.

Workshop Wrap-Up

Organizing your information in lists is easy. The hardest part is thinking of the information that you want to include. Keep in mind that lists can appear differently in your visitors' browsers. While you develop your site, have a few different browsers on hand to check the appearance of your pages.

Chapter Summary

In this chapter, you learned how to format information in different types of lists. You learned how to add extended attributes to change the appearance of your lists. You also learned an easy way to develop hot lists without typing any URLs.

Next Steps

In Chapter 11, "Sprucing Up Your Pages," you learn how to create your own style sheets and how to add images and animation to your pages. You learn how to make images appear as though they float on your pages by using transparent GIFs. Read on to learn how to use color and images effectively. You even get tips on how to create your own images.

Q&A

Q: I inserted a normal paragraph after a definition list, and the insertion point did not return to the beginning of the line. How do I get back to the beginning?

A: Click the Decrease Indent button twice to get back to the beginning.

Q: How do I increase the indent in a definition list? When I select the items in the definition list and try to move them inward, they do not go anywhere.

A: You might have multiple normal paragraphs within the definition list. If the entire list does not become selected, you probably broke up the list during construction. This occurs when you use the Enter key to start a new term or definition rather than using the Insert | Definition | Term and Insert | Definition | Definition commands. You can tell where your list is broken when you select the list. After you reformat the broken areas, you should be able to select the entire list and indent it.

Q: I am writing instructions on how to plant a garden, but sometimes I want to enter a paragraph or two between steps. When I start a numbered list after the paragraph, I want to continue the numbering from the preceding list. How can I do that?

A: Suppose that you covered steps 1 through 3 in your instruction, and then you wrote a paragraph. When you inserted a numbered list after the paragraph, it began with number 1, but you wanted it to begin with number 4. Place the insertion point within the list item that you want to change, and use the START extended attribute to change the first list item's value to 4. You will not see the numbers change in the FrontPage Editor, but you will notice it in your browser when you call up the page.

ELEVEN

Sprucing Up Your Pages

It's estimated that more than 80 percent of the people who browse the Internet are using graphical browsers. When I first started browsing the Internet, the Web didn't offer too much in the way of graphics. Being a person who enjoys the visual side of electronic media and communications, I quickly lost interest and didn't get back on the Web for quite a while.

Graphics are running rampant on the Web now, and people are taking notice. We're able to design past that standard WWW-gray background color now. We can use tiled background images, specify custom colors, use images for links, and even place animations in the pages. The Web is becoming the way I like it! Obviously, there are lots of us out here who enjoy a graphical environment. Give us flash, give us style, but do it in a manner that doesn't tie up our modems too long or distract us, okay?

Some people have the knack for using images effectively, and others don't. This chapter gives you some tips on color combinations and when and when not to use images in your pages. You'll soon be building pages like a pro.

In this chapter you

❏ Learn how to change page properties and create your own style sheets that customize background, text, and link colors

❏ Learn how to use horizontal lines and dividers

❏ Learn how to insert and align images with the text on your pages and to use line breaks to enhance alignment

❏ Learn how to place animated GIFs on your pages that can be viewed in Netscape 2.0

❏ Learn how to use extended attributes to place animations on your pages that can be viewed in Internet Explorer

❏ Learn how to create transparent GIFs that make your images look like they're floating on your page background

❏ Get some tips on designing visual elements for your pages

Tasks in this chapter:

❏ Creating a Style Sheet

❏ Changing Page Properties

❏ Using Horizontal Lines

Show It with Style

It's always a good idea to maintain some consistency on your site. If you use different color combinations on your pages, users might think that they have landed in a different site on the Web. Even if you don't use images on your pages, you can use custom background colors or images and custom text and link colors to give your pages a unique and consistent appearance.

The easiest way to accomplish this is to create a style sheet. Any page can be used as a style sheet for another page, but the easiest way is to use a page that is easily identifiable as a style sheet. On this style sheet, you specify the color combinations you want to use in all the pages in your web or in a section of your web.

Keep in mind that people expect certain colors to represent certain things. The standards are blue for links, purple for visited links, and red for active links. It's a good idea to stay within these color guidelines, but there's nothing wrong with changing hues a little bit to complement your background and text colors. For example, if your background is a light tan color, you can use dark brown for your text color. Then you can create a nice teal blue for a link color, a deep purple for a visited link color, and a tomato red for an active link color. Those colors are a bit more earthy-looking and would blend in well with the light tan background.

You often see color formulas expressed in graphics software as hue, saturation, and luminance values (HSV) or in red, green, and blue values (RGB). For other color formula examples, refer to Table D.18 in Appendix D, "HTML Quick Reference." Custom colors created using these formulas are much easier on the eyes.

TIP: While we're on the subject of color, here's another tip: Consider how stark contrasts in color can affect people's eyes. You might like how that red text looks on that lime green background, but other people might not like it. If color differences are too drastic, the colors vibrate and cause eyes to tire quickly. For this reason, try not to keep your colors pure. Rather than create a blue that's pure blue (an RGB value of 0,0,255), for example, use a value more like 0,0,240. Rather than use pure white (255,255,255), use a white that has a little bit of gray or other color undertone in it. The goal is to make your pages easy on the eyes.

Creating a Style Sheet

You'll find it helpful to keep a record of the color combinations and backgrounds you use. As you develop your graphics (especially graphics that blend with your background and text colors), you'll need to remember the color formulas you've used. It's helpful to put the formulas right on the style sheet.

Here's a great way to create a style sheet:

1. Open a blank page and type a heading or two in it. Then type in the following lines using normal text. Underline the last three lines of text to simulate links:

   > For a background, I used:
   > For normal text color, I used:
   > <u>For link color, I used:</u>
   > <u>For visited link color, I used:</u>
   > <u>For active link color, I used:</u>

2. Choose the File I Page Properties command to apply a background color or image to your page as described later in the task "Changing Page Properties." This step lets you test your text and link colors while you design them.

3. If you have any finished header graphics, insert one of them into your page for reference as you select your colors.

4. Check the box beside Use Custom Text Color. Then, click the Text Color's Choose button to open the Color dialog box. (See Figure 11.1.)

Figure 11.1.
Create custom colors in the Color dialog box.

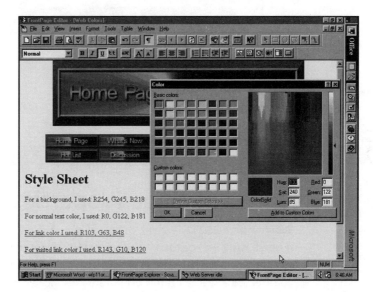

5. Click the Define Custom Colors button to expand the Colors dialog box. As you create your colors, write down the HSV or RGB values of the colors so that you can type them on your page later. I tend to note the RGB values because most shareware and commercial software programs support RGB color formulas.

6. Apply the colors to the appropriate text that appears on the page. Also add the colors to the Custom Colors slots at the left side of the Colors dialog box. This step allows you to select the same colors when you apply them to the page properties.

7. After you create your background, text, and link colors, enter the color formulas on the style sheet, as shown in Figure 11.2.

8. Use the File I Page Properties command to apply the text and link colors to your page.

9. Save the page to your web, titling the page "Web Colors" or something similarly descriptive. You now have a record that you can easily refer to.

Figure 11.2.
After you make your selections, apply the colors to your sample text and enter the color formulas on your style sheet.

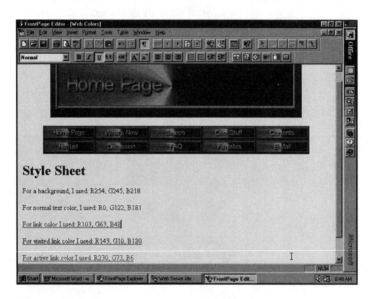

 # Changing Page Properties

When you create a style sheet, or any other page for that matter, you can change the properties of the page to use the page's own custom colors, or you can base the page's style on another page. You learned about assigning some of these properties when you created a web with the Corporate Presence Web in Chapter 4, "If You Mean Business." Now it's time to assign page properties yourself.

To assign colors and other properties to your page, follow six steps:

1. Choose File I Page Properties. The Page Properties dialog box, shown in Figure 11.3, appears.

2. Enter a title for your page in the Title field. You can't edit the URL field in this dialog box.

Figure 11.3.

The Page Properties dialog box allows you to define the colors used in a page.

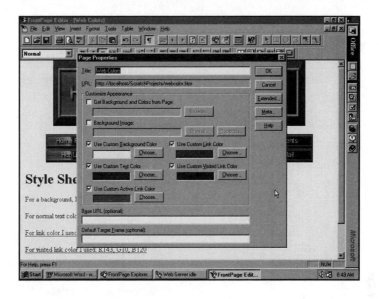

3. In the Customize Appearance section, you have a few choices:

Get Background and Colors from Page. Check this option if you want to use the colors from another page in your web (such as your Web Colors style sheet). If you know the name of the page, you can type it in the field. Click the Browse button to choose the page by name or URL from your currently opened web. When you choose this option, all other Custom Appearance selections are disabled.

Background Image. If you want to use a tiled image for your background, choose this option. Click the Browse button to select an image.

To learn how to insert an image, see "Adding an Image to Your Page," later in this chapter.

Use Custom Background Color. Check this option if you would rather use a solid color background. Click the Choose button to select a custom color from the Color dialog box.

NOTE: The Background Image option takes precedence over the Custom Background Color. The solid background color displays while the background image is loading. If you want to use only a solid background color, be sure that Background Image is unchecked.

Use Custom Link Color, Use Custom Text Color, Use Custom Active Link Color, and *Use Custom Visited Link Color*. Choose any of these checkboxes if you want to specify custom colors for any of these elements on your page. Click the Choose button to select a custom color from the Color dialog box.

The Page Properties dialog box contains two other options. For Base URL, refer to Chapter 1, "Learning Your Way Around." For Default Target Frame, see Chapter 14, "Frames— Pages with Split Personalities."

4. To apply extended attributes to your page, click the Extended button. The procedures for adding an extended attribute are similar to those covered ahead for images. Attributes you can add are shown in Table 11.1.

5. To apply Meta information to your pages, click the Meta button. Enter System or User Meta variables in the Meta Information dialog box. An example of values you can add is shown in Table 11.2.

6. Click OK to exit the Page Properties dialog box.

Table 11.1. Body page property tags.

Name	*Value*	*What It Does*
BGPROPERTIES	FIXED	Specifies a watermark (a background that doesn't scroll). Internet Explorer 3.0 feature.
LEFTMARGIN	*n*	Specifies a left margin, which overrides the default. When set to 0, the left margin is exactly on the left edge of the page. Internet Explorer 3.0 feature.
TOPMARGIN	*n*	Specifies a top margin, which overrides the default. When set to 0, the top margin is exactly on the top edge of the page. Internet Explorer 3.0 feature.

Meta tags are used to describe information about a Web page. For example, Web robots and searches use Meta information to display information about pages on the Web. The following Web page provides information and good links to pages that describe how to use Meta variables with your Web pages:

`http://www.stars.com/Search/Meta.html`

Table 11.2 shows an example of how Meta variables are entered in FrontPage.

Table 11.2. Meta page property tags.

Name	*Value*	*What It Does*
HTTP-EQUIV	REFRESH	Tells the browser to refresh the document.

Name	Value	What It Does
CONTENT	n	Tells the browser to reload in a specified number of seconds.
CONTENT	URL	Tells the browser to load the URL after the specified time has elapsed. If no URL is specified, it reloads the current document.

What Are Extended Attributes?

You've seen the term *extended attribute* in other parts of this book, but I've put the explanation in this chapter because it's the most likely place you'll use extended attributes.

If you've never touched HTML code, you might need some background information first: In simplistic terms, there are several varieties of HTML *tags* that perform a specific function. For example, the IMG tag indicates an image. Each tag has a subset of *attribute names* that apply to different types of functions the tag can perform. Each of these attribute names can (but not always) have a *value*. For an analogy, compare a car to an HTML tag, color to an attribute name, and the color blue to the attribute value.

There are other HTML tags that you'll need to use the HTML Markup bot to enter. These are covered in Chapter 21, "Using Your Own HTML Code."

Why do you need extended attributes? Doesn't FrontPage have a lot of built-in attributes? First, there are some attributes that aren't yet supported by FrontPage. For the most part, those that aren't covered are either seldom-used, under development or discussion, or browser-specific. For the majority of them, you can use extended attributes to cover the bases, but remember that when you use an extended attribute, the feature you're adding might not be viewable by all browsers. Second, because HTML standards are constantly being developed, extended attributes allow for future growth. It's a well-thought-out plan.

For a complete cross-reference of HTML tags and the FrontPage commands used to implement them, see Appendix D.

For properties dialog boxes that allows you to add extended attributes, this book contains a table of HTML tags that you can add and explains what they do. If you don't find a table for a dialog box that allows you to enter attributes, it means that FrontPage covers all the attributes for those tags.

Using Horizontal Lines

You use horizontal lines (traditionally known as horizontal rules) to distinguish the beginning or end of sections on your pages. For example, if you have a page that describes the main sections on your site, you would use horizontal lines at the end of each section's description.

NOTE: If you want a fancier divider, insert a divider graphic into your page. Your dividers can be gradients, dots, stars, metallic bars, or whatever else you can think of. See the task "Using Images in Your Pages," later in this chapter.

To insert a horizontal line into your page, follow five steps:

1. Position the insertion point on the line before which you want to insert the horizontal line.

2. Choose Insert I Horizontal Line. You'll get either a default line (2 pixels wide, 100 percent of window width, center-aligned with shading) or the same type of line you used in your page the last time.

3. To change the appearance of the horizontal line, position the insertion point at the beginning of the line on which the horizontal line appears. Choose Edit I Properties or right-click and choose Properties from the pop-up menu. The Horizontal Line Properties dialog box, shown in Figure 11.4, appears.

Figure 11.4.
Specify settings for horizontal lines in the Horizontal Line Properties dialog box.

4. Choose any of the following options:

    Percent of window. Choose this option to specify a line that spans across a percentage of the screen. Enter the percent value in the Width field. For example, for a line that spans 90 percent of the screen, you would enter **90** in the Width field.

    Pixels. Choose this option to specify a line that spans across a certain number of pixels. Enter the number of pixels in the Width field. If you choose this setting, be sure to keep in mind that some people use 640×480 resolution to browse the Web. Make sure your horizontal line isn't too wide.

    Align. Choose an alignment for the horizontal line. Available choices are Left, which aligns the line with the left edge of your page; Center, which centers it; and Right, which aligns it with the right side of your page.

    Height. Specify the height of the horizontal line in pixels.

    Solid line (no shading). Choose this checkbox if you want to create a horizontal line that is the same color as your text.

5. If you want to add extended attributes to the horizontal line, click the Extended button. These attributes allow you to specify a horizontal line of a different color, which Internet Explorer 3.0 supports. They are shown in Table 11.3.

Figure 11.5 shows several examples of horizontal lines. The top example shows the horizontal line that is created using the default settings. Its width is 100 percent of the screen, and it is 2 pixels high. Beneath it are several other examples with different width, height, and shading settings. You can also align the horizontal lines to the left, center, or right of the browser window.

Figure 11.5.

Examples of horizontal lines with different widths, heights, and shading.

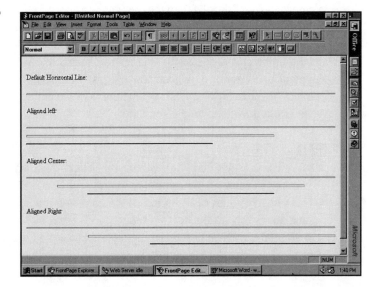

Table 11.3. HR property tags (horizontal line properties).

Name	Value	Comment
COLOR	#rrggbb	Enter color value in hex.
COLOR	See Appendix D	Specify custom color as shown in Table D.18 in Appendix D.

Images—To Be or Not to Be?

As mentioned at the beginning of this chapter, 80 percent of the people who use the Internet are using graphical browsers. This percentage should increase even more in the near future; however, that doesn't necessarily mean that all the people who use graphical browsers actually view the graphics. Some people don't like the added download time and turn the feature off if they can.

How do you keep these people happy? One way is to keep your graphics small. It might not take a person with a 28.8 modem very long to download that 300KB header graphic you have, but think about the user who is using a 2400- or 9600-bps modem. It would take a long time to download a header graphic of that size on a slower modem.

So, keep the file size down, either in dimension or through JPEG compression. You can also decrease the file size by reducing the number of colors in an image. Even though GIF files can contain as many as 256 colors, you can create good artwork with as few as 16 colors.

Whether you use GIF or JPEG images (you'll learn about the differences between them in "Choosing Between GIF and JPEG Images," later in this chapter), try to limit the total page size (including the images) to 50KB or less. If your images exceed that size, make small thumbnail versions of the images to use as previews. The user can click the thumbnails to view or download the images, if desired. Be sure to note the larger graphics' file sizes (in kilobytes) somewhere near the link so that the user can decide whether the download time is too long.

TIP: If you simply can't live without those large pictures or animations on your pages, here's another tip that might work: Place all your important text and smaller images near the top of the page and the large images and animations toward the bottom. Warn people about what's coming, telling them that the lower portion of the page takes some time to load. This way, they can at least explore a portion of your page while the larger files are being downloaded. If you get people's attention at the top of the page, they are more likely to check out what's at the bottom.

 # Using Images in Your Pages

Web pages normally use two types of images—GIF and JPEG. FrontPage can also import several other types of common image formats. If any of these other file types are imported into your web and placed on your pages, they are automatically converted to either GIF or JPEG format. When FrontPage sees an image that uses 256 or fewer colors, it converts the file to GIF format. Images that use more than 256 colors are converted to JPEG.

FrontPage can convert several image formats:

GIF. CompuServe GIF format. 256-colors. Viewable in all graphical browsers.
JPG. JPEG format. Compressed hi-color or true-color images. Currently not supported in all browsers, but support is increasing.

BMP. Windows or OS/2 bitmaps.
EPS. Encapsulated PostScript files.
MAC. MAC format.
MSP. Microsoft Paint format.
PCD. Photo CD format.
PCX. Z-Soft Paintbrush format.
RAS. Sun Raster Image format.
TIFF. Tagged Image File Format.
WPG. WordPerfect raster image file format.
WMF. Windows Metafile format (available only when the image is embedded within an RTF file).

Choosing Between GIF and JPEG Images

Pardon the pun, but choosy Web developers choose GIF. They choose GIF because most browsers support this format. GIF images have some advantages over JPEG, and vice versa:

❑ GIF images can be *interlaced*—rendered on your screen in progressive steps. The image appears blocky at first, but at least something appears on the page fairly quickly. As the image is downloaded to a local computer, the blockiness gives way to a clear image.

❑ You can designate *transparent* areas in a GIF image, giving the appearance that the image is floating on the background of your page.

❑ GIF images can be *animated*. You insert an animated GIF file the same way you would an ordinary GIF; however, at this time you can view these animated files only in Netscape 2.0.

❑ GIF images are best used for gray-scale photographs, cartoon-type images, small icons, buttons, bars, dividers and bullets, and small- to medium-sized header graphics, providing that the file size doesn't get too large.

Appendix C, "Directory of Resources," points you to some shareware programs that allow you to build animated GIF files.

If GIF images can do all that great stuff, why do you need JPEG images? Consider how many colors can exist in a photograph. The human eye can see approximately 11 or 12 million colors, and a computer can display even more—up to 16 million different colors. Photographs can contain millions of colors as well. When you reduce this monstrous amount of colors down to 256 colors, you don't get quite the same effect. Banding, loss of subtlety and detail, and objectionable dithering can occur.

NOTE: Banding occurs when you reduce a true color image down to a limited amount of colors, such as those found in a 256-color palette. The colors in the original image are replaced with the closest value found in the limited palette. Areas that originally contained many subtle color differences convert to an area of solid color, giving the image a banded effect.

With JPG images, you have a fighting chance. By using various compression schemes, JPG images can reduce the size of a true-color image substantially. In most cases, a true-color JPG image that uses good- to high-quality compression is smaller than a 256-color image of the same dimension, yet it contains more colors. Colors can be reduced by applying image compression, but you won't see a lot of difference if you use compression ratios wisely. When allowed to specify compression levels in percentages, I usually use 60 to 85 percent quality (depending on the richness of the image), with 100 percent quality being best. When given a range of choices, such as Low, Good, and High, I never go below Good. Too much deterioration occurs when compression ratios are set too low.

TIP: Don't recompress a compressed JPG image. If you think your image might need to be modified again at some point, keep a true-color version of it on your hard drive (TIF, TGA, true-color PCX, true-color BMP, and so on). Make the changes to the original, and compress again.

Importing Images to Your Webs

Now that you know the basics about different kinds of images, how to use them, where to put them, and so on, you need to learn how to import them into your web. You can import graphics files to your web from a drive on your local computer or from a network drive. FrontPage allows you to import several graphics types. Importing graphics into your web before you place the images on your pages allows you to import multiple files at once and to change the URLs to point to another existing directory in your web. It also allows easier selection of images later.

NOTE: If you change any image that has been imported into your web, you have to import it again.

To import images to your web, follow nine steps:

1. From the FrontPage Explorer, choose File | Import. The Import File to Web dialog box, shown in Figure 11.6, appears.

Figure 11.6.

Import graphics, Web pages, and other Web files using the Import File to Web dialog box.

2. Click the Add File button. The Add File to Import List dialog box, shown in Figure 11.7, appears.

Figure 11.7.

Use the Add File to Import List dialog box to select the images and files you want to import from your local computer into your web.

3. Use the Look in field in the Add File to Import List dialog box to locate the folder in which your images are stored.

4. After you find the directory that holds your images, select one or more images to import into your web. Multiple selections can be made by using the Shift key to select contiguous files and the Ctrl key to select items manually.

5. Click Open. You'll return to the Import File to Web dialog box, where your files appear in the Import List.

6. To change the URL of the images, choose the Edit URL button. The Edit URL dialog box, shown in Figure 11.8, appears. Enter the URL for the file if it's destined for another directory. For example, say you store your GIF and JPG images in separate directories named /images/gif and /images/jpg. Use the Edit URL button on each image and edit the URL to save the files to your custom directories rather than to the default /images directory. Click OK after each change.

7. To import the graphics into your web, highlight the file or files you want to import from the Import File to Web dialog box. Multiple selections are allowed.

8. Click Import Now. The file or files are added to the web and can be viewed in Summary View.

Figure 11.8.

Use the Edit URL dialog box to save your files into directories other than the FrontPage default directories.

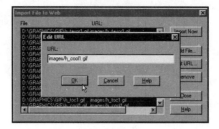

9. Click Close to exit the Import File to Web dialog box after all files are imported.

Adding an Image to Your Page

You can insert graphics files into your pages from a drive on your local computer, from a network drive, from a location on the World Wide Web, or from your currently opened web. FrontPage allows you to insert several graphics types.

To insert an image into your page, follow three steps:

1. Move the insertion point to the place where you want to insert the image.

2. Choose Insert I Image. The Insert Image dialog box, shown in Figure 11.9, appears.

Figure 11.9.

Use the Insert Image command to insert an image into your page.

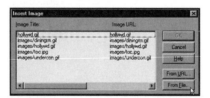

3. Choose one of the following options:

   To insert an image from the current web, select the image you want to insert. You can select by image title or URL. Click OK, and the image appears on your page.

   To insert an image from a local or network drive, click the From File button. Use the Look In box to choose a folder and file from which to insert the image. Select the file you want to insert and click Open.

   To insert an image from the World Wide Web, click the From URL button. The Open Location dialog box appears. Enter the Absolute URL of the image you want to insert and click OK.

NOTE: When you insert an image from the World Wide Web, the image is inserted from its location on the Web. You cannot import the image into your web.

When you save your page to the Web, you are asked if you want to save the images you inserted on your pages to the Web.

NOTE: The Save Image to Web dialog box appears when you save images that you inserted with the Insert I Image command. It also appears when you save images that you pasted into your page through the Clipboard.

The Save Image to Web dialog box appears as FrontPage attempts to save each image to the Web. To save your images, follow three steps:

1. In the Save as URL field, enter a page URL for the image. You have the opportunity to specify custom directories in which to save your images.
2. If an image with that filename exists on your web, you are prompted to enter a new URL. To overwrite the current version, leave the filename as is.
3. Click Yes to save the image to the Web.

Using Line Breaks with Images

Line breaks can help you to lay out images and text in your pages. They force text to appear after images in a few ways. To insert line breaks, follow two steps:

1. Choose Insert I Line Break.
2. Choose one of three options:

   Clear Left Margin. The next line of text moves to the next clear line after an image that appears in the left margin.

   Clear Right Margin. The next line of text moves to the next clear line after an image that appears in the right margin.

   Clear Both Margins. If an image is in either or both margins, the next line of text moves until both margins are clear.

Changing the Image Properties

You can change several of the image properties with the Image Properties dialog box, shown in Figure 11.10. You can open this dialog box using a few methods:

❏ Click the image you want to change, and choose Edit I Properties.

❏ Click the image you want to change, and press Alt + Enter.

❏ Left-click the image you want to change. Then right-click the mouse and choose Properties from the pop-up menu.

Figure 11.10.
Edit the properties of the image with the Image Properties dialog box.

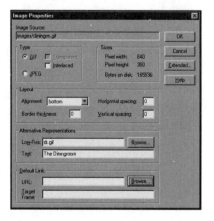

The Image Properties dialog box appears. To set your image properties, follow eight steps:

1. To convert from GIF to JPEG, or vice versa, click the radio button beside the image type in the Type field. If you want to interlace the GIF file, check the Interlaced checkbox. You cannot interlace a JPEG file.

2. In the Layout Alignment field, choose one of the following options:

    bottom. Aligns the bottom of the image with the text.

    middle. Aligns the middle of the image with the text.

    top. Aligns the top of the image with the text.

    absbottom. Aligns the bottom of the image with the bottom of the current line.

    absmiddle. Aligns the middle of the image to the middle point of the top and bottom text in the line.

    texttop. Aligns the top of the image with the top of the tallest text in the line.

    baseline. Aligns the bottom of the image with the baseline of the current text line.

left. Aligns the image to the left of the text. Good for wrapping text around an image.

right. Aligns the image to the right of the text. Another choice for wrapping text around an image.

3. In the Border thickness field, enter a value, in number of pixels, for how wide you would like a border to be. This draws a solid border around the image.

4. Select values for horizontal and vertical spacing. These are Netscape enhancements that set the amount of spacing between the nearest text or image on the line above or below the current line. Enter the value, in pixels, in either or both of the Horizontal spacing or Vertical spacing fields.

5. To specify Alternative Representations, choose from two options:

Low-Res. This setting allows you to choose an image of lower resolution to display while the larger version is being downloaded.

Text. This field lets you specify text that is displayed in the image's boundaries while the image is being downloaded. The text is displayed even if users have graphics turned off in their browsers.

6. To complete Default Link information, choose one or both of the following options:

URL. Click the Browse button to choose the file you want to link to with this image.

Target Frame. See Chapter 14 for information on this field.

7. To specify extended attributes, click the Extended button. Follow the procedure outlined below in "Using Image Extended Attributes."

8. Click OK to exit the Image Properties dialog box. The image changes to the position you specify.

Using Image Extended Attributes

Some extended attributes can be applied to images. The HTML specification includes two attributes—HEIGHT and WIDTH—which allow you to resize an image. Your image is stretched or reduced to fit the dimensions that you specify with these settings. When you attempt to add either of these two extended attributes to an image, however, a message informs you that FrontPage recognizes and handles the attribute directory. You are instructed to change the values in the appropriate dialog box. In this case, the settings for image height and width appear in the Size section of the Image Properties dialog box. However, the dialog box does not allow you to edit these fields.

There is a good reason why you are not allowed to resize an image through these attributes: When you resize images in this manner, you might get objectionable results. Graphics programs know how to resize an image and maintain a good appearance while doing so—Web browsers don't; that's not what they were made for. Rather than resize your pages using these attributes, resize the image properly with your graphics software and put it on your page in its actual size. You'll be glad you did.

You can use the attributes shown in Table 11.4 to add inline animations (AVI) files to your pages. These animations can be viewed only in Internet Explorer 2.0 at this time. Beta versions of Internet Explorer 3.0 and Netscape 3.0 also display inline animations. It's fun to see an animation on a page every now and then. To place an animation on a page, you need to add more than one attribute. You start with the DYNSRC attribute and go from there.

Table 11.4. IMG **tags for animation (Internet Explorer only).**

Name	Value	Comment
CONTROLS		If a video clip is present, a set of controls is displayed beneath the video clip.
DYNSRC	URL	Specifies the address of a video clip or VRML world to be displayed in a window.
LOOP	*n*	Specifies how many times a video clip loops when activated. If *n*=-1, the video loops indefinitely.
LOOP	INFINITE	Video clip loops indefinitely.
START	FILEOPEN	Video clip plays as soon as the file is opened. When used in conjunction with MOUSEOVER, it plays once as soon as it opens and thereafter whenever the user moves the mouse.
START	MOUSEOVER	Video clip plays when user moves mouse cursor over the animation. When used in conjunction with FILEOPEN, it plays once as soon as it opens and thereafter whenever the user moves the mouse.

Say you want to add a small AVI file on your page. The animation is going to go on your guest book, and it's an animation of pages turning in a book. You want the animation to play as soon as the page is loaded, and you want it to play as long as the user is on the page. Here's how you would add the animation and its attributes:

1. Import the AVI file into your web as outlined previously in "Importing Images to Your Webs."

2. Create a GIF or JPG file for the first frame (or the best frame) of the animation and import that into your web also. This single image displays in place of the animation in browsers that don't support inline AVI files.

3. Insert the single image on your page where you want the animation to be located.

4. Select the image and choose Edit I Properties, or right-click and choose Image Properties from the pop-up menu. The Image Properties dialog box appears.

5. Click the Extended button to open the Extended Attributes dialog box shown in Figure 11.11.

6. To attach the animation to your image, click the Add button. Enter the following for name and attribute:

   Name: DYNSRC

   Value: pageturn.avi (or your filename)

7. To start the animation as soon as the page opens, click the Add button and add the following:

   Name: START

   Value: FILEOPEN

8. To loop the animation as long as the page is displayed in the browser, click the Add button and enter the following:

   Name: LOOP

   Value: INFINITE (entering a value of -1 also works)

   When you're done entering these values, the entries in the Extended Attributes dialog box should appear as shown in Figure 11.11.

Making an Image Transparent

When you use GIF images, you have the opportunity to make one of the colors in the image transparent. The term *transparent* is a bit deceiving because the color you pick doesn't really go away—it's just hidden so that the page background can show through. This option makes the GIF image look like it's floating on the page.

Figure 11.11.

An example of attributes entered for an AVI file.

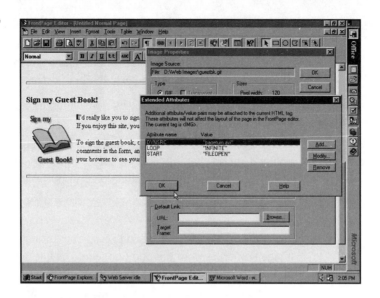

NOTE: You can make a JPEG image transparent; however, when you save the page to your web, you are prompted to convert the image to GIF format. Because JPEG image formats can contain more than 256 colors, you might see a reduction in the number of colors, which could affect image appearance. Also, because JPEG images use various compression schemes to reduce file size, you might also see an increase in file size when you convert the image to GIF, even though the GIF image contains fewer colors.

Only one color in the image can be transparent. If you select a new color, the previous transparent color returns to its opaque value. You can choose a transparent color with four steps:

TIP: When you create a GIF image, fill the areas that you want to make transparent with a color that doesn't appear anywhere else in the image. You don't want holes in your transparent GIF in the wrong places.

1. Select the image that you want to change.
2. Click the Make Transparent button on the Image toolbar.
3. Place the pointer inside the image. It becomes a Make Transparent pointer. Position the pointer over the color you want to make transparent.
4. Click the left mouse button. The color you clicked on turns transparent.

NOTE: When you save the page, your original version of the image is overwritten. Don't add transparencies to animated GIFs after the fact.

Removing Image Transparency

As mentioned, when you choose a new transparent color, the previous one becomes opaque again and returns to its original color. However, you might want to return a transparent color to its original color and not have any transparent area in your image.

You use either the Make Transparent Pointer or the Image Properties dialog box to make a color nontransparent. A description of each method follows.

To make a color in an image nontransparent using the Make Transparent Pointer, follow these four steps:

1. Select the image that you want to change.
2. Click the Make Transparent button.
3. Place the pointer inside the image. Position it over a transparent area.
4. Click the left mouse button. The transparent color returns to its original color.

To make a color in an image nontransparent using the Image Properties dialog box, follow these four steps:

1. Select the image that you want to change.
2. Open the Image Properties dialog box.
3. In the Image Properties dialog box, uncheck the Transparent field.
4. Click OK to exit the Image Properties dialog box. The transparent color returns to its original color.

Cutting, Copying, and Deleting Images

You can select images to cut or copy to the Clipboard by using the following procedure:

1. To select the image, do one of the following:
   - ❏ Move the pointer to the selection bar at the left side of the page. The cursor changes from a standard pointer (facing left) to a selection pointer (facing right). Click the left mouse button to select the image.
   - ❏ Move the pointer to the right side of the image, and then click the left mouse button and drag the pointer over the image.

2. When the image is selected, it appears in inverse video, a negative representation of the image. You can cut or copy the image to the Clipboard when the image is selected in this manner.

Use the Copy command to copy an image to the Clipboard:

1. Select the image you want to copy.

2. Choose Edit I Copy or click the Copy button. The image is copied to the Clipboard.

To remove an image from your page, follow these steps:

1. Select the image you want to cut or delete.

2. Choose one of the following methods to remove the image from your page:

   ❏ To remove an image and place it into the Clipboard, choose Edit I Cut or click the Cut button.

   ❏ To remove an image without placing it into the Clipboard, choose Edit I Clear or click the Delete button.

   ❏ To delete an image without selecting it, position the insertion point before the image and press Delete; or position the insertion point after the image and press Backspace.

To paste an image that you cut or copied from your page, perform one step:

1. Choose Edit I Paste or click the Paste button.

Do's and Don'ts

This chapter has given you lots of tips regarding graphics. Let's review some do's and don'ts about adding graphics to your pages:

❏ **Do** design graphics that blend well with your background and text choices.

❏ **Do** add text alternatives for graphics you use as links, in case users have graphics turned off.

❏ **Do** try to keep the file size of your images small. Provide the option to download large graphics and animations at the user's discretion.

❏ **Do** add images where they are most effective. Sometimes an image can describe a process more efficiently than words.

❏ **Do** use images and other effects that keep the same tone of the other content on your page. If you're discussing a serious topic, cartoon images might be inappropriate. Conversely, if the tone of your page is light and humorous, a serious picture might break the mood.

❑ **Do** try to keep background tiles simple. Use light backgrounds with dark text and dark backgrounds with light text. Try to stay away from medium-toned backgrounds because they make it difficult to choose text and link colors. Busy backgrounds can interfere with the content of your page. If you have a hard time reading your text, other users will, too.

❑ **Do** avoid using pure colors. Back off a bit on that brightness.

❑ **Don't** put images on your pages just because you can.

❑ **Don't** clutter your pages with images. Use white space to separate images from text. Use books, magazines, or other Web pages you like for layout ideas.

❑ **Don't** overuse animated GIFs or video files; too many on a single page make the page overwhelming. The user won't know where to look first and might be distracted from reading the text on your page. Save animated GIFs and video files for emphasis.

❑ **Don't** use colors that clash; they make users' eyes tire quickly.

Workshop Wrap-Up

Graphics, when used effectively, can really make a page. On the other hand, when graphics aren't used properly, they can break a page. The best way to learn how to use graphics effectively is to carefully examine pages that catch your eye. You'll find lots of "picks of the week" on the Web—check them out for various ideas. How were colors used on the page? What was it about the page that caused you to explore it? Try to apply the same principles to your own pages.

Chapter Summary

In this chapter, you learned how to combine colors for text, links, and backgrounds with images. You learned how to insert files into your webs in a variety of ways. You even learned how to add animated GIFs and animations to your pages using extended attributes. The groundwork is set—the rest is up to your imagination.

Next Steps

In the next chapter, you'll learn how to combine everything you've learned so far to create Web pages of your own. You'll design a style sheet, a home page, and some favorite links pages from the ground up and make a navigation bar that will satisfy graphics enthusiasts and nonenthusiasts alike. For topics related to what you've learned in this chapter, see these chapters:

❏ To learn how to use tables to enhance page and graphics layout, see Chapter 13, "Your Tables Are Ready."

❏ To learn how to use images in frames, see Chapter 14, "Frames—Pages with Split Personalities."

❏ To learn how to use images in forms, read Chapter 19, "Fields—The Building Blocks of Forms."

❏ To learn how to add other multimedia elements into your page, such as sound, Java applets, Shockwave features, and more, see Chapter 21, "Using Your Own HTML Code."

Q&A

Q: I put an animated GIF on my page and then I made it transparent in the FrontPage Editor. It doesn't animate anymore. What's wrong?

A: When you make an image transparent in FrontPage, it saves the image over the previous version, with the transparent data in it. Animated GIFs are a special animal—there are actually multiple images (called frames) within that single file, and they are grouped together as one image in a special way. Think of an animated GIF as an electronic flip-book. When you add transparency to an animated GIF, you are adding the transparency only to the first frame. FrontPage (and many other graphics programs for that matter) doesn't know how to recognize the additional frames in an animated GIF, so it just writes out the first frame with the transparent data in it. That's why you don't see animation anymore—what was originally a GIF file with multiple frames became a single frame with transparency.

To make transparent GIFs, you need to break apart that special GIF file into separate frames again, add the transparency to each frame, and then rebuild the animated GIF. (Or, if you're creating the animation from scratch, add the transparency to each frame to begin with.) This sounds like a lot of work, but that's what it takes to make an animation of any kind. Unfortunately, because of the wide variety of graphics and animation programs available, I can't go into much more detail than this. Check out my support site for this book at `http://frontpage.flex.net/dtyler/FPSite/index.htm`, though I'll be adding tips and tricks that are a bit more application-specific.

Q: What software should I use to make images and animations of my own?

A: There are so many graphics programs to choose from that it's difficult to know which one to use. No one graphics program does it all, and sometimes you need multiple programs to create your Web graphics. Refer to Appendix C for comments about some shareware and commercial graphics programs that can help you to get the job done. Check out the Web site mentioned in the previous answer, too. I'm planning to add tips and tricks that can help you.

Q: Can a user click on an animated GIF or AVI file to go on to another page?

A: You can assign an animated GIF or AVI file as a link as you would any other image. Click on the image, click the Create or Edit Link button, and away you go!

TWELVE

Real-Life Examples

Roll up your sleeves, because it's time to start building your own Web site. You're going to take what you've learned in this section and combine all the features to create your own pages. You'll find out that it's not as hard as you think. You're going to create a Web site that contains several different sections, beginning in this chapter with a style sheet, your not-quite-so-standard-everyday home page, and some links pages. You know—the usual. Except here, you'll learn how to give those pages some punch.

About the Web Site Project

The Web project for this book will include a few different sections you'll be developing in the remaining "Real-Life Examples" chapters in this book. These combine all the techniques from the chapters in the book into (you guessed it) a real-life example. You can customize this site in any way you choose as far as the content goes. The examples here should give you enough ideas and groundwork to get you started.

In this chapter, you

- ❏ Create a color set for your Web site that has a little more flash and uses custom colors
- ❏ Create a home page complete with graphics, image map, animated GIF, and *very little text*
- ❏ Create a Favorite Links main page, which links to other Links pages
- ❏ Create a template for the Links pages and use it to create your first page for links to the Web
- ❏ Create a What's New page and add your new pages to it
- ❏ Begin a header and footer that can be included on all the main pages on your web

Tasks in this chapter:

- ❏ Creating a Normal Web
- ❏ Creating the Web Colors Style Sheet
- ❏ Creating Your Home Page
- ❏ Working on the Favorites Page
- ❏ Creating a Template from the Favorite Links Page

Your Web project will consist of the following:

❏ A home page (of course) that links back to the home page on your root Web as well as all the main pages on your Web project. This isn't your standard Hi, I'm Joe home page. It's going to have just enough flash to get people's interest so that they will want to peek inside the wrapper.

❏ A Favorite Links section, where people who browse the Web and sometimes don't know where to go for good information or great pages can look. That's why a lot of people put lots of links on their sites. You'll satisfy those Web users, too. Your site's Favorite Links section will include links to your favorite sites and arrange them in categories. You'll also develop a template you can use whenever you want to create a new Links page.

❏ A What's New page to keep folks informed about the new additions to your site.

What Else Will You Get?

The pages you develop in this chapter are only the beginning. Wait until you start learning how to automate and enhance your pages in the next section! To give you an idea of what you can expect in your Web project in future chapters, here's a brief description of the other features your Web site will contain:

❏ A Table of Contents page that displays the pages in each section of your Web site.

❏ A Search page, which enables visitors to search for words or phrases contained on your pages.

❏ A Guest Book, which enables people to sign in and place comments about your pages on your site.

❏ A Happenings page, where you'll tell people each month about things that are happening in your related fields of interest.

❏ A Cool Stuff section, where you'll incorporate advanced features into your pages: marquees, multimedia, sound, video, and more.

❏ A discussion on the topic of your choice.

 ## Creating a Normal Web

You're going to create a Far Out There Web site. Given the title, you're free to be as creative as you want. Make it humorous, make it tongue-in-cheek, and pull out all the stops.

To begin your Web site, you want to start with a normal web:

1. From the FrontPage Explorer, choose File I New Web (or press Ctrl+N). The New Web dialog box appears.
2. In the Template or Wizard field, select Normal Web and click OK. The New Web from Template dialog box appears.
3. In the Web Name field, type `FarOutThere` to name your web.
4. Click OK. The web is created with a single normal page.

 # Creating the Web Colors Style Sheet

The images for this project are provided on the CD-ROM included with this book in both GIF and JPG format. They were designed against a white background, so you'll want to choose a light background color or the background image provided on the CD-ROM. If you use a dark background, you'll see some ghosting around the images, which is caused by the antialiasing of the image. I've also provided a true-color (TGA) version of the images on the CD-ROM so that you can edit them for a dark background.

To create your Web Colors style sheet, follow these steps:

1. From the FrontPage Editor, choose File I New or Ctrl+N. The New Page dialog box appears.
2. Choose to base your new page on the Normal Page template and click OK. A new blank page appears in the FrontPage Editor window.
3. Choose Insert I Image to display the Insert Image dialog box. Click the From File button, and locate the `farouthd.gif` (or `.jpg`) image on the CD-ROM. Highlight the file and click Open.
4. Place the insertion point immediately after the image. Choose Insert I Heading 2 and enter the following text:

   `Sample Heading`

5. Choose Insert I Paragraph I Normal. The insertion point moves to the next line. Enter some sample text using Normal Paragraph font. In the example shown in Figure 12.1, the following text is added:

   `Sample text. Sample text. Sample text.`

6. Choose File I Page Properties. The Page Properties dialog box appears. You'll be working against a light background, so you shouldn't have any problem choosing colors that work well. Generally, it's best to use dark text on light backgrounds and light text on dark backgrounds.

Figure 12.1.

Placing some graphics and text on your page helps you see how the colors work together.

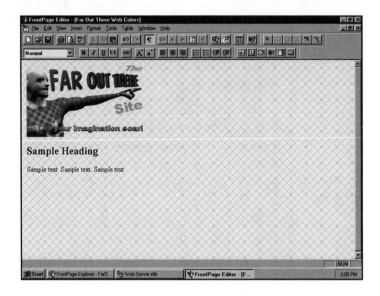

See Chapter 11, "Sprucing Up Your Pages," for instructions on creating custom colors.

From the Page Properties dialog box, select and enter the following settings. To specify the custom color formulas listed below, check the Use Custom Link, Text, or Active Link Color checkbox, and click the Choose button to define the custom colors in the Colors dialog box.

> Page Title: Far Out There Web Colors
> Background Image: `backgrnd.gif` (or `.jpg`)
> Link Color: R 0 G 0 B 240 (toned-down blue)
> Text Color: R 0 G 0 B 128 (navy blue)
> Visited Link Color: Default color (deep purple)
> Active Link Color: R 240 G 0 B 0 (toned-down red)

Figure 12.2 shows the Page Properties dialog box with the properties set for this page. Click OK after you complete the property settings. The page updates with the selections you made.

7. Choose File I Save. The Save As dialog box appears. Enter the following Page Title and URL in the dialog box, and click OK. The page is saved to your web.

> Page Title: Far Out There Web Colors
> Page URL: `faroutwc.htm`

8. You are asked whether you want to save the images to your Web; click Yes or Yes to All. The page properties update in the FrontPage Editor after the file is saved. Now you have an idea of what your pages will look like.

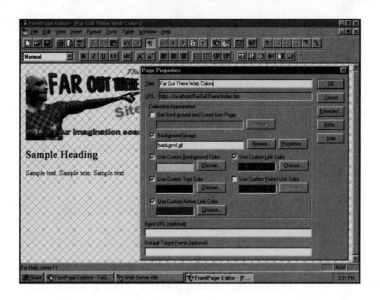

Figure 12.2.

Set the properties for your style sheet in the Page Properties dialog box.

9. You might want to save this page in the _private directory of the Web, which is a special directory that can't be accessed by Web crawlers and searches. To do this, go to the FrontPage Explorer. Right-click on the page title in any view, and choose Properties from the pop-up menu. The Properties dialog box appears.

10. Type the following in the Page URL field:

    _private/faroutwc.htm

11. Click the Apply button. The page is relocated to the new directory.

NOTE: This is the procedure you should use when relocating any file to a new directory. If the directory doesn't exist, the FrontPage Editor creates it. If there are any existing links to the page, you are asked whether you want to update those links.

 ## Creating Your Home Page

A home page doesn't always have to have a lot of text on it. You can use colorful graphics and some fancy effects to attract peoples' interest. This home page has very little text, as you will soon see. It does have a pile of images on it (which probably will take some time to download on slower modems). The sizes of the header graphics are reduced on subsequent pages.

When you created your normal web, a page titled Normal Page, with a filename of `index.htm` was placed into it. You will use this page as your home page. To create the content in your home page, follow these steps:

1. Choose File I Open from Web. The Current Web dialog box appears.

2. Choose the Normal Page (`index.htm`) from the list of files in your current web.

3. Click OK. The page opens in the FrontPage Editor.

4. Choose File I Page Properties. The Page Properties dialog box appears.

5. In the Customize Appearance section, check the Get Background and Colors from Page checkbox, and click Choose to assign the Far Out There Web Colors page as a style sheet.

6. Click OK. The page updates with your web colors.

Adding the Home Page Content

How do people know how to size their browsers when they visit a site? Well, most times they don't, so it's a good idea to let them know. One way you can do this is with a graphic that's sized at least as wide as the widest graphic on your site. The layouts for the pages on this site are designed to fit within a 525-pixel-wide screen, so I created a guide that is exactly that width. This guide tells people that, for optimum viewing, they should size their browser screen until they see both arrows on each side of the graphic. That's the first thing you want to put on the page. Then, you'll add some text for links, the home page graphic, an animated GIF, and some footer text. That's it for this page. Ready?

Follow these steps:

1. With the insertion point in the upper-left corner of the page, choose Insert I Image. The Insert Image dialog box appears.

2. Click the From File button, and use the Look In box to locate the guide.gif file from the CD-ROM included with this book. Click Open to place the image on your page.

3. Click the Center button in the Format toolbar to align the graphic to the center.

4. Right-click the image and choose Properties from the pop-up menu. The Image Properties dialog box appears. Enter the following text in the Alternative Representations Text field:

   `Browser Width Guide`

NOTE: The alternative text displays while the graphic is loading. It also appears in place of the graphic if users have graphics turned off in their browsers.

5. If you're using GIF images, click the image to select it. Then click the Make Transparent button on the Image toolbar to specify white as the transparent color. Click OK to return to the FrontPage Editor.

NOTE: You can make a JPG image transparent, but it will be converted to GIF in the process. All the GIF images on the CD use the same custom palette to avoid *palette shift* when viewing in 256-color mode. Palette shifting occurs when images that have different 256-color palettes exist on the same page. When you convert a JPG image to GIF, it will use a different palette and create some shifting.

6. Place the insertion point at the end of the graphic, and insert a Normal paragraph by choosing Insert | Paragraph | Normal. Align the insertion point to the center of the page by clicking the Center button on the Format toolbar.

7. Enter the following line of text:

   `Main Home Page ¦ What's New ¦ Favorites ¦ Search ¦ Guest Book`

TIP: I used a pipe symbol (¦) for the divider between the words. A forward slash (/) works just as well.

8. With the insertion point at the end of the text you just entered, select Insert | Line Break. From the Break Properties dialog box, choose Normal Line Break and press Enter. The insertion point moves to the center of the next line.

9. Enter this second line of text:

   `Contents ¦ Happenings ¦ Cool Stuff ¦ Discussion ¦ E-Mail`

10. With the insertion point at the end of the line of text, insert another normal line break by choosing Insert | Line Break. Choose Normal Line Break from the Break Properties dialog box and press Enter. The cursor moves to the center of the next line.

11. Choose Insert I Image to insert each of the following images on your page, in succession. Use the From File button in the Insert Image dialog box to select each of the following files from the CD.

    After the images are inserted on your page, right-click on each image and choose Properties from the pop-up menu. The Image Properties dialog box appears. In the Alternative Representations I Text field, enter the alternative text shown after each filename below:

    > `b_home.gif` (or `.jpg`): Home Page
    > `b_new.gif` (or `.jpg`): What's New
    > `b_favs.gif` (or `.jpg`): Favorites
    > `b_srch.gif` (or `.jpg`): Search
    > `b_gstbk.gif` (or `.jpg`): Guest Book

12. Click the Make Transparent button on the Image toolbar to make white the transparent color in each GIF image.

13. Place the insertion point after the last image in the row and insert a Normal paragraph using the Insert I Paragraph I Normal command. Center it by clicking the Center button on the Format toolbar.

14. Choose the Insert I Image command. The Insert Image dialog box appears. Use the From File button to insert `light.gif` from the CD-ROM included with this book. This is an animated GIF that already has transparency applied to it.

15. Click the image to select it. Then, right-click the image to choose Properties from the pop-up menu. From the Image Properties dialog box, assign the image an alternative text representation of Animation in the Alternative Representations I Text field.

16. Click to select the animated GIF and copy it to your clipboard by pressing Ctrl+C or clicking the Copy button on the standard toolbar.

17. Choose Insert I Image again. Use the From File button in the Insert Image dialog box to insert `farouthd.gif` (or `.jpg`) from the CD immediately after the animated GIF. Right-click the image to choose Properties from the pop-up menu. Assign the image an alternative text representation of Home Page Header Graphic in the Alternative Representations I Text field of the Image Properties dialog box. Use the Make Transparent button on the Image toolbar to make white the transparent color in each image.

18. With the insertion point immediately after the header graphic, paste the animated GIF from your clipboard onto the page using Ctrl+V.

19. Click to select the animated GIF you just pasted onto the page. Right-click and choose Properties from the context menu. The Image Properties dialog box appears. In the Layout section, choose Alignment: Top. Your page now should look like Figure 12.3.

Figure 12.3.
Your page should look like this after several graphics are placed on it.

20. Now you'll insert another row of navigation buttons. Choose the Insert | Image command. In the Image Properties dialog box, use the From File button to insert the following graphics from the CD-ROM. Right-click each image to choose the Properties command from the pop-up menu. In the Image Properties dialog box, assign them the alternative text representations shown. Click the Make Transparent button in the Image toolbar to make white the transparent color in each GIF image.

> b_cont.gif (or .jpg): Contents
> b_happn.gif (or .jpg): Happenings
> b_cool.gif (or .jpg): Cool Stuff
> b_disc.gif (or .jpg): Discussion
> b_mail.gif (or .jpg): Send EMail

Adding the Footer Information

You have all the images placed on your page now. To complete the contents of the page, you want to add some footer information that tells who to contact for information about the site, and you also want to place copyright information on the page.

Follow these steps:

1. Place the insertion point immediately after the last graphic in the bottom navigation button row, and insert an address paragraph by choosing Insert | Paragraph | Address. The insertion point moves below the home page graphic on a new line. Align the insertion point to the center of the page by clicking the Center button.

2. Enter the following line of text:

   ```
   For questions or comments about this page, contact (followed by your
   E-Mail address).
   ```

3. With the cursor at the end of your e-mail address, insert a normal line break by choosing Insert I Line Break. From the Break Properties dialog box, select Normal Line Break and choose OK.

4. On the new line, enter the following text, adding a space afterwards:

   ```
   Copyright
   ```

5. Immediately after the space, choose Insert I Special Character. Select the copyright symbol from the Insert Special Character dialog box, and choose Insert. Then click Close to return to the FrontPage Editor.

6. Add a space after the copyright symbol and enter the current year, followed by your name. For example:

   ```
   1996, Denise Tyler
   ```

   Figure 12.4 shows a completed example of this line.

7. Choose File I Save to save the page to your web with what you've completed so far. When you are asked whether you want to save the images to the Web, click Yes to All. Save the home page with these settings:

   > Title: Far Out There Home Page
   > URL: `index.htm` (or whatever you normally name your home page)

Figure 12.4.

The bottom portion of the home page now is complete.

Adding the Links to the Home Page

Now it's time to add the links to the text located near the top of the page. For the home link on this page, you want to create a link back to the main home page on your root Web. You'll also create links to eight new pages that you'll be working on throughout this book. Finally, you'll create a link to your e-mail address.

Follow these steps:

1. In the first line of text below the guide graphic, highlight the following. Don't include the bracket (¦) after the phrase:

   `Main Home Page`

2. Click the Create or Edit Link button on the standard toolbar. The Create Link dialog box appears.

3. Select the World Wide Web tab. Select (other) from the Protocol drop-down menu. In the URL field, enter the following:

   `../index.htm`

   (or whatever you named the home page in your root directory).

   This is a relative link that goes back one level to your root directory (`../`) and loads your home page (`index.htm`).

4. Click OK to create the link.

5. Click the Home Page button in the top line of navigation buttons to select it. Then, click the Create or Edit Link button in the Standard toolbar. Repeat steps 3 and 4 to add the same link to the graphic that is associated with the home page.

For the next eight links, you select the text, click the Create Or Edit Link button, and select the New Page tab to create links to pages that don't yet exist on your Web. For each page, choose to add the pages to your To Do list. After you click OK to create each page, base the first page on the What's New Page template and the remaining ones on the Normal template. Assign the following page titles and URLs.

You'll also want to add the same links to the navigation button graphics associated with each page, as outlined in step 5 above.

> Selected Text: What's New
> Page Title: What's New at Far Out There
> Page URL: `whatsnew.htm`
> How to Create: Add new page to To Do list
> Based On: What's New template
> Will Complete In: This chapter

Selected Text: Favorites
Page Title: Favorite Far Out There Links
Page URL: `favorite.htm`
How to Create: Add new page to To Do list
Based On: Normal template
Will Complete In: This chapter

Selected Text: Search
Page Title: Search Far Out There
Page URL: `search.htm`
How to Create: Add new page to To Do list
Based On: Normal template
Will Complete In: Chapter 22

Selected Text: Guest Book
Page Title: Far Out There Guest Book
Page URL: `guestbk.htm`
How to Create: Add new page to To Do list
Based On: Normal template
Will Complete In: Chapter 22

Selected Text: Contents
Page Title: Far Out There TOC
Page URL: `toc.htm`
How to Create: Add new page to To Do list
Based On: Normal template
Will Complete In: Chapter 17

Selected Text: Happenings
Page Title: Far Out There Happenings
Page URL: `happen.htm`
How to Create: Add new page to To Do list
Based On: Normal template
Will Complete In: Chapter 17

Selected Text: Cool Stuff
Page Title: Far Out There Cool Stuff
Page URL: `cooltoc.htm`
How to Create: Add new page to To Do list
Based On: Normal template
Will Complete In: Chapters 17 and 22

Selected Text: Discussion
Page Title: Far Out There Discussion
Page URL: `disctoc.htm`
How to Create: Add new page to To Do list
Based On: Normal template
Will Complete In: Chapter 22

For the final link (E-Mail), create a link to your e-mail address:

1. Highlight the E-Mail text and click the Create Or Edit Link button in the Standard toolbar.

2. Select the World Wide Web tab from the Create Link dialog box.

3. In the Protocol drop-down listbox, select mailto: and enter your e-mail address.

4. Click the E-Mail navigation button graphic to select it. Then click the Create Or Edit Link button in the Standard toolbar, and repeat steps 2 and 3 to add the same E-Mail link to the footer of the page. Figure 12.5 shows the completed home page.

Figure 12.5.
The completed home page.

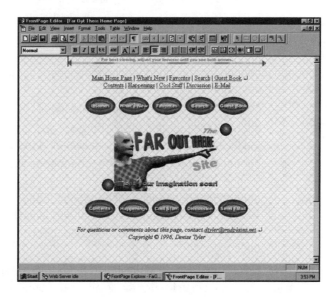

5. Choose File I Save to save the page to your Web. Click Yes to All to save the images to the Web.

TIP: If you want to see that animation in action, make sure that the FrontPage server is running. Then open a browser that can view animated GIFs.

Netscape 2.0 supports animated GIFs, and Internet Explorer 2.0 supports AVIs. Netscape 3.0 and Internet Explorer 3.0 support both file formats.

Use the following URL to view the page:

```
http://localhost/FarOutThere/index.htm
```

 # Working on the Favorites Page

When you created the links from your home page, you added the Favorites page to your To Do list. You can open the Favorites page from there and complete it now. Here's what you do:

1. Open the To Do list by choosing Tools I Show To Do List. If you don't see the To Do list, this means it is minimized and appears in your Windows 95 taskbar. Click the FrontPage To List button in the taskbar to bring it to the foreground.

2. In the Task column of the FrontPage To Do List dialog box, click Finish Favorite Far Out There Links and then click the Do Task button. The page opens in the FrontPage Editor window.

3. Choose the Insert I Image command. From the Insert Image dialog box, use the From File button to insert `faroutsm.gif` (or `.jpg`), located on the CD, at the beginning of the page. Then align it in the center of the page by clicking the Center button on the Format toolbar. Next, right-click the image to choose Properties from the pop-up menu, and assign it an alternative text representation of Small Far Out Header in the Alternative Representations I Text field of the Image Properties dialog box. Finally, click the Make Transparent button in the Image toolbar to make white the transparent color in the image.

4. Using the procedures outlined in the previous step, insert `favorite.gif` (or `.jpg`) immediately after the small header graphic. Assign it an alternative text representation of Favorites.

5. Position the insertion point immediately after the Favorites graphic and insert `divider.gif` (or `.jpg`) from the accompanying CD-ROM. Use the Make Transparent button in the Image toolbar to make white the transparent color. Right-click the image and choose Properties from the pop-up menu. In the Alternative Representations: Text field of the Image Properties dialog box, enter an alternative text representation of Divider.

6. Position the insertion point immediately after the divider graphic and choose Insert | Heading 2. Enter the following text:

   `Favorite Far Out There Links`

7. Position the insertion point at the end of the heading and choose Insert | Paragraph | Normal. Then enter some introductory text that lets people know the kind of links you're providing in this section of the web, as shown in Figure 12.6.

Figure 12.6.

Add some text to your Favorites page that describes the types of sites you're linking to.

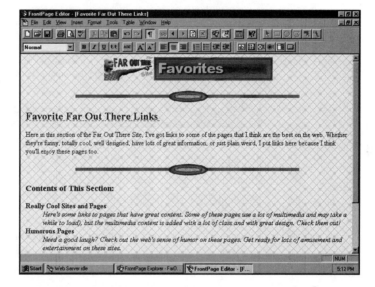

8. Position the insertion point at the end of the text you entered in step 7 and press Enter. Paste the divider graphic onto your page again. Center it by clicking the Center button on the Format toolbar.

9. Position the insertion point immediately after the graphic. Choose Insert | Heading 3. Enter the following text:

   `Contents of This Section:`

10. Choose Insert | Definition | Term for each link name, followed by Insert | Definition | Definition for each link description to enter your list of link categories. After the definition list is complete, format the terms and definitions. Format each of the terms in bold text. Format each of the definitions in italic text.

    When you finish, your page should look similar to the page shown in Figure 12.7.

11. Place the insertion point at the end of the last definition in the list and press Ctrl+Enter. This places the insertion point in a new Normal paragraph.

Figure 12.7.

An example of what your Favorite Links page should look like.

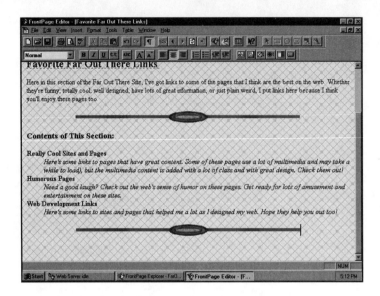

12. Paste the divider graphic onto your page again, using Ctrl+V.

13. Choose File | Page Properties. In the Page Properties dialog box, check the Get Background and Colors from Page checkbox to assign the Far Out There Web Colors style sheet to the page.

14. Choose File | Save to save the page to your web. When FrontPage asks whether you want to remove the task from the To Do list, click No. (You'll add text links and a footer to this page in Chapter 17, "Real-Life Examples.") FrontPage then asks if you want to save the images to your web. Click Yes to All to save the images to your web.

Creating a Template from the Favorite Links Page

Now you're going to create a new page and copy the contents you just entered in the Favorites page to it. You'll modify the contents a bit to add placeholder text for the Links pages. You'll save this new page as a template that can be used for all the Links pages on your site.

Follow these steps:

1. Choose Edit | Select All, or press Ctrl+A. Everything on the page is selected in inverse video. Copy the contents to the clipboard by pressing Ctrl+C or by clicking the Copy button on the standard toolbar.

2. Use the File I New command to create a new page based on a Normal Page template. Paste the contents onto the new page by pressing Ctrl+V or by clicking the Paste button on the standard toolbar.

3. Choose File I Page Properties. In the Page Properties dialog box, check the Get Background and Colors from Page checkbox, and assign the Far Out There Web Colors style sheet to the page.

4. Select the Favorite Far Out There Links heading. Choose Edit I Bookmark or press Ctrl+G to access the Bookmarks dialog box. Assign a bookmark name of top, as shown in Figure 12.8.

Figure 12.8.

Create a bookmark called top *for the page title.*

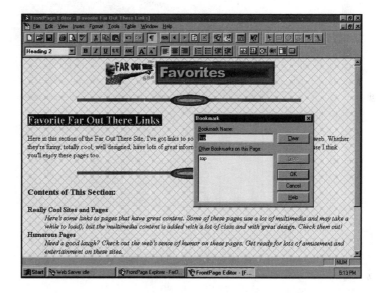

5. Place the insertion point at the end of the first heading in the page. Enter a space and then choose Insert I Line Break. Choose Normal Line Break from the Break Properties dialog box and choose OK.

6. Below the first heading, enter a second heading:

   Subtitle

7. Format the second heading as italic text by clicking the Italic Text button on the Format toolbar.

8. Select the descriptive text you entered below the original heading and replace it with the following:

   Description of the sites on this page.

9. Select the following text:

   Contents of This Section:

Then use Ctrl+G to open the Bookmark dialog box. In the Bookmark Name field, enter Contents.

10. Position the insertion point at the end of the Contents of This Section: heading, and choose Insert I List I Bulleted. Add a few generic list items, as shown in Figure 12.9.

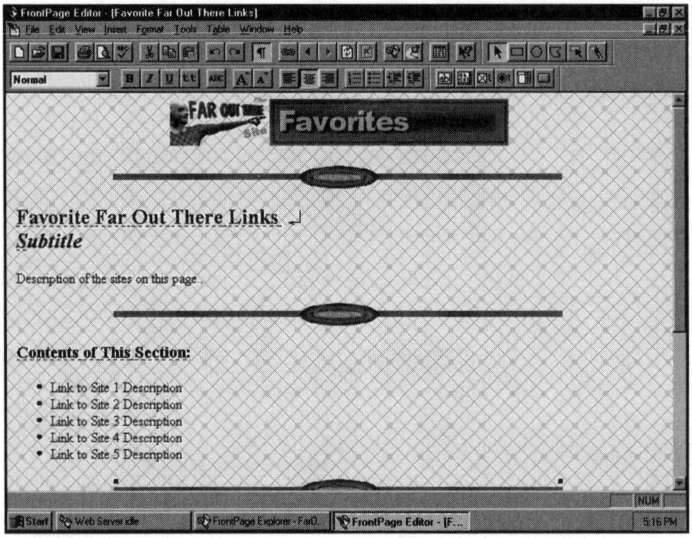

Figure 12.9.

The Contents section of the Links template is revised.

11. Press Ctrl+Enter at the end of the bulleted list to insert a Normal paragraph. Copy the divider graphic from anywhere else on the page, using Ctrl+C, and paste it onto this line using Ctrl+V. Center it by clicking the Center button on the Format toolbar.

12. Modify the Term and Definition list to use generic text as placeholders for the links you'll put on your pages. Create as many terms and definitions as the number of items in the bulleted list above this list. For example, Figure 12.10 shows the term for the first generic link as follows:

    Link to Site 1

    The definition for the first generic link reads as follows:

    Description of Site 1

13. With the insertion point at the end of the Definition list, press Ctrl+Enter to begin a new Normal paragraph. Then type the following:

    Back to Contents ¦ Back to Top

14. Choose Edit I Bookmark (or press Ctrl+G) to format each of the terms in the Definition list as bookmarks. Give the bookmarks generic names also, such as Site1, Site2, and so on. When you're done, the list should look like Figure 12.10.

Figure 12.10.

The Term and Definition list is revised for generic content, and bookmarks are added.

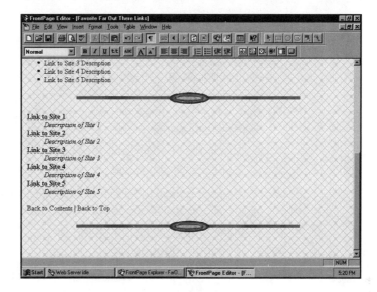

15. Return to the bulleted list in the Contents of This Section portion of the page. Add links to the appropriate bookmarks on the page for each Site item. Highlight one of the items in the bulleted list, and use the Create or Edit Link button to open the Create Link dialog box. Select the Open Pages tab and choose the appropriate bookmark from the Bookmark drop-down listbox, as shown in Figure 12.11.

Figure 12.11.

Choose the bookmark from the Open Pages tab in the Create Link dialog box.

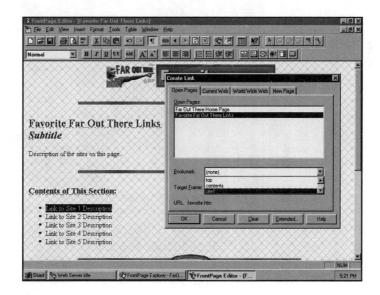

16. Go to the line below the definition list—Back to Contents I Back to Top. Highlight Back to Contents and click the Create or Edit Link button on the Standard toolbar. In the Open Pages tab of the Create Link dialog box, create a link to the Contents bookmark. Do the same for the Back to Top text, adding a link to the Top bookmark.

17. Choose File I Page Properties to access the Page Properties dialog box. Then change the properties of the page:

> Page Title: Far Out Links Template
> Select Background and Colors from Page: `_private/faroutwc.htm`

18. Don't save this page to your web. Instead, choose File I Save As to save this page as a template. In the Save As dialog box, enter the title and URL:

> Page Title: Far Out Links Template
> Page URL: `farlinks.htm`

19. Click the As Template button. The Save As Template dialog box shown in Figure 12.12 appears. Complete the information for the directory and description of the template by entering the following:

> Title: Far Out Links Template
> Name: `farlinks` (limited to eight characters, no extension)
> Description: Links template for the Far Out There site

Figure 12.12.

Save the page as a template by using the Save As Template dialog box.

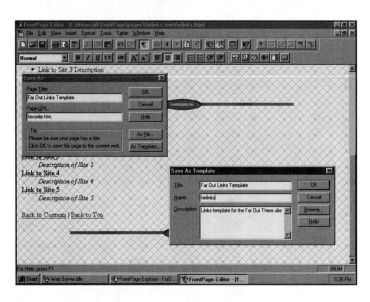

20. Click OK to create the template. When you are asked whether you want to save the images, click Yes to All.

Creating a Link Page from Your Template

When you saved your page as a template, it was saved in the `Microsoft FrontPage\pages\farlinks.tem` directory. The images were placed in an `\images` subdirectory. The template now is available for selection from the New Page dialog box, as shown in Figure 12.13.

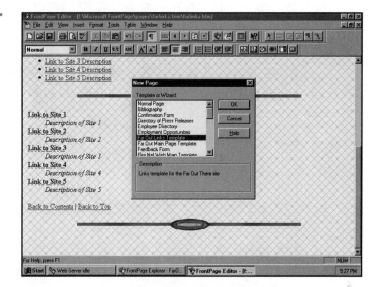

NOTE: You'll make some minor layout changes and additions to this template in Chapter 17. You might want to hold off making any pages from this template until after those changes are made. If you want to skip ahead, you can find the steps in the "Revising the Far Out There Links Template" section of that chapter.

To create a page based on your `farlinks` template, follow these steps:

1. Use the File | Open from Web command to open the Favorite Far Out There Links page.

2. Create the text on which the user will click to navigate to your new links page, and highlight it. Click the Create or Edit Link button in the Standard toolbar. The Create Link dialog box appears.

3. Click the New Page tab in the Create Link dialog box. Enter a title for your new links page in the Page Title field. Enter a URL for your new links page in the Page URL field.

4. Verify that the Edit New Page Immediately radio button is selected (it is selected by default), and choose OK. The New Page dialog box appears.

5. Select Far Out Links Template from the Template or Wizard drop-down listbox.

6. Click OK. The page appears in the FrontPage Editor.

7. Customize the contents of the pages as applicable to the types of links you want to include on the page. Figures 12.14 and 12.15 show a completed example of the page. You can use the definition below each link to enter a description of the page or site, or to list its URL below the link. Of course, the description can be as brief or as long as you like.

Figure 12.14.

The upper portion of a links page contains the header graphics, a page introduction, and the contents of the page.

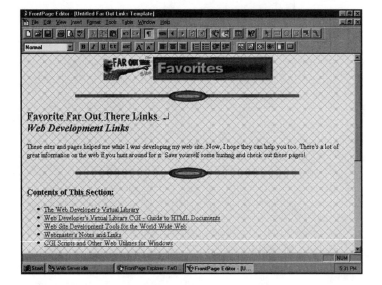

8. Save the page to your web using the File I Save command. When asked whether you want to save the images to the Web, click Use Existing.

Figure 12.16 shows one of the links on the Favorite Far Out There Links page completed. When the user clicks on this link, the browser navigates to the links page created in the previous steps.

Figure 12.15.

The lower portion of a links page contains the links to your favorite sites and a description of each link.

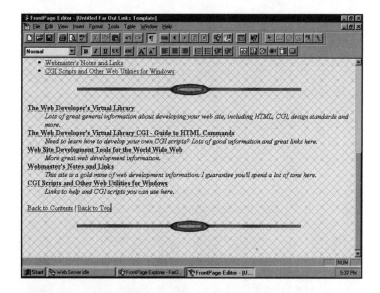

Figure 12.16.

One of the links on the Favorite Far Out There Links page navigates to a new page created with your template.

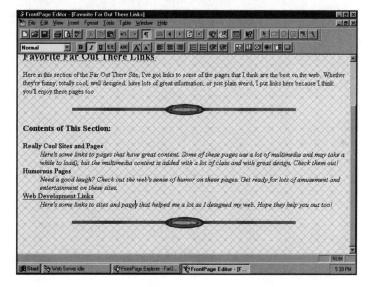

Editing the What's New Page

When you created a link to the What's New page from your home page, you based it on the What's New template. Now you're going to modify this page a bit to better suit your site. Follow these steps:

1. From the FrontPage Editor, choose the Tools I Show To Do List command or use the To Do List button in the Standard toolbar. The To Do List dialog box appears.

2. From the list of tasks, select the task for the What's New page and click Do Task.

3. Position the insertion point at the beginning of the Annotation bot text, and press Enter. This begins a new Normal paragraph at the top of the page. Center the paragraph by clicking the Center button on the Format toolbar.

NOTE: You can delete the annotation text if you like. It might be nice to keep it there, however, so that you will know how to add contents in the future.

4. Insert the `faroutsm.gif` (or `.jpg`) image onto the page. (You can copy and paste it from the Favorites page if it's still open or insert it from the current web.)

5. Insert the `whatsnew.gif` image from the accompanying CD-ROM onto your page. In the Image Properties dialog box, assign it the following alternative text:

`What's New`

6. Reformat the What's New title to Heading 2 using the style bar on the Format toolbar. Change the title to the following:

`What's New at Far Out There?`

7. Center the heading on the page by clicking the Center button on the Format toolbar.

8. Replace the horizontal line with `divider.gif`, which should already exist on your web. You can copy and paste it from another open page as well. Double-click to select the line and then choose Insert I Image to replace it with the divider graphic.

9. Add the dates and pages you've added so far, as shown in Figure 12.17. Create links to the new pages on your Web so that your site visitors can navigate to them from the What's New page.

10. Replace the second horizontal line with the `divider.gif` graphic.

11. Position the insertion point before the first dated item on your page and choose Insert I Image to insert the `newicon.gif` image located on the accompanying CD-ROM. Make white the transparent color in the image by clicking the Make Transparent button on the Image toolbar.

12. Click and drag to select the `newicon.gif` image, and paste it before the remaining new items on your page.

13. Right-click each of the new icons, and choose Properties from the context menu to access the Image Properties dialog box. Align each of the images to the left of the text (Layout: Alignment: Left). When you're done, your page should look as shown in Figure 12.17.

Figure 12.17.
Add the New icon before each date and align them to the left of the text.

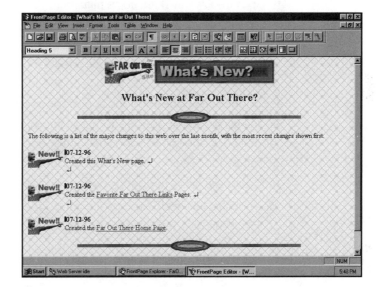

NOTE: When you assign alignment properties to an image, it might be a little confusing to figure out how to select it afterward. If you turn on the Show/Hide button (in the standard toolbar), you'll notice a solid bar before the text on your page. If you select that bar, you'll be able to delete the image or copy it to your clipboard.

14. Choose File I Page Properties to assign the web's style sheet to the page.

15. Choose File I Save to save the page to the web.

16. Click No when FrontPage asks whether you want to remove the page from the To Do list. (You'll make some minor revisions and additions in Chapter 17.)

17. Click Yes to All to save any new images to the web.

Creating the Navigation Bars and Footer Pages

You might notice that the Favorites pages and the What's New page don't have any links to other pages yet. That's because you'll be adding them at the beginning of Chapter 17 by using Include bots. In that chapter, you'll create the navigation bars and footer pages that will be included on the other pages. After you save the pages, you might want to move them to the _private directory.

To create the Text navigation bar, follow these steps:

1. Open the Far Out There home page from your web if it is not still open.
2. Copy the Text navigation bar from the top of the page to your clipboard.
3. Create a new Normal page. Paste the Text navigation bar onto it, and align it to the center of the page by clicking the Center button on the Format toolbar.
4. Edit the Main Home Page link to read Home Page.
5. Change the Home Page link to link to the home page on the current Web rather than the home page in the current directory.
6. Choose File I Page Properties to assign the Web colors to the navigation bar.
7. Choose File I Save to save the page as the following:

> Title: Included Text Navigation Bar
> Page URL: `textnav.htm`

To create the footer, follow these steps:

1. Return to the Far Out There home page.
2. Copy the two lines in the footer to the clipboard.
3. Create a new Normal page. Paste the footer onto it, and align it to the center of the page by clicking the Center button on the Format toolbar. Use the style bar to format the content as an Address paragraph.
4. Choose File I Page Properties to assign the web colors to the navigation bar.
5. Choose File I Save to save the page as the following:

> Title: Included Footer
> Page URL: `footer.htm`

To create the Image navigation bars, follow these steps:

1. Open the home page if it is not still open.
2. Select the first row of navigation buttons by placing your cursor at the left of the row, where it turns into a selection pointer. Click to select the row of buttons, which then appear in inverse video.

You'll learn how to include these navigation bars and footers on your pages in Chapter 17.

3. Copy the navigation buttons to your clipboard.

4. Create a new Normal page. Paste the navigation buttons onto it, and align them in the center of the page.

5. Edit the Home link to link to the home page in the Far Out Web.

6. Choose File | Page Properties. The Page Properties dialog box appears. Select the Get Background and Colors from Page checkbox, and choose the Far Out There Web Colors page for your style sheet. Click OK to return to the FrontPage Editor.

7. Choose File | Save to save the page as the following:

> Title: Included Navigation - Top
> Page URL: `topnav.htm`

To create the bottom navigation bar, follow these steps:

1 Copy the bottom row of navigation buttons from the home page to your clipboard.

2. Create a new Normal page. Paste the navigation buttons onto it, and align them in the center of the page.

3. Assign the Web Color style sheet to the page by choosing File | Page Properties.

4. Choose File | Save to save the page as the following:

> Title: Included Navigation - Bottom
> Page URL: `botmnav.htm`

Move the Text navigation bar, Footer, and Navigation Button pages to the `_private` directory as you did with the Web Colors page earlier in this chapter.

Workshop Wrap-Up

Well, there you have it; you're well on the way to building your site. The main pages exist on your Web now, and you have a fairly good idea of the direction in which the Web is going. You have a unique home page complete with animation. A custom template enables you to easily add links to your site. You let people know what you've added to your site in the What's New page. Other pages await completion, with the To Do list telling you what you need to complete.

Chapter Summary

You created many pages in this chapter, some of which are nearly complete and others that appear in your To Do list. The pages include custom backgrounds and images, and text and link colors that blend together nicely. The home page features animation. The pages soon will be interlinked through navigation bars and text links that enable visitors to easily navigate to the main pages on your web. It wasn't that hard, was it?

Next Steps

You'll continue your web in Chapter 17, after you learn some advanced features you can use on your pages. You'll take full advantage of the techniques you'll learn in the following chapters:

- ❏ See Chapter 13, "Your Tables Are Ready," to learn how to use tables to enhance your page layout.
- ❏ See Chapter 14, "Frames—Pages with Split Personalities," to learn how to display more than one page at a time within the space of a single page, using links to change the contents in each of the sections.
- ❏ See Chapter 15, "Automating Pages with Bots," to learn how to use the basic bots to simplify your page creation even further.
- ❏ See Chapter 16, "Going Beyond the FrontPage Editor," to learn how to use other types of editors with FrontPage and how to use different types of content on your pages.

Q&A

Q: There's some space left after that second animation on the home page. I want to put some text there, but I can't. How can I do that?

A: The center graphic defines the height of the line in that case. Other items appearing on that line look to that image as the deciding factor for alignment. You'll modify the home page in Chapter 17, using tables to control the layout of the text and graphics on this and other pages. Tables really help you plan your page layout to the max!

Q: What about image maps? Couldn't you have put all those navigation buttons on one of those?

A: Yes, I could have done that (and you'll be working with an image map in Chapter 17). The reason I didn't do it here is because I wanted a different layout for the navigation buttons on the home page than the layout that will be used for the Favorites page, the What's New page, and the other pages you'll add in Chapters 17 and 22. You'll be using tables to enhance the layout of the graphics on those pages, arranging the navigation buttons along the sides of the page. By creating individual navigation buttons, you can use the same graphics in both cases (as you'll see).

Q: There's a whole bunch of files on the accompanying CD-ROM for this chapter. What are they?

A: All the `.htm` files on the page are the pages that should appear on your web at this time, completed to the point they should be at the end of this chapter. The Favorite Links template also is included. The images are those that you'll place on your pages in this chapter.

You'll also find some other graphics in TGA and GIF format on the accompanying CD-ROM. These are versions of the Web graphics with no text on them; this way, you can use the Far Out There Web graphics to make links to other pages you might want to create for the Web. I've provided the graphics in TGA format (a true-color format) so that you don't have to worry about recompressing something that already has been compressed.

P A R T

III

Advanced Techniques

THIRTEEN

Your Tables Are Ready

We asked for it, and we got it. A welcome addition to FrontPage 1.1 is the inclusion of table support. Using tables, you can really control the layout of a page in a great number of ways, placing content and images where you want them. Well…sort of.

In the HTML tag family, tables are still growing up. For this reason, browsers handle tables differently. Some older browsers don't recognize tables at all; they leave your hard layout work lying in the dust, displaying a jumble of text and images. You should keep several different browsers around to test your tables as you design them and make compromises when you can.

There is good news, though. The latest versions of Internet Explorer and Netscape handle tables quite well. Each of these browsers has its own nifty little tricks up its sleeve—particularly Internet Explorer, which gives you the opportunity to specify different colors for individual cells. The proposed tags for Internet Explorer 3.0 sound even wilder. You'll have the capability to specify a separate background image for each cell as well. Tables are the way to go if you want to create a fancy layout.

In this chapter, you

❑ Become acquainted with the elements that make up a table

❑ Learn how to insert a basic table onto your page

❑ Learn how to align tables, include borders, choose cell padding and spacing, and change the width of your tables

❑ Learn how to create advanced tables by splitting and merging cells, and creating nested tables

❑ Work with extended table and cell attributes to give your pages that "Microsoft look"

❑ Learn how to insert images, bots, and forms into tables

Tasks in this chapter:

❑ Inserting a Basic Table

❑ Entering Text into Your Tables

❑ Editing Tables

❑ Captions—Giving Your Table a Purpose

❑ Building a Fancy Table

What Makes Up a Table?

A table has several elements, and to understand them is to understand the terminology needed to create them. Figure 13.1 shows an example of a basic table.

Figure 13.1.
The basic elements of a table are rows, columns, cells, borders, and a caption.

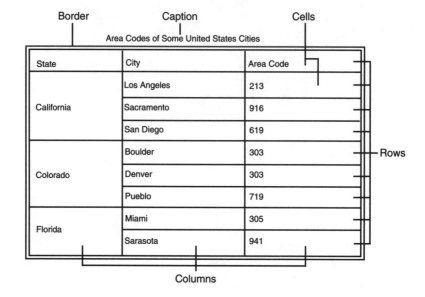

You'll see the following elements:

- ❏ **Rows and columns:** A table usually consists of multiple rows and columns. Rows run horizontally and columns run vertically.
- ❏ **Cells:** Each data field in a table is called a *cell*, which can sometimes be referred to as a *data cell*. Cells used for table headings are called *header cells*.
- ❏ **Captions:** The table caption is a title or description of the contents of the table. Typically, it is located immediately above the table.
- ❏ **Borders:** A table can be created with or without a border. It can appear on all sides of the table or on selected sides through the use of extended attributes.

Setting the Basic Table

You enter a basic table in your page first by choosing the Insert I Table command. This command invokes the Insert Table dialog, from which you can specify several table attributes.

Inserting a Table

By default, FrontPage creates a table that contains two columns and two rows and spans the entire width of your page. The table is aligned in the center of your page, has no border, has a cell padding of 1, and has a cell spacing of 2 pixels.

You can specify several different values for your basic table. Follow these steps:

1. Place the insertion point on the line on which you want to insert the table.

2. Choose Table | Insert Table, or click the Insert Table button on the FrontPage toolbar. The Insert Table dialog shown in Figure 13.2 appears.

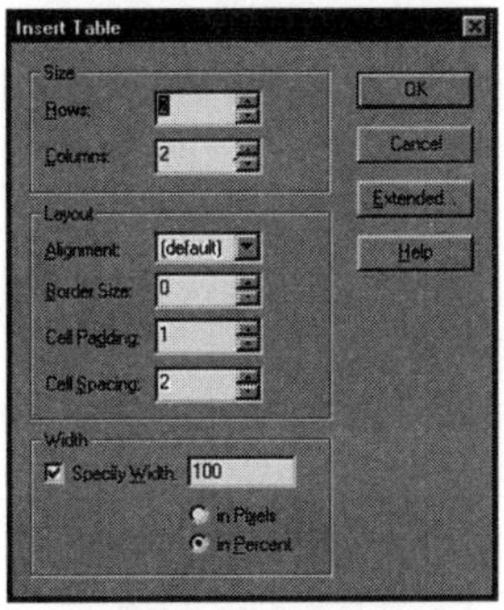

I explain what cell padding and cell spacing do later in this chapter, in "Setting Table Properties."

Figure 13.2.
Choose the table settings in the Insert Table dialog.

3. Enter the settings for your table. Each setting is described in the following sections.

TIP: You can preview your settings by clicking the Apply button in the Table Properties dialog.

4. To add extended attributes to your table, click the Extended button. Follow the procedures outlined in "Using Extended Table Attributes," later in this chapter.

5. When all table settings are entered, click OK to create the table.

Setting Table Properties

The Insert Table dialog enables you to specify the number of rows and columns your table contains. You also can specify how the table aligns on the page and choose a table width in percentage of screen or pixels. You can specify the overall cell padding and cell spacing values in this dialog, too.

Rows and Columns

You set the number of rows or columns in the Size section of the Insert Table dialog. First, enter the number of rows in the Rows field, or use the up and down arrows to select a value from 1 to 100. Then, enter the number of columns in the Columns field, or use its up and down arrows to select a value from 1 to 100. Figure 13.3 shows a table that contains five rows and three columns.

Figure 13.3.
A basic table with five rows and three columns.

Season	Begins	Things I like about it
Winter	December 21	About the only thing I like about winter is the first snowfall because it's pretty. After that it gets boring.
Spring	March 21	Everything is new and fresh. It's exciting to see the leaves on the trees coming back in full bloom.
Summer	June 21	Time to go to the beach and enjoy the waves!
Fall	September 21	The leaves on the trees start to turn to beautiful shades of gold, orange, red and brown.

Table Alignment

The Table Alignment setting is the first in the Layout section of the Insert Table dialog. This setting is not for the alignment of the contents within the cells; it controls how the entire table is aligned on your page.

NOTE: If you want to design tables that display fairly consistently in several browsers, you need to make some compromises. Some browsers don't recognize the right-alignment setting and align the table to the left side of the page instead.

To choose a table alignment, select one of the following options from the Alignment drop-down listbox in the Layout section of the dialog:

- ❏ **Default:** Aligns the table to the position that was specified when the table was created.
- ❏ **Left:** Aligns the table to the left edge of your page.
- ❏ **Center:** Aligns the table to the center of your page.
- ❏ **Right:** Aligns the table to the right of your page. Not recognized in some browsers.

Figure 13.4 shows examples of left, center, and right alignment applied to the table in our example. The Alignment setting won't be noticeable unless the table width is set to a value of less than 100 percent.

Figure 13.4.

Tables aligned to the left, center, and right of a page.

75% Width, Left-Aligned

Row 1, Column 1	Row 1, Column 2	Row 1, Column 3
Row 2, Column 1	Row 2, Column 2	Row 2, Column 3
Row 3, Column 1	Row 3, Column 2	Row 3, Column 3
Row 4, Column 1	Row 4, Column 2	Row 4, Column 3

75% Width, Center-Aligned

Row 1, Column 1	Row 1, Column 2	Row 1, Column 3
Row 2, Column 1	Row 2, Column 2	Row 2, Column 3
Row 3, Column 1	Row 3, Column 2	Row 3, Column 3
Row 4, Column 1	Row 4, Column 2	Row 4, Column 3

75% Width, Right-Aligned

Row 1, Column 1	Row 1, Column 2	Row 1, Column 3
Row 2, Column 1	Row 2, Column 2	Row 2, Column 3
Row 3, Column 1	Row 3, Column 2	Row 3, Column 3
Row 4, Column 1	Row 4, Column 2	Row 4, Column 3

Border Size

The Border Size setting controls the width of the border that appears around the outer edge of the table. Many people use tables to enhance page layout, placing graphics and text in fixed areas of the page. Most commonly, the tables used in this manner don't have borders; using them would detract from the effect of the layout. When you specify a border of 0, the FrontPage Editor displays the borders of the table and cells in dotted lines. Not to worry—this is just a guide for you to place your content in the cells. When you view the table in other browsers, you won't see those border designations. Figure 13.5 shows the table from Figure 13.3 with a border added. Cell padding and cell spacing are set to 0 in this example.

Figure 13.5.

A border is added to the table.

Season	Begins	Things I like about it
Winter	December 21	About the only thing I like about winter is the first snowfall because it's pretty. After that it gets boring.
Spring	March 21	Everything is new and fresh. It's exciting to see the leaves on the trees coming back in full bloom.
Summer	June 21	Time to go to the beach and enjoy the waves!
Fall	September 21	The leaves on the trees start to turn to beautiful shades of gold, orange, red and brown.

The Border Size setting is found in the Layout section of the Insert Table dialog. To set the border size, you can do one of two things:

❏ Enter a value in the Border Size field of the Layout section in the dialog.

❏ Use the up and down arrows at the right side of the Size field to select a value between 0 and 100 pixels.

Cell Padding

The Cell Padding setting controls how far from the edge of the cell's border its contents appear. To see what I mean, compare the top table in Figure 13.6 to the middle table, which does not use cell padding.

Figure 13.6.
Examples of cell padding and cell spacing.

Border=5, Cell Padding=10, Cell Spacing=0

Row 1, Column 1	Row 1, Column 2	Row 1, Column 3
Row 2, Column 1	Row 2, Column 2	Row 2, Column 3

Border=5, Cell Padding=0, Cell Spacing=10

Row 1, Column 1	Row 1, Column 2	Row 1, Column 3
Row 2, Column 1	Row 2, Column 2	Row 2, Column 3

Border=5, Cell Padding=10, Cell Spacing=10

Row 1, Column 1	Row 1, Column 2	Row 1, Column 3
Row 2, Column 1	Row 2, Column 2	Row 2, Column 3

TIP: For text content, you probably will want to use cell padding and cell spacing to improve the appearance of your tables. If you want graphics to get as close to each other as possible to give the illusion that the table is one solid graphic, you might want to set cell padding and spacing to 0.

You specify Cell Padding settings in the Layout section of the Insert Table dialog in one of two ways:

❏ In the Cell Padding field, enter the number of pixels for cell padding.

❏ Use the up and down arrows to select a value between 0 and 100. A value of 0 results in cell contents appearing immediately adjacent to its borders.

Cell Spacing

The Cell Spacing setting controls the width of the borders between cells (the row and column dividers, so to speak). Refer to Figure 13.6, where the center and bottom tables have cell spacing added. Compare them to the top table, which does not.

To set cell spacing, you use one of the following two methods:

❏ In the Cell Spacing field, enter the number of pixels for cell spacing.

❏ Use the up and down arrows to select a value between 0 and 100. A value of 0 results in no borders between cells.

Table Width

You can format tables to different widths by using the Width section of the Table Properties dialog. Figure 13.7 shows some examples of different table widths that are center aligned. You set table width in percentage of screen or in pixels.

Figure 13.7.

You can specify a table width other than 100 percent in the Table Properties dialog.

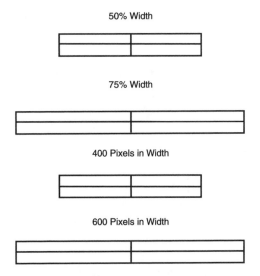

50% Width

75% Width

400 Pixels in Width

600 Pixels in Width

TIP: In most cases, you'll want to specify the table width in percentage of screen because users may have their browser windows sized differently instead of maximized. Also, some users browse the Internet in 640×480 resolution, whereas others use 800×600 or 1024×768. If you specify the width in percentage of screen, the table resizes to accommodate the user's browser window.

On the other hand, if you're adding graphics to your tables, pixel settings help you visualize the table layout before the graphics are inserted. You should note, however, that when a user resizes his browser window or views it in a different resolution, portions of your table may not be visible. Perhaps a good rule of thumb here is to size your pixel table width for 640×480 resolution, and size your graphics accordingly. You should be fairly safe with that setting in most cases.

To specify table width, follow these steps:

1. Enable the Specify Width checkbox in the Width section. (It is checked by default.)

2. Select the In Pixels or In Percent radio button.

3. Specify the percentage or number of pixels in a whole number. You don't need to add a percent sign or decimal point for percent value.

4. Continue specifying other table properties, or click OK to exit the Table Properties dialog box.

Using Extended Table Attributes

Several new tags in HTML 3.0 enable you to enhance a table's appearance. Table 13.1 lists these tags. You add these attributes by specifying extended attributes for the table.

NOTE:
You won't be able to view the results of these extended attributes in the FrontPage Editor. You can, however, view the results in Internet Explorer 2.0 or 3.0, as well as Netscape 3.0.

Table 13.1. Table tags (HTML 3).

Name	Value	Function
ALIGN	BLEEDLEFT	Aligns the table to the left edge of the window border.
ALIGN	BLEEDRIGHT	Aligns the table to the right edge of the window border.
COLSPEC	Cn, Ln, or "	Specifies column alignment and Rn each column in the table. Acceptable values are Cn, Ln, and Rn. A table with four columns, for example, could have

Name	Value	Function
		the following value entry: `L20 R25 C100 C150`. The first column will be 20 pixels wide and left-aligned, the second column will be 25 pixels wide and right-aligned, the third column will be 100 pixels wide and centered, and the fourth column will be 150 pixels wide and centered.
FRAME	ABOVE	Displays a border at the top of the table frame.
FRAME	BELOW	Displays a border at the bottom of the table frame.
FRAME	BOX	Displays a border on all sides of the table frame.
FRAME	HSIDES	Displays a border on the top and bottom sides of the table frame.
FRAME	LHS	Displays a border on the left of the table frame.
FRAME	RHS	Displays a border on the right of the table frame.
FRAME	VOID	Removes all outside table borders.
FRAME	VSIDES	Displays a border on the left and right sides of the table frame. This is an Internet Explorer 3.0 feature.
RULES	none	Removes all interior table borders.
RULES	ALL	Displays a border around all rows and columns.
RULES	BASIC	Displays horizontal borders between the table head, table body, and table foot.
RULES	COLS	Displays horizontal borders between all table columns.
RULES	ROWS	Displays horizontal borders between all table rows.

To add extended attributes for a table, follow these steps:

1. Position the insertion point anywhere within the table.

2. Right-click and choose Table Properties from the context menu. The Table Properties dialog appears (shown at the left in Figure 13.8).

3. Click the Extended button. The Extended Attributes dialog appears (shown at the upper right in Figure 13.8).

4. To add an attribute, click the Add button. Add the attribute's name and value (refer to Table 13.1) in the Set Attribute Value dialog. This dialog is shown in the lower right portion of the screen in Figure 13.8.

5. Choose OK to exit each of the dialogs and return to the FrontPage Editor.

Figure 13.8.
Adding an extended table attribute.

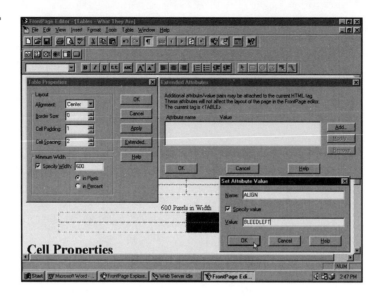

 Inserting a Basic Table

If you want to create your own table, create a new page in the FrontPage Editor. Use the example shown in Figure 13.9 to try a table yourself.

Figure 13.9.
Insert a table with five rows and three columns.

Season	Begins	Things I like about it
Winter	December 21	About the only thing I like about winter is the first snowfall because it's pretty. After that, it gets boring
Spring	March 21	Everything is new and fresh It's exciting to see the leaves on the trees coming back in full bloom.
Summer	June 21	Time to go to the beach and enjoy the waves!
Fall	September 21	The leaves on the trees start to turn to beautiful shades of gold, orange, red, and brown

To insert the table, follow these steps:

1. Place the cursor on the line before the location where you want to insert the table. Choose Table I Insert Table. The Insert Table dialog appears.

2. Specify the following settings:

   Alignment: Center
   Border Size: 5
   Cell Padding: 3
   Cell Spacing: 3
   Width: 75%

3. Click OK to create the table.

 # Entering Text into Your Tables

After you place your table on your page, it's easy to place text, images, bots, or forms into the cells. Start first with a basic text table to learn how easy it is. Enter the text shown in Figure 13.9 into your table, or make up your own example.

To enter text into your table, follow these steps:

1. Place the insertion point inside the cell where you want to add content.

2. Enter the text for the cell. You can use any character-formatting options for text in a cell that you can use in any other area on your page.

3. To place content in another cell, position the insertion point into the cell and left-click. You cannot tab to another cell.

 # Editing Tables

After you place a basic table on your page, you begin to edit the contents in the table. In the process, you can assign different properties to any or all of the cells in the table. You'll run into situations where you might need to add a row or two, reformat widths of cells, align your text differently, and all sorts of other things. Have no fear; it's easy to edit the tables to enhance appearance.

TIP: If you're working along with these examples, you can use the Edit I Undo command to clear your work quickly and easily.

You can edit table properties in the Table Properties dialog shown in Figure 13.10. The basic steps follow:

1. Position the cursor anywhere within the table.

2. Right-click and choose Table Properties from the context menu. The Table Properties dialog appears.

Figure 13.10.
Use the Table Properties dialog to change the settings of your table.

To add rows or columns to your table, see "Inserting Rows and Columns," later in this chapter.

All the settings you specified when you created the table can be modified, with the exception of the number of rows and columns. The procedures to modify them are the same as outlined earlier in "Setting Table Properties."

Working with Cells

You're looking at the table you just created and saying, "So, what's the big deal? Just looks like a standard table to me!" As you are about to learn, you can reformat the cells in your table in a variety of ways.

You can apply cell formatting to a single cell or to multiple cells at once. To do this, you need to select the cells first. You can select a group of cells, an entire row or column, or the entire table.

Selecting Cells

To apply cell formatting to cells, you just select the cells you want to apply the formatting to before you choose the Edit I Properties or Cell Properties command.

To select a single cell or multiple cells, follow these steps:

1. Place the insertion point in the first cell you want to select.
2. Choose Table I Select Cell. The cell appears in an inverse highlight.

After you merge or split cells, it can be a bit confusing as to how to select them. See "Notes on Selecting Split or Merged Rows," later in this chapter.

3. To select additional cells, hold down the Shift key. You can drag the mouse to select a range of contiguous cells, or click any remote cell to add it to the selection.

Selecting Rows

You can select an entire row or multiple rows at a time. A good example for doing this is formatting all the cells in the row as header cells.

To select an entire row, use one of these methods:

❑ Place the insertion point in one of the cells in the row you want to select, and choose Table I Select Row.

❑ Position the insertion point outside the left edge of the table, where it becomes a selection pointer. Click to select the table row. You can drag the arrow to select additional contiguous rows.

Selecting Columns

If you want to change the width of an entire column of cells, you can select one or more columns using one of these methods:

❑ Place the insertion point in one of the cells in the row you want to select, and choose Table | Select Column.

❑ Position the insertion point above the top edge of the table, where it becomes a selection pointer. Click to select the table column. You can drag the arrow to select additional contiguous columns.

Selecting the Entire Table

You also can apply cell formatting to every cell in your table. To select the entire table, use one of these methods:

❑ Place the insertion point in one of the cells in the row you want to select, and choose Table | Select Table.

❑ Move the cursor to the selection bar located on the left edge of your page, where it becomes a selection pointer. Double-click to select the entire table.

Changing Cell Properties

After you select your cells, you use the Cell Properties dialog to change the properties of the cells. This dialog enables you to set the properties of a single cell or a group of selected cells in your table. (See Figure 13.11.) The settings you can choose from are described in the following sections.

Figure 13.11.
The Cell Properties dialog enables you to reformat your cells in a variety of ways.

Horizontal Alignment

You set horizontal alignment in the Layout portion of the Cell Properties dialog. You can choose left, center, or right alignment. The first row of the table in Figure 13.12 shows examples of these alignments.

Figure 13.12.
Contents of cells can be aligned horizontally and vertically.

Horizontal and Vertical Alignment

Horizontal Alignment positions text or image at Left, Center, or Right of Cell (Examples are all aligned Vertical=Middle)	Horiz=Left	Horiz=Center	Horiz=Right
Vertical Alignment positions text or image at Top, Middle or Bottom of Cell (Examples are all aligned Horizontal=Left)	Vertical=Top	Vertical=Middle	Vertical=Bottom

To specify horizontal alignment, follow these steps:

1. In the Layout section's Horizontal Alignment drop-down listbox, choose Left, Center, or Right alignment.
2. Click Apply if you want to preview the results before applying the command.
3. Click OK to apply the setting to your cells.

Vertical Alignment

You also set vertical alignment in the Layout portion of the Cell Properties dialog. You can choose to align the contents of your cell at the top, middle, or bottom sides of the cell. Refer to the second row of Figure 13.12 for examples of these types of alignments.

To specify vertical alignment, follow these steps:

1. In the Layout section's Vertical Alignment drop-down listbox, choose Top, Middle, or Bottom alignment.
2. Click Apply if you want to preview the results before applying the command.
3. Click OK to apply the setting to your cells.

Creating or Removing Header Cells

It's typical to assign the top row and/or the first column in your table as header cells. Figure 13.13 shows a table where the top row is formatted as header cells.

Figure 13.13.
Header cells enable you to distinguish what the contents of the cells represent.

Season	Begins	Things I like about it
Winter	December 21	About the only thing I like about winter is the first snowfall because it's pretty. After that, it gets boring
Spring	March 21	Everything is new and fresh. It's exciting to see the leaves on the trees coming back in full bloom.
Summer	June 21	Time to go to the beach and enjoy the waves!
Fall	September 21	The leaves on the trees start to turn to beautiful shades of gold, orange, red, and brown

NOTE: When you format cells as header cells, the contents of the cell become what appears to be emphasized (or bold) text. You won't be able to use the Bold button on the Format toolbar to remove the bold formatting from the header cell. You'll need to convert the header cells back to normal cells for this. You can also italicize, underline, or use fixed-width font in a header cell.

To change selected cells into header cells, enable the Header Cell checkbox in the Layout section of the Cell Properties dialog. To remove header cell formatting, disable the Header Cell checkbox.

Specifying Minimum Cell Width

Notice that there is a lot of wasted space in the table shown in Figure 13.13. You can specify a minimum width for the cells in your tables. Before you get too deep into this, though, you should know that some browsers ignore cell width settings and automatically size columns to fit the content in the cells below them. If you don't want this to happen, there are ways to work around it, which I'll describe in a bit.

To specify the minimum width of a cell, follow these steps:

1. In the Minimum Width section of the Cell Properties dialog, enable the Specify Width checkbox. (It should be enabled by default.)

2. In the Width section of the dialog box, choose whether you want to specify the width in percentages or pixels.

3. Enter the percentage or number of pixels for the width in the Specify Width field.

It's important to note that the values entered for minimum cell widths are exactly that: minimums. If all the column widths in your table total less than 100 percent, the columns expand as necessary to accommodate cell contents until the table reaches 100 percent width. If all the column widths do total 100 percent, the contents of the cells wrap around as necessary. Figure 13.14 shows a table in which the first and second columns are formatted for 15 percent width, and the last column is formatted for 70 percent width. Notice that the contents of the second column wrapped to accommodate the contents instead of taking width away from the longer row.

Figure 13.14.

You can force the table columns to fixed widths by formatting the columns to total 100 percent.

Season	Begins	Things I like about it
Winter	December 21	About the only thing I like about winter is the first snowfall because it's pretty. After that it gets boring.
Spring	March 21	Everything is new and fresh. It's exciting to see the leaves on the trees coming back in full bloom.
Summer	June 21	Time to go to the beach and enjoy the waves!
Fall	September 21	The leaves on the trees start to turn to beautiful shades of gold, orange, red and brown.

The same rule applies for tables that have a pixel width. If your table was created with a 500 pixel width, for example, format each of the column widths so that their values total 500 pixels. Notice in Figure 13.15 that words too large to display in the column are cut off. The same applies to graphics, so you should coordinate your graphics sizes with the same values you specify in your columns.

Figure 13.15.

For tables that specify pixel width, format the columns to equal the same total.

Table Width = 500 Pixels

75 pixels	35 pixels	150 pixels	240 pixels
DICTIONARY	DICTIONARY	DICTIONARY	DICTIONARY
75 pixels	35 pixels	150 pixels	240 pixels

Now for a little oddity. Suppose that you try to get fancy with table layout for graphics. You format the first row in your table as shown here:

```
Col 1 = 10%   Col 2 = 10%   Col 3 = 10%   Col 4 = 70%
```

So far, so good: It totals 100 percent. The table should be happy. Let's say for the next row, you format the cells this way:

```
Col 1 = 25%  Col 2 = 25%  Col 3 = 25%  Col 4 = 25%
```

Again, they all add up to 100 percent. Will these two rows work together? Well, take a look at the first table in Figure 13.16 to see what happens.

Figure 13.16.

Don't combine different cell widths in the same column. Strange things happen.

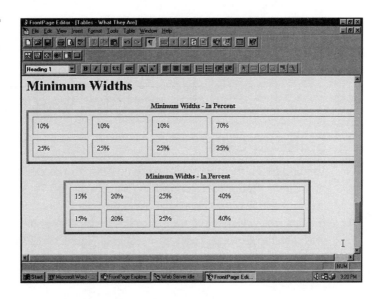

As you can see, strange things brew up. The table expands to fit the widest cell in each column. The first three columns in the second row take precedence over the three columns in the first row because they are wider. The last column in the first row takes precedence over the last column in the second row for the same reason. So, what you originally hoped would be two rows that spanned 100 percent in different ways becomes a table that is 145 percent wide (three columns at 25 percent plus one column at 70 percent). Note that 45 percent of your table will go off the screen. Situations like this make table layout tedious at times, but you can compensate with cell spanning, merging, or splitting.

Cell Spanning and Merging

You can make a cell or group of cells span more than one row or column. Select an entire row, an entire column, or a range of contiguous cells, as shown in the top table in Figure 13.17, and choose the Table I Merge Cells command. The bottom table shows what the cells look like after they are merged.

Figure 13.17.
You can merge cells for advanced layout.

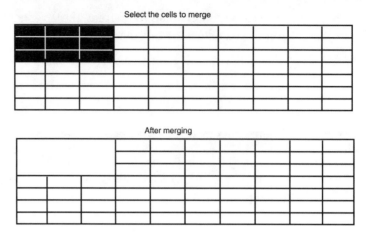

Splitting Cells

If you want to split a cell into both rows and columns, you can insert another table within that cell. See "Inserting a Table Within a Table," later in this chapter.

Splitting cells is the opposite of merging cells. You can split a cell into multiple rows or columns. Figure 13.18 shows an example of this. The top table, which has two columns and two rows, was split using the Split Cells command. The first column in the first row was split into four columns, and the second column in the second row was split into six rows. The bottom table of Figure 13.18 shows the results.

Figure 13.18.
Cells can be split into multiple rows or columns.

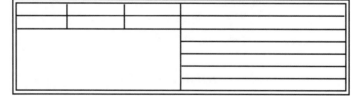

To split a cell, follow these steps:

1. Select the cell or cells you want to split.

2. Choose Table I Split Cells.

3. Choose how you want to split the cell.

To split the cell into columns, choose Split Into Columns. Enter the number of columns that you want to split the cell into.

To split the cell into rows, choose Split Into Rows. Enter the number of rows that you want to split the cell into.

4. Click OK. The cells you selected are split as specified.

Notes on Selecting Split or Merged Rows

After you split cells, it sometimes can be a little confusing as to how to select them. How do you find out which row the big area is in? And how do you select the smaller cells to the right of that big cell?

In Figure 13.19, you easily can see how to find out. Position the insertion point at the left edge of the table near the row you want to select. The cursor becomes a small arrow. Click to select the row.

Figure 13.19.

Selecting rows after splitting.

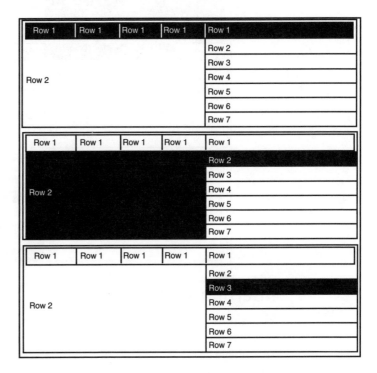

As you can see in the top table of Figure 13.19, the first row (which contains the cell that you split into columns) is still intact as a row.

Now look at the center table in the figure. The second row contains that big cell. To select it and its corresponding cell in the second column, place the mouse at the left side of the table, directly opposite the cell in the second row of the second column.

To select the cells in rows 3 through 7 of the table, position the mouse at the left side of the table, directly opposite the cell or cells you want to select. Click to select the row. The bottom table in Figure 13.19 shows this.

A similar situation occurs with the cells that were split into columns. The first column contains the big cell and first cell in the first row, because those were the cells that originally were there. The second through fourth columns (the ones you split) don't have any additional cells associated with them in the example. All three of these cells are selected in the center table shown in Figure 13.20. And the fifth column is still intact as a column, as shown in the bottom table of Figure 13.20.

Figure 13.20.
Selecting columns after splitting.

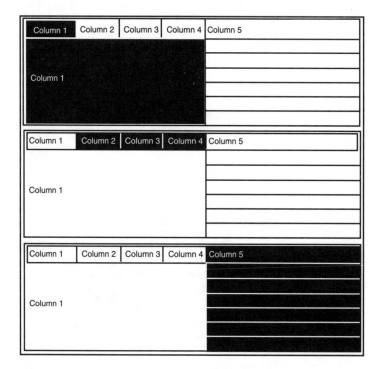

Inserting a Cell

You can insert a new cell into your table. When you do this, the contents of the other cells shift over. You might need to reformat cell widths in that row to compensate. There might be situations in which you want this to occur, but you might be better off splitting the cell that appears before the cell you want to insert. That way, your table layout isn't affected.

To insert a cell, follow these steps:

1. Position the insertion point at the point where you want to insert the new cell.

2. Choose Table I Insert Cell. A new cell appears in the table, and the contents of the table shift over.

Inserting Rows and Columns

You also can insert new rows or columns into your tables by using the Insert Rows or Columns dialog.

To insert new columns, follow these steps:

1. Select the column before or after the location where you want to insert the new column.

2. Choose Table I Insert Rows or Columns. The Insert Rows or Columns dialog appears.

3. Select the Columns radio button.

4. In the Number of Columns field, enter the number of columns you want to insert, and choose whether you want to insert the new columns to the left or right of your current selection.

5. Click OK to insert the columns.

To insert new rows, follow these steps:

1. Select the row before or after the location where you want to insert the new row.

2. Choose Table I Insert Rows or Columns. The Insert Rows or Columns dialog appears.

3. Select the Rows radio button.

4. In the Number of Rows field, enter the number of rows you want to insert, and choose whether you want to insert the new rows above or below the current selection.

5. Click OK to insert the rows.

NOTE: When you insert rows or columns in your table, the new row uses the same number of cells as the row that you select to insert before or after. This is important to keep in mind when you insert new rows in tables that have split and merged cells.

Inserting a Table Within a Table

You also can create a *nested table*—a table within a table. It is sometimes easier to create more complex tables using this approach. Follow these steps:

1. Place the insertion point within the cell in which you want the table inserted.

2. Choose Table I Insert Table.

3. Specify the table properties as outlined in "Setting Table Properties," earlier in this chapter.

4. Click OK to insert the table within the selected cell.

Deleting Cells

It's pretty easy to delete cells from your table. Actually, all you have to do is select the cells, rows, or columns you want to delete and press the Del key. To delete the entire table, select it by choosing the Table I Select Table command or by double-clicking in the selection bar in the left margin of your page. The entire table appears in reverse video, and then you can delete it.

Using Extended Cell Attributes

You add extended attributes to cells in a similar manner as described earlier in "Using Extended Table Attributes." Tables 13.2 and 13.3 list the attributes you can add. Attributes that apply to cells fall in three categories: TH (for header cells), TR (for rows), and TD (for data cells).

Table 13.2. TH, TR, or TD tags (HTML 3).

Name	Value	Function
COLALIGN	LEFT	Left-aligns contents of all cells in the column.
COLALIGN	RIGHT	Right-aligns contents of all cells in the column cell.

Table 13.3. TH, TR, or TD tags (Internet Explorer only).

Name	Value	Function
BACKGROUND	URL	Defines a background image for the cell. Cell contents appear above the background image.

Name	Value	Function
BGCOLOR	#rrggbb	Defines a background color for the cell by its hexadecimal value.
BGCOLOR	colorname	Defines a background color for the cell by color name. Allowed color names are listed in Figure D.18 in Appendix D.
BORDERCOLOR	#rrggbb	Defines a border color in hexadecimal value.
BORDERCOLOR	colorname	Defines a border color by name. Allowed color names are listed in Figure D.18 in Appendix D.
BORDERCOLORDARK	#rrggbb	In a border with a 3-D appearance, selects the dark color by hexadecimal value.
BORDERCOLORDARK	colorname	In a border with a 3-D appearance, selects the dark color by color name. Acceptable values are shown in Figure D.18 in Appendix D.
BORDERCOLORLIGHT	#rrggbb	In a border with a 3-D appearance, selects the light color by hexadecimal value.
BORDERCOLORLIGHT	colorname	In a border with a 3-D appearance, selects the light color by color name. Acceptable values are shown in Figure D.18 in Appendix D.

To add extended attributes to a cell or group of cells, follow these steps:

1. Select the cell or cells to which you want to add attributes.
2. Right-click and choose Cell Properties from the context menu. The Cell Properties dialog appears.
3. Click the Extended button. The Extended Attributes dialog appears.
4. To add an attribute, click the Add button. Add the attribute's name and value in the Set Attribute Value dialog. (Refer to Tables 13.2 and 13.3.)
5. Click OK to exit each of the dialogs and return to the FrontPage Editor.

Figure 13.21 shows an example of applying Internet Explorer's BGCOLOR attribute to cells. The attributes were added to each cell individually. When you apply the extended attributes, you don't see the results in the FrontPage Editor (the top table in Figure

13.21). If you view your tables in Internet Explorer 2.0, however, you'll be able to see the results. Check out the bottom table in the figure.

Figure 13.21.

Internet Explorer tags as viewed in the FrontPage Editor (top example) and in Internet Explorer (bottom example).

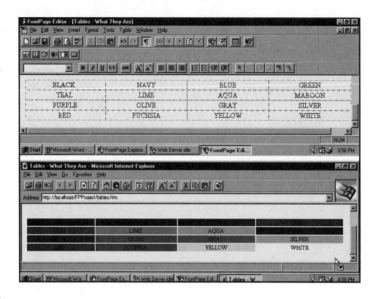

Captions—Giving Your Table a Purpose

Tables don't always have a caption, but, in some cases, they are necessary. They help you point out what the table is about. When you apply a caption to a table, it actually becomes part of the table instead of a separate line of text. Generally, a table caption uses one line.

Adding a Table Caption

To add a caption to a table, follow these steps:

1. Position the insertion point anywhere within the table.

2. Choose Table I Insert Caption. The insertion point moves to a center location above the table, where you can type the table caption.

Selecting a Table Caption

To select a table caption, move the pointer to the left of the table caption. Double-click the mouse to select it.

Inserting an Image into a Table

You also can insert bots and forms into tables, using the same procedures you would for any other part of the page. See "Next Steps" at the end of this chapter for chapter references.

You insert an image into a table in the same manner you would insert an image onto any part of your page. The only special considerations you really need to remember are that the table columns are sized sufficiently to handle the image. You don't want to insert a graphic that is too big for the column, which is why I recommend sizing your columns for pixels rather than percentage when you apply cell properties. To demonstrate this and the other items I've covered in this chapter, build the fancy table in the next section.

Building a Fancy Table

Build a quick example of a table that combines some of what you've learned here:

1. Create a new page. Place a heading on the first line that says something like `Building a Fancy Table.`

2. Insert a new table. Assign it the following properties:

   Number of Rows: 2
   Number of Columns: 2
   Alignment: Center
   Border Size: 5
   Cell Padding: 0
   Cell Spacing: 0
   Width: 600 pixels

3. Place the insertion point in the upper right cell and insert another table. Assign the following properties to it:

   Number of Rows: 1
   Number of Columns: 3
   Alignment: default
   Border Size: 0
   Cell Padding: 0
   Cell Spacing: 0
   Width: 300 pixels

4. From the new table you just inserted into the first table, choose the Table I Split Cells command to split the first and third cells into two rows.

5. The following graphics are located on the CD-ROM that accompanies this book. Choose the Insert I Image command to insert them into the new table. You'll want to use the From File option in the Insert Image dialog.

Insert `small1.gif` into the top cell in the first row.

Insert `small2.gif` into the bottom cell of the first row.

Insert `small3.gif` into the top cell of the third row.

Insert `small4.gif` into the bottom cell of the third row.

Insert `medium1.gif` into the middle cell.

6. Position the insertion point in the lower right cell of the main table. Insert `large1.gif` into this cell.

When you're finished, your table should look like Figure 13.22. Links can be assigned to the images in the upper right portion of the main table, and you can add text to the other cells in the table to describe the things to which you are linking.

Figure 13.22.
A fancier table, with graphics and alignment.

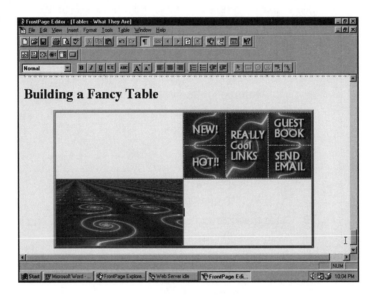

Workshop Wrap-Up

I hope I've got the wheels turning now. I think you can see from what you've learned in this chapter that tables aren't just for data anymore. They go a long way in dressing up your pages and can sometimes compensate for using image maps on your pages.

Chapter Summary

You've covered a lot of ground in this chapter. You learned what tables are and the many ways you can use them. You built a basic table and applied table properties to it. And then, after learning the many ways in which you can format cells, you got a taste of building a more advanced table, complete with graphics. You also learned ways in which you can give your tables a fresh look for those using Internet Explorer for a browser. Well done—you deserve a hearty pat on the back!

Next Steps

In the next chapter, you'll learn about one of the latest hot features of pages: *frames*. The chapter is aptly titled "Frames—Pages with Split Personalities," because that's exactly what they are. You'll see when you get there.

For information that relates to this chapter, refer to the following chapters:

❏ See Chapter 11, "Sprucing Up Your Pages," for procedures on how to add images to pages. The same principles can apply to tables.

❏ See Chapter 15, "Automating Pages with Bots," to learn how to place basic bots into your pages. Bots also can be inserted into your tables.

❏ See Chapter 18, "Adding Interactivity—Forms the Easy Way," to learn how to develop a form. Like any other item on your page, you can insert forms into tables as well.

Q&A

Q: Are there any other compromises that can be made for browsers that don't support tables very well?

A: One workaround is to build your table as you normally would and then do a screen capture of it while viewing the table in the FrontPage Editor or another browser that supports tables. Insert the graphic of the table onto your page instead of the actual table.

For browsers that don't support graphics, or for folks who have graphics turned off, create a text alternative of your table on another page. Use formatted paragraphs or typewriter font to align the contents of the page nice and neat. Then provide a link to the text version on the page that contains your original table.

Q: I inserted a table at the very beginning of my page, and now I want to add text up there. I can't figure out how to do that, because my cursor won't go above the table. Help!!!

A: If your table has a caption, position the insertion point at the beginning of the caption and then choose one of the Insert I Paragraph or Insert I Heading commands to enter your text. If your table doesn't have a caption, insert one, enter its contents, and then insert your paragraph.

Q: I'm using a background that puts a really neat design at the left side of my page. I used paragraph alignment to position my text beyond that border, but some browsers put the text at the beginning of the page over the border. How can I fix that?

A: Put your page contents in a table. Create a table that contains one row and two columns and spans 100 percent of the page width. Size the left column wide enough to cover the border, and size the right column for the remainder of the page. For more information, see Chapter 17, "Real-Life Examples," because this is one of the examples you'll be working on. There are many more tips there.

Q: I formatted my tables for 50 percent width and aligned them to the right side of my page. Now I want to put text next to it but I can't. What gives?

A: Tables are an entity unto themselves. The table may be formatted to display in a portion of your screen, but the areas to the right and left are also a part of that table. What you can do is insert another table on your page that spans 100 percent page width and has one row and two columns. Size each column for 50 percent width. Next, reformat your original table for 100 percent width. Cut or copy it to the Clipboard and paste it in one of the cells in the new table. Then you can add your text in the other empty cell.

FOURTEEN

Frames—Pages with Split Personalities

Frames are a relatively new addition to the Internet scene. They were first introduced in Netscape 2.0, and soon many other browsers will support them. You cannot view frame sets directly in FrontPage, but the package includes an easy way to develop them.

What Are Frames?

You can think of a frame as multiple pages in one. They really are what the title of this chapter implies: pages with split personalities. Each region of a framed page displays a separate page that is scrollable, just like any other Web page.

Frames Terminology

Figure 14.1 shows a basic diagram of how frames and pages connect together. A *frame set* is a special kind of page that is divided into multiple sections, called *frames*. The page at the top of Figure 14.1 designates the frame set. You assign it a URL, just as you would any other page. The frame set gets loaded first when a user navigates to the URL. Next, the frame set loads the pages referenced by *source URLs,* and it displays each page in a separate frame.

Figure 14.1.
A simplified diagram of what a frame set does.

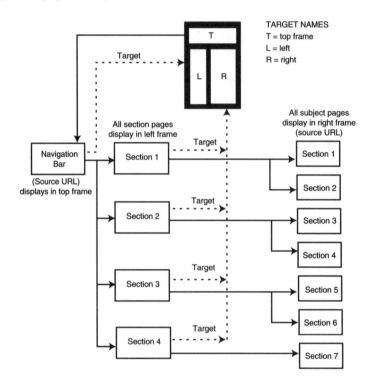

Each frame within the frame set has a source URL. Figure 14.1 shows three source URL pages on the second row. The navigation bar (`navbar.htm`), section 1 (`section1.htm`), and subject 1 (`subject1.htm`) load into the frame set when the user navigates to it for the first time.

For the source URL, use the name of the page that you want to display first in the frame. It can belong to a page, a file, or another frame set in your web. If one of the frames in the frame set contains another frame set, the initial frame is called a *parent frame*, or the master frame that displays another frame set within it.

You learn how to enter target frame names in the "Designing Frame Grids" task later in this chapter.

Target frames are applicable when you create links from a framed page to another framed page. You must designate in the source frame's properties the frame in which the target page displays. To do this, assign a default target frame in the page properties of the originating page—that is, the page from which you are linking. The target frame is not the URL of the page to which you are linking. Instead, it is the name of one of the frames in the page, such as left, right, top, or bottom.

Take a look again at Figure 14.1. The frame set first loads into your browser, dividing the viewing window into three sections named topframe, left, and right. The source URLs then load into their respective frames.

The first source URL, the navigation bar, initially displays in the top frame. The navigation bar contains links to four section pages, indicated by solid lines in Figure 14.1. The navigation bar page also includes a default target link of left, indicated by a dotted line. This instructs the browser to load the linked pages in the left frame in the frame set.

The second source URL, section 1, initially displays in the left frame of the frame set. Each section contains links to different subjects, indicated by solid lines in Figure 14.1. Each section page includes a default target link of right, which displays the section's subject matter in the right frame of the frame set.

The third source URL, subject 1, initially displays in the right frame of the frame set. The subject pages do not need default target frames associated with them. When the user clicks links in the subject pages, the new subject matter appears in the same frame.

When to Use Frames

One frame, such as a navigation bar or a table of contents, is commonly used to link to other pages that display in another frame. This makes for easier navigation through a site. Instead of having to return with a link or the Back button in a browser as with standard web pages, the table of contents displays in its own frame while its links appear in another frame.

Frames also work well for an online book. The table of contents for each section of the book can appear in one frame, the content of each chapter in another frame, and footnotes for a page in yet another frame.

A formal presentation is another good candidate for frames. The outline of the presentation appears in one frame and the graphics in another. You can use a third frame in the set for navigation buttons.

Not All Browsers Are Frame-Compatible

Frames offer you great flexibility in displaying pages. Don't let your Web site rely totally on that flexibility, though. Many people use browsers that are not compatible with frames. Others use different browsers at different times for various reasons. For example, a user might prefer the way one browser views mail and newsgroups over another, and that choice might not have frame compatibility.

It is frustrating to browse the Web and find someone talking about a great site. You want to check it out, so you navigate to the page. A message pops up that reads, "Your browser is not frame-compliant. You cannot see this site unless you use a frame-compatible browser." It gives you no clue about which browser to use, and there is no way to exit out unless you use the Back button in your browser.

Be considerate to those out there who do not have frame-compatible browsers or who do not use them all the time. Provide alternatives for navigating to the pages that you display within the frames. Otherwise, you might potentially lose visitors to your site.

Creating Frame Pages

Because a frame set involves multiple pages that are linked together, you must have a web open to save the pages when they are created. Open a web in the FrontPage Explorer before you create pages with the Frames Wizard. You can select a predefined frame template, or you can design your own.

To create a frame set:

1. Create or open a web in the FrontPage Explorer. The frame set and its associated pages are saved to this web after the wizard generates them.

2. From the FrontPage Editor, select File | New. The New Page dialog box appears.

3. From the list of available page templates and wizards, choose the Frames Wizard. The Choose Technique panel of the Frames Wizard appears. (See Figure 14.2.)

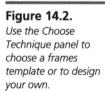

Figure 14.2.
Use the Choose Technique panel to choose a frames template or to design your own.

Creating Frames with Templates

Several frame templates have already been built for you. To use one of these predefined templates, select the Pick a Template option in the Choose Technique panel of the Frames Wizard. The steps are

1. From the Choose Technique panel of the Frames Wizard, select Pick a Template.

2. Click Next. The Pick Template Layout panel appears. (See Figure 14.3.)

Figure 14.3.
Use the Pick Template panel to select a template.

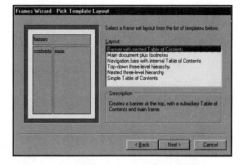

3. Select a frame layout from the list of options. As you make a selection, a preview of the layout appears on the left of the panel. Each frame in the frame set is labeled with a name. A description of the template also appears in the Pick Template Layout panel.

4. After you choose a template, click Next. The Choose Alternate Content panel appears. (See Figure 14.4.) This is where you select an alternate page for users without frame-compatible browsers.

Figure 14.4.
Use Choose Alternate Content panel to select a page that can be viewed with browsers that do not support frames.

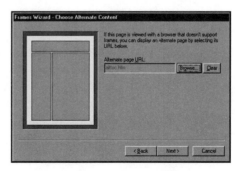

5. To specify an alternate page to display instead of the frame set, click the Browse button to choose another page in your web. If you do not already have an alternate page, you can create one and select it later. Use the HTML

Page, Image, or Any Type tabs to choose an alternate page. After you make your selection, click Next. The Save Page panel appears.

6. Enter the title of the frame set in the Title field.

7. Enter the URL of the frame set in the URL field.

8. Click Finish to create the frame set. The frame set and its associated pages are saved to the currently opened web.

The Frames Wizard Frame Templates

FrontPage comes with six frame templates. They are

Banner with nested Table of Contents
Main document plus footnotes
Navigation bars with internal Table of Contents
Top-down three-level hierarchy
Nested three-level hierarchy
Simple Table of Contents

Try to create one of the templates to find out how it works. You will learn a lot. The following sections describe what frame template produces.

Banner with Nested Table of Contents

The Banner with nested Table of Contents frame set generates four pages, as shown in Figure 14.5. They are

❏ *The frame set.* The title of this document is that which you enter in the Frames Wizard. It holds the other three pages. If you open this frame in the FrontPage Editor, the Frames Wizard appears again, and you can edit the frame set. A link to the alternate page that you specified appears in the HTML code for the page.

❏ *The banner frame.* This page contains the main navigation links. The default target frame for this page is the table of contents frame. In other words, when the user clicks the navigation links in this frame, the referenced page appears in the table of contents frame.

❏ *The table of contents frame.* The pages this frame references contain links to main pages in a section of the web. It can also contain links to all the bookmarks on a long page. Its default target frame is the main frame. When the user clicks a link in this frame, the referenced page appears in the main frame of the frame set.

❏ *The main frame.* The pages this frame references contain the main document that the user views. It does not cause changes in other frames.

Figure 14.5.

The Banner with nested Table of Contents frame set displays three pages in separate frames.

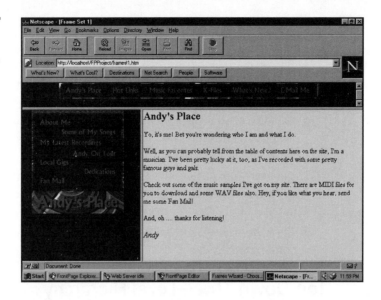

Main Document Plus Footnotes

The Main document plus footnotes frame set generates three pages. They are

❏ *The frame set.* The title of this document is that which you enter in the Frames Wizard. It holds the other two pages. If you open this frame in the FrontPage Editor, the Frames Wizard appears again, and you can edit the frame set. A link to the alternate page that you specified appears in the HTML code for the page.

❏ *The main frame.* The pages this frame references contain the main document that the user views. When the user clicks a link in this frame, footnotes appear in the Footnotes frame.

❏ *The footnote frame.* The pages or bookmarks this frame references contain the footnotes mentioned in the main document. It does not cause changes in other frames.

Navigation Bars with Internal Table of Contents

You create a similar frame set in the "Designing Frame Grids" task later in this chapter.

The Navigation bars with internal Table of Contents frame set generates five pages. They are

❏ *The frame set.* The title of this document is that which you enter in the Frames Wizard. It holds the other four pages. If you open this frame in the FrontPage Editor, the Frames Wizard appears again, and you can edit the frame set. A link to the alternate page that you specified appears in the HTML code for the page.

❏ *The top navigation bar frame.* The pages this frame references contain images with hotspots or links to table of contents pages. The table of contents pages are loaded in the table of contents frame.

❏ *The table of contents frame.* The pages this frame references contain links to the main pages in the web or to all the bookmarks on a single page. Clicking these links causes changes in the main frame.

❏ *The main frame.* The pages this frame references contain the main pages being viewed. Clicking links in these pages does not cause changes in other frames.

❏ *The bottom navigation bar frame.* This frame can be used to display additional navigation bars.

Top-Down Three-Level Hierarchy

The Top-down three-level hierarchy frame set generates four pages. They are

❏ *The frame set.* The title of this document is that which you enter in the Frames Wizard. It holds the other three pages. If you open this frame in the FrontPage Editor, the Frames Wizard appears again, and you can edit the frame set. A link to the alternate page that you specified appears in the HTML code for the page.

❏ *The top frame.* The pages this frame references contain links to the main sections in the web. Clicking these links causes changes in the middle frame.

❏ *The middle frame.* The pages this frame references contain links to the main pages in a section. Clicking these links causes changes in the bottom frame.

❏ *The bottom frame.* The pages this frame references contain the main pages being viewed. Clicking links in these pages does not cause change in other frames.

Nested Three-Level Hierarchy

The Nested three-level hierarchy frame set generates four pages, as shown in Figure 14.6. These pages are similar to those in the Top-down three-level hierarchy frame set, but the frame layout differs slightly. The pages are

❏ *The frame set.* The title of this document is that which you enter in the Frames Wizard. It holds the other three pages. If you open this frame in the FrontPage Editor, the Frames Wizard appears again, and you can edit the frame set. A link to the alternate page that you specified appears in the HTML code for the page.

❏ *The left frame.* The pages this frame references contain links to the main sections in the web. Clicking these links causes changes in the right top frame.

❏ *The right top frame.* The pages this frame references contain links to the main pages in the section. Clicking these links causes changes in the right bottom frame.

❏ *The right bottom frame.* The pages this frame references contain the main pages being viewed. Clicking links in these pages does not cause changes in other frames.

Figure 14.6.
The Nested three-level hierarchy frame set displays three pages.

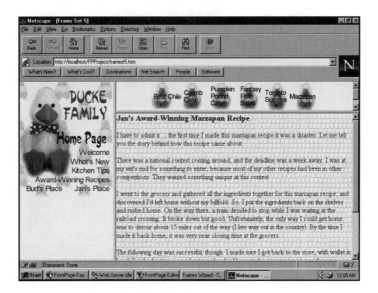

Simple Table of Contents

The Simple Table of Contents frame set generates three pages. They are

❏ *The frame set.* The title of this document is that which you enter in the Frames Wizard. It holds the other two pages. If you open this frame in the FrontPage Editor, the Frames Wizard appears again, and you can edit the frame set. A link to the alternate page that you specified appears in the HTML code for the page.

❑ *The table of contents frame.* The pages this frame references contain links to the main pages in the web or to all the bookmarks on a long page. Clicking these links causes changes in the main frame.

❑ *The main frame.* The pages this frame references contain the main pages being viewed. Clicking links in these pages does not cause changes in other frames.

Designing Frame Grids

If the frame set templates provided with the Frames Wizard do not strike your fancy, you can design your own frame sets. Indeed, designing a frame set can help you better understand how frame sets and frames work.

Create or Import the Initial Source URL Pages

The CD that accompanies this book contains pages for you to work with as you design your frame set.

In Chapter 17, "Real-Life Examples," you create a frame set that has much more punch.

You need to create the frames that are initially displayed in the frame set before you use the Frames Wizard to create the frame set. Save these pages to the currently opened web. You do not have to worry about that for this project because the CD that accompanies this book contains pages for you to work with. This project builds an online book that is displayed in four different frames. Two frames are used as navigation links—one for navigating through the sections of the book and the other frame for navigating to other pages in the web that are not contained in the frame set. The third frame displays the contents for each section of the book. The fourth frame displays the chapter contents. These are simple pages with generic links that help you see how frames work together.

Build the Frame Set

Now you can build the frame set. The steps are

1. Create an empty web in the FrontPage Explorer. The frame set and its associated pages are saved to this web after the wizard generates them.

2. Import into your web the following files, which are located on the CD that accompanies this book. Use the File I Import command from the FrontPage Explorer. The first four files are the source URLs for the frame set. They are the pages that are initially displayed in the frame set when it is opened by the browser.

File	Content
botbar.htm	Bottom navigation bar
topbar.htm	Top navigation bar
chap01.htm	Chapter 1

`s1toc.htm`	Section 1 table of contents
`alttoc.htm`	Alternate table of contents for the frame set
`chap02.htm`	Chapter 2
`chap03.htm`	Chapter 3
`chap04.htm`	Chapter 4
`chap05.htm`	Chapter 5
`chap06.htm`	Chapter 6
`chap07.htm`	Chapter 7
`chap08.htm`	Chapter 8
`chap09.htm`	Chapter 9
`chap10.htm`	Chapter 10
`chap11.htm`	Chapter 11
`chap12.htm`	Chapter 12
`s2toc.htm`	Section 2 table of contents
`s3toc.htm`	Section 3 table of contents
`s4toc.htm`	Section 4 table of contents
`s5toc.htm`	Section 5 table of contents

3. Open the FrontPage Editor and select File I New. The New Page dialog box appears.

4. From the list of available page templates and wizards, choose the Frames Wizard. The Choose Technique panel of the Frames Wizard appears.

5. Select the Make a Custom Grid option. Click Next. The Edit Frameset Grid panel appears. (See Figure 14.7.)

Figure 14.7.
Design the frame set grid in the Edit Frameset Grid panel.

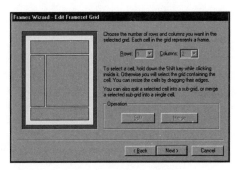

6. Enter the number of rows and columns that you want in your frame set. As you make your selections, the preview in the left side of the panel updates to reflect your entries. Remember that these frame sets are displayed within the confines of a browser window, so don't add too many frames to the frame set. If you add too many frames, the user must rely too heavily on

scroll buttons to see the contents of your frames. For this project, enter **3** for the number of rows and **1** for the number of columns.

TIP: Don't go overboard on the number of frames in your frame set. Keep in mind that some people browse the Web with low screen resolutions.

7. To move the dividers between the rows, position the mouse in the preview screen and place the cursor over the divider line. Directional arrows appear. Move the divider toward the top edge of the page until the top section of the frame set is about one fifth or one sixth of the height of the page preview. Move the bottom divider line to about the same distance from the bottom.

8. Shift+click to select the middle portion of the frame set in the page preview. The Split button enables. Enter the number of columns in which to split the middle portion. You can merge the split columns back together with the Merge button if you do not like how it looks. For this project, enter 1 for the number of rows and 2 for the number of columns.

9. Move the vertical divider line between the two new columns toward the left of the page. This creates a larger area for the main content of the frame set, which should now look as it does in Figure 14.7.

10. Click Next. The Edit Frame Attributes panel appears.

11. Click the top frame in the frame set preview window. This frame includes links to all the section tables of content in the online book.

When you pick the source URL for the page, click the Browse button to choose the page from the currently opened web, or type the source URL given in this step and in steps 14, 16, and 17 that follow.

The margin width and height designate the size of the borders between frames. The scrolling setting determines whether a scroll bar is located at the left and bottom edges of the frame. It is generally a good idea to leave it set to Auto unless the page length is less than two or three lines of text. Likewise, in case the user has his browser window set to less than full screen, consider keeping the Not Resizeable option unchecked. This enables him to resize the frame windows to better fit his browser screen.

Assign the following attributes to the top frame in the frame set, as shown in Figure 14.8.

Attribute	Value
Name	top
Source URL	topbar.htm (the top navigation bar)
Margin Width	2
Margin Height	2
Scrolling	Auto
Not Resizeable	Unchecked

Figure 14.8.
Each frame is assigned a name, a source URL, and margin and border options.

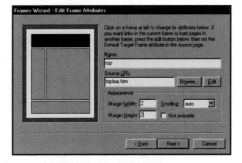

TIP: Because the navigation bar contains only a single line of text, you can set scrolling to No if you want. Choose Auto if the contents of the frame are too large to display in the height of the frame. It is generally a good idea to leave the Not Resizeable field unchecked, in case the user wants to resize the frameset to fit a smaller window.

12. Click the Edit button to edit the topbar.htm page. After the page opens in the FrontPage Editor, select File | Page Properties. The Page Properties dialog box appears.

13. In the Default Target Frame field, located at the bottom of the Page Properties dialog box, enter the name of the frame that changes its content when the user clicks a link in this frame. This field is shown in Figure 14.9 with a frame name assigned to it.

    For this project, the current frame contains links to the section's table of contents pages. These pages appear in the center left frame of the frame set. Enter cleft for the name of the default target frame.

The files included on the CD accompanying this book already have the name of the default target frame value entered for you.

Figure 14.9.

*The default target frame
is the name of a
frame—not of a file.*

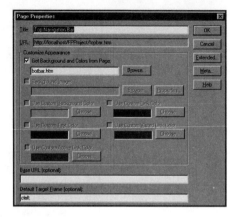

14. Click the center left frame in the frame set preview window. This frame displays each section's table of contents pages when the user clicks a link in the top navigation bar. When the user first opens the frame set, you want the contents of section 1 to appear in this frame. Each section contains links to its chapters and to bookmarks within the pages. Assign the following attributes to this frame:

Attribute	Value
Name	`cleft`
Source URL	`section1.htm` (section 1)
Margin Width	2
Margin Height	2
Scrolling	Auto
Not Resizeable	Unchecked

15. Click the Edit button to edit the `section1.htm` page. In the FrontPage Editor, select File I Page Properties. Enter `cleft` for the name of the default target frame. This causes the correct chapter or subheading of a chapter to appear in the center left window when the user clicks a link in this frame.

NOTE: When you create a similar frame set of your own, you need to complete the Default Target Frame field for each page that is referenced in the links here. For example, all the section table of contents pages on the CD have their default target frames set to `cright`. Use the File I Page Properties command for each page to enter this value.

16. Click the center right frame in the frame set preview window. This is the frame that contains the chapter content for the online book. When the user

first opens the frame set, you want to display the first chapter in this frame. Assign the following attributes to it:

Attribute	Value
Name	`cright`
Source URL	`chap01.htm` (chapter 1)
Margin Width	2
Margin Height	2
Scrolling	Auto
Not Resizeable	Unchecked

NOTE: You do not need to specify a default target frame for any of these pages. When a user clicks any links that appear in these pages, the new page displays in the same frame. This enables you to create links between chapters.

17. Click the bottom frame in the frame set preview window. Assign the following attributes to it:

Attribute	Value
Name	`bottom`
Source URL	`botbar.htm` (the bottom navigation bar)
Margin Width	2
Margin Height	2
Scrolling	Auto
Not Resizeable	Unchecked

18. Click the Edit button to edit the `botbar.htm` page. In the FrontPage Editor, select File | Page Properties. Enter `_top` for the name of the default target frame.

NOTE: `_top` is one of four special names that are recognized by browsers. It causes the browser to remove the frame set and to display the referenced links from the bottom navigation bar in a full window. If you have pages in your web that are not displayed in frames, such as a home page, use this technique to exit the frame set. Place the `_top` default target frame on any page that contains links to pages outside your site.

19. Click Next. The Choose Alternate Content panel appears.

20. Use the Browse button to select the alternate table of contents for frame set page, or enter `alttoc.htm`.

21. Click Next. The Save Page panel appears. (See Figure 14.10.)

Figure 14.10.

Assign a title and a URL for your frame set in the Save Page panel.

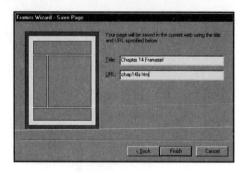

22. Enter `Chapter 14 Frameset` as the title of frame set page. Assign `chap14fs.htm` for its URL.

23. Click Finish to generate the frame set. The frame set page is saved to your web.

24. Select File I Save All to update the source URL pages to save the default target frame values that you entered when you created the frame set.

Create the Alternate Content Page

The CD that accompanies this books includes a completed example of an alternate content page.

Now you can generate the content of the alternate table of contents. Figure 14.11 shows a portion of the alternate page. It begins by mentioning that these pages appear in links. It also tells the user where to download a frame-compatible browser.

As for the links on this page, you want to include links to the pages that do not have default target frames associated with them. If your alternate table of contents includes links to pages that have default target frames specified, the browser might load the page in a new window.

You can also use Table of Contents bots to create an alternate Table of Contents page. Refer to Chapter 17 for an example of this.

In the pages that you just completed, the chapters pages do not reference target frames. You can include them in the alternate table of contents. You also should add links to some of the other pages in your web and put copyright or footer information on the page.

It is easy to generate the content for this page. Copy the contents of each section page to the clipboard and paste them in the alternate table of contents page. Then mention that this table of contents was loaded because the user did not have a frame-compatible browser. Provide links to sites where the user can download a browser that can handle frames.

Figure 14.11.

Begin your alternate page with a mention of where the user can download a frame-compatible browser.

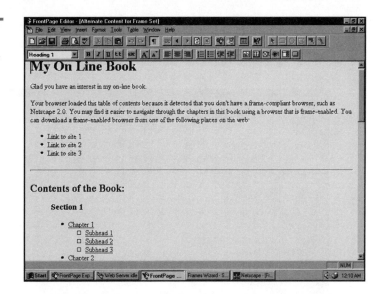

View the Frame Set

To see how your frame set looks, open a frame-compatible browser, such as Netscape 2.0. Enter a URL similar to the following, replacing the server name and web name with the one you created your frame set in:

```
http://localhost/yourwebname/chap14fs.htm
```

The browser loads the frame set. It should look like the one in Figure 14.12.

Figure 14.12.

How your frame set actually looks.

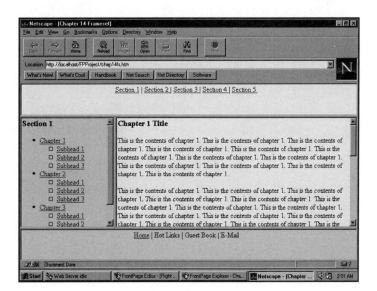

This frame set does not have to be used for a book. Figure 14.13 shows the same frame set being used with graphics for the top and bottom navigation bars and an image map for the table of contents. As you can see, the content is all up to you.

Figure 14.13.
The frame set that you created does not have to be used with a book. The content is up to you.

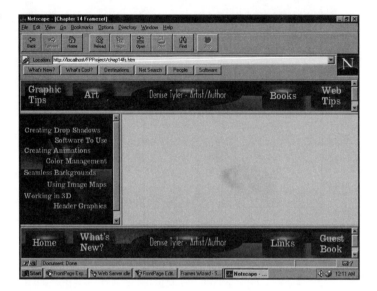

Name the Target Frames

When you design a frame grid, you assign each frame in the frame set a name, such as top, cleft, cright, or bottom. Typically, you assign a name that describes the frame's location in the frame set. Four frame names have special meanings. They are described in Table 14.1.

Table 14.1. Frame names with special significance.

Name	Description
_blank	Loads the referenced page in a new window
_parent	Loads the referenced page in the parent frame if the current frame is one that has a parent frame
_self	Loads the referenced page in the same window as the link
_top	Removes the frame set and displays the referenced page in the full browser window

Editing Frame Sets

You can edit a frame set after you create it. For example, you might want to remove, add, or rename frames. The steps are

1. Use the File I Open from Web command to open the frame set from the FrontPage Editor. The Current Web dialog box appears.
2. Choose the frame set, and click OK. The Frames Wizard appears again.
3. To change the layout of the frameset, use the Edit Frameset Grid panel. Click Next to continue.
4. To rename frames or to change other frame attributes, use the Edit Frame Attributes panel. Click Next to continue.
5. To specify or change alternate content for your frames, use the Change Alternate Content panel. Click Next to continue.
6. Save revisions to your web with the Save Page panel.
7. To accept the changes that you made, click Finish in the Save Page panel. To discard the changes, click Cancel.

 # Choosing a Default Target Frame for a Page

You added default target frames to the frame set that you created in this chapter while you used the Frames Wizard. You also can add or edit a default target frame. The steps are

1. Open the page in the FrontPage Editor using the File I Open from Web command.
2. Select File I Page Properties. The Page Properties dialog box appears.
3. In the Default Target Frame field, enter the name of the default target frame.
4. Click OK.

Loading Pages into Frames

It is possible to display another page in your web inside one of the frames in a frame set. The steps are

1. Create a link to the page.
2. Select the link, and choose Edit I Properties. The Edit Link dialog box appears.

3. In the Default Target Frame field, enter the name of the frame in which you want the page to appear.

4. Click OK. When the frame set is loaded in a frame-compatible browser, the page displays in the specified frame. If the frame set is not loaded, the browser may create a new window to display the page.

Displaying Clickable Images in Frames

If you have a clickable image, you do not necessarily have to assign a default target frame for each hotspot link that appears on the page. When you set the default target frame in a clickable image, you can use the Image Properties dialog box to assign a global default target frame. This means that all links in the clickable image that do not have target frames associated with them are associated with the global default target frame.

To add a default target frame to a clickable image:

1. Select the clickable image.

2. Choose Edit I Properties. The Image Properties dialog box appears.

3. In the Default Link area, type the name of the default target frame in the Target Frame field, as in Figure 14.14.

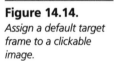

Figure 14.14.
Assign a default target frame to a clickable image.

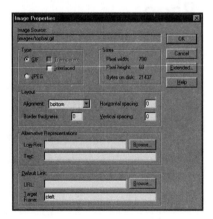

4. Click OK to exit the Image Properties dialog box.

You also can add a target frame to a hotspot when you create it. Immediately after you draw the hotspot, the Create Link dialog box appears. Choose the Current Web tab, and specify the target frame, as in Figure 14.15.

Figure 14.15.
You can specify a target frame in the Create Link dialog box.

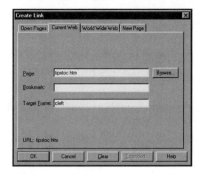

Workshop Wrap-Up

You now know what frames are and what they do. It is time to hit the ground running and develop some frame sets of your own.

Chapter Summary

In this chapter, you learned how to give your pages multiple personalities by using frame sets. With the Frames Wizard, you designed a frame set and learned how to include page content in specified frames. You even learned how to use the same content for people who do not use frame-compatible browsers.

Next Steps

More challenging projects with frames await. In Chapter 17, "Real-Life Examples," you design a frame set into which you will insert multimedia content in Chapter 22, "Real-Life Examples."

❏ Refer to Chapter 13, "Your Tables Are Ready," to learn how to create tables that can be inserted into a page.

❏ Refer to Chapter 20, "Runtime Bots: The Heartbeat of FrontPage Forms," to learn how to display forms in a frame.

Q&A

Q: Can I put anything I want into frame sets?

A: More or less, yes. You can insert picture presentations, animations, video files, Java applets, forms (such as those used in the discussion groups), and even links to your favorite sites.

Exercise caution when you use links to other sites in your frame pages, however. When you include a link to a page on someone else's site, assign it a default target frame _top. Otherwise, the pages at the other sites are displayed in your frame set. This gives the illusion that the pages from the other sites are part of your site. The user will continue down the Net with those pages displaying in your frame. You can see what a mess that might cause.

Q: When I divide pages into frames, how large should I make the graphics?

A: The resolutions most commonly used when browsing the Web are 640×480 and 800×600, with the latter being most common. In 640×480 resolution, Netscape's viewing screen measures close to 626 by 278 pixels. Internet Explorer's measures 610 by 312 pixels; release 3.0 will support frames. In 800×600 mode, Netscape's screen measures 786 by 398 pixels, and Internet Explorer measures 764 by 408 pixels. You can use these figures to estimate sizes for graphics.

Alternatively, design your frame set and open it up in a frame-compatible browser. Using a screen capture program, take a screen shot of the frame set exactly as it appears in your browser at each resolution. That way, you can determine the exact measurements for your graphics. The hard part is deciding whether you want to design your graphics for 640×480 resolution or for 800×600 resolution. It is probably best to design for 640×480 resolution.

Q: How many frames can I put in a page?

A: As many as you want. Remember, though, that some users display pages at lower resolutions. You do not want to use so many frames that the content of your pages becomes unreadable. If your frame sets contain many sections, check them out at 640×480 resolution before you put them on the Web.

FIFTEEN

Automating Pages with Bots

As your web grows—and it will—it becomes difficult to keep track of the content that you want to include on your pages. You find yourself using the same contact information or navigation links repeatedly on your pages. At times, you forget about a page or a graphic that you wanted to place on your site on a certain date, only to remember it weeks later. You forget to add new pages to your table of contents, and it soon becomes incomplete. When you move your web site, you must change all the pages that have your contact information on them.

There is an easier way to handle these situations. FrontPage's bots help automate your pages so that you can keep these situations well under control.

What Is a Bot?

Advanced Web page developers use custom scripts to automate or enhance their pages. These scripts are written in languages such as CGI, Perl, Java, and JavaScript. For the novice Web page designer, learning how to do this can be time-consuming. It can seem like an insurmountable task.

In this chapter, you

- ❏ Learn which bots can be used with or without the FrontPage Server Extensions
- ❏ Place comments on pages with the Annotation bot
- ❏ Include the contents of one page in another with the Include bot
- ❏ Place web and page configuration variables in your pages with the Substitution bot
- ❏ Generate a table of contents for your pages automatically with the Table of Contents bot

Tasks in this chapter:

- ❏ Annotating a Page
- ❏ Changing the Contents of an Annotation
- ❏ Including Pages Within Pages
- ❏ Editing Included Pages
- ❏ Following Links on Included Pages
- ❏ Inserting Content at Specified Times
- ❏ Inserting Images at Specified Times
- ❏ Generating an Automatic Table of Contents

Through the use of *bots,* FrontPage enables even novice Web page designers to use advanced features that are normally handled with scripts. These bots are basically custom-made scripts that are configured to perform certain tasks. With FrontPage, you just need to plug in the variables that each bot requires, and you are on your way to automating your pages.

Basic Bots Described

Other FrontPage bots do require the FrontPage Server Extensions to operate. They are discussed in Chapter 20, "Runtime Bots: The Heartbeat of FrontPage Forms."

The bots discussed in this chapter can be used regardless of whether your Internet service provider has the FrontPage Server Extensions installed on its server. You can use these bots to enhance your pages so that making changes down the road will be much easier.

Annotation Bot

In the chapters in the "Basic Techniques" section of this book, you created webs and pages with templates. Some of those pages contained purple text that suggested content for you to enter. That text was placed in the page using an Annotation bot.

You use the Annotation bot to place reminders or preliminary placeholder text on your pages. The text that you enter in an Annotation bot can be viewed in the FrontPage Editor. However, when you open the same page in a Web browser, you do not see the text.

TIP: When you enter code in an HTML Markup bot, discussed in Chapter 21, "Using Your Own HTML Code," a small yellow icon is placed on your page. You can use the Annotation bot to note on your page what the code in the HTML Markup bot does.

 ## Annotating a Page

You can insert an Annotation bot on your page in two ways:

❏ To insert an Annotation bot that uses the same text formatting as the line before it, place the insertion point at the end of the line before which you want to insert the Annotation bot. Then choose Insert I Bot. The Insert Bot dialog box, shown in Figure 15.1, appears.

❏ To insert an Annotation bot with its own text formatting, place the insertion point at the beginning of a line. Select the paragraph or list type as you normally would. Then choose Insert I Bot. The Insert Bot dialog box, shown in Figure 15.1, appears.

Figure 15.1.

Use the Insert Bot dialog box to select the type of bot to place on your page.

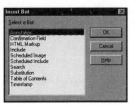

To complete the Annotation bot:

1. From the Insert Bot dialog box, highlight Annotation and click OK. The Annotation Bot Properties dialog box appears.

2. Enter the annotation text in the dialog box, as in Figure 15.2.

Figure 15.2.

Enter the text for the annotation in the Annotation Bot Properties dialog box.

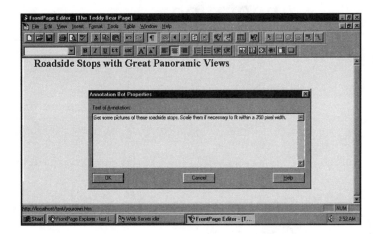

3. Click OK. Purple annotation text appears on your page.

You can apply any text formatting to an annotation after it is placed on your page. For example, you can change it to bold or italic, increase the font size, or change the paragraph or list style. You can also change the color of the text. As long as the annotation remains an annotation, however, it appears in the color purple. When you replace the annotation text with the final contents, you will see the font color that you selected during formatting. Figure 15.3 shows examples of annotations with various types of formatting.

Figure 15.3.
Annotations can be formatted just like regular text.

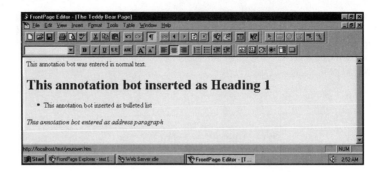

 # Changing the Contents of an Annotation

You sometimes need to edit an annotation and keep it as an annotation. The steps are

1. Place the insertion point over the annotation, where it changes into a bot pointer.
2. Click to select the annotation. It appears in inverse video.
3. Choose Edit I Properties, or right-click and choose Properties from the pop-up menu.
4. Edit the contents of the annotation, and click OK.

 # Replacing an Annotation with Page Content

You can replace an annotation with content that will appear in Web browsers. The steps are

1. Place the insertion point over the annotation, where it changes into a bot pointer.
2. Click to select the annotation. It appears in inverse video.
3. To replace the annotation with text, enter the text with which you want to replace it; the text appears in the same formatting as for the Annotation bot. To replace the annotation with an image, choose Insert I Image while the annotation is highlighted; the image appears in place of the annotation.

Include Bot

As you design your pages, you often enter the same information on several pages. Examples of repetitive information include

❑ Navigation links that appear on all pages within a section of your web

❑ Copyright and contact information that appears at the bottom of each page in the footer

❑ A logo graphic that appears at the top of several pages

It is easy to cut and paste information like this from one page to another. Consider, though, how much work it is to go back and change that information, especially if it appears on dozens of pages. You can use an Include bot to simplify and automate the task.

An Include bot inserts the contents of one page into another page. Rather than change the information in the dozens of pages in which the repeated content appears, you need change it only in the page that gets included in the others. If you study the pages in the Web templates and wizards, you will find Include bots used frequently. They are real time-savers.

When you use Include bots, note that the page you include must be an HTM or HTML page—in other words, another web page. You cannot insert a text file, a graphic, or any other type of file using an Include bot. Likewise, the page you include must exist in your current web. If you include a page from another web on your server or if you include a page that does not yet exist in your web, a line appears in italic text surrounded by brackets, such as

[badpage.htm]

What you should see after you include another page with the Include bot are the actual contents of that page inserted into your current page. If you do, you know that the Include bot did its job.

 # Including Pages Within Pages

Using the Include bot is straightforward. It involves only a few steps. They are

1. Position the insertion point at the end of the line before which you want to include the contents of another page.

2. Choose Insert | Bot. The Insert Bot dialog box appears.

3. Highlight Include and click OK. The Include Bot Properties dialog box, shown in the upper example in Figure 15.4, appears.

4. If you know the URL of the page that you want to include, enter it in the Page URL to Include field, or click the Browse button to choose a page from your current web. The Browse button will not be highlighted if you don't have a web open in the FrontPage Explorer.

5. Click OK. The contents of the other page are inserted into your current page, as in the lower example in Figure 15.4.

Figure 15.4.

Include the contents of another page with the Include Bot Properties dialog box. The contents of the referenced page appear in your current page.

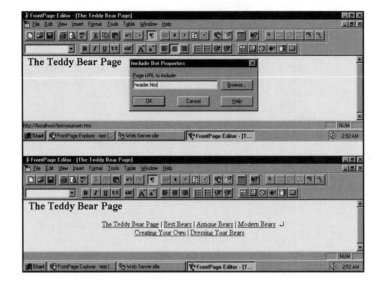

TIP: Consider placing content that is included in other pages with the Include, Scheduled Include, and Scheduled Image bots in your web's `_private` directory. This directory serves as a storage area for pages and content to which you do not want to provide public access.

 Editing Included Pages

You might decide at a later point to include a different page in an Include bot that has already been configured. To revise the Include bot so that it includes a different page:

1. Move the cursor over the text of the current included page, where it becomes a bot cursor.

2. Double-click to bring up the Include Bot Properties dialog box.

3. Use the Browse button to open the Current Web dialog box. The button will be disabled if you don't have a web open in the FrontPage Explorer.

4. Select another page from those in your current web, and click OK to return to the Include Bot Properties dialog box.

5. Click OK to return to the FrontPage Editor. The contents of the new included page appear on your current page.

If you want to edit the page contents of an included page, you must open the originating page. You can open the page by selecting the Include bot. The steps are

1. Move the mouse over the contents of the included page. The mouse pointer becomes a bot pointer.

2. Click the Include bot to highlight it. It appears in inverse video.

3. Right-click and choose Open *webpage.htm* from the pop-up menu, where *webpage.htm* is the name of the originating file. The page must already be saved to your current web for this to work. Figure 15.5 shows an example.

Figure 15.5.

Navigate to the included page by using the pop-up menu.

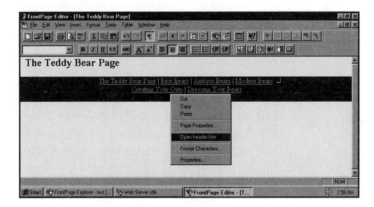

4. After the originating page appears in the FrontPage Editor, make the changes and save the edited page to your current web.

5. Return to the page that contains the Include bot. Use the Tools | Reload command or the Reload icon to view the updates in the page.

 # Following Links on Included Pages

A common use for Include bots is to place the same navigation links on many pages. If you try to follow a link from an included navigation links page, you will see the bot pointer appear when you position your mouse cursor over any of the links on the included page. To follow these links, you must open the original navigation links page. You can follow a link from an included navigation links page as follows:

1. Move the mouse over the contents of the included navigation links page. The mouse pointer becomes a bot pointer.

2. Click the Include bot to highlight it. It appears in inverse video.

3. Right-click and choose Open *webpage.htm* from the pop-up menu, where *webpage.htm* is the name of your navigation links page. The navigation links page appears in the FrontPage Editor.

4. Place the insertion point anywhere in the link that you want to follow. Choose Tools I Follow Link. The linked page that you want to view appears in the FrontPage Editor.

Scheduled Include Bot

Suppose that you want to post information on your web on a certain date. Eventually that day goes by, and you forget to include the page on the site. FrontPage provides a way to help you avoid this situation effortlessly: the Scheduled Include bot.

The Scheduled Include bot is similar to the standard Include bot, except that you can specify a date range in which the page appears in your web. You prepare your pages beforehand, and specify the date when they are posted to your web. The page displays on your site until the end date specified in the Scheduled Include bot.

Scheduled Include bots and Scheduled Image bots require proper timing. They execute only if changes occur to the web. Because of this, you are advised to make daily changes to your web. The help file suggests incrementing the value of a configuration variable. Use the FrontPage Explorer's Tools I Web Settings command, and specify a variable with the Parameters tab of the Web Settings dialog box.

That solution works well if you use FrontPage on your own server with a 24-hour connection to the Internet. For the average user who relies on an Internet service provider, though, another solution is necessary. Instead, create a page titled Updater (`updater.htm`), and place a Timestamp bot on it. Set the Timestamp bot to update each time the page is manually updated. Save this page to a private area on your web, to which only you have access; a directory named `_private` is included in your FrontPage webs automatically. If you are like most people who browse the Web, you do so frequently. Before you log into the Web, make a tiny change to this Updater page on your local computer, and use an FTP program or the FrontPage Publishing Wizard to send the new version of the page to your remote site. This makes a change to your web that will keep the schedule timers functioning properly, and the Timestamp bot keeps track of when you last made the change.

You might want to use Scheduled Include bots for

❑ Content that changes on a regular basis, such as a monthly newsletter

❑ Press releases or announcements that you want to post on a given date

❑ Links to other pages or downloadable files that you want to make available for a limited amount of time

❑ A tip, joke, or thought of the day

Inserting Content at Specified Times

To insert a scheduled page into your web on a specified date, you need to create a master page that holds its contents. It can be a blank page whose contents change based on the values specified in the Scheduled Include bot.

To display a page in your web on a given date and for a specified length of time, use the Scheduled Include bot. The steps are

1. Create a master page that holds the contents of the included page.
2. Position the insertion point at the end of the line before which you want to include the contents of another page.
3. Choose Insert I Bot. The Insert Bot dialog box appears.
4. Highlight Scheduled Include and choose OK. The Scheduled Include Bot Properties dialog box, shown in Figure 15.6, appears.

You create a page that updates both content and images on a monthly basis in Chapter 17, "Real-Life Examples."

Figure 15.6.
Use the Scheduled Include bot to place the contents of a page into your web on a specified time.

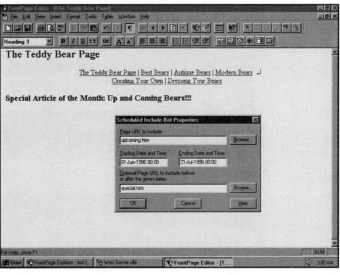

You can place several Scheduled Include bots on a single page, loading pages in sequence one after another. You create a similar set of pages in Chapter 17.

5. Enter the URL of a page in your current web in the Page URL to Include field, or click the Browse button to select a page from the currently opened web.
6. Enter the starting date and time and the ending date and time in the designated fields. The format to enter the date and time is exactly as it appears in the dialog box, including hyphens, spacing, and colons. Time is entered in 24-hour format. For example:

`01-Jun-1996 00:00`

is midnight on June 1, 1996.

7. You can also add a page URL that is displayed before or after the Scheduled Include page. This is not a bad idea, because you might have links to the page on which the Scheduled Include bot appears. If you do not specify an alternate page, the user receives an error message indicating that the page does not appear on the site. Enter the URL of an alternate page in your current web, or click the Browse button to select one from your currently opened web.

8. Click OK. If you create the page before the Scheduled Include date, you see either the alternate page or the following text:

    `[Expired Scheduled Include]`

NOTE: If you see `[Expired Scheduled Include]` during the time period specified by the Scheduled Include bot, the page that you included may not exist in your current web. Verify the name of the included file, or check to see if a file by that name exists in your current web.

If you open the page in the FrontPage Editor during the time period specified by a Scheduled Include bot, you see the page specified in the bot, as in Figure 15.7.

Figure 15.7.

The content from the included page appears within the master page during the scheduled time frame.

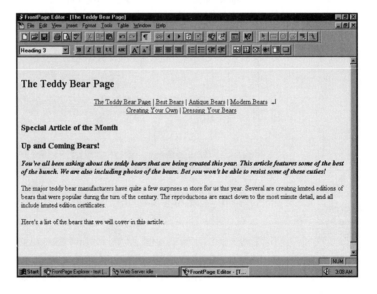

Scheduled Image Bot

The Scheduled Image bot is similar to the Scheduled Include bot, except that it places an image on a page during a specified time period. Use it to display, for example, calendar graphics or an image of the week. The same rules and cautions applicable to a Scheduled Include bot apply here as well.

Inserting Images at Specified Times

You can insert a scheduled image anywhere on a page. Note that you cannot apply image formatting to a scheduled image after it is placed on your page, because you cannot access the Image Properties dialog box. Apply image transparency or hotspots to an image before you place it on the page with a Scheduled Image bot. Likewise, because you cannot access the Image Properties dialog box, you also cannot specify layout options. Instead, insert the scheduled image in a table, as in Figure 15.8.

Figure 15.8.
Use tables to assist with laying out scheduled images.

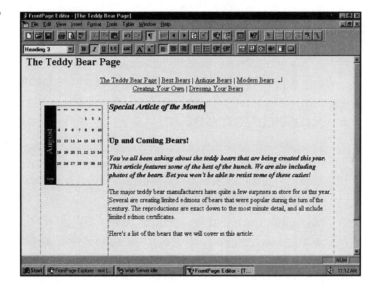

TIP: To maintain the table widths, create a general graphic image or a transparent GIF file that has the same dimensions as the image or images that you want to include. Specify this transparent GIF as an optional page URL to include before or after the given date.

To insert a scheduled image on a page:

1. Position the insertion point where you want the image to appear.

2. Choose Insert I Bot. The Insert Bot dialog box appears.

3. Highlight Scheduled Image and choose OK. The Scheduled Image Bot Properties dialog box appears. It is similar to the Scheduled Include Bot Properties dialog box.

4. Enter the URL of an image in your current web in the Image to Include field, or click the Browse button to select an image from the currently opened web.

5. Enter the starting date and time and the ending date and time in the designated fields.

6. If you want, add an image URL that is displayed before or after the scheduled include page. Enter the URL of an image in your current web, or click the Browse button to select one from the currently opened web.

7. Click OK. If you create the scheduled image before the scheduled date, you see either the alternate image or the following text:

   `[Expired Scheduled Image]`

   If you open the page in the FrontPage Editor during the time period specified by a Scheduled Image bot, you see the image specified in the bot.

Substitution Bot

If you are familiar with word processors, you might be aware of the concept of fields. Fields enable you to set up a form letter or a master mailing label, placing variable names in certain locations. The fields are replaced with data set up in a database or an another word processing document.

The Substitution bot works almost the same way, although the variables that it places on pages are settings applicable to the current web. It enables you to place on your pages the names of generic variables whose contents are replaced with values specified in the web configuration settings.

Suppose, for example, that you design a product data sheet that you want to use as a template for several different companies or for divisions of a company. You want to save this page as a template that can be used in many instances. On this page, you place Substitution bots with the following values:

```
[CompanyName]
[CompanyAddress]
[CompanyEMail]
[CompanyHomePage]
```

When you create a web for the company, you configure the web settings to specify the information that is placed on these fields in your pages.

Another good use for the Substitution bot is to place your own contact information on your pages. You might move, change Internet service providers, or upgrade your web site with your own domain name. If you placed your contact information on dozens or hundreds of pages without using Substitution bots, you would have many page changes ahead of you. Using Substitution bots for this information enables you to enter the changes only once—in your Web configuration settings. After that, if you store your pages on a remote site, it is just a matter of transferring them to your remote web.

Substitution bots need configuration variables associated with them. In this chapter, you learn how to add general configuration variables in your Web settings. You can also add configuration variables to forms, as discussed in Chapter 20.

NOTE: To add a configuration variable to your Web settings, you need to have access to the Web as an administrator. If you use FrontPage on your own personal computer, you established administrator status when you installed FrontPage under the Typical installation procedures, through the FrontPage Server Administrator.

If you are working in a multiauthor environment, you might not have administrator status and might be unable to perform all the steps in the following task. Find out from your web administrator the names of the configuration variables that you can use.

Entering Substitution Bots and Configuration Variables

In this task, you create an example of a footer that can be inserted into several pages. The footer is designed to substitute your actual contact information with the values specified in Web settings. The steps are

1. On the first line of the footer, enter the following text:

   `For questions or comments regarding this page, contact`

2. Enter a space and choose Insert I Bot. The Insert Bot dialog box appears.

3. Highlight Substitution and click OK. The Substitution Bot Properties dialog box, shown in Figure 15.9, appears.

Figure 15.9.
Use Substitution bots to place variable names on your pages.

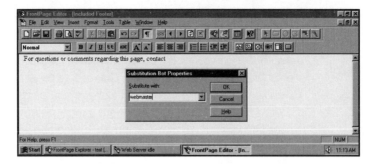

4. In the Substitution bot, enter the text that describes the variable that you want to insert. This text cannot contain any spaces or colons. Though the Substitution Bot Properties dialog box will accept spaces and colons, the Substitution bots might not work properly. For this example, enter

   `webmaster`

5. Click OK. If the configuration variable exists in your Web settings, the value set for it appears on the page, as in the top portion of Figure 15.10. If the variable does not yet exist in your Web settings, the line on your page looks like

   `For questions or comments regarding this page, contact [webmaster].`

6. To complete the next line of the footer, insert a normal line break after the Substitution bot. The insertion point moves to the next line.

Figure 15.10.
The variable name specified in the Substitution bot is replaced with configuration variables you enter in the Web settings.

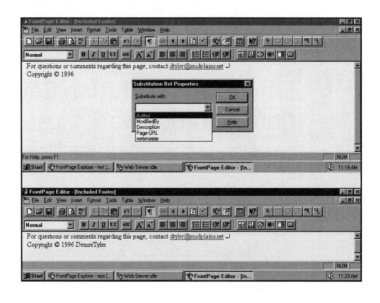

7. For the second line of the footer, type the word `Copyright` and insert a space. Next, choose Insert I Special Character, select the copyright symbol, and click Close to exit the Insert Special Character dialog box. Then, insert a space, type 1996, and insert another space.

8. Insert another Substitution bot, this time using one of the four standard configuration variables. From the drop-down list box, choose `Author`, as in the top portion of Figure 15.10. This configuration variable places the name of the author who created the page in the Substitution bot field.

NOTE: Four configuration variables are standard to every web or page created in FrontPage. They are

`Author`	Replaced with the name of the author who created the page. The author name is based on the name as entered in the FrontPage Server Administrator, or by using the Tools I Permissions command, where spaces are not allowed in the name.
`ModifiedBy`	Replaced with the name of the author who most recently modified the page.
`Description`	Replaced with a description of the current page as entered in the Comments field of the Properties dialog box.
`Page-URL`	Replaced with the page URL of the page.

The values of each configuration variable can be viewed from the FrontPage Explorer. Highlight the page whose properties you want to view, and choose Edit I Properties.

9. Click OK. The Substitution bot places the author name on your page, as shown in the bottom portion of Figure 15.10.

10. Highlight the Substitution bot text that was entered in the first line, and create a link to the webmaster's email address.

Now you need to add the configuration variable for the webmaster Substition bot to your web. To do this:

1. Open the FrontPage Explorer. Choose Tools I Web Settings. The Web Settings dialog box, opened to the Parameters tab, appears.

2. Click the Add button. The Add Name and Value dialog box, shown in Figure 15.11, appears.

Figure 15.11.
Use the Add Name and Value dialog box to add the configuration variable for the Substitution bot to the web.

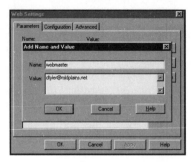

3. In the Name field, enter

   webmaster

4. In the Value field, enter the e-mail address of the person who designs and maintains the web. Click OK to exit the Add Name and Value dialog box. The variable appears in the Parameters tab of the Web Settings dialog box.

5. Click the Apply button in the Web Settings dialog box.

6. Click OK to exit the dialog box and return to the FrontPage Explorer. The webmaster configuration variable becomes an option that you can select from the drop-down menu in the Substitution Bot Properties dialog box.

7. Return to the footer page in the FrontPage Editor, and save the page to your web. You can now include this footer on any page in your web. Figure 15.12 shows an example.

Figure 15.12.
After you save the footer, it can be included on any page.

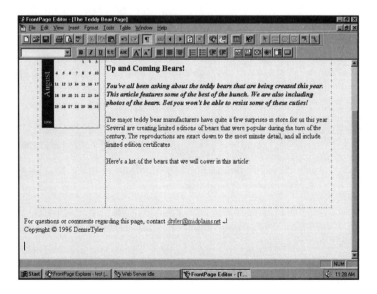

Table of Contents Bot

The Table of Contents bot enables you to generate a list of the pages that appear in your Web site automatically. Any pages in your web that appear beneath that page are listed in the table of contents in a hierarchical manner using nested lists. You can include—or not include—pages that are not linked from anywhere in your table of contents.

You do not have to generate a table of contents from your home page; it can start from any page that appears in your web. For example, if your home page provides links to several different sections, some of which you do not want to include in the table of contents, you can automatically generate a table of contents that starts at the beginning of each of the sections you do want to include. Multiple Table of Contents bots can appear on a single page, each generating contents that begin at a specified page.

Generating an Automatic Table of Contents

When you generate a table of contents using the Table of Contents bot, it inserts a generic heading and three dummy links on your page. That is what you see in the FrontPage Editor. Your first reaction is probably that you did something wrong. When you open a Web browser and navigate to the page while your server is running, though, you see the results.

To insert a table of contents on a page:

1. Position the insertion point where you want the table of contents to appear.

2. Choose Insert I Bot. The Insert Bot dialog box appears.

3. Highlight Table of Contents and click OK. The Table of Contents Bot Properties dialog box, shown in Figure 15.13, appears.

Figure 15.13.

Use the Table of Contents Bot Properties dialog box to choose options for your table of contents.

4. In the Page URL for Starting Point of Table field, type the name of the page from which you want to begin generating the table of contents, or click the Browse button to choose a page from the currently opened web.

Specifying your home page as the starting point generates a table of contents that lists all the pages in your web. If you do not want to include all the pages in your table of contents, you can selectively choose pages. For example, you can insert several Table of Contents bots on a single page, each listing the pages in specific sections in your web.

5. Select a heading size for the first entry in the table of contents in the Heading Size field. Choose None if you do not want a heading to appear.

6. Select one or more of the following options:

    Show each page only once. Sometimes, several pages in your web contain links to the same page. You might not want the same page to appear in multiple locations in your table of contents. Keep this box checked to list pages only once in the table of contents. Uncheck it if you want to show the page each time a link to it appears.

    Show pages with no incoming links. If you want to include orphan pages—that is, pages that cannot be reached by clicking links in your pages—check this option. However, this might produce links to pages to which you do not want users to navigate, such as header and footer pages that are placed on your pages with Include bots. The table of contents does not include links to any pages placed in your _private directory.

    Recompute table of contents when any other page is edited. By default, this option is unchecked. If your web site is fairly small, it is safe to check this option. Whenever you save a new or revised page to your web, checking this option causes the table of contents to regenerate and add the new pages. If you leave this option unchecked, you can regenerate the table of contents by opening and saving the page that contains the Table of Contents bot.

7. Click OK to exit the dialog box. The Table of Contents bot appears on your page, showing three dummy links. Figure 15.14 shows an example.

To view the table of contents in your browser, make sure that the FrontPage Personal Web Server is running. Open your favorite browser, and enter a URL similar to the following, replacing the server name, web name, and page URL with your settings:

```
http://localhost/yourwebname/yourtoc.htm
```

or

```
http://yourservername/yourwebname/yourtoc.htm
```

The browser loads the table of contents page, and you can see each page listed, beginning with the page that you specified in the Table of Contents Bot Properties dialog box. The pages are listed in the table of contents by their title, as in Figure 15.15.

Figure 15.14.

In the FrontPage Editor, the table of contents appears to be incomplete.

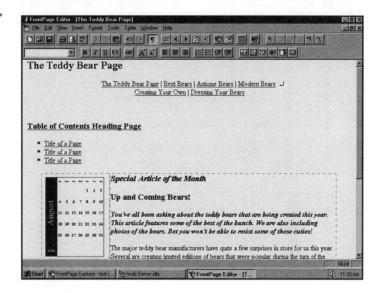

NOTE: If you are having difficulties viewing the table of contents page in your browser, one of two things may remedy this situation. First, verify that the Table of Contents page and other open pages in the FrontPage Editor are saved to your current web. Secondly, use the View I Refresh command in the FrontPage Explorer to refresh the web. Check in the FrontPage Explorer's Outline View to see if the pages appear beneath the Table of Contents page. If they do, you should be able to view them in your browser as well.

Timestamp Bot

The Timestamp bot helps you and your visitors keep track of the date when a page was most recently updated—manually or automatically. In most cases, you specify manual updating. However, there are some instances when you want to specify automatic updating.

TIP: Include a Timestamp bot at the beginning of your pages. This tells users whether your pages have changed since their last visit.

Figure 15.15.

When you view the table of contents in a Web browser, the titles of the pages appear.

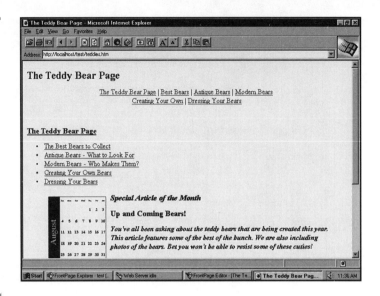

Indicating When a Page Was Last Revised

To place a Timestamp bot on your page:

1. On your page, enter some text that appears before the timestamp. For example, enter

   ```
   This page was last edited on
   ```

   and follow that line with one space.

2. Choose Insert l Bot. From the Insert Bot dialog box, choose Timestamp and click OK. The Timestamp Bot Properties dialog box, shown in Figure 15.16, appears.

3. In the Display field, choose one of the following options:

   Date this page was last edited. Choose this option if you normally edit the page manually. This is the most common way to specify a timestamp.

   Date this page was last automatically updated. Choose this option if the page includes any features that are generated automatically. Examples include tables of contents, discussion group articles, or guest book pages in which users' comments are inserted automatically.

4. In the Date Format field, choose the format for displaying the date on your pages from the drop-down menu.

5. If you also want to specify the time when your page was last updated, choose a time format from the Time Format drop-down menu.

Figure 15.16.

Use the Timestamp Bot Properties dialog box to choose date and time options for the timestamp.

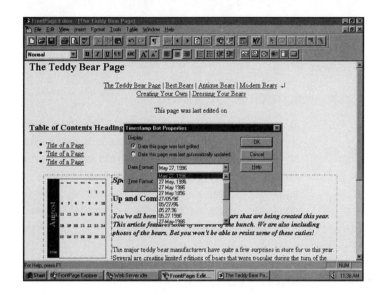

6. Click OK. The timestamp appears on your page, as shown in Figure 15.17. The timestamp updates whenever you save a page to your web.

Figure 15.17.

The timestamp appears on your page, and it updates whenever a new version of the page is saved to your web.

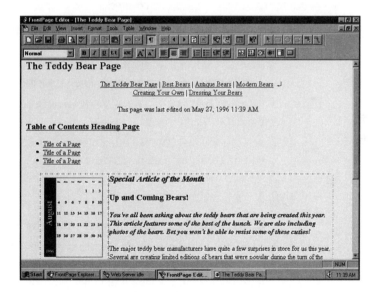

Workshop Wrap-Up

Now you have solutions to the problems described at the start of this chapter. You can use FrontPage bots to resolve them quickly and easily. Bots allow you to add reminders or notes to your pages, reduce repetitive typing of links or other text, schedule web content, and automatically keep track of all the pages in your web. Your Web creation tasks are greatly simplified, and making changes to your Web site in the future requires less time to complete.

Chapter Summary

In this chapter, you learned about the basic bots available to you in FrontPage. Using them, you can automate your pages in several different ways. You learned how to annotate pages, include content from one page in another, schedule content and images to appear in your web at specified times, generate a table of contents automatically, use and apply configuration variables to your webs, and advise yourself and others when changes were last made to your pages. Automating your pages in this manner involves only a few steps, and it makes your work much easier down the road.

Next Steps

In the next chapter, you learn how to use other editors in conjunction with the FrontPage Editor to edit other types of content from within FrontPage. For more information on the subjects covered in this chapter:

- ❏ Refer to Chapter 20, "Runtime Bots: The Heartbeat of FrontPage Forms," to learn how to use the advanced bots used in forms. The form bots must be used on a server that has the FrontPage Server Extensions installed. Other options are mentioned in the chapter as well.
- ❏ Refer to Chapter 21, "Using Your Own HTML Code," to learn how to use the HTML Markup bot.
- ❏ Refer to Chapter 23, "Web Maintenance and Administration," for information on configuring administrators and authors for your web.

Q&A

Q: Can I use these bots without using the FrontPage Explorer?

A: Many of the bots rely on links to pages that exist in the current web. This means that you must have your server running, and the FrontPage Explorer must be open to the web that holds the pages with which you are working.

Q: How do the bots work if my service provider does not have the FrontPage Server Extensions?

A: When you view the HTML code—source or generated—using the View I HTML command in the FrontPage Editor, you see references to bots placed in your code. However, if you view the source code of the same page through a Web browser, you see quite a difference. The contents inserted with bots become an integral part of the page. References to the bots are stripped out. For this reason, you should keep a copy of your pages in your FrontPage web if you plan to make changes to them. When you import your web pages into your web from your server, you need to insert the bots again to bring them back to automation status.

Q: I put a Timestamp bot in a footer and used the Include bot to place it on several pages. When I changed some of the pages that included the footer, the dates were not updated. What happened?

A: The Timestamp bot updates when you change a page. In this case, though, the timestamp is tied to the footer—not to the page on which it is included. If you place a Timestamp bot on your pages with an Include bot, the date does not change unless you save the footer again. This might place an incorrect date on all the pages in which the timestamp is included. Rather than use an Include bot to place a Timestamp bot on several pages, place the timestamp on each page individually.

Q: I inserted a logo at the beginning of my page by using an Include bot. I want to add something before it. I cannot place the cursor at the beginning of the page now. How do I do that?

A: To place the cursor before the Include bot, select the Include bot so that it appears in inverse video. Then press Ctrl+Enter. This places the cursor on a new line above the Include bot. The new line is formatted as a normal paragraph.

SIXTEEN

Going Beyond the FrontPage Editor

There will be times when you need to work with existing content or use editors besides the FrontPage Editor. You might want to use a text editor to edit text or ASCII files that are located in your web. You might want to touch up a graphic. You might even want to use another Web page editor to incorporate features that the FrontPage Editor does not support. You can access other editors easily through FrontPage by configuring them with the Tools I Configure Editors command.

Using Existing Content

FrontPage enables you to import any type of file into your web. Besides HTML documents, you can open or insert two types of files, which are converted to web pages for you. They are

❏ Text files
❏ Rich text format (RTF) files

Working with HTML Files

You can open existing HTML documents from your local or network hard drive or from the World Wide Web. You use the FrontPage Editor in both cases. The steps are

1. In the FrontPage Editor, select File I Open File. The Open dialog box, shown in Figure 16.1, appears.

Figure 16.1.
Use the Open dialog box to open existing HTML, text, or RTF documents from your local or network hard drive.

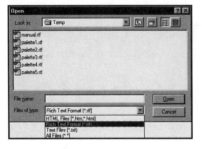

2. Use the Look In field to locate the drive and directory where the HTML file appears.
3. From the Files of type drop-down menu, choose HTML Files (*.htm, *.html).
4. Select the file, and click Open. FrontPage opens the file in a new window.

You can insert an HTML file into another web page in the FrontPage Editor. The file is inserted at the current insertion point. The steps are

1. In the FrontPage Editor, select Insert I File. The Insert dialog box, shown in Figure 16.2, appears.

Figure 16.2.
Use the Insert dialog box to insert an HTML document into another web page.

2. Use the Look In field to locate the drive and directory where the HTML file appears.
3. From the Files of type drop-down menu, choose HTML Files (*.htm, *.html).
4. Select the file, and click Open. FrontPage inserts the file at the current insertion point.

You also can open a Web page from the World Wide Web. In this case, you use the File I Open Location command. The steps are

1. Establish a connection to the Internet.
2. In the FrontPage Editor, select File I Open Location. The Open Location dialog box, shown in Figure 16.3, appears.

Figure 16.3.
Use the Open Location dialog box to open a page from the World Wide Web.

3. Enter the URL of the page to which you want to navigate in the Location (URL) field.
4. Click OK. You navigate to the page, and it opens in the FrontPage Editor.
5. Select File I Save As to save the page to your current web.

You learn about HTML markup bots in Chapter 21, "Using Your Own HTML Code."

If the pages that you open contain any HTML code that FrontPage does not support, small yellow rectangles with question marks in them appear, as in Figure 16.4. These marks look like gibberish on your page, but they serve a good purpose. They are HTML markup bots. If you double-click them, you can view or edit the HTML code that they contain.

Figure 16.4.
Code that the FrontPage Editor does not recognize is inserted into an HTML markup bot.

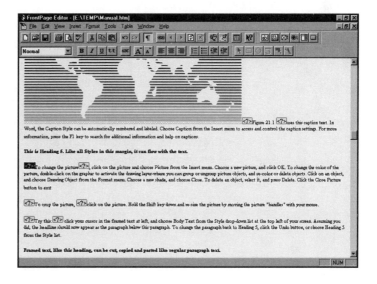

Working with Text Files

When you open a text file in the FrontPage Editor, it is converted to a new HTML document that can be added to the current web.

To open a text file from the FrontPage Editor:

1. In the FrontPage Editor, choose File | Open File. The Open dialog box appears.

2. Use the Look In field to locate the drive and directory where the text file appears.

3. From the Files of type drop-down menu, choose Text Files (*.txt).

4. Select the file, and click Open. The Convert Text dialog box, shown in Figure 16.5, appears.

Figure 16.5.

Use the Convert Text dialog box to choose how you want to convert a text file.

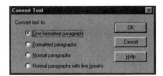

5. Choose one of the following conversion options, and click OK. In Figures 16.6 through 16.9, the `fpreadme.txt` file, located in the Microsoft FrontPage directory, is imported.

   One formatted paragraph. All the text is converted to a single paragraph of formatted text with line breaks. (See Figure 16.6.)

   Formatted Paragraphs. Each paragraph in the text file is converted to formatted text. (See Figure 16.7.)

   Normal Paragraphs. Each paragraph in the file is converted to normal text. (See Figure 16.8.)

   Normal Paragraphs with Line Breaks. Each paragraph in the text file is converted to normal text with line breaks. (See Figure 16.9.)

6. Use the File | Save command to save the page to the current web.

Figure 16.6.

When you choose one formatted paragraph, each line ends with a line break. The entire page is one continuous formatted paragraph.

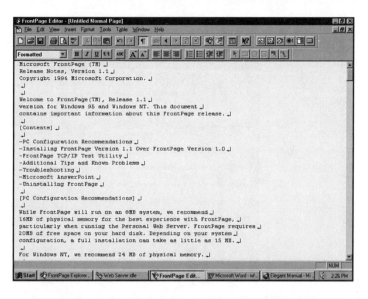

Figure 16.7.

When you choose formatted paragraphs, each paragraph begins as a new formatted paragraph. The lines within each paragraph use line breaks.

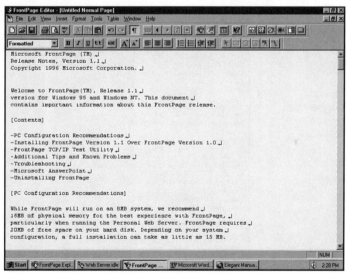

Figure 16.8.

When you choose normal paragraphs, each paragraph is formatted as a normal paragraph. No line breaks are included.

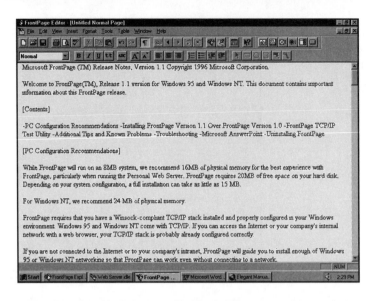

Figure 16.9.

When you choose normal paragraphs with line breaks, each paragraph is formatted as a normal paragraph. Line breaks retain the original formatting of the text document.

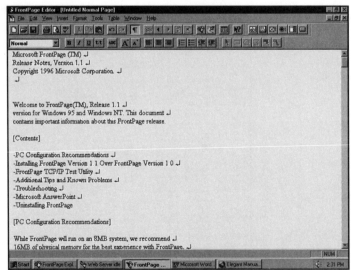

When you insert a text file, FrontPage converts the file and inserts it at the insertion point in the current page. The steps are

1. In the FrontPage Editor, select Insert I File. The Insert dialog box appears.

2. Use the Look In field to locate the drive and directory where the text file appears.

3. From the Files of type drop-down menu, choose Text Files (*.txt).

4. Select the file, and click Open. The Convert Text dialog box appears.

5. Choose a conversion option and click OK. The text file is inserted at the insertion point.

Working with RTF Files

You can save any word processing document as an RTF file and open or insert its content into a page that can be saved in your current web. The steps are

1. From the FrontPage Editor, select File I Open File. The Open dialog box appears.
2. From the Files of type drop-down menu, choose Rich Text Format (*.rtf).
3. Locate the drive and directory where the RTF file is located.
4. Highlight the page that you want to open, and click Open. FrontPage converts the RTF document to HTML format and creates a new page for you. Any graphics that are contained in the RTF document are converted to GIF or JPG format, as appropriate.
5. Save the page to your current web with the File I Save command. Assign it a title and a URL.

TIP: A graphic might appear larger or smaller in a FrontPage web page than it does in the original RTF file. If this is the case, open it in a graphics editor, and check what dots per inch setting it was saved at. Graphics convert best if their dpi setting is 72.

You also can insert an RTF document into any web page. The steps are

1. Open or create a new web page in the FrontPage Editor, using the Normal page template.
2. Position the insertion point where you want to insert the RTF file.
3. Select Insert I File. The Insert dialog box appears.
4. From the Files of type drop-down menu, choose Rich Text Format (*.rtf).
5. Locate the drive and directory where the RTF file is located.
6. Highlight the page that you want to open and click Open. FrontPage converts the RTF document to HTML format and inserts it at your insertion point. Any graphics that are contained in the RTF document are converted to GIF or JPG format, as appropriate.
7. Save the page to your current web with the File I Save command. Assign it a title and a URL.

Associating File Types with Editors

You will come across other types of files as you develop your webs. If you include or add links to multimedia files—such as sounds, animations, or VRML worlds—you can configure FrontPage to start their associated editors by clicking the file in your web that you need to edit.

To associate a file type with another editor, use the Tools I Configure Editors command in the FrontPage Explorer. After an editor is configured, you can open any file with the extension that you configured. The associated editor is invoked automatically.

To configure an editor and file type:

1. In the FrontPage Explorer, select Tools I Configure Editors. The Configure Editors dialog box, shown in Figure 16.10, appears.

Figure 16.10.
The Configure Editors dialog box enables you to associate an editor with a file extension.

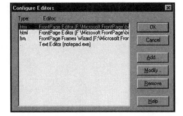

2. Click the Add button. The Add Editor Association dialog box appears. (See Figure 16.11.)

Figure 16.11.
You associate an editor with a file extension in the Add Editor Association dialog box.

3. In the File Type field, specify a file extension for the file type. You do not need to enter a period before the extension. To indicate files that have no extensions, use a period by itself.

NOTE:
FrontPage enables you to configure only one editor per extension. If you try to add an editor association for a file extension that is already configured, you get an error message.

4. In the Editor Name field, enter the name of the editor.

5. In the Command field, enter the full path to the executable file for the editor, or use the Browse button to choose the executable file from a drive and directory on your hard drive.

6. Click OK. The new editor appears in the Configure Editors dialog box.

After an editor is configured, you can open it from the FrontPage Explorer. In the FrontPage Explorer's Link View or Summary View, just double-click the file that you want to edit. Its associated editor is opened.

NOTE:
When you open a file with another editor, FrontPage places a copy of it in the `\Microsoft FrontPage\temp` directory. Some editors will not open the file automatically, so you might have to open it from within the configured editor. You should open the copy of the file in the temporary directory, instead of the original one in your current web. After you save the file, it appears in the FrontPage Explorer's Import List in the Import File to Web dialog box. Use the File I Import command to import the new version into your web.

Changing Editor Associations

If you want to use another editor to edit a specific type of file, it is simple to edit the association. The steps are

1. In the FrontPage Explorer, select Tools I Configure Editors. The Configure Editors dialog box appears.

2. Select the editor configuration that you want to change.

3. Click the Modify button. The Modify Editor Association dialog box appears. (See Figure 16.12.)

Figure 16.12.
You change the associated editor for a file type in the Modify Editor Association dialog box.

4. In the Editor Name field, enter the name of the new editor.

5. In the Command field, enter the full path to the executable file for the editor, or use the Browse button to choose the executable file from a drive and directory on your hard drive.

6. Click OK. The revised editor configuration appears in the Configure Editors list.

 ## Removing Editor Associations

If you find that you no longer work with files of a certain type, you can remove their editor associations from FrontPage. The steps are

1. In the FrontPage Explorer, select Tools | Configure Editors. The Configure Editors dialog box appears.

2. Select the editor configuration that you want to remove.

NOTE: You cannot remove the default editor and file type associations supplied with FrontPage.

3. Click the Remove button. To confirm the removal, click OK. To undo the removal, click Cancel.

HTML Editors

FrontPage enables you to assign only one editor for a specific file type. What if you want to use another HTML editor in conjunction with the FrontPage Editor? This is what you can do:

1. Configure the editor association for the HTM or HTML extension—whichever you use more frequently—to the FrontPage Editor. This enables you to use the FrontPage Editor to design the bulk of your page while you take advantage of the bots and other enhancements in the program.

2. Configure a second editor to use the other extension. Now you have two different HTML editors in your editor configuration.

To open the HTML document in the secondary editor:

1. From any view in the FrontPage Explorer, right-click the Web page that you want to open. A pop-up menu appears, as in Figure 16.13.

Figure 16.13.

You can open a file with any configured editor by using the Open With command in the pop-up menu.

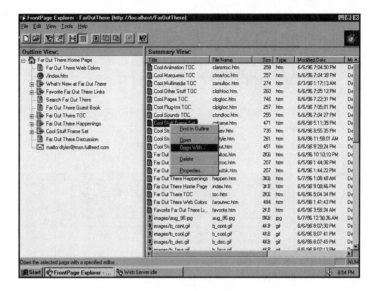

2. From the pop-up menu, choose Open With. The Open With Editor dialog box appears.

3. Select the secondary HTML editor and click OK. The editor opens, and you can edit the file.

Keep in mind these points:

❏ You lose the capability to use bots in your pages when you work with another HTML editor.

❏ If the page that you are opening in another editor was originally designed in the FrontPage Editor and contains bots, the commands that reference them are likely to be stripped out in the other editor. When you import back into your FrontPage web, you must add the bots again.

❏ Many HTML editors check code for compliance before the web page opens in the editor. Your FrontPage web pages might contain code that another HTML editor will not accept.

The solution to these problems is to create as much as you can in the FrontPage Editor. Use the HTML markup bot discussed in Chapter 21 to add additional HTML code.

Text Editors

You can configure a text editor to work with any extension for which you normally use a text, or ASCII, editor. If you use Windows 95, configure these files to use Notepad or WordPad. With WordPad, the files retain their formatting and indentation much better.

Word Processors

If you want to include word processing documents in your web, you can save them in rich text format—that is, with an RTF extension. Figure 16.14 shows a Microsoft Word document in RTF format.

Figure 16.14.
This Microsoft Word document has been saved in RTF format.

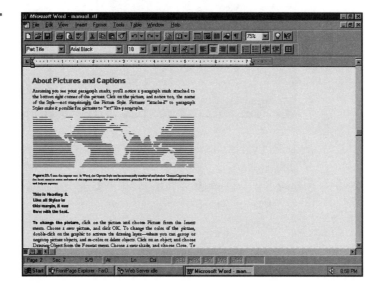

Figures 16.15 and 16.16 show the RTF document as it appears in the FrontPage Editor. There are some minor differences in formatting:

❑ In Figure 16.14, the Arial font is used for the headings. In the FrontPage Editor's HTML version in Figures 16.15 and 16.16, the headings are format-ted in FrontPage's default heading style, which uses the Times Roman font.

❑ In Figure 16.14, the area beneath the picture caption is formatted into four individual lines that are aligned with the left side of the page. In Figure 16.16, the same text is arranged in a single line.

Figure 16.15.

The upper portion of the RTF file converted perfectly, with the exception of the font style of the heading.

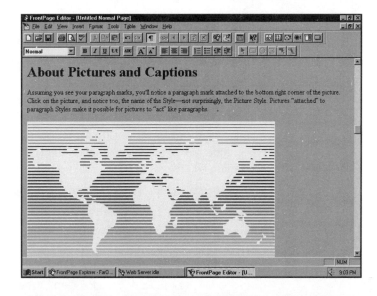

Figure 16.16.

The lower portion of the RTF file is formatted slightly differently.

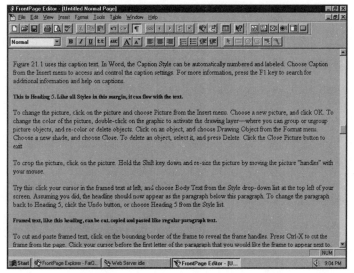

There is a way around these differences. If you use Microsoft Office or Microsoft Word 95, you have two alternatives. If you use another word processor, check whether similar options are available.

❏ Import the original Word document—doc extension—into your web with the File I Import command. Provide a link on another web page that enables users to download or view it. To view the document in its original Word format, users need the Word Viewer.

You can provide a link on your page for users to download the current version of the Word Viewer. The URL is

`http://www.microsoft.com/msword/internet/viewer/default.htm`

❏ Use Internet Assistant for Word to save the Word document in htm format. (Save a Word document in its native doc format, and then save a copy of it in HTM format after you have revised it.) This adds font formatting commands to the web page, which Internet Assistant for Word includes in its HTML code. When FrontPage imports this HTML command, it places the font formatting commands in HTML markup bots.

You can download the current version of Internet Assistant for Word from

`http://www.microsoft.com/msword/internet/ia/default.htm`

After you save the HTML document from Internet Assistant, use the File I Open command to open it in the FrontPage Editor. Save the page to your web with the File I Save As command. (If you use the File I Save command, it saves the file back to its original location.) When you open the page in Microsoft Internet Explorer, you will see the fonts used in the original document, providing they exist on your system. For users to see the same fonts, the fonts must exist on their system. Otherwise, the default font is used.

NOTE: You might need to add size attributes to the fonts. You learn how to do this in Chapter 21.

Spreadsheet and Database Software

FrontPage currently does not provide direct support for spreadsheet or database files. When you work with spreadsheet or database software, your options are

❏ Open the spreadsheet or database program, and select the cells that you want to insert into your web page. Copy them to the clipboard. Then open or create a page in the FrontPage Editor. Position the insertion point where you want to insert the data, and format the line as a formatted paragraph. Paste the data to the web page. (See Figure 16.17.)

❏ Save the spreadsheet or database data as a tab-delimited text file, and insert it into your FrontPage web page. The data appears as formatted text. (See Figure 16.17.)

Figure 16.17.

Cut and paste data from your spreadsheet or database files into a formatted paragraph on your web page.

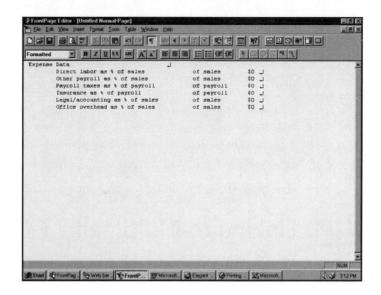

If you use Microsoft Office or Microsoft Excel for Windows 95, Internet Assistant for Excel 95 can enhance the use of Excel files in your web. It converts Excel spreadsheets into HTML format and places the cell data in tables. This Excel add-on is provided in Excel (XLA) format. You can download this utility from

```
http://www.microsoft.com/msexcel/internet/ia/default.htm
```

You also can import an Excel spreadsheet into your web and provide a link to it on another page. Likewise, provide a link to the following URL so that users can download the Excel Viewer:

```
http://www.microsoft.com/msexcel/internet/viewer/default.htm
```

An Internet Assistant for Microsoft Access for Windows 95 is also available. This free utility allows you to publish native HTML documents from your Access or ODBC-compliant databases. You can download it from

```
http://www.microsoft.com/msaccess/internet/ia/default.htm
```

Presentation Software

If you use Microsoft Office or Microsoft PowerPoint 95, Internet Assistant for PowerPoint 95 can enhance the use of PowerPoint presentations in your web. It converts PowerPoint presentations into a series of consecutively numbered HTML files and provides navigation between them. The presentation screens are converted to graphics that are placed on each page. You can download this utility from

```
http://www.microsoft.com/mspowerpoint/internet/ia/default.htm
```

You also can import a PowerPoint presentation into your web and provide a link to it on another web page. Likewise, you can provide a link to the following URL so that users can download the PowerPoint Viewer:

`http://www.microsoft.com/mspowerpoint/internet/viewer/default.htm`

If your PowerPoint presentation includes animation, check out what is available in the PowerPoint Animation Player for ActiveX. Internet Explorer 3.0, which is currently available in beta version from Microsoft's site, provides built-in ActiveX support. You can download the PowerPoint Animation Player for ActiveX from

`http://www.microsoft.com/mspowerpoint/internet/player/default.htm`

 # Linking to Multimedia Files

You can link to multimedia files in your web. To play the files, however, users must have a helper associated with the file type.

To create links to multimedia files:

1. From the FrontPage Explorer, select File | Import. The Import File to Web dialog box appears.

2. Click the Add File button. The Add File to Import List dialog box appears.

3. Choose All Files (*.*) from the Files of type drop-down menu. Then use the Look in box to locate the drive and directory in which your files appear.

4. Select the files you want to import, and click Open to add the multimedia files to the import list. You return to the Import File to Web dialog box.

5. Highlight the file or files to import, and click the Import Now button. The files are imported into your web one by one.

6. Close the Import File to Web dialog box by clicking the Close button.

7. Create links to the multimedia files on a page with the Edit | Link command.

To play the multimedia files, make sure that your browser has a helper application associated with the file type. You can run the files from the FrontPage Editor by using the Tools | Follow Link command.

Workshop Wrap-Up

FrontPage works with a wide variety of file formats. You can import just about any type of file into your web, as well as recommend helper applications or viewers to visitors to your site. You can open these files by configuring editors in the FrontPage Explorer. You can open and insert text or rich text format files in your web documents directly, and you can save them in standard HTML format to your web.

Chapter Summary

In this chapter, you learned how to work with other types of files. You learned how to configure FrontPage to open an editor associated with a specific file type by clicking on the file that you want to edit. You also learned about using other Microsoft Office documents in your web.

Next Steps

In the next chapter, you continue your web project by working on the techniques that you learned in this section. You create new content for your web and rearrange some of what you have already worked on. The following chapters provide information that relates to this chapter:

- ❑ Refer to Chapter 9, "Composing and Editing Page Content," to learn about adding more formatting to the text or rich text format files that you import into your web.
- ❑ See Chapter 21, "Using Your Own HTML Code," to learn more about the HTML markup bot.

Q&A

Q: I used an editor to change a graphics file, but the change does not show up in my web. Why?

A: Check whether the file is still in your import list. Choose the File I Import command from the FrontPage Explorer. The file might be waiting to be imported into your web again. After you import the new version, refresh the page in the FrontPage Editor or in your web browser. Then you will see the changes.

Q: I made my graphics smaller and saved them to my web. When I loaded the page that had those graphics in my Web browser, the images looked odd and took up the same amount of space as before. Did I do something wrong?

A: If you resize your graphics and do not update the pages on which they are contained, the browser stretches to fit them in the area that they used to contain. The dimensions are saved in the HTML code, which is written when you save the page to your web. Open the pages that contain the graphics, and save them again. Pay particular attention to graphics that you include on other pages with Include bots, such as navigation bars.

Q: I used Internet Assistant for Word to create an HTML document. I imported it into FrontPage, and several markup bot symbols appeared. When I look at the web page in Internet Explorer, all the fonts are sized differently and do not look the same as in the original document. How can I fix that?

A: For the most part, the HTML documents translate fairly well. As for the font size, though, it is more confusing. Word processors handle font formatting differently than a web page does. In some cases, you must add the size attribute to that HTML markup bot tag to specify how large the font is. You learn how to do this in Chapter 21.

SEVENTEEN

Real-Life Examples

Well, you're about to learn about one of the facts of life about developing Web pages. As new features are added to the HTML standards, the first thing you want to do is add those new features to your pages. Some of the things you learned in this section of the book incorporate some of the latest and greatest enhancements to the HTML standard. So, you'll get a crash training course in modifying some existing pages to apply the features as well as adding some automation to your pages with those bots you've been hearing so much about.

In this chapter, you

❑ Modify your home page, adding enhanced layout through the use of tables

❑ Create a master template that can be used for the main pages in your web

❑ Apply some extended attributes to the tables

❑ Learn how to convert decimal Red/Green/Blue color formulas to their hexadecimal equivalents for use in extended attributes that require a color value

❑ Complete the Far Out Links page and the What's New page

❑ Use the new template to revise your Far Out Links template

❑ Create a table of contents for your web

❑ Create a frameset and start the associated pages that appear in the Cool Stuff section of your web

❑ Create the Happenings page

❑ Complete the What's New page and add your new pages to it

Changing Your Home Page

You're going to change the layout of the home page a little bit by inserting the contents that are already there into a table. This brings the footer from the bottom of the page to directly below the Star Map animation file.

See Chapter 13, "Your Tables Are Ready," for additional information on table formatting.

Open the Far Out There Web in the FrontPage Explorer. Then, open the home page and edit it by following these steps:

1. Open the Far Out There home page in the FrontPage Editor by choosing File I Open from Web. The screen shots show this page against a white background, so you easily can see the table guides on the page.

2. Position the insertion point at the end of the guide graphic at the top of the page. Choose Table I Insert Table to insert a table with the following properties:

   Rows: 5
   Columns: 3
   Alignment: Center
   Border Size: 0
   Cell Padding: 0
   Cell Spacing: 0
   Width: 456 Pixels

TIP: Click the Show/Hide button on the Standard toolbar to see the guides around borderless tables as well as other formatting marks.

3. Select the cells in the first and third columns of the table. To select the first row, place your cursor directly above the column, where it changes to a small arrow. Click to select the cells. Shift+click to select the third column in a similar manner.

4. Right-click and choose Cell Properties from the context menu. Set the properties for the selected cells to the following:

   Horizontal Alignment: Center
   Vertical Alignment: Middle
   Specify Width: 88 Pixels

5. Select the cells in the second column and use the Cell Properties dialog to change their settings to the following:

   Horizontal Alignment: Center
   Vertical Alignment: Middle
   Specify Width: 280 Pixels

6. Select the first row of cells by placing the cursor just outside the left side of the table. Click to select the cells, and choose Table | Merge Cells to merge them into one cell.

7. Select the text in the text navigation bar, and press Ctrl+X to cut it and place it on the Clipboard. Then paste it into the first row of the table by pressing Ctrl+V.

8. Merge the cells in the bottom row into one cell. Cut the footer from the page and paste it into this cell. See Figure 17.1 to see what your table should look like at this point.

Figure 17.1.

You begin to enhance your page layout by using tables.

9. Click and drag to select the three navigation buttons in the middle of the top row of buttons on the page. They appear in inverse video when selected. Cut them and move them to the Clipboard by pressing Ctrl+X. Then paste them into the center cell in the row below the text navigation bar, using Ctrl+V.

10. Cut and paste the animated GIFs in the first and third cells in the same row as the navigation buttons you just added.

11. Cut and paste the remaining two buttons from the top navigation bar into the first cell in the third row. Figure 17.2 shows what your table should look like at this point.

12. Cut the Far Out There Site graphic from the page and paste it into the center cell of the third row (the cell next to the two navigation buttons).

13. Cut the three navigation buttons from the center of the bottom navigation bar on your page, and paste them into the cell below the header graphic.

Figure 17.2.

The animations and first row of navigation buttons are relocated to the table.

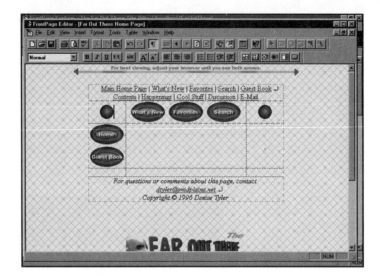

14. Select the two remaining navigation buttons from the bottom navigation bar and paste them into the cell at the right of the main header graphic.

15. Click and drag your mouse in the page area below the table to select any stray formatting that may still exist from the previous contents. Delete any selection by pressing Delete.

16. Your page is now complete and should look like the page shown in Figure 17.3. Save the updated page to your web by choosing File | Save.

Figure 17.3.

The layout of the home page is greatly improved with a table.

Creating a Template for Your Main Pages

In Chapter 12, "Real-Life Examples," you created new pages while you generated links from the navigation text and graphics. It would have been easier if you had a custom template of your own on which to base the pages. I held off on creating that template first, because I wanted you to use tables to enhance the layout for those pages as well. After you create and save the following template, you'll use it to revise the pages that already exist on your web.

You'll create a template that you can use for all the main pages in your web. This template features table layout for the text and graphic navigation bars. You'll also place bookmarks and links on the template to prepare for pages that might be long. This way, your pages can have a consistent layout from one section to the next.

See Chapter 8, "Getting from Here to There," for additional information on creating and using bookmarks and links.

Follow these steps:

1. Create a new page in the FrontPage Editor by choosing File I New. Choose to base the page on the Normal page template.

2. Assign the Far Out There Web colors to the page by choosing File I Page Properties.

3. You'll be inserting a table into this page. Keep the Insert Table dialog open after you assign the following table properties, because you'll be adding some extended attributes in the next step:

   Rows: 2
   Columns: 3
   Alignment: Center
   Border Size: 5
   Cell Padding: 0
   Cell Spacing: 0
   Width: 460 Pixels

   The following attributes enhance the appearance of the table when you view it in Internet Explorer (2.0 or 3.0) and the upcoming version of Netscape 3.0 (now available in beta from Netscape's site). The values make the background color of the cells the same shade of light blue as the background image. The border around the cells has a 3-D appearance, with the light purple from the background color as the lighter shade and the dark shade of purple from the background as the darker shade.

A complete list of table and cell attributes appears in Chapter 13.

4. From the Insert Table dialog box, click the Extended button. The Extended Attributes dialog appears. Add extended attributes to the table using the following names and values:

Name: BGCOLOR
Value: #C8EDFF

Name: BORDERCOLORLIGHT
Value: #ECC8FF

Name: BORDERCOLORDARK
Value: #C8D3FF

TIP:

How'd I get those weird values to enter in the Extended Attributes dialogs? I used one of my graphics programs to determine the RGB formulas for the light blue and purple in the background:

Background: R 200 G 237 B 255
Light Purple: R 236 G 200 B 255
Dark Purple: R 200 G 211 B 255

There are a couple of ways you can convert to hexadecimals. One is to use the calculator built into Windows 95. Select the calculator from the Start menu (it's in the Accessories submenu). After the calculator opens, follow these steps:

1. From the View menu, choose Scientific.

2. Select the Dec radio button in the Number System group, and enter the decimal number you want to convert to hexadecimal.

3. Select the Hex radio button in the Number System group. The equivalent hexadecimal number appears in the calculator display.

If you're the type of person who likes visual references that you can put your hands on, I made up a table so that I could easily translate each of these decimal numbers to its hexadecimal equivalent. Take a look at Table 17.1, and you can use it, too! The first row of the table contains the hexadecimal values of the decimal numbers 0 through 15, the second row contains the hexadecimal values for the numbers 16 through 31, and so on. You'll have to do a bit of counting using this table, but it's a lot easier than calculating it.

Using the first color as an example, 200 (red) translates to C8; 237 (green) translates to ED, and 255 (blue) translates to FF. Put these together, and you get the value I entered for the background of the table: C8EDFF.

Table 17.1. Hexadecimal equivalents of decimal numbers.

Decimal Values	Hexadecimal Equivalent															
0–15	00	01	02	03	04	05	06	07	08	09	0A	0B	0C	0D	0E	0F
16–31	10	11	12	13	14	15	16	17	18	19	1A	1B	1C	1D	1E	1F
32–47	20	21	22	23	24	25	26	27	28	29	2A	2B	2C	2D	2E	2F
48–63	30	31	32	33	34	35	36	37	38	39	3A	3B	3C	3D	3E	3F
64–79	40	41	42	43	44	45	46	47	48	49	4A	4B	4C	4D	4E	4F
80–95	50	51	52	53	54	55	56	57	58	59	5A	5B	5C	5D	5E	5F
96–111	60	61	62	63	64	65	66	67	68	69	6A	6B	6C	6D	6E	6F
112–127	70	71	72	73	74	75	76	77	78	79	7A	7B	7C	7D	7E	7F
128–143	80	81	82	83	84	85	86	87	88	89	8A	8B	8C	8D	8E	8F
144–159	90	91	92	93	94	95	96	97	98	99	9A	9B	9C	9D	9E	9F
160–175	A0	A1	A2	A3	A4	A5	A6	A7	A8	A9	AA	AB	AC	AD	AE	AF
176–191	B0	B1	B2	B3	B4	B5	B6	B7	B8	B9	BA	BB	BC	BD	BE	BF
192–207	C0	C1	C2	C3	C4	C5	C6	C7	C8	C9	CA	CB	CC	CD	CE	CF
208–223	D0	D1	D2	D3	D4	D5	D6	D7	D8	D9	DA	DB	DC	DD	DE	DF
224–239	E0	E1	E2	E3	E4	E5	E6	E7	E8	E9	EA	EB	EC	ED	EE	EF
240–255	F0	F1	F2	F3	F4	F5	F6	F7	F8	F9	FA	FB	FC	FD	FE	FF

5. Select the cells in the first and third columns and format them as the following:

> Horizontal Alignment: Center
> Vertical Alignment: Top
> Specify Width: 90 Pixels

6. Select the cells in the center column and format them as the following:

> Horizontal Alignment: Center
> Vertical Alignment: Top
> Specify Width: 280 Pixels

7. Select the cells in the first row and merge them into a single cell by choosing Table | Merge Cells.

8. Insert the `faroutsm.gif` file (or `.jpg`) from your web into the cell in the top row.

9. The insertion point should be at the end of the image at this point. Insert the following Annotation bot:

```
Replace this Annotation with the appropriate title bar graphic.
```

See Chapter 15, "Automating Pages with Bots," for further information on using Annotation, Timestamp, and Include bots on your pages.

10. With the insertion point at the end of the Annotation bot, press Enter. This starts a new normal paragraph on the next line. Enter the following text:

    `This page was last updated on (space)`

11. Choose Insert I Bot and choose Timestamp. Select your date and time preferences, and choose to update the timestamp the last time the page was edited.

12. With the insertion point at the end of the timestamp, insert an Include bot. Choose to include the Included Text navigation bar from your current web (`_private/textnav.htm`). Figure 17.4 shows the upper portion of the complete table.

Figure 17.4.

The upper portion of the table contains the header graphics, a timestamp, and some text links.

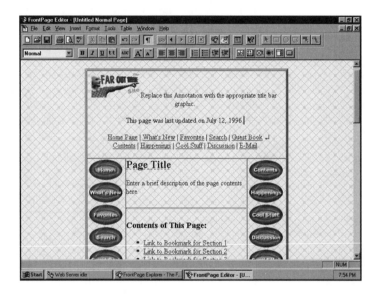

13. In the left cell in the bottom row of the table, insert another Include bot, placing the Included Navigation – Top page (`_private/topnav.htm`) into the cell.

14. In the right cell in the bottom row of the table, insert another Include bot, placing the Included Navigation – Bottom page (`_private/botmnav.htm`) into the cell.

15. Place the insertion point in the center cell and right-click. Choose Cell Properties from the context menu. Choose Horizontal Alignment: Left for this cell.

16. Place the insertion point at the top of the center cell. Choose Heading 2 from the style bar and enter `Page Title`.

17. Select the Page Title text, and press Ctrl+G or choose the Edit I Bookmark command to assign it a bookmark name of `top`.

18. Position the insertion point after the page title and insert the following Annotation bot:

    `Enter a brief description of the page contents here.`

19. Use the Style Bar in the FrontPage Editor Format toolbar to format the Annotation bot as a normal paragraph.

20. With the insertion point at the end of the annotation, insert a horizontal line. Leave the line at its default settings.

21. Format the next line as Heading 3, and enter the following text:

    `Contents of This Page:`

22. On the next line, insert a bulleted list, and enter some placeholders for links to sections on your page, as shown in Figure 17.5. You can delete these links if the contents of the pages you develop from the templates don't need them.

Figure 17.5.

Enter a bulleted list for links to bookmarks that might appear on longer pages.

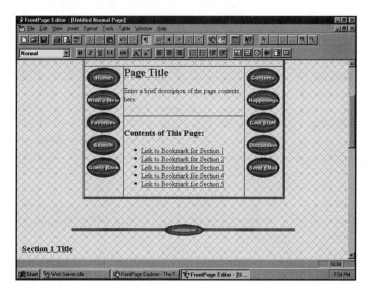

> **NOTE:** Most of the pages you develop in this project are fairly short and don't require the bulleted list and bookmarks, but you might have pages that need to be arranged into several sections down the road. This template covers the bases.

23. Below the table, insert `divider.gif` from the images in your Web. Align it to the center of the page by clicking the Center button on the Format toolbar.

24. Place the insertion point at the end of the divider, and insert Heading 3. Enter the following text:

    `Section 1 Title`

25. Insert the following Annotation bot:

    `Insert section contents here`

26. Press Enter to add a normal paragraph to your page. Enter the following text:

    `Back to Top`

27. Select the text you just entered and click the Create Link button to create a link to the Top bookmark (the page title in the table). Figure 17.6 shows the results so far.

Figure 17.6.
A divider and placehold-ers are added for each section of the template.

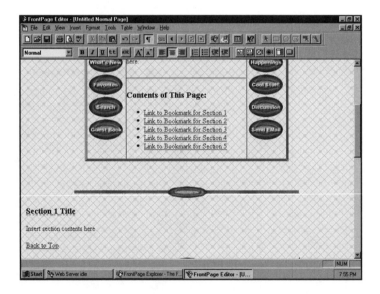

28. Copy the divider, Section 1 Title, the Annotation bot, and the link to the Top bookmark to your Clipboard.

29. Paste these items onto your page so that you have as many sections on the bottom of the page as you added links to them in the table (in the example shown, there are five items in the bulleted list in the table, so four additional copies were pasted in). To paste each item, place the insertion point on the line after the Back to Top link, and press Ctrl+V to paste the contents of the Clipboard. Center the divider graphic on the page if necessary.

30. Edit the titles of each new section appropriately (Section 2 Title, Section 3 Title, and so on).

31. Select each section title and choose Edit I Bookmark or press Ctrl+G to create a bookmark for each. Call the bookmarks sect1, sect2, and so on. Figure 17.7 shows additional sections with bookmarks added.

Figure 17.7.

Additional sections are added, and bookmarks are created for them.

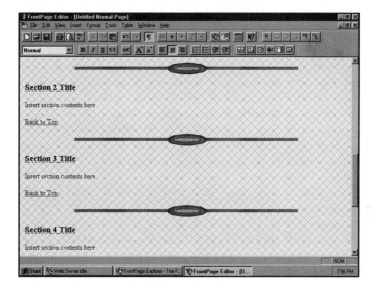

32. Copy the divider graphic and paste it on the line after the last Back to Top link on the page. Center the divider.

33. Position the insertion point at the end of the divider and insert an Include bot. Include the footer (_private/footer.htm). Figure 17.8 shows the results.

34. Return to the bulleted list in the table, and add the links to the bookmarks on the page. Select the Open Pages tab in the Create Link dialog, and choose the bookmark from the Bookmark drop-down listbox.

35. The template now is complete. Choose File I Save As. In the Save As dialog, enter the following:

> Page Title: Far Out Main Page Template
> Page URL: faroutmn.htm

36. Click the As Template button in the Save As dialog. In the Save As Template dialog, enter the following:

> Title: leave as is
> Name: faroutmn
> Description: Template for main pages in Far Out Web

37. Click OK to save the template. FrontPage asks whether you want to save the images to a file. Click Yes to All.

Figure 17.8.

The footer is added to the page with an Include bot.

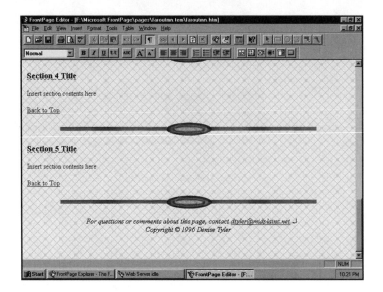

Finishing the Favorite Far Out There Links Page

You saw how much work it was to create that template for your main pages; now you'll see how much time it can save you in the long run. You'll start by using your new template to complete the Far Out There Links page you started in Chapter 12.

To complete your Far Out There Links page, follow these steps:

1. From the FrontPage Editor, choose File | New. Select the Far Out Main Page template and click OK. There's everything already in place for you: the bots, the navigation links, the whole shooting match.

2. Choose File | Open from Web to open the Favorite Far Out There Links page.

3. Click on the Favorites header graphic to select it. Copy it to your Clipboard.

4. Choose Window | Tile to display both pages in the FrontPage Editor window.

NOTE: If you have other pages open in FrontPage Editor, you can minimize them before you choose the Window | Tile command. They won't become part of the tiled display that way.

5. Return to the template page, and click the Annotation bot at the top of the page to select it. It appears in inverse video. Paste the header graphic in its place.

6. Edit the title in the new page to read `Favorite Far Out There Links`. You can edit the title without removing the bookmark. Place the insertion point after the first letter in the bookmark and type your new title. Use the backspace and Delete keys to remove the letters that were originally there.

   Figure 17.9 shows what your page should look like at this point.

Figure 17.9.

Contents from the original page are pasted into the new page created with the main page template.

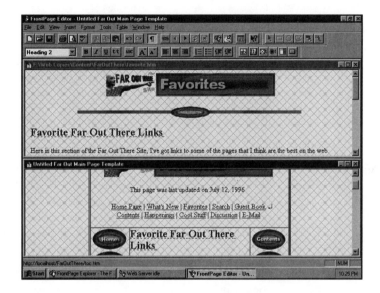

7. Select the text below the title in the original page (the text that describes what your Favorites section is all about) and copy it to your Clipboard.

8. Select the Annotation bot below the heading in the template page and paste the contents of the Clipboard in its place.

9. This page is brief enough that you won't need the bulleted list and sections that are in the Template page. Select the bulleted list and the horizontal line before it, and delete them from the Template page by pressing Delete. In the example shown in Figure 17.10, I added the Definition list from the original Template page to the table in the template because it was brief enough to fit there.

10. Delete the dividers, section titles, Annotation bots, and links from the Template page. Leave only one divider and the footer below the table, as shown in Figure 17.10.

11. Choose File | Save to save the page to your Web, using the same title as the previous version:

    Title: Favorite Far Out There Links
    URL: `favorite.htm`

Figure 17.10.

If the contents of your Favorite Links page are brief enough, you can insert them in the table in the new Template page.

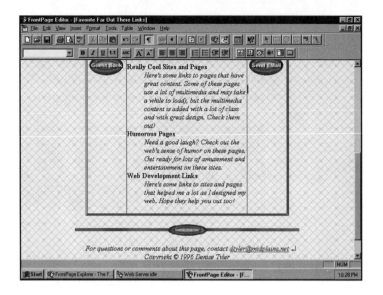

12. When FrontPage asks whether you want to overwrite the previous version of the page, click Yes. When you are asked whether you want to replace the existing graphics, click Use Existing.

13. Close the old version of the Favorite Far Out There Links page. That way, you won't mistakenly get confused between the two and overwrite the newer one with the older one. When FrontPage asks whether you want to save the changes to the original version, click No.

14. Open the To Do list and mark the task for the Favorite Far Out There Links page as complete.

Revising the Far Out There Links Template

The Far Out There Links template creates pages that are subsections of the Favorites section of the Web. You won't place the navigation buttons on this template, but you will include the text links, timestamp, and the footer on this page. You can copy these items from the Favorites page you currently have open in the FrontPage Editor.

You need to choose File I Open File in the FrontPage Editor to open this file and save it back to the correct directory. Follow these steps:

1. From the FrontPage Editor, choose File I Open File.

2. Open the `farlinks.htm` page. If you installed FrontPage using the default typical installation, it appears in the following directory:

```
c:\Microsoft FrontPage\pages\farlinks.tem
```

3. Return to the Favorites page. Select the first row of the table by placing the insertion point to the left of the table, where it turns into a small arrow. Click to select the row (it appears in inverse video). Copy the contents of the row to your Clipboard.

4. Return to the Far Out There Links template. Highlight the small header graphic and the title plate so that they appear in inverse video. Paste the contents of the Clipboard in their place. Figure 17.11 shows what your page should look like.

Figure 17.11.

The header cell from the table in your Master Page template is pasted into the Links template.

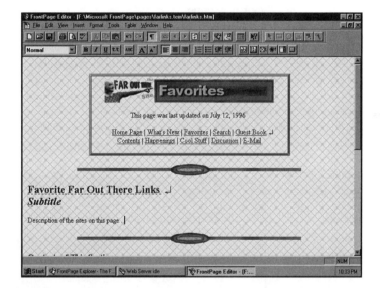

NOTE: Copying and pasting the contents of the cell from the Far Out There Links template does something nice. The Clipboard didn't contain only the items in the cell; it also took a copy of the table cell along with it. The graphics, text navigation, and timestamp stand out from the rest of the page. In Internet Explorer, the Links pages look as though they have one large header graphic.

5. Choose Insert I Bot to include the footer at the bottom of the page, or you can copy it from the Favorites page and paste it at the bottom of the Far Out There Links Template page.

6. Save the page by choosing the File I Save command. The template is saved back to its original template directory. When you are asked whether you want to replace the graphics, click Use Existing.

Creating a Table of Contents Page

Now you're going to work on the Table of Contents page. This page also appears in your To Do list, but you won't open it from there. You'll use the main Page template to create the table of contents and overwrite the blank version that already exists on your web. Then you'll mark the task as complete when you're done.

Follow these steps:

1. Choose File I New and select the Far Out Main Page template to generate your new page.

2. Highlight the Annotation bot that appears at the top of the page. With the annotation text selected, replace this text by choosing Insert I Image to insert `contents.gif` (or `.jpg`) from the CD-ROM that accompanies this book.

3. Replace the page title in the table with the following text:

   `Table of Contents`

4. Replace the bulleted list and horizontal line in the center cell with some introductory text for the table of contents, as shown in Figure 17.12.

Figure 17.12.
Enter some introductory text in the second row.

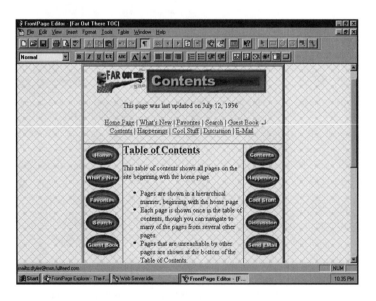

See Chapter 15 for more detailed instructions on using the Table of Contents bot.

5. Position the insertion point immediately after the divider below the table, and insert a Table of Contents bot. Assign it the following settings:

   Page URL for Starting Point: `index.htm` (or the name of your home page)

   Heading Size: 3

   Show Each Page Only Once: Checked

   Show Pages with No Incoming Links: Checked

Recompute Table of Contents: Choose your preference here. There won't be many pages in this site, so it shouldn't take long to recompute the contents. If your site gets very large, you might want to leave this option unchecked.

6. Delete the extra content from the Table of Contents page, leaving the last divider and the footer at the bottom. Figure 17.13 shows what your page should look like at this point.

Figure 17.13.
The Table of Contents page is now complete.

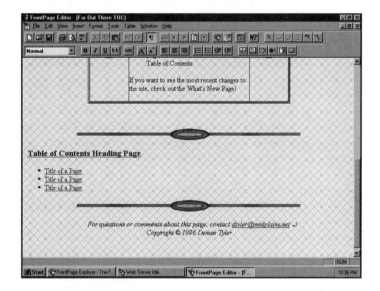

7. Choose File I Save As to save your page to the web, overwriting the previous version of the Table of Contents page. When FrontPage asks whether you want to overwrite the previous version, click Yes. Save the page with the following title and URL:

    Page Title: Far Out There TOC
    Page URL: `toc.htm`

8. FrontPage asks whether you want to save the graphics to your web. The first graphic already exists on your web, so you can click Use Existing. The second graphic is new, so you'll want to save that graphic to the web. The third graphic exists on the current web, so you can click Use Existing for that one.

9. Open the To Do list and mark the task for the What's New page as complete.

 # Creating Your Frameset Content

The Cool Stuff section of your web features advanced techniques that you'll learn how to incorporate in Chapter 22, "Real-Life Examples." These techniques are presented in a frameset, which you'll create now. In order to complete the frameset, though, you'll need to create some pages that load into the frameset when it first opens. You'll create those pages now and add the content to them in Chapter 22.

The frameset is divided into four frames. The left-most frame contains navigation buttons that take the user to the main pages in the Cool Stuff section of your web. The upper middle frame contains the table of contents for each of the sections. The lower middle frame is the main viewing window for the contents in the Cool Stuff section. Finally, the right frame contains navigation buttons that take the user back to some of the main pages on your web.

See Chapter 14, "Frames—Pages with Split Personalities," for further information on creating and using framesets.

The Cool Stuff Main Window Style Sheet

The main viewing window of the Cool Stuff frameset has a different background than what you've been using on the Web so far. You'll use the same background color that you applied to the tables with extended attributes in your other pages. This time, applying the background color to the page is easier; you can specify it by its RGB values. The text and link colors are the same as those used by the main style sheet.

To create the style sheet, follow these steps:

1. From the FrontPage Editor, choose File l New.

2. Choose to create the page from the Normal template.

3. After the page opens in the FrontPage Editor window, assign the following properties to the page:

> Page Title: Cool Stuff Main Window Style Sheet
> Background color: Custom Color – R 200 G 237 B 255
> Link Color: R 0 G 0 B 240 (Toned-Down Blue)
> Text Color: R 0 G 0 B 128 (Navy Blue)
> Visited Link Color: Default Color (Deep Purple)
> Active Link Color: R 240 G 0 B 0 (Toned-Down Red)

4. Choose File l Save to save your page to the Web. Assign it the following URL:

```
_private/csstyle.htm
```

The Cool Stuff Main Navigation Page

The Main Navigation page contains an image map that navigates to the main pages in the Cool Stuff section of the Web. When the user clicks one of the hotspots in this frame, it changes the contents of the upper middle frame in the frameset, which is the target frame for this page.

To create the Cool Stuff Main Navigation page, follow these steps:

1. From the FrontPage Editor, choose File | New.

2. Choose to create the page from the Normal template.

3. After the page opens in the FrontPage Editor window, assign the following properties to the page:

   > Page Title: Cool Stuff Main Navigation
   > Background Color: R 0 G 0 B 128 (Navy Blue)
   > Text/Link Colors: Leave as default. There won't be any text on this page
   > Default Target Frame: `cssect`

4. Choose Insert | Image to place the `climgmap.gif` image onto your page.

You use the Rectangle button in the Image toolbar to place a rectangular hotspot around each of the navigation areas on the image. After you create each hotspot, the Create Link dialog appears. You'll create links to new pages that appear in the upper middle frame in the frameset. For each of these new pages, use the following steps:

See Chapter 8 for further information on using images for links. Also see Chapter 23, "Web Maintenance and Administration," for instructions on how to configure image-map handling if your service provider does not have the FrontPage Server Extensions installed.

1. Use the Rectangle tool in the Image toolbar to create a rectangular hotspot around each of the navigation areas on the image map in the Cool Stuff Main Navigation page. The Create Link dialog appears.

2. Create a link to a new page for each hotspot. Assign the following page titles, URLs, and target frame to the appropriate page, using the New Page tab in the Create Link dialog.

NOTE: Assign the target frame of cssect to all the links you create here, using the New Page tab of the Create Link dialog. When users click on links from these new pages, they generate changes in the upper middle frame of the frameset.

Page Title	Page URL	Target Frame
Cool Pages TOC	`clpgtoc.htm`	cssect
Cool Sounds TOC	`clsndtoc.htm`	cssect
Cool Marquees TOC	`clmartoc.htm`	cssect
Cool Animation TOC	`clanmtoc.htm`	cssect
Cool Plug-Ins TOC	`clplgtoc.htm`	cssect
Cool Other TOC	`clothtoc.htm`	cssect

3. Choose to edit each new page immediately. Base each new page on the Normal Page template.

4. Each of these new pages uses the style sheet that is used in the main pages of your Web. Assign the default target frame of `csmain` to these new pages after they appear in the FrontPage Editor. To complete both these items, choose the File I Page Properties dialog for each new page and assign the following properties:

    Get background from Page: `_private/faroutwc.htm`
    Default Target Link: `csmain`

5. Save each new page to your current web by choosing File I Save.

6. Choose Edit I Add To Do Task while each new page is opened to add a task to complete the contents of each page. The task would look something like this:

    Name: Complete Cool Pages TOC
    Description: Add links to pages in main frame

After all the hotspots are completed on the Cool Stuff Main Navigation page, it should look as shown in Figure 17.14. Now you can save the Cool Stuff Main Navigation page to your web by choosing File I Save. Save this page to your web with the following URL:

Title: Cool Stuff Main Navigation
URL: `csnav.htm`

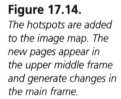

Figure 17.14.
The hotspots are added to the image map. The new pages appear in the upper middle frame and generate changes in the main frame.

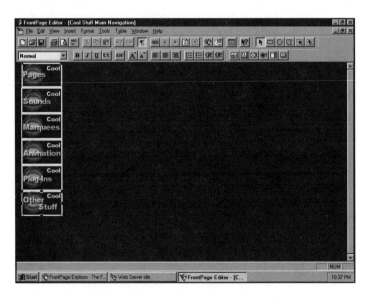

The Cool Pages TOC

The Cool Pages TOC appears in the upper middle frame of the frameset when it first opens. The other TOC pages you created (Cool Sounds TOC, Cool Multimedia TOC, and so on) should appear similar to the page you'll create in this example.

In the Cool Pages section, you'll place the best pages you've designed—pages that incorporate lots of fancy graphics, effects, multimedia, Java applets, and whatever else you can think of. So, you want this TOC to list those pages. As you create your new pages, don't forget to add links to them on this page.

Because this is the first table of contents that appears in the frameset when it first loads, you might want to include a link that displays a master table of contents in the main frame. You should have a page named Far Out There Cool Stuff (`cooltoc.htm`) on your web, which fits the bill quite nicely.

To complete the Cool Pages TOC page, follow these steps:

1. From the FrontPage Editor, choose File l Open from Web, or switch to the Cool Pages TOC page if it still is open in the FrontPage Editor.

2. Add a brief introduction to the table of contents. Keep in mind that this page appears in a very narrow window. One or two sentences should be sufficient, as shown in Figure 17.15.

Figure 17.15.
A brief introduction and list of files in the Cool Pages section appears on this page.

3. Add a bulleted list to prepare for links to pages you'll place in this section. Place text that links to the Far Out There Cool Stuff page on the first line.

4. Highlight the Far Out There Cool Stuff text and click the Create Link button.

5. From the Current Web tab in the Create Link dialog, select the Far Out There Cool Stuff page from your current web, or enter `cooltoc.htm` in the Page field.

6. Click OK to exit the Create Link dialog. Choose File | Save to save the Cool Pages TOC to your current web.

The Cool Stuff Navs to Main Web

The final frame in the frameset contains the navigation buttons that take the user back to the main pages on your web. You'll use the same navigation links you've already created here, through the use of Include bots.

NOTE: You'll need to use one of those "special" default target frame names I discussed in Chapter 14 for this page. You want the frameset to be removed after the user clicks the buttons in this frame.

Follow these steps:

1. From the FrontPage Editor, choose File | New.

2. Choose to create the page from the Normal template.

3. When the page opens in the FrontPage Editor window, assign the following properties to the page, leaving the remaining settings at their default values:

> Page Title: Cool Stuff Navs to Main Web
> Get Background: Far Out There Web Colors
> Default Target Frame: `_top`

4. Use two Include bots, one right after the other, to include the following two pages within this page. When they are inserted, your page should look like Figure 17.16.

> Upper row: Included Top Navigation Links (`_private/topnav.htm`)
> Lower row: Included Bottom Navigation Links (`_private/botmnav.htm`)

5. Save the page to your web using the following URL:

`csout.htm`

Figure 17.16.

Make it easy; include what you've already created on your pages when you can.

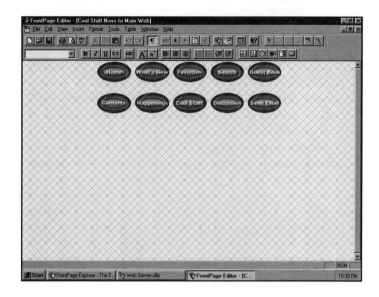

The Alternate Table of Contents Page

In Chapter 14, you cut and pasted contents from the other pages in your frameset to generate an alternate table of contents for the frameset. Although it wasn't that difficult a job to do it that way, it created a situation where you'd have to keep track of your pages and add links to two different pages. Things could get out of sync that way.

Now that you know how to automate your pages with bots, you can use the Table of Contents bots to your advantage here. Use them to generate an automatic list of the pages in each section of your frameset. Then you can use this for an introductory page in your frameset and for an alternate page for those who don't have frame-compatible browsers.

To create the page, follow these steps:

1. The Far Out There Cool Stuff page should be in your To Do list. Choose Do Task from the To Do list to open the page.
2. Choose File I Page Properties to assign the Cool Stuff Main Window style sheet (_private/csstyle.htm) to the page.
3. Insert Heading 3 (remember, this will also be in a frameset, so you don't want the heading too large!). Enter the following text:

    `Far Out There Cool Stuff`
4. Switch to Normal text and enter a brief introduction for those who don't have frame-compatible browsers. Figure 17.17 shows an example.

Figure 17.17.

A heading, some introductory text, and six Tables of Contents bots are placed on the page.

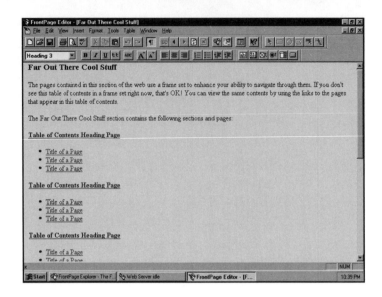

5. Now you'll place a Table of Contents bot on your page for each of the sections in the Cool Stuff frameset (those that appear on the left navigation bar). Choose Insert I Bot I Table of Contents for each of the sections. The Table of Contents Bot dialog appears.

6. Start the Table of Contents bots with the following pages in your current web, in this order so that the automatic table of contents agrees with the order of the buttons on the left navigation bar. You can use the Browse button in the dialog to choose the pages by their names, or you can enter the URL in the URL field.

> Cool Pages TOC (`clpgtoc.htm`)
> Cool Sounds TOC (`clsndtoc.htm`)
> Cool Marquees TOC (`clmartoc.htm`)
> Cool Animation TOC (`clanmtoc.htm`)
> Cool Plug-Ins TOC (`clplgtoc.htm`)
> Cool Other Stuff TOC (`clothtoc.htm`)

7. For the remaining properties for the Table of Contents bots, choose the following for each:

> Show Pages Only Once: Checked
>
> Show Pages with No Incoming Links: Unchecked—otherwise, every page on your site will be listed
>
> Recompute TOC: Your choice

8. Click OK to place each Table of Contents bot on your page.

9. After all six Table of Contents bots are complete, insert an Include bot at the bottom of the page. Include the footer (_private/footer.htm) here.

10. Save the page to your web by choosing File I Save. When FrontPage asks whether you want to remove the page from your To Do list, click Yes.

 ## Creating the Cool Stuff Frameset Page

Now that you've completed all the prep work for the frameset, you'll probably get mad at me for saying this. You didn't really have to put all that content in your pages before you generated your frameset. I had you do that so that you would have a good idea of what would be in each section *before* you got to this point. It also saved the fun part for last.

Chapter 14 gives step-by-step instructions for creating framesets with built-in templates as well.

To generate your frameset, follow these steps:

1. Choose File I New. Select to base the page on the Frames Wizard. The first screen in the Frames Wizard appears.

2. Choose to make a custom grid, and click Next to continue.

3. Start the table off with one row and three columns. Adjust the columns so that the center column takes up the largest amount of space. The outer columns are narrow (the graphics within them are 100 pixels wide).

4. Shift+click to select the center column. Click the Split button and split it into two rows and one column.

5. Adjust the height of the center top section to match the width of the two columns on the side. This portion of the frameset holds brief text and bulleted lists. When you're finished, your frame grid should look like Figure 17.18.

6. Click Next to continue. Now you assign frame names and the content pages you created earlier to the frameset.

7. Click the left column, where your Cool Stuff Main Navigation page appears. Assign the following settings:

> Name: csnav
> Source URL: csnav.htm (Cool Stuff Main Navigation)
> Margin Width: 0
> Margin Height: 0
> Scrolling: Auto
> Not Resizeable: Unchecked

Figure 17.18.
*Your frameset contains
four sections.*

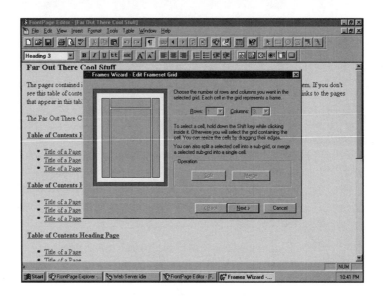

8. Click the upper middle frame, where the Cool Pages TOC appears. Assign the following settings:

    Name: `cssect`
    Source URL: `clpgtoc.htm` (Cool Pages TOC)
    Margin Width: 0
    Margin Height: 0
    Scrolling: Auto
    Not Resizeable: Unchecked

9. Click the larger middle frame, where your automatic table of contents appears, and assign it the following settings:

    Name: `csmain`
    Source URL: `cooltoc.htm` (Far Out There Cool Stuff)
    Margin Width: 0
    Margin Height: 0
    Scrolling: Auto
    Not Resizeable: Unchecked

10. Click the right frame and assign it the following settings:

    Name: `csout`
    Source URL: `csout.htm` (Cool Stuff Navs to Main Web)
    Margin Width: 0
    Margin Height: 0
    Scrolling: Auto
    Not Resizeable: Unchecked

11. Click Next to continue. You are asked to specify an alternate page URL for the frameset. Choose the Far Out There Cool Stuff page here as well (`cooltoc.htm`).

12. Click Next to continue. You are asked to save the frameset. Save it with the following title and URL:

> Title: Cool Stuff Frame Set
> URL: `csframe.htm`

13. Click Finish to generate the frameset.

If you want to see your frameset page, you'll need to open it in a frame-compatible browser. With the Personal Web server running, open your browser and enter the following URL:

`http://localhost/FarOutThere/csframe.htm`

Your frameset should appear in the browser, complete with the pages you created in this chapter, as shown in Figure 17.19.

Figure 17.19.
Viewing your frameset in a frame-compatible browser.

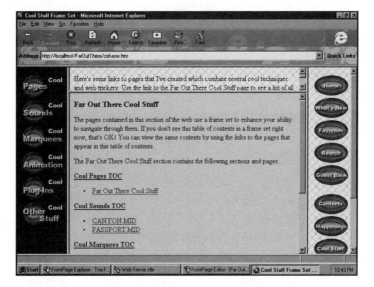

Editing the Home Page and Navigation Links

When you created the links on your home page and on the Included Navigation Links pages, you didn't know how to create framesets. The following pages contain links to the page that you now use as your alternate table of contents. You want to change the links so that they open the frameset instead. Open each of the following pages and edit the links:

❏ Open the Included Text navigation bar from your current web. Edit the Cool Stuff text link in the second row. You can place the insertion point anywhere within the text and click the Create or Edit Link button on the toolbar to bring up the Edit Link dialog. Change the link from `cooltoc.htm` to `csframe.htm`. Save the page to your web when you're done.

❏ Open the Included Navigation – Bottom page and edit the link for the Cool Stuff button. Change it from `cooltoc.htm` to `csframe.htm`. Save the page when you're done.

❏ Open the Far Out There home page. This page has two links to the Cool Stuff section. The first appears in the second row of the text link below the page-width guide. The second appears in the row of navigation buttons below the main graphic. Change both of these links from `cooltoc.htm` to `csframe.htm` and save the page when you're done.

Creating the Happenings Page

What's the Happenings page all about? It's a page that tells your site visitors about monthly happenings on a topic or subject of interest. You'll use Scheduled Include bots to insert a list of upcoming events, meetings, conferences, or other newsworthy events that are to occur over the next month. A Scheduled Image bot places a calendar graphic on the page as well. If you're in the know about a topic and want to share the latest and greatest events about it, this is the place to share.

To complete the Happenings page, follow these steps:

1. Create a new page based on the Far Out There Main Page template.

2. Delete the horizontal line and bulleted list from the table.

3. Delete the section bookmarks and dividers from below the table, leaving only one divider and the footer at the bottom of the page.

4. Replace the Annotation bot text in the table with the `happen.gif` (or `.jpg`) image located on the CD-ROM that accompanies this book.

5. Enter some introductory text below the title, as shown in Figure 17.20.

6. Position the insertion point at the beginning of the divider below the table and press Enter. This adds a new normal paragraph to the page and also provides an area between the two tables in case you want to add content between them later.

Figure 17.20.

Enter the header graphic, revise the title, and add a brief description of what the Happenings page is all about.

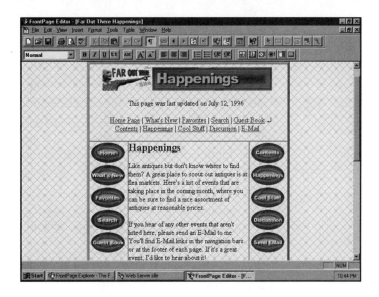

7. Choose Table I Insert Table. Format this table with the following settings. I also used extended attributes to apply the same background colors from the table in the main page template to this new table.

> Number of Rows: 2
> Number of Columns: 1
> Alignment: Center
> Border Size: 5
> Cell Padding: 5
> Cell Spacing: 5
> Table Width: 90 percent

Extended Attributes:
> BGCOLOR: #C8EDFF
> BORDERCOLORLIGHT: #ECC8FF
> BORDERCOLORDARK: #C8D3FF

8. Select the cell in the first row and choose Table I Split Cells to split it into two columns.

9. Place the insertion point in the left cell of the first row. Format the line as Heading 3. Enter a title that's descriptive of what the Happenings page is about.

10. Return to the FrontPage Explorer and choose File I Import to import one or more of the calendar images into your web. These calendar images are provided on the CD-ROM included with this book in the Miscellaneous Graphics section in .jpg format only. If a graphic doesn't exist on your web, you can assign a name to it in advance by entering it in the URL field.

For the example, I imported the following:

```
aug_96.jpg
sep_96.jpg
oct_96.jpg
```

11. Position the insertion point in the right cell in the top row. Use the Scheduled Image bot for each of the calendar graphics you want to import. Use the Browse button to select the image from your current web. Start each image on the first day of the month that the calendar represents, at midnight (00:00), and end each scheduled image on the first day of the following month at midnight. For example, the August calendar would have a start and end date:

> Starting Date and Time: 01-Aug-1996 00:00
> Ending Date and Time: 01-Sep-1996 00:00

12. Before you insert a Scheduled Include bot into the table, place an extra space in the table. Insert the Scheduled Include bot on the line above the extra space.

13. Place three Scheduled Include bots in the cell in the bottom row, using the same procedure as you did for the Scheduled Image bots. You can enter the URLs of pages that do not yet exist in your Web or click the Browse button to choose pages from those in your current Web. The pages I include by Scheduled Includes, for example, have the monthly happenings for those who like to haunt flea markets.

After you enter your bots, the page is complete.

14. Save the page to your web as Far Out There Happenings, with the URL of happen.htm.

15. Click Yes to overwrite the previous version of the file.

16. Click Yes to save the new graphics to your Web also.

17. Mark the task as complete in your To Do list.

All that remains is to generate the content that will be included on those given dates, and that can be done at your leisure. Figure 17.21 shows an example of what the page looks like during the month of August. The page that was included through the Scheduled Image bot contained yet another table with a row for each day of the month. That table was inserted inside this table through the Scheduled Include bot.

Figure 17.21.

When the month of August rolls around, the page contains the correct calendar and page content.

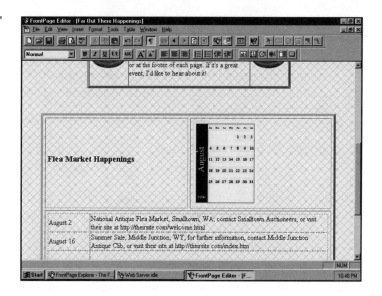

Completing Your What's New Page

Complete your What's New page using the same steps as outlined for the Favorite Far Out Links page:

1. Generate a new page with the Far Out There Main Page template.
2. Cut and paste the contents from the original `whatsnew.htm` page into the new page where appropriate.
3. Add the pages you created in this chapter to the What's New page.
4. Save the new version of the page over the version that exists on your web, using the same title and URL.
5. Remove the What's New page from the To Do list.

Workshop Wrap-Up

Many of the features you added to the pages in this chapter are fairly new to the Web. For certain, Netscape and Internet Explorer handle tables very well. The next versions of both these browsers offer greater features still. You probably want to check out your pages now in several different browsers to see how you like the look.

Chapter Summary

In this chapter, you incorporated many features that are relatively new to the Web. You've come a long way! You learned how to use tables to enhance page layout. You learned how to apply special cell and border colors to tables using extended attributes.

You learned how to convert decimal numbers to their hexadecimal equivalents. You generated an automatic table of contents in a couple of different ways. Through the use of Scheduled Image and Scheduled Include bots, you created a page that automatically updates its content on a monthly basis. Finally, you created a frameset and many related pages, in which you will soon add multimedia and other, even more advanced features.

Next Steps

❑ See Chapter 18, "Adding Interactivity—Forms the Easy Way," to learn how to generate forms using FrontPage's Form Wizard. What a great way to create a form!

❑ See Chapter 19, "Fields—The Building Blocks of Forms," to learn how to edit the form fields on your pages.

❑ See Chapter 20, "Runtime Bots: The Heartbeat of FrontPage Forms," to learn how to assign form handlers to the forms so that they will work properly when they are out on the Web.

❑ See Chapter 21, "Using Your Own HTML Code," to learn how to incorporate HTML code into pages you create with FrontPage.

❑ See Chapter 22, "Real-Life Examples," to learn how to add all these new features to your web.

Q&A

Q: Can I create any kind of template I want for my webs?

A: Sure you can! You might not want to do this for page styles you think you'll only use once in a while, but for pages you use repeatedly (section pages, links pages, and so on), templates help maintain a degree of consistency in the look of your web while saving you time in the process.

Q: Do I have to use a Scheduled Image bot and Scheduled Include bot separately, or can I put regular images on a page and include them along with the page content in a Scheduled Include bot?

A: Scheduled Image bots and Scheduled Include bots don't have to be used separately. I put them separate in this chapter for two reasons: one, to have you work with both in a real-life example, and two, to arrange the calendar beside the heading of the page content rather than below it. A Scheduled Include bot can include anything a "normal" Include bot does.

Q: Why are color numbers entered in hexadecimal? Isn't that really confusing?

A: Yes, and tedious. But it's one of those "computer things" we have to live with. It would be nice to enter those color values by clicking on a color somewhere, and I hope that as the standards for page development are set in stone, we'll see this capability in future releases of FrontPage. I'd much rather click a button than calculate a hexadecimal value myself!

P A R T

IV

Still More Advanced Techniques

EIGHTEEN

Adding Interactivity— Forms the Easy Way

Everyone has filled out countless forms—order forms, registration forms, personal information forms, surveys, and so on. Even when you enter a message or article in a discussion, you are using a form. Essentially, whenever information is exchanged, it is done through a form.

Designing a form can be tedious, especially if you want to ask many questions. Suppose, for example, that you want to design an online IQ test of 50 questions. Each question has a multiple choice answer. That is a lot of form fields to place on a page. Laying the form out and aligning the fields is a task in itself. It could take you hours to complete the form.

Have no fear. In FrontPage, creating forms is a breeze. The Form Page wizard does much of the work for you. It takes care of the layout and enables you to present questions in several different categories. You think of a question, pick the category that best handles how you want to present it, assign a few variables, and away you go. You can design your IQ test in a matter of minutes.

Setting the Groundwork

To edit the types of fields contained in the forms that the Form Page wizard generates, refer to Chapter 19, "Fields—The Building Blocks of Forms."

Always create a form on a new page. After you complete the form, you can add additional content to it or copy its contents to the clipboard to paste into another page. To create a form with the Form Page wizard, use FrontPage Editor's File I New command. From the New Page dialog box, choose the Form Page wizard and click OK.

Examining the Form Page Wizard

The Form Page wizard is a gem. You use it to design just about any type of form you can think of. If you know the type of form you want to design and the questions or responses you need, the rest is absolutely simple. After you choose the wizard, its introductory screen appears.

Introducing the Form Page Wizard

The first screen of the Form Page wizard is an introductory screen. It explains what the Form Page wizard does. You navigate forward and backward through the wizard by using the navigation buttons at the bottom of each dialog box.

Click the Cancel button to leave the Form Page wizard without creating the page. Click the Back button to review the questions or choices that you made in previous screens. Click the Finish button to generate the page with the content you have chosen up to that point. Click the Next button to proceed to the next step.

NOTE: In some cases, you cannot go back unless you assign a name to the group of fields for the question on which you are working. You can go back and review the question after you assign the name.

Naming a Form Page

On the second screen of the Form Page wizard, shown in Figure 18.1, you enter a URL for the page and a page title.

Figure 18.1.
Enter a page URL and a page title.

In the Page URL field, enter the filename of the page. Filenames are restricted to eight characters plus the `.htm` extension. For example, if you are designing a survey form, you might enter

`survey.htm`

In the Page Title field, enter the title for the page. This title appears in browsers. The title for the survey form might be

`Web Site Survey`

After you enter the URL and title, click Next to continue.

Adding, Modifying, Removing, and Arranging Questions

The third screen of the Form Page wizard, shown in Figure 18.2, appears next. You use it to

- ❏ Add a question to your form
- ❏ Modify a question while designing it
- ❏ Remove a question from the question list
- ❏ Rearrange the order in which the questions appear in the form

Figure 18.2.
You can add, modify, remove, or rearrange questions.

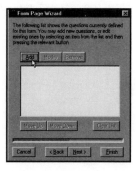

To add a question to a form:

1. Click the Add button shown in Figure 18.2. The screen shown in Figure 18.3 appears.

Figure 18.3.

Choose the type of question you want to ask and enter a question in this screen.

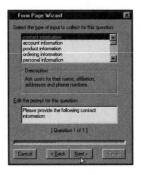

2. Choose a category for the question. In the lower portion of the screen, type the question or prompt that you want to include on the form. Click the Next button. A screen that is applicable to the type of question that you are asking appears.

3. Choose the options for the question's form fields. Click Next to return to the screen shown in Figure 18.2.

Options for form fields are discussed later in this chapter.

4. To enter another question, repeat steps 1 through 3.

5. Click Next to continue with the Form Page wizard after you have added all your questions to the list.

To modify a question:

1. From the screen shown in Figure 18.2, highlight the question that you want to modify.

2. Click the Modify button. The question's option screen appears, and you can modify the question.

To remove a question from the list:

1. From the screen shown in Figure 18.2, highlight the question that you want to remove.

2. Click the Remove button. The question is removed from the list.

NOTE: To remove all the questions from the list, click the Clear List button.

To rearrange the order of the questions in the list:

1. Highlight the question that you want to move.
2. Click the Move Up or Move Down button to change its location in the list.

 # Choosing a Question Type

You can choose from fourteen categories for your question. They are

- ❏ Contact information
- ❏ Account information
- ❏ Product information
- ❏ Ordering information
- ❏ Personal information
- ❏ One of several options
- ❏ Many of several options
- ❏ Boolean
- ❏ Date
- ❏ Time
- ❏ Range
- ❏ Number
- ❏ String
- ❏ Paragraph

 # Choosing Options for the Question's Form Fields

Based on the type of question that you select, one of fourteen screens appears. The following sections discuss options for each type of question.

Contact Information

The contact information fields are displayed in text boxes. To learn how to edit these fields, refer to Chapter 19.

Use a contact information question when you need to know how to contact the person filling out your form. Information request forms often ask for contact information. A typical prompt is `Please let us know how we can contact you`. Figure 18.4 shows examples of the fields available for contact information.

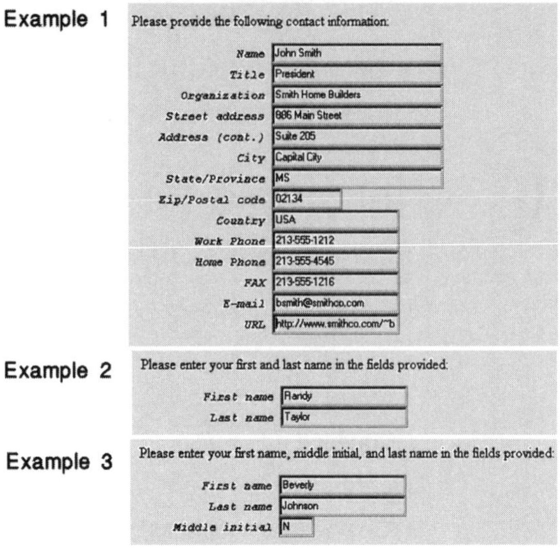

Figure 18.4.

You can request different types of contact information.

Example 1

Please provide the following contact information:

Name	John Smith
Title	President
Organization	Smith Home Builders
Street address	986 Main Street
Address (cont.)	Suite 205
City	Capital City
State/Province	MS
Zip/Postal code	02134
Country	USA
Work Phone	213-555-1212
Home Phone	213-555-4545
FAX	213-555-1216
E-mail	bsmith@smithco.com
URL	http://www.smithco.com/~b

Example 2

Please enter your first and last name in the fields provided:

First name	Randy
Last name	Taylor

Example 3

Please enter your first name, middle initial, and last name in the fields provided:

First name	Beverly
Last name	Johnson
Middle initial	N

To complete a contact information question:

1. Select how you want to receive name information. The options are

   Full. The user enters his name in a single field, as in Example 1 of Figure 18.4.

   First, last. The user enters his name in two separate fields, as in Example 2 of Figure 18.4.

   First, last, middle option. The user enters his first name, last name, and middle initial in three separate fields, as in Example 3 of Figure 18.4.

2. Check or uncheck the boxes to include the contact information that you want to obtain. The choices are title, organization, postal address, work phone, home phone, fax number, e-mail address, and URL. (See Figure 18.4.)

> **TIP:** It is most efficient—for you and for the person filling out the form—to ask for no more information than you need in response to a question.

3. Enter a base name for the variables. This name is used as a reference in the information retrieved from the form and as bookmark names in the form's table of contents if one exists. Give it a descriptive name. The default name is `Contact`.

4. Click Next to return to the screen shown in Figure 18.2.

Account Information

Use an account information question to obtain a user name and password. Account information questions are often used on registration forms, such as those used to gain access to a protected web. A typical prompt is `Please enter your name and password in the following fields`. Figure 18.5 shows examples of the options available for account information.

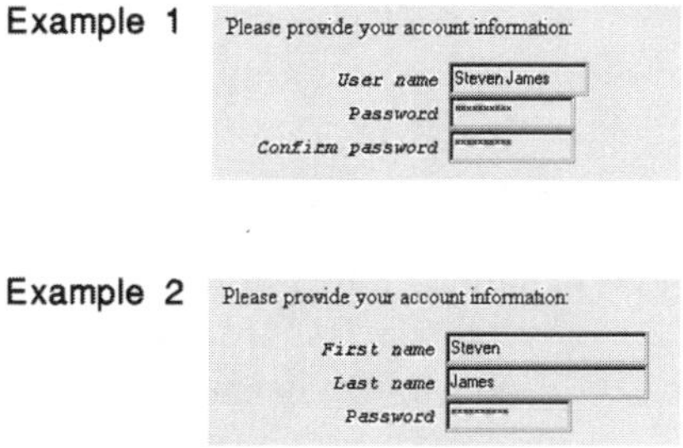

Figure 18.5.

Account information questions ask for a user's name and password.

Example 1

Example 2

To complete an account information question:

1. Select how to include user name information on your form. If you do not want to include a user name, uncheck the option.

   As separate field. The user types his full name, as in Example 1 of Figure 18.5.

   As first and last names concatenated. Choose this option when you use the registration bot to create a registration form for a protected web. This option is shown in Example 2 of Figure 18.5.

2. Choose how you want to receive password information. If you do not want to include password information, uncheck the option. If you require confirmation, the user confirms his password in a separate field, as in Example 1 of Figure 18.5. If you do not require confirmation, the user enters his password once, as in Example 2 of Figure 18.5.

Refer to Chapter 20, "Runtime Bots: The Heartbeat of FrontPage Forms," for more information on the registration bot.

3. Type a descriptive name for this set of variables. The default name is `Account`.

4. Click Next to return to the screen shown in Figure 18.2.

Product Information

Use a product information question to obtain warranty or registration information on a product. A form for this type of question might be a software registration form or a warranty service request. A typical prompt is `Please enter the following information on the product for which you are requesting warranty service`. Figure 18.6 shows the options available.

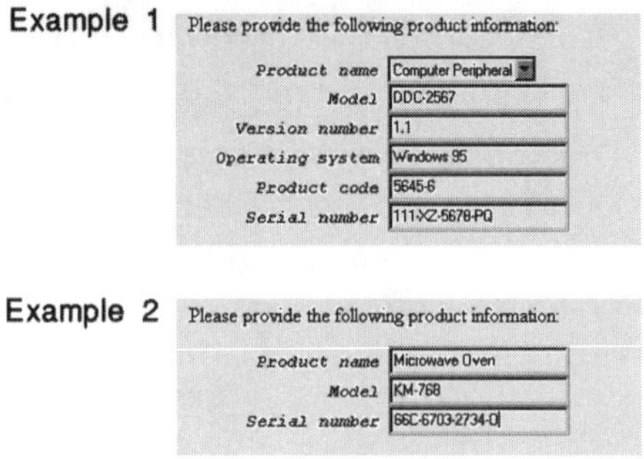

Figure 18.6.

Use product information questions to register software or to request warranty service information.

To complete a product information question:

1. Choose how you want to receive the product name. Users can select from list products in a dropdown menu, as in Example 1 of Figure 18.6. They also can type the name of the product, as in Example 2 of Figure 18.6.

2. Check or uncheck the information that you want to request on the product. The choices are model, platform and version (for software products), product code, and serial number.

3. Type a descriptive base name for this set of variables. The default name is Product.

4. Click Next to return to the screen shown in Figure 18.2.

Ordering Information

Use an ordering information question when you want users to order products online. You can create order forms easily. A typical prompt is Order your products and provide method of payment and delivery information below. Figure 18.7 shows examples of the fields for this type of question.

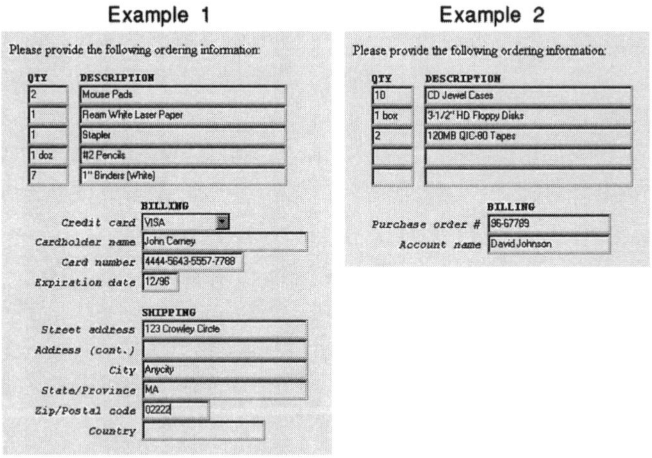

Figure 18.7.

Use ordering information in an online order form.

To complete an ordering information question:

1. Check the List of products and quantities checkbox to include an order form in your question. By default, the order form has five entries, as in Figure 18.7. You can specify more or fewer entries in the Maximum Number field.

2. Check Billing Information to ask for the method of payment, and choose the type of field for billing information. If you choose the Credit Card option, the user specifies his credit card type from a dropdown menu. The name of the cardholder and the card's number and expiration date are entered in text fields, as in Example 1 of Figure 18.7. If you choose the Purchase Order option, the user enters a purchase order number and account name in text boxes, as in Example 2 of Figure 18.7.

3. Check whether you want to request a shipping address, as in Example 1 of Figure 18.7.

4. Type a descriptive base name for this set of variables. The default name is Ordering.

5. Click Next to return to the screen shown in Figure 18.2.

To learn how to edit a drop-down menu field, refer to Chapter 19.

Personal Information

You can ask for personal information in your forms, including age, sex, height, weight, ID number, and hair and eye color. A typical prompt is Enter optional personal information below. Figure 18.8 shows examples of the fields.

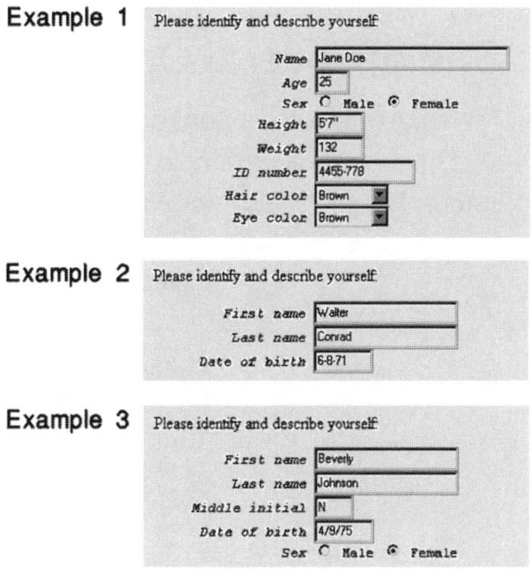

Figure 18.8.

You can request several types of personal information.

Example 1

Please identify and describe yourself

Name	Jane Doe
Age	25
Sex	○ Male ● Female
Height	5'7"
Weight	132
ID number	4455-778
Hair color	Brown
Eye color	Brown

Example 2

Please identify and describe yourself

First name	Walter
Last name	Conrad
Date of birth	6-8-71

Example 3

Please identify and describe yourself

First name	Beverly
Last name	Johnson
Middle initial	N
Date of birth	4/9/75
Sex	○ Male ● Female

To complete a personal information question:

1. Select how to request name information on the form. If you do not want to request a name in this section of the form, uncheck the option. The options are

    Full. The user enters his name in a single text field, as in Example 1 of Figure 18.8.

    First, last. The user enters his first and last names in individual fields, as in Example 2 of Figure 18.8.

    First, last, middle. The user enters his first name, last name, and middle initial in individual fields, as in Example 3 of Figure 18.8.

2. Select how you want the user to enter his age:

    Years old. The user enters his age in years, as in Example 1 of Figure 18.8.

    Date of birth. The user enters his date of birth, as in Example 2 of Figure 18.8.

3. Check or uncheck the additional types of information that you want to request. The choices are sex, height, weight, ID number, hair color, and eye color. Examples are shown in Example 1 of Figure 18.8.

4. Type a descriptive base name for this set of variables. The default name is `Personal`.

5. Click Next to return to the screen shown in Figure 18.2.

One of Several Options

Ask a one of several options question when you want to obtain a single response from a list of choices. An example of a question in this category is `What is your favorite color?`. Figure 18.9 shows examples of the options for this question.

Figure 18.9.

A one of several options question enables you to obtain responses through drop-down menus, a series of radio buttons, or a scrollable menu list.

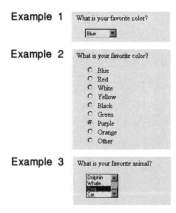

To complete a one of several options question:

1. Enter the choices from which the user chooses in the scrolling text box at the upper portion of the screen. Enter each item on an individual line.

2. Select how you want to display the list:

   Drop-down menu. The list is displayed in a drop-down menu, as in Example 1 of Figure 18.9.

   Radio buttons. The list is displayed in a series of radio buttons, as in Example 2 of Figure 18.9.

   List. The list is displayed in a scrollable menu list, as in Example 3 of Figure 18.9.

3. Type a descriptive base name for this set of variables. There is no default name for this question.

4. Click Next to return to the screen shown in Figure 18.2.

Any of Several Options

Ask an any of several options question when you want to provide one or more choices from a list of several. A typical question in this category is `What other peripherals do you have in your computer?`. Figure 18.10 shows an example of the output that you receive.

To learn how to edit these fields, refer to Chapter 19.

Figure 18.10.
An any of several options question enables the user to make multiple choices. The checkboxes can be displayed in a single column or in multiple columns as shown here.

To complete an any of several options question:

1. Enter the labels for the choices that you want to include in the scrolling text box on the form. Put one option on each line. If you want to display the questions in multiple columns, as in Figure 18.10, keep the descriptions fairly short.

2. Check the box that reads "Use multiple columns to present the options" if you want to arrange the list in multiple columns. If you do not check the box, the choices are arranged in a single column.

3. Type a descriptive base name for this set of variables as a reference for the report. The default name is `AnyOfSeveral`.

4. Click Next to return to the screen shown in Figure 18.2.

Boolean

Use a Boolean question when you want to ask a question that requires an either/or response. A typical question is `Do you want express delivery? (Additional charges apply)`. Figure 18.11 shows other examples.

Figure 18.11.

Boolean questions can be answered with checkboxes or radio buttons.

Example 1

Example 2

Example 3

To complete a Boolean question:

1. Select the type of response area that you want to include in the form. The options are as checkboxes (see Example 1 of Figure 18.11), as Yes/No radio buttons (see Example 2 of Figure 18.11), and as True/False radio buttons (see Example 3 of Figure 18.11).

NOTE:
The True/False radio buttons are labeled Yes and No. You can easily change their labels to True and False if you want.

2. Type a descriptive name for this variable. There is no default name.

3. Click Next to return to the screen shown in Figure 18.2.

Date

A date question asks the user for a date—a calendar date, not the romantic kind. The user can enter a date response in one of three ways. A typical question is `On what date was this product purchased?`. Figure 18.12 shows some examples.

Figure 18.12.
Users can enter dates in three ways.

Example 1

What date is your appointment?

06/14/96 -- mm/dd/yy

Example 2

On what date were you born?

14/06/96 -- dd/mm/yy

Example 3

On what nights will you be booking your reservation?

5/4/96 to 5/9/96

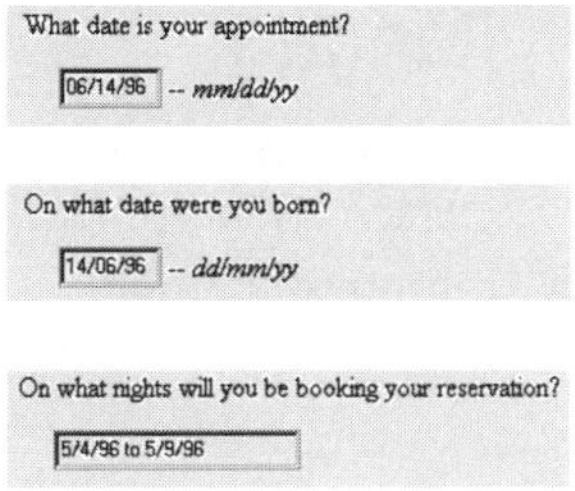

To complete a date question:

1. Select how you want the date to appear on the form. The options are mm/dd/yy (see Example 1 of Figure 18.12), dd/mm/yy (see Example 2 of Figure 18.12), and free format (see Example 3 of Figure 18.12).

2. Type a descriptive name for this variable. There is no default name.

3. Click Next to return to the screen shown in Figure 18.2.

Time

A time question asks the user for a specific time. A typical question is `After what time can we contact you at this number?`. Figure 18.13 shows other examples.

Figure 18.13.
Time can be entered in 12-hour, 24-hour, or free format.

Example 1

What time is your appointment?

12:00 AM -- hh:mm:ss am/pm

Example 2

Enter your time of birth in Greenwich Mean Time:

17:45 -- hh:mm:ss

Example 3

What time frame would work best for you?

7:00 to 7:30

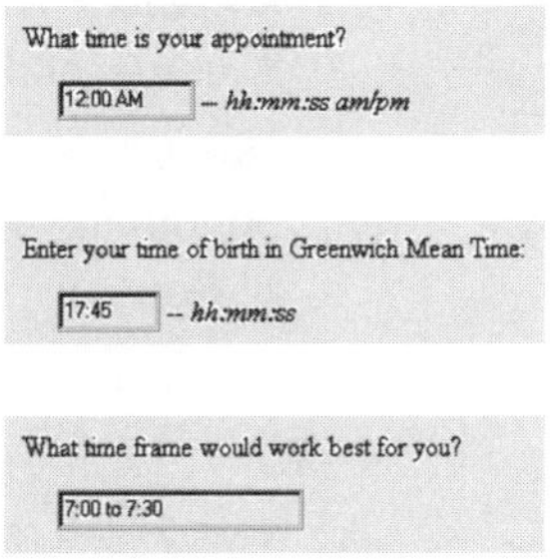

To complete a time question:

1. Select how you want the time to appear on the form. The options are 12-hour format (see Example 1 of Figure 18.13), 24-hour format (see Example 2 of Figure 18.13), and free format (see Example 3 of Figure 18.13).

2. Type a descriptive name for this variable. There is no default name.

3. Click Next to return to the screen shown in Figure 18.2.

Range

Use a range question when you want the user to rate satisfaction or to provide an opinion on something. A typical question is How do you rate our customer service department?. Figure 18.14 shows other examples.

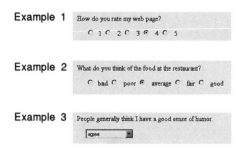

Example 1

How do you rate my web page?

C 1 C 2 C 3 C 4 C 5

Example 2

What do you think of the food at the restaurant?

C bad C poor C average C fair C good

Example 3

People generally think I have a good sense of humor.

agree

To complete a range question:

1. Select the type of scale. You can use on a scale of 1 to 5 (see Example 1 of Figure 18.14), bad to good (see Example 2 of Figure 18.14), or disagree strongly to agree strongly (see Example 3 of Figure 18.14).

2. Select the presentation option:

    Mid-range choice is default. If you choose this option, the number 3, Average, and Neutral are the default values.

    Use drop-down menu instead of radio buttons. If you choose this option, the list is displayed in a drop-down menu list, as in Example 3 of Figure 8.14. The default is radio buttons.

3. Enter a descriptive base name for this set of variables. There is no default name.

4. Click Next to return to the screen shown in Figure 18.2.

Number

Use a number question when you need numerical input from the user. A typical question is How many fingers are on your right hand?. Figure 18.15 shows other examples.

Figure 18.15.
You can specify the length of a numerical response. You also can specify a currency symbol.

Example 1

How many computers do you have?

2

Example 2

What is your current salary?

$30000

To complete a number question:

1. Enter the maximum number of digits that you want for the response. The default value is five.

2. Check the set currency prefix box if you want to allow additional space for a currency symbol. Enter the currency symbol in the designated field.

3. Type a descriptive name for this variable. There is no default name.

4. Click Next to return to the screen shown in Figure 18.2.

String

Ask for a string response when you need a single line of text input from the user. A typical question is `What is the name of your pet?`. Figure 18.16 shows an example.

Figure 18.16.

Use a string question when a single-line text response is sufficient.

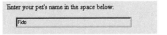

To complete a string question:

1. Specify the length of the text field. The default length is 50 characters. To specify a different length, check the Set Maximum Length checkbox. Enter the maximum number of characters that you want in the text field.

TIP: Make sure that the field is long enough to handle anything that your user might enter. This type of question is intended for short responses. If the length of the textbox is too long, it will not be displayed fully in the window of the user's browser. If you think you need a long response, use a paragraph question.

2. Type a descriptive name for this variable. There is no default value.

3. Click Next to return to the screen shown in Figure 18.2.

Paragraph

Use a paragraph question when you need a multiline response. A typical question for this category is `What is the nature of the problem you are having?`. Figure 18.17 shows an example.

Figure 18.17.
Use a paragraph question when several lines of text are required for a response.

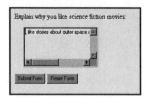

To complete a paragraph question, simply type a descriptive name for the variable. Then click Next to return to the screen shown in Figure 18.2.

 # Presenting Your Questions

After you complete your question list, select how you want to present it. You use the screen shown in Figure 18.18 to do this.

Figure 18.18.
Choose how you want to present your questions.

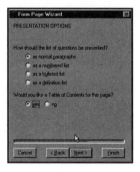

To present your questions:

1. Select a format for displaying your questions:

   Normal Paragraphs format displays the questions without any preceding numbers or bullets.

   Numbered List format displays the questions in a numbered list.

   Bulleted List format displays the questions with a bullet preceding them.

   Definition List format displays the questions as terms. You can place additional text and instructions beneath each question as definitions.

NOTE: You must edit the table of contents manually to reflect the questions on your form.

2. Select Yes if you want the questions to be listed in a table of contents. If your form is lengthy, you should choose Yes. The table of contents provides links to the questions, which are bookmarked on the page.

3. Click Next to proceed to the next screen.

Storing Your Responses

The screen shown in Figure 18.19 asks how you want to retrieve the information from the form. The options are

❏ Save results to a web page

❏ Save results to a text file

❏ Use a custom CGI script

Figure 18.19.
Choose the output option.

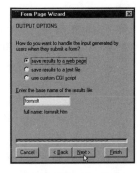

Click Finish to create your form. Your page appears in the FrontPage Editor window. At this point, you can save it to your web, or you can copy it to the clipboard and paste it into another page in your web.

There's More

Chapter 20 describes what form handlers do and how to apply them to your custom forms.

Your form is now designed correctly, but you still need to tell your server how to handle it. The form cannot function unless you assign a form handler to it. Some of FrontPage's bots—such as the Save Results bot and the Registration bot—act as form handlers. For you to use these types of bots, your Internet Service Provider or target server must have the FrontPage Server Extensions installed. If that is not possible, you can assign a custom CGI script to process the form for you.

Workshop Wrap-Up

You can design forms quickly and easily with the Form Page wizard. Start with a list of questions, and decide how you want to display them. The wizard does the rest.

Chapter Summary

In this chapter, you learned how to design a customized, interactive form using the FrontPage Form Page wizard to ask a variety of questions. Based on your selections, the wizard tailors your form so that you can gather information from visitors to your site.

Next Steps

The next two chapters help you edit your form fields and assign form handlers to them. To learn more about the fields in your form, refer to Chapter 19, "Fields—The Building Blocks of Forms." To learn how to assign a form handler to your form, refer to Chapter 20, "Runtime Bots: The Heartbeat of FrontPage Forms."

Q&A

Q: I designed a form and put it on my web site, but it does not do anything when I try to test it. What is happening?

A: If you assigned a form handler to your form, check whether the FrontPage Server Extensions or custom CGI scripts have been installed on your remote server. You might need to coordinate this with the server administrator at your site. Refer to Chapter 24, "Working with the FrontPage Servers," for more information.

Q: Which is the better choice to use when I specify a results file—web pages or text files?

A: Generally, it is more efficient to store your results files as text files. When you store them in a web page, it requires extra time for the server to process and format the results. You can find more information on the different types of results files in Chapter 20.

Q: Are Boolean questions stored as 1s and 0s or as "True and False"?

A: When a user responds to a Boolean question, the names and values that you specify in the form field properties dialog box are reported back to you.

If, for example, you create a question that asks "Do you like cats" and specify a checkbox with a name of likecats, an initial value of ON, and an initial status of not checked, the results would appear as follows if the user checks the box:

likecats ON

If the same question were asked using a Yes/No radio button with a Group Name of likecats, a Yes radio button that is initially selected, and a No radio button that is initially deselected, the results would appear as follows if the user selects No:

likecats No

You learn more about configuring form fields in Chapter 19.

NINETEEN

Fields—The Building Blocks of Forms

In Chapter 18, "Adding Interactivity—Forms the Easy Way," you learned how to generate a form using the FrontPage Form Page Wizard. The Form Wizard created the form by prompting you with a series of questions. The form fields and the layout were handled automatically.

What if you want to create your own layout, add additional form fields, or edit the content of the forms that you designed with the wizard? This chapter shows you how to do that. You learn how to work with the elements that make up a form.

What Every Form Needs

Every form has some basic elements within it. Form fields are the areas where users enter data. Each form field has a name so that the data can be arranged by category. Every form has a button that users press to submit information to your site. Finally, every form also has a form handler—a set of instructions that tells your server how to process the information that users submit.

Form Fields

When you ask users a question or need input from them, they enter their responses in a form field. For example, the form fields shown in Figure 19.1 are textboxes and radio buttons. You insert a form field on your page with the Insert I Form Field command.

Figure 19.1.

Users enter data on your form with form fields.

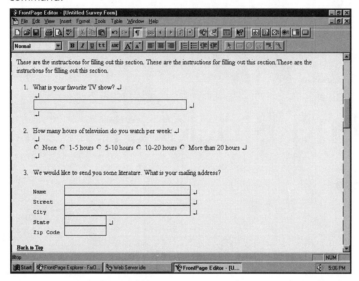

Whenever you insert a form field on a page, you automatically create a form. If you have the Show/Hide button on the Standard toolbar enabled, the form fields are surrounded by a dashed box. This shows you the area of the page where the form appears.

Form Field Names

Each form field is assigned a name through its respective Properties box, as shown in Figure 19.2. The name of the field is passed first to the form handler and then to you through the use of *name/value pairs*—that is, the name you assign to the form field and the value the user enters.

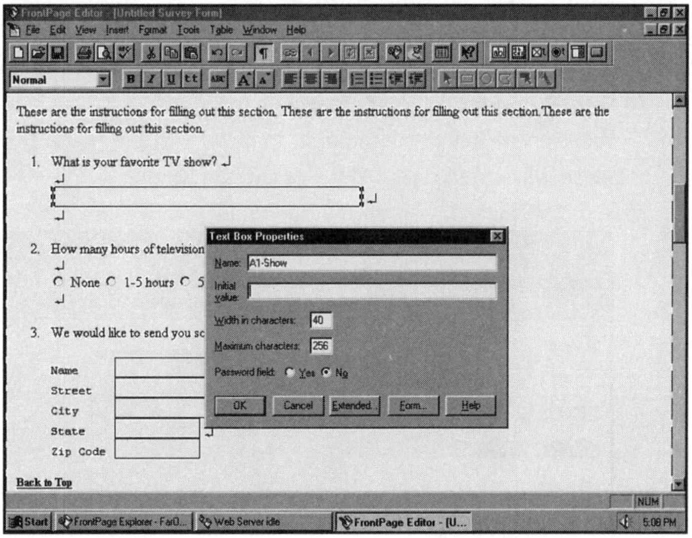

Figure 19.2.

Each form field has a name that is matched with the user's value. Together, they make up a name/value pair.

Buttons

Unless you place a button on your page, the form cannot do anything. A form must contain, at a minimum, a button that the user presses to submit the information to you. Most forms include a second button that enables the user to reset or clear the data from the form fields already completed. These buttons are shown in Figure 19.3.

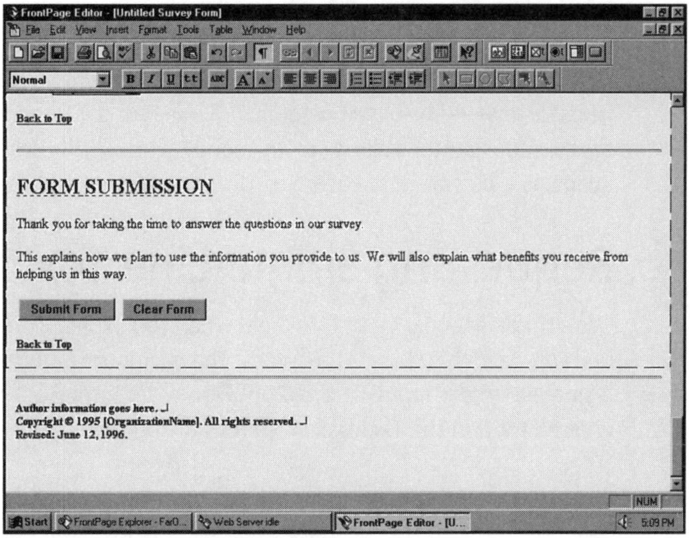

Figure 19.3.

Every form must contain at least one button, which is used to submit the information. A reset button is optional, although usually included.

Form Handlers

After you design a form, you need to assign a form handler to it. You do that with the Form Properties dialog box, shown in Figure 19.4. The form handler resides on your Web server. It accepts the data that the user enters on the form and processes it in some way. Then it passes the results on to you.

Figure 19.4.
Every form requires a form handler. It is assigned in the Form Properties dialog box.

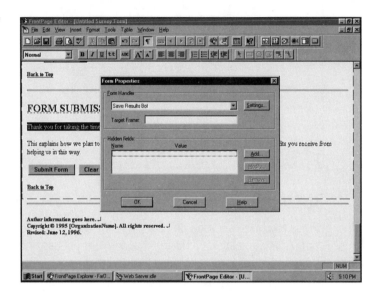

What Form Fields Do

You learn more about the types of form handlers that you can use in Chapter 20, "Runtime Bots: The Heartbeat of FrontPage Forms."

HTML enables you to place several different types of form fields on a page. There are fields for a single line of text or for multiple lines or paragraphs. You also can use checkboxes, radio buttons, drop-down menus, and pushbuttons. You can even use an image as a pushbutton. Each type of form field requests an input from the user.

Requesting Single-Line Text Input

Use a single-line text input form field when you expect a brief response from the user or if you need to request a password. The maximum number of characters allowed in a single-line text input field is 256. Figure 19.5 shows a textbox and the settings entered for it in the Text Box Properties dialog box.

To place a one-line textbox on your form:

1. From the FrontPage Editor, position the insertion point where you want to insert the textbox field.

Figure 19.5.

Textboxes are used for brief text responses.

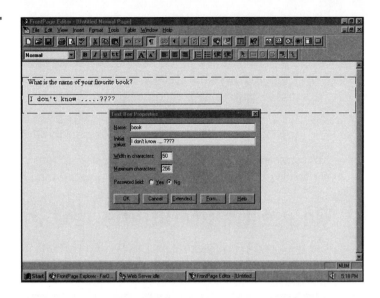

TIP: If you want to align your forms similarly to how the Form Page Wizard does, format the line on which you want to insert the form field as a formatted paragraph. Use the arrow keys to move back and forth through the alignment; use the backspace and space keys to alter the spacing of the labels and the form fields.

2. Choose Insert | Form Field | One-Line Text Box, or click the One-Line Text Box button on the Forms toolbar. The Text Box Properties dialog box appears.

3. In the Name field, enter a name for the text field. This name does not appear on the form; it is the name that coincides with the name/value pair reported to the form handler. In the example shown in Figure 19.5, the question asks the user the name of his favorite book, so the form field is named **book**.

4. If you want your text box to have a default value when the form initially appears on the page, enter the text in the Initial Value field. In Figure 19.5, I don't know ..... ???? appears in the Initial Value field. This text appears in the actual form field by default. The user must delete the default value and enter a new value.

5. Enter the width, in characters, for the textbox in the Width in Characters field. The default width is 20 characters. In Figure 19.5, the width entered is 50 characters. This setting refers to the width of the textbox; it does not reflect the maximum length of the data that can be entered in it. Make sure that the width of the textbox is not too wide for the screen.

6. Enter the maximum number of characters for the response in the Maximum characters field. The maximum number is 256, which is also the default value.

7. If this textbox will be used for a password entry, select the Yes radio button in the Password field section. Select No for any other type of text input.

8. Click OK. The textbox appears on your page. Enter a label for the textbox on your page, or write an appropriate question above it, as in Figure 19.5.

You can change any property for the textbox after it appears on your page by selecting the textbox and choosing Edit I Properties, or by pressing Alt+Enter.

Requesting Multiline Text Input

Use the Insert I Form Field I Scrolling Text Box command to insert a multiline, or paragraph, textbox field on your form. Figure 19.6 shows a scrolling textbox.

Figure 19.6.
Scrolling textboxes are used for lengthy text responses.

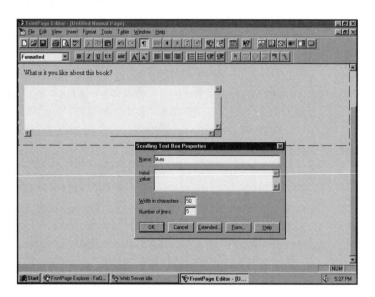

To place a scrolling textbox on your form,

1. From the FrontPage Editor, position the insertion point where you want to insert the textbox field.

2. Choose Insert I Form Field I Scrolling Text Box, or click the Scrolling Text Box button on the Forms toolbar. The Scrolling Text Box Properties dialog box appears.

3. In the Name field, enter a name for the scrolling text field. This name coincides with the name/value pair that is reported to the form handler.

4. If you want the scrolling textbox to have a default value when the form initially appears on the page, enter the text in the Initial Value field.

5. Enter the width, in characters, for the scrolling textbox in the Width in characters field. The default width is 20 characters. Make sure that the width of the textbox is not too wide for the screen.

6. Enter the height of the scrolling textbox in the Number of Lines field. The default height is 2.

7. Click OK. The scrolling textbox appears on your page. Enter a label for the scrolling textbox on your page.

You can change any property for the scrolling textbox after it appears on your page by selecting the scrolling textbox and choosing Edit I Properties, or by pressing Alt+Enter.

Requesting Input from Checkboxes

Use checkboxes to give the user a Boolean choice, such as Yes/No or True/False. Checkboxes also are used to present a multiple list of items from which the user can select single or multiple choices. Figure 19.7 shows several checkboxes.

Figure 19.7.
Checkboxes allow the user to select or deselect a choice in your form.

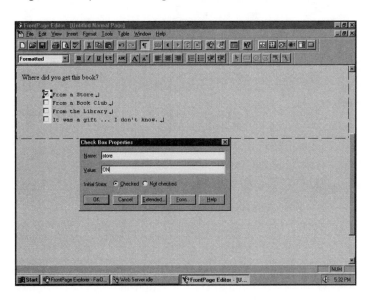

TIP: Checkboxes are often arranged in groups. You can place the first one on your form and copy it and its label to your clipboard. Then you can paste in the additional checkboxes and edit the properties of the copies. This saves you a few extra steps, and it helps you visualize the layout.

To place a checkbox on your form:

1. From the FrontPage Editor, position the insertion point where you want to insert the checkbox.

2. Choose Insert I Form Field I Check Box, or click the Check Box button on the Forms toolbar. The Check Box Properties dialog box appears.

3. In the Name field, enter a name for the checkbox. This name coincides with the name/value pair that is reported to the form handler. The name should relate to the label that you put beside the checkbox.

4. In the Value field, enter a value for the checkbox. It is easiest to enter a value that makes sense when you receive the results for the form. Usually, you enter the value that represents the checked state of the checkbox. The default value is "ON" when the box is checked. The value `No if checked` helps avoid confusion if the response requires a negative answer.

5. In the Initial State field, select either the Checked or Not Checked radio button. The default value is Not Checked, which means that the user must check the box.

6. Click OK. The checkbox appears on your page. Enter a label for the checkbox on your page.

You can change any property for the checkbox after it appears on your page by selecting the checkbox and choosing Edit I Properties, or by pressing Alt+Enter.

Requesting Input from Radio Buttons

Radio buttons are similar to checkboxes in that they are used to give the user a Boolean choice. Typically, radio buttons are arranged in a group and are assigned a group name. The user selects only one option, as in Figure 19.8. The group name and the value assigned to each selected button are sent to the form handler after the user submits the form.

To place radio buttons on your form:

1. From the FrontPage Editor, position the insertion point where you want to insert the first radio button.

2. Choose Insert I Form Field I Radio Button, or click the Radio Button on the Forms toolbar. The Radio Button Properties dialog box appears.

3. In the Group Name field, enter a name for the group of radio buttons. This name is assigned to all the radio buttons in the group, and it coincides with the name/value pair that is reported to the form handler.

Figure 19.8.

Radio buttons are used to give the user a Boolean choice. They typically are arranged in groups, and usually one button of the group is selected.

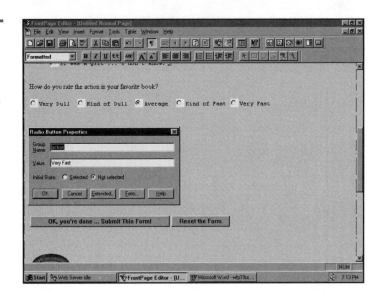

TIP: Inserting radio buttons is one time when copying the first button and pasting copies to your form really helps. You can keep the group name consistent if you enter the properties for the first radio button and copy additional radio buttons on the page.

4. In the Value field, enter a value for the individual radio button.

5. In the Initial State field, select either the Selected or Not Selected radio button. The default value is Not Selected, which means that the user must select a button.

6. Click OK. The radio button appears on your page. Enter a label for the radio button.

7. Repeat steps 1 through 6 for each radio button in the group.

You can change any property for the radio button after it appears on your page by selecting the radio button and choosing Edit | Properties, or by pressing Alt+Enter.

 Providing a Menu of Choices

Menus are used to present the user with a list of defined choices. Items are displayed in either a drop-down list or a scrolling list. You can configure a drop-down menu list to permit single or multiple selections. Figure 19.9 shows a single-selection drop-down list.

Figure 19.9.

Drop-down lists contain a list of selections from which the user can choose. They can be configured for single or multiple selections.

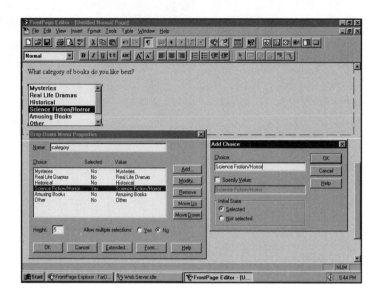

To place a drop-down menu on your form:

1. From the FrontPage Editor, position the insertion point where you want to insert the drop-down menu.

2. Choose Insert I Form Field I Drop-Down Menu, or click the Drop-Down Menu button on the Forms toolbar. The Drop-Down Menu Properties dialog box appears.

3. In the Name field, enter a name for the drop-down menu field that appears on your page. This name coincides with the name/value pair that is reported to the form handler.

For each item that you want to add in the drop-down menu, complete these steps:

1. Select Add Choice.

2. In the Choice field, enter the name of the item.

3. Normally, the menu choice name you enter in step 2 is sent to the form handler along with its value (selected or not selected). You can specify an optional value to be sent to the form handler in place of the choice name. To do this, check the Specify Value checkbox. In the Optional Value field, enter an optional value to send to the form handler.

4. In the Initial State field, select either the Selected or Not Selected radio button. The default value is Not Selected.

5. Click OK. The menu items appear in the order in which you created them.

After you enter your menu list items, complete the menu list as follows:

1. In the Allow Multiple Selections field, choose Yes if you want to permit multiple selections from the drop-down menu. Choose No for single selections.

2. In the Height field of the Drop-Down Menu Properties dialog box, enter the number of rows that drop-down menu list should display.

3. Choose OK to apply all the settings to the drop-down list.

Based on the Height and Allow Multiple Settings values, the drop-down menu can appear in several ways. Table 19.1 shows how most browsers display a drop-down menu based on your choices.

Table 19.1. Drop-down menu appearances.

Height	Multiple	Appearance
1	No	Displays as a drop-down list
1	Yes	Displays as a scrollable list with half-height arrows
2 or above	No	Displays as a scrollable list with half-height arrows
2 or above	Yes	Displays as a scrollable list with half-height arrows (may be difficult to use unless the list height is sufficient to display all or most items in the drop-down menu list)

Inserting Buttons on Forms

Pushbutton fields are used to submit or reset the data that the user enters in form fields. You can insert more than one pushbutton on a form, as Figure 19.10 shows.

FrontPage provides two types of pushbuttons that can be used with the FrontPage form handling bots: a Submit button and a Reset button. You can write custom CGI scripts to add additional buttons to your form and to assign other names and values to them.

To place a pushbutton on your form:

1. From the FrontPage Editor, position the insertion point where you want to insert the pushbutton.

2. Choose Insert I Form Field I Push Button or click the Push Button button on the Forms toolbar. The Push Button Properties dialog box appears.

3. In the Name field, enter a name for the pushbutton. This name coincides with the name/value pair that is reported to the form handler.

Figure 19.10.

Pushbuttons are used to submit or clear the data from the form.

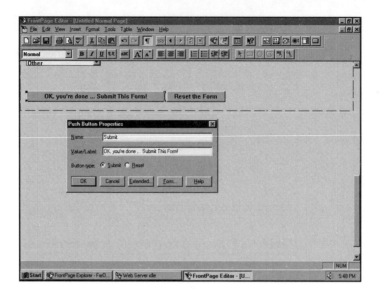

4. In the Value/Label field, enter a value for the pushbutton. By default, the value Submit appears as a label for a Submit button, and the value Reset appears as a label for a Reset button. The default labels are replaced with the values that you enter in this field.

5. Select the type of button that you want to insert. The choices are Submit and Reset.

6. Click OK. The pushbutton appears on your page.

You can change any property for the pushbutton after it appears on your page by selecting the pushbutton and choosing Edit I Properties, or by pressing Alt+Enter.

 # Using Image Form Fields

If you write custom form handlers, you can use image form fields to submit data entered on your forms. The button shown beneath the standard form buttons in Figure 19.11 is an image form field. When a user submits a form by clicking an image field, FrontPage passes the coordinates from the image's coordinate system to the form handler. The bots do not use this coordinate information, so you must create a custom form handler to process the coordinates.

To place an image form field on your form:

1. From the FrontPage Editor, choose Insert I Form Field I Image. The Insert Image dialog box appears.

2. Choose an image. The method that you use depends on the source of the image.

Figure 19.11.

You can use images as buttons in a form field if you use custom CGI scripts.

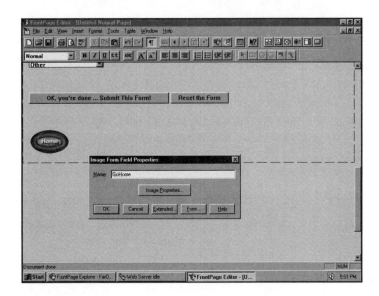

To insert an image from the current web, click the image title or URL that appears in the Insert Image dialog box. Then click OK.

To insert an image from a file on your local or network hard drive, click the From File button. Locate the file in its drive or directory. Choose a file type from the Files of Type drop-down menu to list all the files of a single type. Select the file that you want to insert, and click Open, or double-click the filename to open it.

To insert an image from the World Wide Web, click the From URL button. Enter the URL of the image, and click OK. This image is not added to the current web. Instead, it is inserted from its remote location on the Web.

3. After you select the image, the Image Form Field Properties dialog box appears. Assign a name to the image form field in the Name field. This name is sent to the form handler.

4. To change the image properties, click the Image Properties button. The Image Properties dialog box appears. The default link field is disabled because you cannot create a link from an image field. Click OK to exit the Image Properties dialog box.

5. Click OK to insert the image form field on your form.

 # Using Hidden Form Fields

Use hidden form fields to pass information from one form to another. For example, the Product Data Sheet that you created with the Corporate Presence Web (see

See Chapter 20,
"Runtime Bots: The
Heartbeat of FrontPage
Forms," for an example
of how hidden form
fields are used.

Chapter 6, "Real-Life Examples") contains an information request form. This information request form uses a hidden form field to pass the name of the product to the results file and to the confirmation form that is sent to the user.

You can use hidden form fields in other ways as well. Suppose, for example, that your first form has a question such as How long ago did you read this book? and that the user responds 16 days. A custom CGI script looks at that value and determines that the user read the book within the last month. The CGI script returns a hidden form field from the first form, shown in Figure 19.12, to the user in a form on another page that says You read your favorite book in the last 1 month.

Figure 19.12.
Hidden form fields are used to pass information from one form to another.

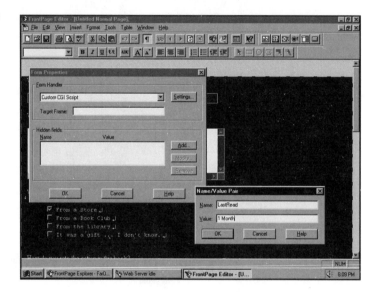

To create a hidden form field:

1. In the FrontPage Editor, double-click any form field to open its Properties dialog box. The Form Field Properties dialog box appears.

2. Click the Form button. The Form Properties dialog box appears.

3. Click the Add button. The Name/Value Pair dialog box appears.

4. Enter a name in the Name field.

5. Enter a value to associate with the name in the Value field. The value can be any text string.

6. Click OK to close the Name/Value Pair, Form Properties, and Form Field Properties dialog boxes.

To modify a hidden form field:

1. In the FrontPage Editor, double-click any form field to open its Properties dialog box. The Form Field Properties dialog box appears.
2. Click the Form button. The Form Properties dialog box appears.
3. In the Form Properties dialog box, select the field to change from the Hidden Fields section.
4. Click the Modify button. The Name/Value Pair dialog box appears.
5. Edit the values in the Name field or the Value field.
6. Click OK to close the Name/Value Pair, Form Properties, and Form Field Properties dialog boxes.

To delete a hidden form field:

1. In the FrontPage Editor, double-click any form field to open its Properties dialog box. The Form Field Properties dialog box appears.
2. Click the Form button. The Form Properties dialog box appears.
3. In the Form Properties dialog box, select the field to change from the Hidden Fields section.
4. Click the Remove button. The hidden form field is removed from the list.
5. Click OK to close the Hidden Form Field, Form Properties, and Form Field Properties dialog boxes.

Workshop Wrap-Up

You already learned how to create forms quickly by using the Form Page Wizard. In this chapter, you learned how to add your own form fields and edit their properties. There now remains one major step in designing your forms, which you learn about in the next chapter.

Chapter Summary

In this chapter, you learned about the various form fields that you can use. You learned how to insert them in your Web pages and how to configure each type of field. You also learned some tips to help you align your form fields just as the Form Page Wizard does.

Next Steps

In the next chapter, you learn how to assign a form handler to your forms and what the runtime bots do. You can find related information in the following chapters:

❑ Refer to Chapter 3, "Can We Talk?" to learn how to configure a discussion group easily. The steps outlined in this chapter help you edit the form fields created in your discussion groups.

❑ Refer to Chapter 5, "Lots of Pages—The Template Way," to learn which pages contain forms that are already made for you.

Q&A

Q: What about extended attributes? All the Form Field Properties dialog boxes have Extended Attributes buttons on them.

A: FrontPage has all the attributes for each form field built in. The Extended Attributes button is there in case you need them in the future.

Q: Can I design a form from scratch and not use the templates or the Form Page Wizard?

A: Yes, but the Form Page Wizard streamlines the task by taking care of the layout. Using it is a much quicker way of designing a form.

Q: I don't like the way my form looks. What is the easiest way to delete it and start over again?

A: There are a couple of ways in which you can delete a form from a page. For example, delete every object on the form and use the Backspace or Delete key to delete the form. To delete a form field, use the Delete or Backspace key. Alternatively, position the cursor in the upper left corner of the form, where it turns into a selection pointer. Double-click to select the entire form and cut the page to the clipboard, or use the Del key to delete the form from the page.

TWENTY

Runtime Bots: The Heartbeat of FrontPage Forms

Throughout this book, I've noted where pages contain features requiring that the FrontPage Server Extensions be on your remote server's site. The pages I referred to were mostly forms that incorporated one of FrontPage's runtime bots.

For the beginner, adding advanced features to Web pages can be a daunting task. FrontPage puts advanced features well within the capability of beginning page developers with the use of its advanced bots. These bots work with the server at runtime to process information; they allow a user to submit requests or information to your site that you can use many different ways.

What These Bots Do

What are these runtime bots, and why are they so special? Well, if it weren't for these bots, you'd need to write custom scripts to instruct your server how to handle the forms you create. This isn't an easy task for a beginner, which is one reason there are as many books on scripting languages as there are on HTML programming. Scout the shelves in your local bookstore sometime, and you'll see rows of books on CGI, Perl, Java, JavaScript, VBScript, and countless other languages that can be used with your Web pages. With these scripting languages, you can add functionality to your Web pages—if you want to get into programming, that is.

For those who don't want to learn all those other programming techniques, you have the FrontPage bots to fall back on, which are really nothing more than custom CGI scripts designed to work with the FrontPage Server Extensions—like the "plug-and-play" of Web pages.

Five bots work with forms: the Discussion bot, the Registration bot, the Save Results bot, the Search bot, and the Confirmation Field bot. You may choose any but the Search bot and the Confirmation Field bot when you configure a form handler for your form. The Search bot and Confirmation Field bot are inserted with the Insert I Bot command but work with form fields, as you will learn later in this chapter.

Why These Bots Need the FrontPage Server Extensions

You might ask, "Why do these bots need the server extensions, but the ones discussed in Chapter 15, "Automating Pages with Bots," don't?"

The bots you learned about in the "Advanced Techniques" section don't require the FrontPage Server Extensions because they don't need user input to function. You control the content of those bots at design time, and their content is placed onto your pages in conventional form once your pages go out on the Web.

The runtime bots discussed in this chapter are basically CGI scripts written to be compatible with FrontPage and the Windows 95 or Windows NT operating system. They work seamlessly with FrontPage's Personal Web Server, which is why you can test the forms with your favorite browser while the Personal Web Server is running.

More often than not, when your Web pages are placed "out there," they reside on a server that runs on a UNIX or Windows NT operating system. The runtime bots process the user's entries when he or she clicks the Submit button on your form. An executable file in your FrontPage-enabled Web site translates the data from your FrontPage form into language the UNIX or Windows NT Server expects to see. That executable file is part of the FrontPage Server Extensions that need to reside on your remote server. In this case, the server extensions act as the go-between from the FrontPage bots to your server's operating system.

When Your Server Doesn't Have the Server Extensions

You'll learn about the executable files and where they reside in Chapter 24, "Working with the FrontPage Servers."

I'll show you where you can add the configurations for these alternatives in this chapter and in Chapter 21, "Using Your Own HTML Code."

I'll recommend some online sources for you in Appendix C, "Directory of Resources."

You'll learn some of the advantages of using JavaScript or VBScript in Chapter 21.

If your service provider doesn't have the FrontPage Server Extensions installed, you do have other options for adding interactivity to your Web site.

To use these alternative options, you need to understand how to work with CGI (other scripting languages will be discussed in Chapter 21). Unfortunately, it gets rather involved to discuss the different options and types of forms you can configure with CGI scripts on a case-by-case basis. That subject goes far beyond the scope of this book because so many variables come into play, such as using platform-specific scripts, assigning directory permissions, and other advanced topics requiring some knowledge of the CGI scripting language.

Here are some options you can use to add forms to your pages:

❏ Configure your form to use a custom CGI script, as discussed in "How to Assign Custom CGI Scripts," later in this chapter.

❏ Design your Web pages for a Java-enabled browser and use JavaScript to develop a form.

❏ Design the form on your Web page with VBScript.

With the basic information out of the way, the following sections will explain what each of the bots do and how you can use and configure them.

Discussion Bot

In Chapter 3, you learned how to add discussion groups to your Web site by using templates and wizards, but you can also create your own discussion groups with the Discussion bot. This bot enables you to create an online discussion on your Web site. It collects information from a form, formats the results into an HTML page, and adds the new page to a table of contents and to a text index. It also gathers information from the form and stores it in one of several formats.

Registration Bot

In Chapter 6, "Real-Life Examples," you learned how to register an end user for participation in a closed section of your Web site. The registration form you placed in your root Web uses a Registration bot, which lets users register for access to a service or portion of your Web site. A Registration bot adds the user to the server's authentication database, gathers information from the form, and then stores it in one of several formats, as discussed in "Configuring a Results File," later in this chapter.

Save Results Bot

The Save Results bot is the general-purpose form handler in FrontPage. It is used for many types of forms. Survey forms, guest books, information forms, and online ordering forms are some examples of what you can use a Save Results bot for. It gathers information from a form and stores it in a variety of Web page and text formats.

Search Bot

The Search bot creates a list of links to pages containing one or more words—that is, the search term—entered by the user in the form. The results returned to the user list pages in which his or her search term appears. The list can also include the file's date and size and the score for the quality of the search term's match.

Confirmation Field Bot

When a user submits a response to a form on your page, you use a confirmation page to acknowledge his or her post. For this type of page, you use the Insert I Bot command to place a Confirmation Field bot on your page for each name/value pair you want to acknowledge. The Confirmation Field bot retrieves the information the user entered into your form and places his or her response on the confirmation page.

Assigning a Form Handler to a Form

To use any of the bots mentioned in this chapter, you first develop a Web page containing form fields appropriate for the type of bot you're assigning. After you design the form, assign one of the bots as a form handler by following these steps:

1. In the FrontPage Editor, right-click any form field in the form to open the pop-up menu.

2. Choose Form Properties to open the Form Properties dialog box, shown in Figure 20.1.

3. Select the type of form handler from the Form Handler field. You can choose one of the following options:

> Custom CGI Script
> Discussion Bot
> Registration Bot
> Save Results Bot

4. Click Settings to configure the form handler. Edit the form handler settings as outlined in the tasks in the following sections.

5. Click OK to exit the Settings dialog box.

6. Click OK to close the Form Properties dialog box.

Figure 20.1.

Use the Form Properties dialog box to assign a form handler to a form.

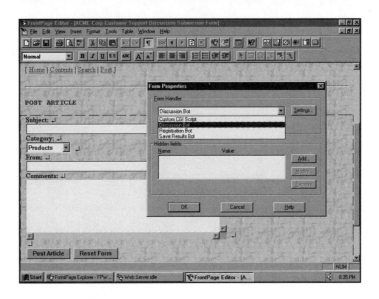

When and Where to Use a Discussion Form

You can add a Discussion bot to a page that you create yourself. You'll need at least the following pages to completely configure a Discussion bot:

❑ A discussion submission form on which to place the Discussion bot. This submission page can include the headers and footers you use on the other pages in your Web site, or you can design a separate header and footer for the submission form.

❑ A header and footer for the discussion articles saved to your Web site.

Creating a Discussion Form

The easiest way to add a discussion group to your Web site is to use the Discussion Wizard, discussed in Chapter 3. This wizard streamlines the process of creating a discussion group because the required forms and pages are automatically created and linked for you. You can then use the procedures outlined in the following numbered steps to configure or revise the Discussion bot on the Discussion Submission form. An example of this form from the ACME Corp Customer Support Discussion project in Chapter 6 is shown in Figure 20.2.

Figure 20.2.

The Customer Support Discussion Submission form you created in Chapter 6 uses a Discussion bot.

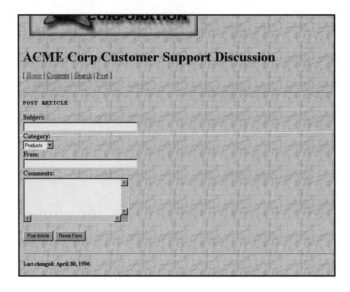

To add and configure a Discussion bot, follow these steps:

1. Design the form fields for your discussion submission form.

2. Using the steps outlined in the earlier section "Assigning a Form Handler to a Form," choose the Discussion bot.

3. Click Settings to configure the Discussion bot. The Settings for Discussion Form Handler dialog box appears. By default, it opens to the Discussion tab.

Configuring the Discussion

Use the Discussion tab of the Settings for Discussion Form Handler dialog box, shown in Figure 20.3, to configure the discussion and its table of contents arrangement. The steps to configure the Discussion bot are as follows:

1. Enter a title for the discussion group in the Title field.

2. In the Directory field, enter a directory name in which to place the discussion group articles. The directory name is limited to eight characters and must be preceded by an underscore (for example, _accsd). The underscore is one of the eight characters in the directory name.

NOTE: To view the discussion group directories in the FrontPage Explorer, choose Tools I Web Settings, click the Advanced tab, and check Show documents in hidden directories.

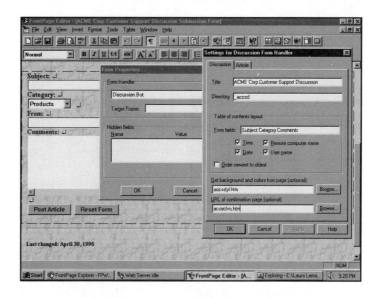

Figure 20.3.

Use the Settings for Discussion Form Handler dialog box to configure your discussion.

3. In the Table of contents layout section, complete the following:

> **Form fields**. In this section of the dialog box, enter the fields you want to appear at the top of the discussion articles, separating each with a space (for example, Subject Category Comments).

> **Time**. If you select this option, the table of contents includes the time an article was written.

> **Date**. If you select this option, the table of contents includes the date an article was written.

> **Remote computer name**. If you select this option, the table of contents includes the remote computer name of the article's author.

> **User name**. If you select this option, the table of contents includes the name of the article's author.

> **Order newest to oldest**. Uncheck this option to sort the articles in the order in which they were created, but check it to place the most recent articles at the top of the table of contents.

4. If you want to use a style sheet from your current Web site, enter the URL of the style sheet in the Get background and colors from page field, or use the Browse button to select a page from your current Web site.

5. If you want to send a confirmation page to the user after he or she submits an article, enter the page's URL in the URL of confirmation page field, or use the Browse button to select a page from your current Web site.

6. Click the Article tab to continue with the article settings.

Configuring the Discussion Articles

You use the Article tab, shown in Figure 20.4, to configure the articles in the discussion.

Figure 20.4.

Use the Article tab to assign a header and footer to your discussion articles.

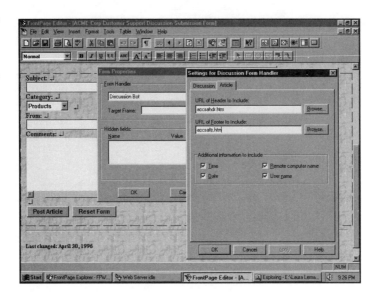

A confirmation page uses a Confirmation Field bot, discussed in the task "Confirming Pages," later in this chapter.

To configure your articles, follow these steps:

1. To configure the discussion articles, click the Article tab in the Settings for Discussion Form Handler dialog box.

2. Enter the URL of the article header in the URL of Header to Include field, or use the Browse button to select a page from your current Web site.

3. Enter the URL of the article footer in the URL of Footer to Include field, or use the Browse button to select a page from your current Web site.

4. Select any or all of the following items to include on each discussion article:

    Time. If you select this option, the article includes the time it was written.

    Date. If you select this option, the article includes the date it was written.

    Remote computer name. If you select this option, the article includes the remote computer name of its author.

    User name. If you select this option, the article includes the author's name.

5. Choose OK to assign the Discussion bot properties to your form.

When and Where to Use the Registration Bot

The Registration bot is used when you design a form that registers a user for an event or to gain entry to a protected Web page on your site. In Chapter 6, you placed the form shown in Figure 20.5 in your root Web. This form uses a Registration bot. FrontPage gives you two templates to help you develop your own registration forms:

❏ The Product or Event Registration page template uses a Registration bot to register a user for product or warranty service or an event taking place.

❏ The User Registration page template registers a user to gain access to a protected Web site.

Figure 20.5.

Registration bots are used on user registration forms or to register for a product or an event.

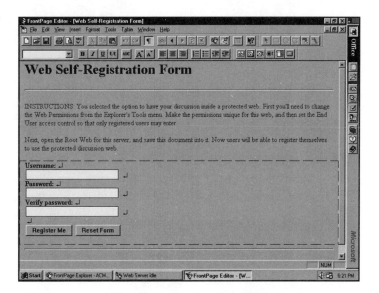

 Creating Your Own Registration Pages

You can use either of the templates as guidelines to create your own registration form; follow these steps:

1. Design the form fields for your registration form.

2. Using the steps outlined in the earlier section "Assigning a Form Handler to a Form," choose the Registration bot.

3. Click Settings to configure the Registration bot. The Settings for Registration Form Handler dialog box, shown in Figure 20.6, appears. By default, it opens to the Registration tab.

Figure 20.6.

Use the Registration tab to assign a restricted web to your registration form and to assign name and password fields.

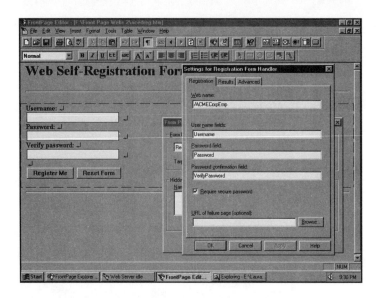

4. In the Web name field, enter the web name you're creating the Registration Form for. The web name relates to the server. The registration form is normally placed in the root web. If you are registering a child web of the root, the URL looks something like this:

   `/ACMECorpEmp`

5. In the User name fields field, enter the names of one or more form fields on the registration form, separating them by commas or spaces. The Registration bot constructs the user name from these fields. The values you enter here should agree with the fields you inserted in your form.

   ❑ If the user enters his or her name in a single field, your entry might look like this:

   `Username`

   ❑ If the user enters his or her name in two fields, your entry might look like this:

   `First, Last`

   ❑ If the user enters his or her name in three fields, your entry might look like this:

   `First, Middle, Last`

6. In the Password field section, enter the name of the form field in which the user enters his or her password.

7. In the Password confirmation field section, enter the name of the form field in which the user enters his or her password confirmation.

8. If you want the user to enter a secure password, check the Require secure password checkbox so that the user must enter a password that has at least six characters and doesn't partially match his or her name. Password fields display an asterisk for each character entered by the user.

9. To specify a failure page, enter its URL in the URL of failure page (optional) field, or use the Browse button to select a page from your current Web site. If the user doesn't enter a name and password that appears in your server's authentication database, a failure page returns. This page can inform the user that he or she needs to enter a correct password to gain access to the page or Web site.

10. Click OK to configure the registration form.

You create the authentication database when you add administrators, authors, or end users to a Web site. See Chapter 23, "Web Maintenance and Administration," for instructions on how to assign permissions for your webs.

See the later sections "Configuring a Results File" and "Configuring a Second Results File" for instructions on how to complete the Results and Advanced tabs in the Settings for Registration Form Handler dialog box.

When and Where to Use the Save Results Bot

The Save Results bot is used as a form handler for general forms you place in your web, such as the Feedback Form template, the Guest Book template, and the Survey Form template. The Information Request Form in the Product Data Sheets you created in Chapter 6 also uses a Save Results bot. This page is shown in Figure 20.7. You can use any of these examples as guidelines to develop your own forms.

Figure 20.7.
The Save Results bot can be used for forms of a general nature.

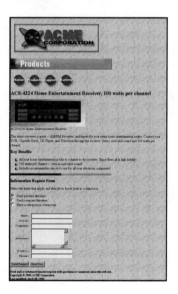

Creating a General Form

To create a general form, use one of the above mentioned templates or design your own form with the Form Page Wizard; these methods help make the form layout a lot easier. After your form is designed, you can assign the Save Results bot as follows:

1. Using the steps outlined in the earlier section "Assigning a Form Handler to a Form," choose the Save Results bot. The Settings for Saving Results of Form dialog box appears.

2. Use the steps outlined in the following section, "Configuring a Results File," to complete the settings in the Results tab. This is the default tab for the dialog box.

3. Use the steps outlined in the subsequent sections, "Configuring a Second Results File" and "Adding Additional Fields," to complete the settings in the Advanced tab.

Configuring a Results File

Both the Registration bot and the Save Results bot offer you a choice of configuring a results file. The Results tab, shown in Figure 20.8, is identical for both bots.

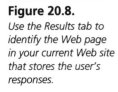

Figure 20.8.

Use the Results tab to identify the Web page in your current Web site that stores the user's responses.

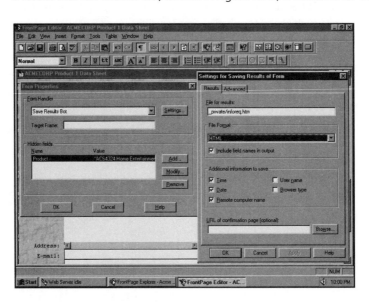

❑ To configure a results file for a Registration bot, click the Results tab (the second tab) in the Settings for Registration Form Handler dialog box.

❑ To configure a results file for a Save Results bot, click the Results tab (the first tab) in the Settings for Saving Results of Form dialog box.

Both bots offer several choices for how you store the results from forms on your Web site. To configure the results file for either of these bots, follow these steps:

1. Enter the name and location of the file to place the form results in the File for results field. If the file does not exist, the bot creates the file the first time the form is submitted. If you want to save your results file in text format, be sure to enter a .txt extension when you specify the filename.

   ❑ To save the results to a file in your current Web site, supply a page URL with a full path and filename.

   ❑ To save the results to a file outside your current Web site (to a location on your server's file system), supply an absolute filename and folder (the full path and filename).

NOTE: When you collect information you will read from a Web browser or from FrontPage, you have the option to supply an .html or .htm extension. This causes the FrontPage Server Extensions to generate the HTML at runtime, which could make your Web site slower as more results are appended to the page. You can also save your results in formatted text format or periodically edit the results page and paste its contents into another Web page on your server.

2. Select the format you would like to store the results file in. The first four options are used when you specify a results file with an .htm or .html extension. The latter four options are used when you specify a results file with a .txt extension. The choices are as follows:

   HTML. This is the default style. When you select this option, your results file is stored in an HTML page that uses normal text with line endings, as shown in Figure 20.9.

   HTML definition list. When you select this option, your results file appears in a definition list. The names of the form fields appear as terms, and the values of the form fields appear as the definition. An example is shown in Figure 20.10.

   HTML bulleted list. When you choose this option, your results file appears in a bulleted list, as shown in Figure 20.11.

   Formatted text within HTML. When you choose this option, your results file appears in formatted paragraphs with line endings, as shown in Figure 20.12.

Figure 20.9.

A results file stored in HTML format.

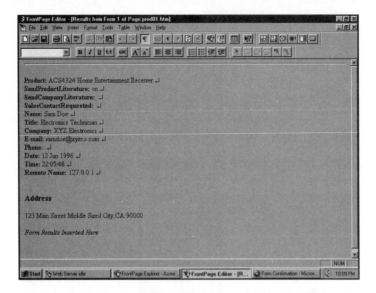

Figure 20.10.

A results file stored in HTML definition list format.

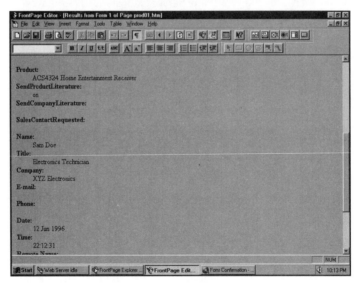

Figure 20.11.

A results file stored in HTML bulleted list format.

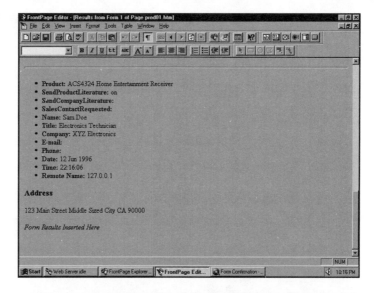

Figure 20.12.

A results file stored in formatted text within HTML format.

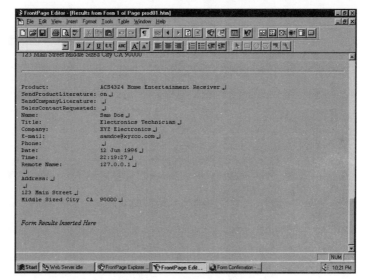

Formatted text. When you choose this option, the results file appears in formatted text, as shown in Figure 20.13.

Text database using comma as a separator. This option specifies a text file that uses commas to separate the values in the results file. An example is shown in Figure 20.14.

Figure 20.13.

A results file stored in formatted text format.

Figure 20.14.

A results file stored in the format text database using comma as a separator.

Text database using tab as a separator. This option specifies a text file which uses tabs to separate the values in a results file. Many database or spreadsheet applications allow you to import files of this type. An example is shown in Figure 20.15.

Figure 20.15.

A results file stored in the format text database using tab as a separator.

Text database using space as a separator. This option specifies a text file that uses spaces to separate the values in a results file, as shown in Figure 20.16. These files can be used with spreadsheet or database applications and are recommended for single-word responses to maintain proper formatting of the items in the database.

3. Check Include field names in output to save both the name and value of each form field. If you uncheck this option, only the responses from the user will be written to the file.

Figure 20.16.
A results file stored in the format text database using space as a separator.

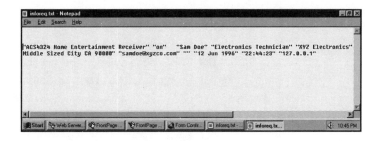

4. In the Additional information to save section, choose any or all of the following additional items to save in the results file:

   Time. If you select this option, the results file includes the time it was written.

   Date. If you select this option, the results file includes the date it was written.

   Remote computer name. If you select this option, the results file includes the remote computer name of the respondent.

   User name. If you select this option, the results file includes the respondent's name.

   Browser type. If you select this option, the results file includes the type of browser the respondent used.

5. In the URL of confirmation page (optional) field, enter the URL of the confirmation page you want to return to the user after he or she submits the form, or use the Browse button to select a page from your current Web site.

NOTE: The confirmation page notifies the user that his or her response has been received to the Web. If you don't specify a confirmation page, the Save Results bot generates and maintains one automatically for you. The confirmation page thanks the user for submitting the form and returns the contents of the form by using Confirmation Field bots.

You can enter one of three special attributes for a Registration bot confirmation page:

❑ Registration-Username designates the name of the user who is registering.

❑ Registration-Password specifies the password of the user who is registering.

❑ Registration-Error designates a sentence or two that describes an error condition at runtime.

Configuring a Second Results File

You can also choose to configure a second results file for the Registration bot or Save Results bot. This is done by using the Advanced tab, shown in Figure 20.17, in the Settings for Saving Results of Form or Settings for Registration Form Handler dialog box.

Figure 20.17.

Use the Advanced tab to configure a second results file or additional field selections.

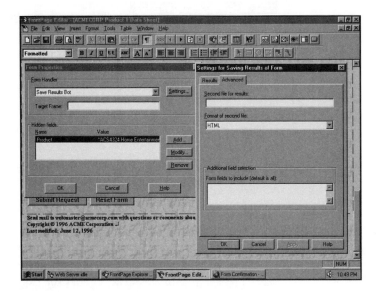

❏ To configure a second results file for a Registration bot, click the Advanced tab (the third tab) in the Settings for Registration Form Handler dialog box.

❏ To configure a second results file for a Save Results bot, click the Advanced tab (the second tab) in the Settings for Saving Results of Form dialog box.

Adding Additional Fields

Your form might have more fields than those available to choose from in the first tab of the Settings for Registration Form Handler or Settings for Saving Results of Form dialog box. By default, the results file returns all information on the form itself. You can use the Advanced tab to specify which additional fields the Registration Form or Save Results bot returns.

❏ To configure additional fields for a Registration bot, click the Advanced tab (the third tab) in the Settings for Registration Form Handler dialog box.

❏ To configure additional fields for a Save Results bot, click the Advanced tab (the second tab) in the Settings for Saving Results of Form dialog box.

When and Where to Use a Search Bot

If your site is very large, including a search form in your Web site allows visitors to find topics of interest quickly and easily. There's really no hard-and-fast rule for where to put a search form in your Web; the following list offers some ideas:

❏ You can place a Search bot on your home page so that users can find it right away.

❏ You can create a search form on a page of its own and provide links to it from the main pages in your Web site.

❏ You can include a search form on your Table of Contents page.

❏ If your Web site contains several child webs, you can place several Search bots on a single page and place the page in your root web.

Creating and Configuring a Search Form

You can create a search form that searches your entire Web site, a portion of it, or just discussion articles. Figure 20.18 shows an example of the search form generated with the Discussion wizard, as discussed in Chapter 3.

Figure 20.18.
A search form can be configured to search your entire Web site or just a portion of it.

ACME CORPORATION

ACME Corp Customer Support Discussion

[Home | Contents | Search | Post]

SEARCH FOR ARTICLE

Find articles posted to this discussion containing matching words or patterns.

Search for:

Start Search   Reset

Last changed: April 30, 1996

To create a search form, follow these steps:

1. Design the page on which you want to insert the Search bot. You'll want to add some text that instructs the user how to enter text into the search form fields.

2. Position the insertion point where you want to place the search form.

3. Choose Insert I Bot, and choose Search from the Insert Bot dialog box. The Search Bot Properties dialog box, shown in Figure 20.19, appears.

Figure 20.19.

You place a Search bot on your page to create a search form.

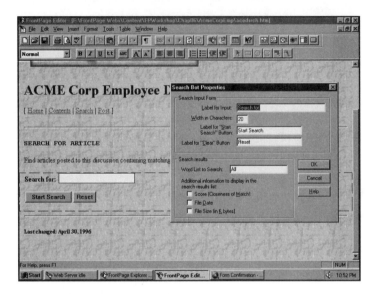

4. Configure the Search bot in the Search Bot Properties dialog box. The following settings can be configured in this dialog box:

Label for Input. Enter the label that you want to appear before the text input field on the search form. The default text is Search for:.

Width in Characters. Enter the width in characters of the input field, or select the default of 20. Note that this doesn't limit the length of text the user can enter in the field; rather, it limits the width of the text entry box. Take care not to make the width too wide for the page.

Label for "Start Search" Button. Enter the text you want to appear on the Start button, or accept the default of Start Search.

Label for "Clear" Button. Enter the text you want to appear on the Clear button, or accept the default of Reset.

5. Select the word list you want the Search bot to search through from the Word List to Search field. Choose one of the following:

   ❑ All. This searches the entire Web site except the discussion groups.

   ❑ Specify a discussion group directory to search a single discussion group. If you want to search a discussion group, its directories begin with an underscore (_).

6. Configure additional options for the Search bot as follows:

    Score. Indicates the quality of the match to the text the user enters.

    File Date. Reports the date and time of the document that matches the user's search entry. The date reported is the date the document was last modified.

    File Size. Reports the size of the matching document in kilobytes.

7. Choose OK to accept your selections and return to the FrontPage Editor.

When and Where to Use the Confirmation Field Bot

When a user sends a response from a form to your site, it's nice to send them a thank you with a confirmation form. It lets users know that their information has been received. The confirmation form can also include information about what you'll do with the information after you get it. For example, if you created a survey form, you can inform the user that once the survey is complete and tabulated, you'll post the results on your site. The confirmation page can be as simple as acknowledging that you received their information, as shown in Figure 20.20.

Figure 20.20.
Confirmation fields, which confirm responses from the user, are placed into pages with the Confirmation Field bot.

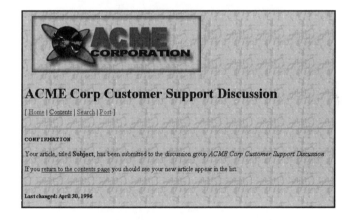

Confirming Pages

The Confirmation Field bot works somewhat the same as the Substitution bot (discussed in Chapter 15), except that it's directly tied to a Save Results bot or Discussion bot. The Confirmation Field bot works at runtime and requires processing from the server to insert its replacement text. It extracts information from the originating form and places the data on the confirming page.

To create a confirmation form, follow these steps:

1. Create the contents of the confirmation form.

2. Position the insertion point where you want to place the confirmation field.

3. Choose Insert I Bot I Confirmation Field to open the Confirmation Field Bot Properties dialog box shown in Figure 20.21.

Figure 20.21.

Enter a confirmation field in a page by using the Confirmation Field Bot Properties dialog box.

4. In the Confirmation Field Bot Properties dialog box, enter the name of one of the fields that appears in the form you're confirming. In the example shown, the Subject field from the Customer Support Discussion is being confirmed.

5. Choose OK. The name of the field is inserted into your confirmation form, surrounded by brackets.

6. Save the page to your Web, using the same URL you entered in the URL of confirmation page field for the form you're confirming.

When and Where to Use Custom CGI Scripts

You'll need to use CGI scripts (or other alternatives discussed in the next chapter) if your Internet Service Provider (ISP) doesn't have the FrontPage Server Extensions installed. You may also want to include advanced features in your form, such as automatically entering the results in a database or spreadsheet or tabulating totals in an online ordering form. In that case, some programming of your own is in order.

What's important to learn here is how to configure your FrontPage form to use that custom CGI script.

A form and CGI script are usually developed in concert with each other. The CGI script contains information on how to handle each of the form fields in the form, along with other instructions for the server. You can find several good examples of CGI scripts you can use, along with the HTML pages associated with them, at the following sites on the Web:

> Matt's Script Archive has several good forms with features similar to those some of the bots accomplish. You can find his site at `http://worldwidemart.com/scripts/`.

> Selena Sol's Public Domain CGI Script Archive also offers some creative examples of how you can use CGI scripts with forms, scripts, and Web page examples. The URL for this site is `http://www.eff.org/~erict/Scripts/`.

However, even if you use ready-made CGI scripts, you can still expect to spend some time on them. The CGI scripts have to be "tweaked" in many cases to get them up and running on your own site. You might also need to check with your service provider to see whether you can use custom CGI scripts on your site—and if so, where you are allowed to place them. Sometimes, CGI scripts must be assigned a `.cgi` extension to be recognized on the server; other times, they have to be placed in a specific directory to function properly. These particulars should be coordinated with your ISP before you configure your form. At that time, ask your service provider how to assign permissions for the form. They may already have a "frequently asked questions" page on their site that deals with these issues.

If all this sounds confusing, don't feel bad. CGI scripts are not something you can learn to work with in a few minutes; if you find you're still scratching your head after a few days of working with them, you won't be the first. There are several good resources on the Web for learning all about CGI scripts. They are listed in Appendix C, "Directory of Resources."

How to Assign Custom CGI Scripts

You assign a CGI script to your FrontPage form in much the same way as you assign any of the other form-handling bots—with the Form Properties command. The steps are as follows:

1. In the FrontPage Editor, double-click any form field in the form to open its Properties dialog box.
2. Click the Form Properties button to open the Form Properties dialog box.
3. Choose Custom CGI Script from the Form Handler field.

4. Click Settings to configure the form handler. The Setting For Custom Form Handler dialog box, shown in Figure 20.22, appears.

Figure 20.22.
Assign a custom CGI script for your form in the Settings For Custom Form Handler dialog box.

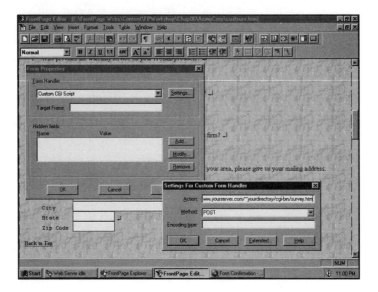

5. In the Action field, enter the absolute URL of the form handler. For example, if your form handler is named `guestbook.cgi` and it resides in the `/cgi-bin` subdirectory of your Web site, the absolute URL might look something like this:

   `http://www.yourserver.com/~yourdirectory/cgi-bin/guestbook.cgi`

6. In the Method field, enter the method the form handler needs to process the form. If you're using one of the examples from either of the sites mentioned earlier, you can see which method was used by examining the HTML page example provided with the CGI script. You typically will have one of the following options:

   Post (default). This method passes the name/value pairs to the form handler as input.

   Get. This method encodes the name/value pairs of the form and assigns the information to a server variable called `QUERY_STRING`.

NOTE:
The choice for the `Get` method is a bit tricky to access. Click the arrow in the Method field to drop the drop-down menu. Then, click the bottom arrow at the right side of the drop-down menu list (it's very narrow). You should see the `Get` method choice beneath the `Post` method choice.

7. In the Encoding type field, enter the default encoding method used for the form. If you leave this field blank, the following encoding method is used by default:

```
application/x-www-form-urlencoded
```

8. Click OK to close each of the Settings for Custom Form Handler and Form Properties dialog boxes.

Adding Extended Attributes to a Form

You can assign extended attributes to any form field that uses a custom CGI script as a form handler. To assign extended attributes to a form, follow these steps:

1. In the FrontPage Editor, double-click any form field to open its Properties dialog box, or select the entire form.

2. Click the Form Properties button. Make sure the Form Handler type is Custom CGI Script.

3. Click Settings to open the Settings for Custom Form Handler dialog box.

4. Click Extended to open the Extended Attributes dialog box.

5. Click Add to open the Set Attribute Value dialog box.

6. Enter the attribute's name in the Name field.

7. To associate a value with the name, check the Specify Value option and enter the attribute's value in the Value field. If the Specify Value option is checked and no value appears in the Value field, FrontPage associates the value with an empty string.

8. Click OK to close each of the Set Attribute Value, Extended Attributes, Setting for Custom Form Handlers, and Form Properties dialog boxes.

Other Ways to Use Forms

You can display forms in tables or frames much as you can any other type of content. To display a form in a table, create the form by using the Form Page wizard, or build your own as you've learned in this section. You can copy the form into the Clipboard and paste it into a table, or you can insert the form into another page with an Include bot.

You can also configure forms to direct their output to a frame. The steps are as follows:

1. In the FrontPage Editor, right-click any form field to open the pop-up menu.

2. Choose Form Properties to open the Form Properties dialog box.

3. In the Target Frame field, enter the name of the default target frame you want your form to appear in.

4. Click OK to close the Form Properties dialog box.

Workshop Wrap-Up

You should now know all the basics about designing forms in FrontPage. If you want to learn more about writing your own scripts, refer to the online sources listed in Appendix C. Other options you can use as an alternative to CGI will be discussed in the next chapter, "Using Your Own HTML Code."

Chapter Summary

In this chapter, you have learned how to configure FrontPage's runtime bots—the backbone of form handling in FrontPage, why you need the FrontPage Server Extensions to use the bots covered in this chapter, and the various ways you could store information you get from the user. You should now have an understanding of what really makes these forms tick.

Next Steps

This is the last chapter that covers the features "built-in" to FrontPage. In the next chapter, you'll learn how to go beyond what's built-in by inserting your own HTML code into your FrontPage pages.

For additional information on topics related to this chapter, refer to these chapters:

❏ Refer to Chapter 3, "Can We Talk?" for more information about discussions.

❏ Refer to Chapter 5, "Lots of Pages—The Template Way," to learn how you can create forms based on page templates.

❏ See Chapter 24, "Working with the FrontPage Servers," for more information about the FrontPage Server Extensions.

Q&A

Q: OK. I designed my form, I've got everything configured, my Internet Service Provider has the FrontPage Server Extensions installed. Is there anything else I need to know about forms?

A: Believe it or not, after three chapters, you've finally got it all. If you want to go beyond what you've learned, you can get even more interactivity if you write custom routines yourself.

Q: Where should I put the results files?

A: It's best to put them in a location where your Table of Contents can't find them. If your service provider has the FrontPage Server Extensions installed, the most likely place is the private directory because your Table of Contents bot doesn't look there. Browsers can't find that one, either.

Q: If I place more than one form on a single Web page, do their results go to the same file?

A: No, you can configure them to go to different files, just as you could if they were on separate pages. Of course, if you want all the forms on a single page to point to one results file, you can do that, too!

TWENTY ONE

Using Your Own HTML Code

What happens if you import a page into your FrontPage Web site that incorporates features that go beyond the capabilities of the FrontPage Editor? Or, better yet, what if you want to incorporate the latest and greatest features into your pages? It often simplifies the process to use an editor that automatically develops the HTML code for your Java, JavaScript, VBScript, or other page enhancements. But how do you bring those features into your Web pages?

FrontPage allows you to add extensibility to your pages for these types of situations. For HTML tags not covered in the FrontPage Editor interface or by extended attributes, use the HTML Markup bot.

In this chapter, you

❏ Learn how to insert code into your pages that goes beyond the capabilities of the FrontPage Editor

❏ Examine some of the tags that can be used to add extended features into your pages

❏ Learn how to add multimedia elements, such as background sounds and Marquees

❏ Learn how to add code that inserts Java, JavaScript, and VBScript applications into your Web pages

❏ Learn how to change the fonts on your Web pages

Tasks in this chapter:

❏ Getting Code into Your Pages

When the FrontPage Features Aren't Enough

The Web is like the weather: Wait five minutes, and it will change. As a result, it's hard for browser and Web page editing software programmers to predict what features they'll need to incorporate in their software. It's one of the reasons FrontPage gives you a couple of ways to add extensibility. For most tags, you can add extended features by using extended attributes. You've covered those already in previous chapters. However, for those tags that aren't covered in the FrontPage Editor, you can use the HTML Markup bot to enter code manually.

Getting Code into Your Pages

What the HTML Markup bot does is allow you to enter "snippets" of code that the FrontPage Editor doesn't write itself. It's really quite simple to use. Here's basically what you do:

1. Create as much as you can in the FrontPage Editor. After all, it's easy to use, and you can get a good idea of what your page layout looks like.

2. Position the insertion point where you want to add additional features by using code.

3. Choose Insert I Bot, then choose HTML Markup. The HTML Markup dialog box, shown in Figure 21.1, appears.

Figure 21.1.

Insert HTML code into your page with the HTML Markup dialog box.

4. Enter the code you want to include on the page in the HTML Markup dialog box, or cut and paste it from other editors.

5. Choose OK. FrontPage then inserts the code into your Web page. What you see on the FrontPage Editor screen is a small yellow rectangle with either an exclamation point (for comments) or a question mark (for code it won't check for correctness).

TIP: It's a good idea to also insert an Annotation bot near your HTML Markup bot to describe what the markup is there for. The Annotation bot text won't appear in other browsers, and you will have a reminder.

6. To edit the code in the HTML Markup bot, all you have to do is double-click that small yellow icon. The HTML Markup dialog box opens again, and you can edit your code.

Make It Easy: Create "Snippet" Pages

If you find you use the same markups over and over again, create a page that places all your Markup Bot icons in one place. Use an Annotation bot or text to describe the contents of each of the markups. To insert the markup into another page, simply highlight the icon you want to reuse, copy it into your Clipboard, and paste it into another page.

Viewing HTML Code with the FrontPage Editor

Choose the View I HTML command in the FrontPage Editor to view your HTML code. You can view the code in one of two ways:

Original HTML is the HTML code as it was when the FrontPage Editor opened the page. To view Original HTML, choose View I HTML and select Original from the View HTML window. The original source code for the current page is shown in Figure 21.2.

Generated HTML is the HTML code that FrontPage generates when it saves your current page. Any editing you added from the time the page was opened can be viewed here. To view Generated HTML, choose View I HTML, and select Generated from the View HTML window. An example of generated HTML is shown in Figure 21.3. Notice where the HTML Markup bot starts and ends. It begins with a statement like this:

```
<!-VERMEER BOT=HTMLMarkup StartSpan->
```

The code included in the HTML Markup bot ends with a statement like this one:

```
<!VERMEER BOT=HTMLMarkup End Span->
```

Figure 21.2.

The original HTML code as it appeared when you opened the page in the FrontPage Editor.

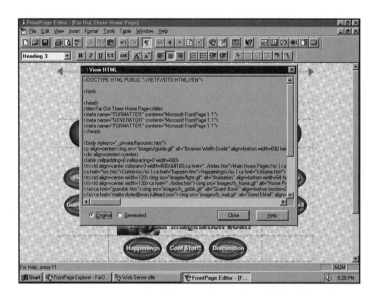

Figure 21.3.

The generated HTML code includes the code you entered since the file was opened.

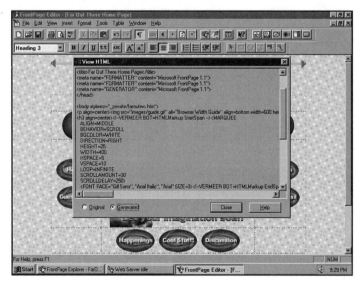

Some Examples for You

To give you an idea of how to use the HTML Markup bot, I've included some examples in this chapter. If you aren't familiar with HTML code and how it's structured, you might want to check out Laura Lemay's *Teach Yourself Web Publishing with HTML 3.0 in a Week — Second Edition*. It's a great book, complete with everything you want to know about every HTML command.

Font Face and Size

Most font attributes are set in the Character Styles dialog box, discussed in Chapter 9, "Composing and Editing Page Content." Microsoft Internet Explorer also supports the ability to display different font faces, which you can apply to your pages by using the HTML Markup bot.

To apply font faces to your pages, use the FACE attribute for the FONT tag. This attribute sets the typeface for the on-screen text (can be viewed only in Internet Explorer). The typefaces listed must be installed on the user's computer to display; otherwise, text is displayed in the default style the user chooses. In some instances, depending on the formatting you used in the FrontPage Editor, you might also need to include the FONT SIZE attribute in the HTML Markup bot.

To add a font face to your FrontPage Web pages, follow these steps:

1. Position the insertion point before the text you want to apply the font face to.

2. Choose Insert I Bot, and select the HTML Markup Bot.

3. In the HTML Markup dialog box, insert a line similar to the following:

   ```
   <FONT FACE="Arial">
   ```

   The text that follows this HTML Markup bot is displayed in Arial font if it's available on the user's computer (this font is installed with Windows). If that font doesn't exist, the text that follows the tag displays in the default font style (usually Times Roman).

   To add a SIZE attribute in addition to the FONT FACE tag, the code looks something like this:

   ```
   <FONT FACE="Arial" SIZE=3>
   ```

   This displays the text that follows in Arial text, if it exists on the user's computer, or the default font if the font does not reside on the user's computer. The font displays in Font Size 3 (12 point).

4. Position the insertion point at the end of the text for which you want to use this font, and enter the following in an HTML Markup bot:

`</FONT>`

Figure 21.4 shows two HTML Markup bots that mark the start and end of two paragraphs formatted in Arial font, Size 3, as described in the preceding example. Figure 21.5 shows what the same area looks like when you view the page in Internet Explorer.

Figure 21.4.

Two HTML Markup bots mark the start and end of the FONT FACE and SIZE formatting.

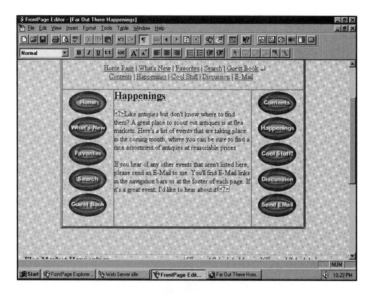

Figure 21.5.

When you view the page in Internet Explorer, the font displays in the specified style if it's available on the user's system.

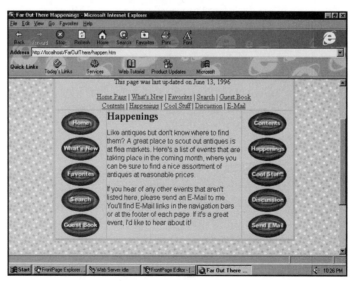

Frame-Related Tags

Frames are designed with the Frames Wizard. If you try to edit the page in the FrontPage Editor, the Frames Wizard opens again so you can edit the frame's configuration. The FrontPage Editor has the majority of the frame tags built in, but Internet Explorer 3.0 (now in beta) offers the ability to display a couple of additional attributes for frames. At present, there's no way to add extended attributes or HTML Markup bots to frame sets by using the Frames Wizard.

If you really want to use either of these tags, there is a workaround method. Use the Open With command (available from the pop-up menu in the FrontPage Explorer) to open your frame set by using a text editor such as Notepad or WordPad. Near the beginning of the page, you'll see each frame described in a line beginning with the following text:

```
<frame src=
```

Add the FRAMEBORDER or FRAMESPACING tags to your HTML code directly:

❏ The FRAMEBORDER command allows you to display or not display borders around the frames. Attribute values are "Yes" or "No".

❏ The FRAMESPACING command allows you to specify the spacing around the frames in pixels.

In the following code example, frame borders of all four frames are set to "No", and 5 pixels of spacing are added around the frames. You see this code added to the frame descriptions at the end of each of the lines:

```
<frameset cols="15%,70%,15%">
  <frame src="csnav.htm" name="csnav" frameborder="No" framespacing="5">
  <frameset rows="13%,87%">
    <frame src="clpgtoc.htm" name="cssect" frameborder="No" framespacing="5">
    <frame src="cooltoc.htm" name="csmain" frameborder="No" framespacing="5">
  </frameset>
  <frame src="csout.htm" name="csout" frameborder="No" framespacing="5">
  <noframes>
```

After you make your modifications, save the file using the same filename and extension. FrontPage adds the new file to the Import List. Use the File | Import command to import the new version of the file back into your Web site. Figures 21.6 and 21.7 show the frames before and after these tags are added. The FRAMEBORDER command gives the frames a much cleaner look.

Figure 21.6.
Frame borders normally look like this.

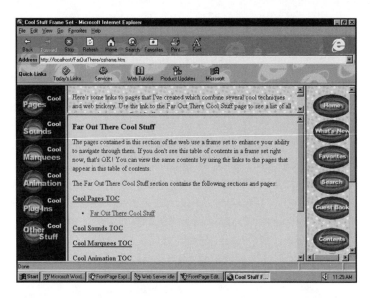

Figure 21.7.
Internet Explorer tags allow you to display borderless frames, giving the page a seamless and clean look.

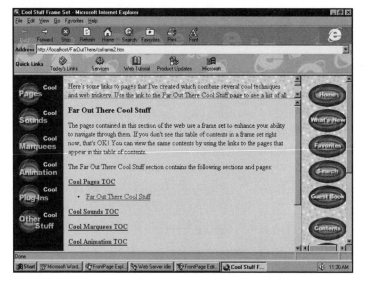

Unfortunately, when you use this procedure, two things occur:

❏ You break the connection with the Frame Editor, so if you want to edit your frame set in the future, you'll need to make the changes manually.

❏ You'll have to reapply any Include bots or other bots that were originally in the pages.

MARQUEE Tags

Marquees are another Internet Explorer invention. You often see text slide onto Web pages if you view them in Internet Explorer. Marquees are a somewhat improved version of blinking text, which is sometimes used for emphasis. Use Marquees sparingly, such as when you want to draw people's attention to a certain portion of your page.

There are several attributes and values associated with the MARQUEE tag. They are as follows:

Attribute	Value	What It Does
ALIGN	TOP	Aligns Marquee text to the top of the Marquee.
ALIGN	MIDDLE	Aligns Marquee text to the middle of the Marquee.
ALIGN	BOTTOM	Aligns Marquee text to the bottom of the Marquee.
BEHAVIOR	SCROLL	The text starts completely off one side, scrolls across and completely off, and starts again. This is the default.
BEHAVIOR	SLIDE	The text starts completely off one side, and then scrolls in and stops as soon as it reaches the other margin.
BEHAVIOR	ALTERNATE	The text bounces back and forth within the Marquee.
BGCOLOR	*colorname*	Defines the background of the Marquee by color name (see Appendix D, "HTML Quick Reference," for acceptable color names).
BGCOLOR	*#rrggbb*	Defines the background of the Marquee by hex value. Refer to Chapter 17, "Real-Life Examples," to see how to translate color values to hex.
DIRECTION	LEFT	The text in the Marquee scrolls from right to left. This is the default.
DIRECTION	RIGHT	The text in the Marquee scrolls from left to right.

continued

Attribute	Value	What It Does
HEIGHT	*n*	Defines the height of the Marquee, with *n* being the height in pixels.
HEIGHT	*n*%	Defines the height of the Marquee, with *n*% being the percentage of screen height.
HSPACE	*n*	Specifies, in pixels, the size of the left and right margins of the outside of the Marquee.
LOOP	*n*	Specifies how many times the Marquee will loop when activated. If *n* = -1, it loops indefinitely.
LOOP	INFINITE	The Marquee loops indefinitely.
SCROLLAMOUNT	*n*	Specifies the number of pixels in between each successive draw of the Marquee. Use when you loop more than once.
SCROLLDELAY	*n*	Specifies the number of milliseconds between each successive draw of the Marquee. Use when you loop more than once.
VSPACE	*n*	Specifies the top and bottom margins of the Marquee in pixels.
WIDTH	*n*	Specifies the width of the Marquee in pixels.
WIDTH	*n*%	Specifies the width of the Marquee in percentage of screen height.

Here's an easy way to add a Marquee to your page:

1. Position the insertion point where you want to place a Marquee.
2. Enter the code in the HTML Markup bot that describes the Marquee. An example is shown in Figure 21.1 in the HTML Markup dialog box.

   To place a Marquee that has all default settings on your page, enter the following in the HTML Markup bot:

   ```
   <MARQUEE>This text scrolls.</MARQUEE>
   ```

   Enter the following code in the HTML Markup bot to create a Marquee that slides in from the right and stops at the left margin, has a white background, and measures 40 pixels high and 350 pixels wide:

   ```
   <MARQUEE DIRECTION=LEFT BEHAVIOR=SLIDE BGCOLOR=WHITE HEIGHT=40
   WIDTH=350>This text scrolls.</MARQUEE>
   ```

Here's a full-featured Marquee. The properties in this Marquee represent the following settings: The text in the Marquee aligns to the Marquee's middle; it scrolls completely on and off from right to left and then starts again; it appears on a silver background; it scrolls from right to left; it measures 40 pixels high and 350 pixels wide; the left and right margins are 5 pixels; the top and bottom margins are 10 pixels; it loops indefinitely; there are 30 pixels in between each successive draw of the Marquee; and each successive draw of the Marquee delays by 250 milliseconds (1/4 of a second). I'll show each property line by line. Ready?

```
<MARQUEE
    ALIGN=MIDDLE
    BEHAVIOR=SCROLL
    BGCOLOR=SILVER
    DIRECTION=LEFT
    HEIGHT=40 WIDTH=350
    HSPACE=5 VSPACE=10
    LOOP=INFINITE
    SCROLLAMOUNT=30
    SCROLLDELAY=250>
    This text scrolls across the page and keeps repeating as long as the
    page is open.
</MARQUEE>
```

All that code and syntax typing makes WYSIWYG a lot more appealing, doesn't it?

To combine the previous example with a specific font, enclose the Marquee within the font tags. The code in your HTML Markup bot might look something like this:

```
<FONT FACE="Arial" SIZE=3>
<MARQUEE
    ALIGN=MIDDLE
    BEHAVIOR=SCROLL
    BGCOLOR=SILVER
    DIRECTION=LEFT
    HEIGHT=40 WIDTH=350
    HSPACE=5 VSPACE=10
    LOOP=INFINITE
    SCROLLAMOUNT=30
    SCROLLDELAY=250>
    This text scrolls across the page and keeps repeating as long as the page is
    open.
</MARQUEE>
</FONT>
```

Figure 21.8 shows the Marquee on the page. The text is nearly scrolled off the screen.

Figure 21.8.
You view the Marquee in a browser that supports the feature.

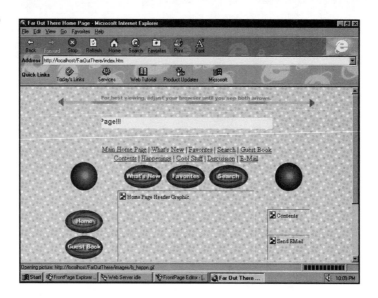

Adding Sound to Your Pages

Internet Explorer allows you to add sound to your pages, so that a WAV, AU, or MIDI format file plays when the page opens. When a user browses to a page that has the background sound tag included, the sound file first gets downloaded to the user. Then the sound plays according to the parameters set in the BGSOUND tag. Of course, the user needs a sound card, the appropriate application to play the sound—and his or her speakers have to be turned on.

If you include sound files in your Web pages, take care to limit the file size. Wave (.WAV) files can get pretty large, so you don't want the user to download the entire Beethoven's Fifth Symphony in this format. If you have a lengthy musical piece, offer the option to download the file instead (indicate its file size near the file's link).

You can also use a MIDI file. Then, of course, you're dealing with something that can sound entirely different, depending on the sound card your user has. It's fantastic to hear a MIDI file in full fidelity on a sound card with a great built-in synthesizer, but many people have SoundBlaster-compatible cards that make that MIDI file sound entirely different.

Each sound format has its advantages and its disadvantages. What you want to keep in mind is that the file should download relatively quickly. Remember, too, you should always use royalty-free or public domain sound files—better yet, make your own originals. It's more creative that way!

To add a sound file to your pages, use the BGSOUND tag, which has a couple of attributes associated with it:

Attribute	Value	What It Does
SRC	URL	Assigns the URL of the sound file you want to play.
LOOP	n	Specifies how many times you want the sound file to loop when activated; n is the number of times the sound repeats. If n = -1, the sound loops indefinitely.
LOOP	INFINITE	The sound loops indefinitely.

Here's how you add a sound file to your page:

1. From the FrontPage Explorer, use the File I Import command to import the sound file into your Web site. The BGSOUND tag works with the following types of sound files:

   .WAV—Wave format (sound clip)
   .AU—Audio file format (sound clip)
   .MID—MIDI file format (data file)

2. Open the page you want to attach the sound file to in the FrontPage Editor.

3. Choose Insert I Bot, and select the HTML Markup bot.

4. Enter text similar to the following examples in the HTML Markup bot:

   To play a .WAV file that loops five times, enter code similar to the following, using the URL of the file you imported to your Web site:

   ```
   <BGSOUND SRC="mysound.wav" LOOP=5>
   ```

   To play an .AU file that loops as long as the page is active, enter code similar to the following, using the URL of the file you imported to your Web site:

   ```
   <BGSOUND SRC="mysound.au" LOOP=INFINITE>
   ```

   To play a MIDI file that plays only once, enter code similar to the following, using the URL of the file you imported to your Web site:

   ```
   <BGSOUND SRC="mysound.mid">
   ```

5. Click OK to enter the code into your page. When you open the page in Internet Explorer, you'll hear the sound file you attached to the page.

Figure 21.9 shows an example of a sound tag being added to a page.

Figure 21.9.
The BGSOUND tag is used to attach a sound to a page.

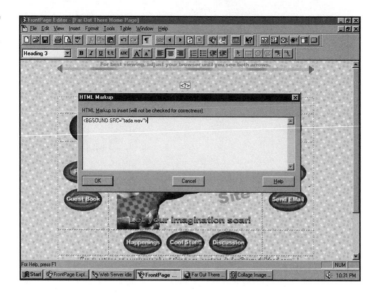

CGI and Perl Alternatives

I have good news for you: If you want to add forms and other types of interactivity but don't have the FrontPage Server Extensions, there are some great alternatives to using CGI scripts. Three hot languages right now are Java, JavaScript, and VBScript. My purpose here isn't to teach you how to use these languages (yikes, that would take a whole book in itself!), but I can show you how to insert code for them into your pages.

Java

Java is a language developed by Sun Microsystems, and many browsers are incorporating its features. It's modeled after C++, which means you can create just about anything you can imagine with it. It's also a multiplatform language, meaning that you don't have the platform-dependent worries that come along with CGI or Perl scripts—no cross-compiling, no headaches. All that's needed is a Java-capable browser to view what you've created. You can find a link to download the most current version of Sun's Java Developer's Kit at the following URL:

```
http://java.sun.com/
```

Laura Lemay's *Teach Yourself Java in 21 Days,* published by Sams.net, is a great way to learn how to use Java!

Java files come in two forms: applets and applications. These items are compiled on the server with a Java compiler. The applets aren't a part of your Web page; rather, you need to insert a reference to the applet much as you do with a sound file or other multimedia file. *Applets* require that the user browse the Web with a Java-capable browser to view what you've created. *Applications* are general programs written in the Java language.

You use the APPLET tag to insert a reference to Java applets in your Web pages. This code is inserted into an HTML Markup bot in much the same manner as the other items mentioned in this chapter. You import the Java applet into your Web site, and then use the following procedure to include code for it in your Web page:

1. Import the Java applet to your current Web site by using the File I Import command in the FrontPage Explorer.

2. Open the page in which you want to insert the Java applet.

3. Choose Insert I Bot, and select the HTML Markup Bot.

4. In the HTML Markup dialog box, enter the code that launches the Java applet, as in the following example:

```
<APPLET CODE="MyJavaApplet.class" WIDTH=350 HEIGHT=100>
This is my Java Applet!
</APPLET>
```

5. Click OK to exit the HTML Markup dialog box and insert the code into your Web page.

JavaScript

JavaScript is similar to Java, except that its code is actually integrated right in your Web page. Rather than compile the code on the server, it is interpreted by the user's browser instead. You must use a browser that has JavaScript capability (they're becoming increasingly popular).

You insert JavaScript commands in their entirety with the HTML Markup bot. Here are some good sources for JavaScript information on the Internet:

❏ JavaScript Authoring Guide (Netscape's site):

```
http://home.netscape.com/eng/mozilla/Gold/handbook/javascript/index.html
```

❏ Andrew's JavaScript Index

```
http://www.c2.org/~andreww/javascript/
```

❏ Yahoo!: Computers and Internet: Languages: JavaScript

```
http://www.yahoo.com/Computers_and_Internet/Languages/JavaScript/
```

VBScript

Microsoft has recently announced its Visual Basic, Scripting Edition (VBScript). This language allows you to create interactive online content for your Web pages and also lets you use Microsoft's ActiveX controls and Java applets. This is not a language to be overlooked, since it seems incredibly flexible and easy to use. Like JavaScript, VBScript is contained directly in your Web page and inserted by using the HTML Markup bot.

You can get more information, as well as examples of VBScript, from the following URLs:

❏ Microsoft VBScript Home Page

`http://www.microsoft.com/vbscript/vbsmain.htm`

❏ VBScript and Forms

`http://www.microsoft.com/vbscript/de/vbstutor/vbscntrl.htm`

Microsoft ActiveX

Coming down the road is Microsoft's ActiveX technology. This capability is built into Microsoft Internet Explorer 3.0, and you can preview its capabilities by downloading the ActiveX Control Pad, Microsoft HTML Layout Control, and Microsoft Internet Explorer 3.0 beta. You can do some pretty neat things with this little package, including layering images and text and adding form controls. Figure 21.10 shows a screen shot of the ActiveX Control Pad and HTML Layout Control in action. After you complete the page in the ActiveX Control Pad, you can import it into FrontPage, which will automatically place HTML Markup bots where it needs them.

Figure 21.10.
The ActiveX Control Pad and HTML Layout Control allow you to add form controls, layer images, and do much more.

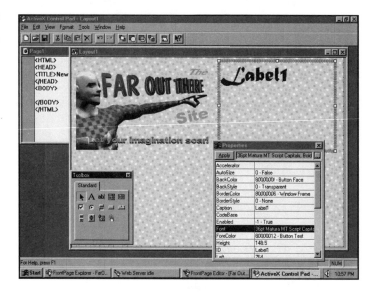

These items are available from Microsoft's Web site at the following URLs:

❏ ActiveX Controls (information)

`http://www.microsoft.com/intdev/inttech/controls.htm`

❏ The Microsoft ActiveX Control Pad

`http://www.microsoft.com/intdev/author/cpad/`

❏ The Microsoft HTML Layout Control (Note: If you download the ActiveX Control Pad, you won't need this because it's already included.)

`http://www.microsoft.com/ie/controls/layout/`

❏ Microsoft ActiveX SDK

`http://www.microsoft.com/intdev/sdk/`

❏ ActiveX Scripting

`http://www.microsoft.com/ie/script/default.htm`

Keeping Up with the Joneses

A ton of other browser plug-ins are available, but how do you keep track of what's hot and what's not? One way is by watching the capabilities that browsers use, and a good source for keeping track of that is the Browser Watch site. From this site, you'll learn everything you wanted to know about browsers, and more. It also maintains a list of all known browser plug-ins, so it's a great site to bookmark. Here's some of what they offer:

❏ Browser Watch Browser List

`http://www.browserwatch.com/browsers.shtml`

❏ Browser Watch Browser Stats

`http://www.browserwatch.com/report-table-browsers.shtml`

❏ Browser Watch Plug-In Plaza

`http://www.browserwatch.com/plug-in-big.shtml`

The FrontPage Developer's Kit

Although this doesn't directly relate to inserting code into your pages, it does address adding customization to your FrontPage Webs. Microsoft has released a FrontPage Developer's Kit, which allows you to create your own Web templates, wizards, and bots, using either Microsoft Visual C++ or Microsoft Visual Basic. If you like the way FrontPage allows you to develop your pages quickly by using these methods, why not learn to create your own? Create a Table Wizard that allows you to configure row, column, and cell widths exactly the way you want them. Create another wizard that allows you to create home pages exactly the way you want them. You can truly customize FrontPage to work in any way you choose.

You can download the FrontPage Developer's Kit from the following URL:

`http://www.microsoft.com/frontpage/freestuff/fs_fp_sdk.htm`

Workshop Wrap-Up

Using the HTML Markup bot, you can insert the latest and greatest features into your Web pages. Some of these features are easier than others, but you get a chance to customize your pages even further by adding your own code. You can extend your knowledge to other programming and scripting languages to enhance your pages even further. It's both fun and exciting to do things your way and to use the latest features in your pages.

Chapter Summary

In this chapter, you have learned how to customize your pages by adding special fonts, sounds, and Marquees with the HTML Markup bot. You have also learned about some other scripting languages that can be used with your Web pages. You're ready now to complete your pages by using FrontPage's features to their fullest!

Next Steps

In the next chapter, you'll combine what you've learned in this section to complete the Far Out There Web. You'll add some forms and some extra coding, and get your Web site ready to publish.

❏ Refer to Appendix C, "Directory of Resources," for a list of sites that can help you with your own HTML code.

❏ Refer to Appendix D, "HTML Quick Reference," for a list of the tags that will require you to use the HTML Markup bot.

Q&A

Q: So, what you're saying is it's actually best to do as much as I can in the FrontPage Editor and then add the rest in with the Markup bot?

A: I find it to be the simplest way, but you may learn different tips and tricks as you become more familiar with how your other editors react with FrontPage. If you can see what you get while you're working on it, why not use that to your advantage while you develop your page? As you learned in this chapter, things can sometimes get a little jumbled when you try to work with other editors. It's best to keep it clean and simple so you can keep the bots intact in your pages. After all, the bots save you a lot of time down the road!

Q: When I import pages into the editor, sometimes it inserts a whole series of HTML Markup bots one right after the other. Can I combine the code?

A: If there's nothing between them, I don't see why not. What you can do is open the second HTML Markup bot and copy its contents into your Clipboard. Then open the first one and paste the contents of your Clipboard at the end of its contents. Continue on down the line in this manner, pasting the contents of the third to the first, and so on. Delete all but the first Markup bot that combines the content of all of them.

Q: If there are a whole bunch of Markup bots scattered around the page, can I put them all in one place?

A: Probably not. Remember, you might have content in between them, and the Markup bot tags are usually arranged in the order in which your code has to appear to make the page flow correctly.

TWENTY TWO

Real-Life Examples

Now that you've learned the rest of the story, you're going to create and configure some forms for your site. You'll take the tasks you've learned in this section and work them in with the pages you've already created! Forms add a lot of interactivity and interest to a site; besides, they're fun to design!

TASK ## Creating a Guest Book

To create your guest book, follow these steps:

1. Choose File | New. From the New Page dialog box, choose the Far Out Main Page Template.

2. Highlight the small Far Out There header graphic, and insert `animbook.gif` (located on the book's CD-ROM) in its place. This is an animated GIF, in which the pages of the book turn. Use the Image Properties dialog box to change the alignment to Middle, and add Guest Book Animation as an alternative text representation.

3. Highlight the Annotation bot at the top of the page. Use the Insert | Image command to insert `guestbk.gif` (or `.jpg`) in its place. Change its alignment to Middle, and enter `Guest Book` for an alternative text representation.

4. Edit the Page Title bookmark to read "Far Out There Guest Book" (without quotes).

5. Delete the horizontal line and bulleted list from the table. Choose Normal paragraph formatting from the Style bar in the FrontPage Editor, and add a welcome statement, as shown in Figure 22.1.

Figure 22.1.

Your guest book page begins to take shape.

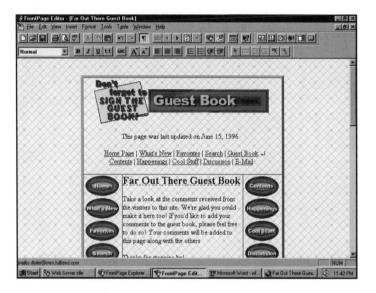

6. Go to the area beneath the table and delete everything except the first and last dividers and the footer.

7. Position the insertion point at the end of the first divider and press Enter. A new line is added between the dividers.

8. Align the new line to the left of the page by using the Align Left button on the Format toolbar.

9. Save the page to your Web site as `Far Out There Guest Book` using a URL of `guestbk.htm`. When FrontPage asks whether you want to overwrite the version that exists in your Web site, answer Yes, and then answer Yes to All to save all the images to the Web site.

Creating the Form

Now you'll create a form that you will paste into your guest book page. To use the Form Page Wizard, you have to create a new page, so follow these steps to create your guest book form:

1. Choose File | New. Select the Form Page Wizard.

2. When the introductory screen appears, click Next to continue.

3. Leave the Page URL and title as is and click Next to continue.

4. Click the Add button, and choose to add a Contact Information question. For the prompt, enter something like the following:

   `Let us know who you are! We'd appreciate it if you could at least add your name and location to the list. Contact information is optional.`

5. Click Next to continue and choose to add the following fields:

   > Full Name
   > Postal Address
   > Email Address
   > Web Address (URL)

6. In the "Enter name for variables" field, leave the variable name as Contact and click Next to continue.

7. Click Add, and choose to add a Paragraph question. For the prompt, enter something like the following:

   `Tell us what you think of the site. Your comments will be added to this page.`

8. Click Next to continue. For the name of the variable for this question, enter `Comments`.

9. Click Next to proceed to the final screen, and then click Finish to generate the form; it should look like the one shown in Figure 22.2.

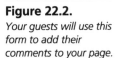

Figure 22.2.

Your guests will use this form to add their comments to your page.

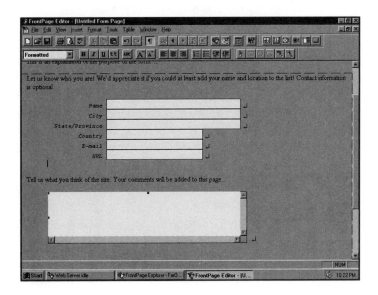

Editing the Form and the Form Fields

You need to edit the fields' properties to assign shorter names that are more applicable to the form. These values are those that will be passed to the form handler for use in the confirmation form and the results file. Currently, these names are preceded by the word Contact, which you want to eliminate.

Some other small modifications have to be made, too. For example, all the form fields are 256 characters except for the URL form field, which contains only 25 characters. This might not be long enough for your guest to add his or her URL. Also, you need to increase the width of the scrolling textbox a little to give the form a more balanced look.

To edit the form and the form fields, follow these steps:

1. From the Contact Information section, delete the street address, additional address, and Zip Code fields.

2. Right-click on the Name textbox, and choose Properties from the pop-up menu. Change the value in the name field from ContactName to Name.

3. In the same manner, assign the following words to each of the properties in their respective Text Box Properties dialog boxes:

   > City textbox: should read City
   > State/Province textbox: should read State
   > Country textbox: should read Country
   > E-mail textbox: should read Email

   Refer to Step 4 for the properties for the URL textbox.

4. Right-click on the URL form field and choose Properties from the pop-up menu. Enter URL in its Name field. In the Text Box Properties dialog box, enter a value of 256 in the Maximum characters field.

5. Right-click on the scrolling textbox, and choose Properties from the pop-up menu. Change the width in characters to 50. When you're finished, your form should look like the one shown in Figure 22.3.

6. Position your cursor at the leftmost corner of the form and double-click to select it. Choose Edit | Copy (or press Ctrl+C) to place the form in your Clipboard.

7. Return to the Guest Book page and paste the form between the two dividers.

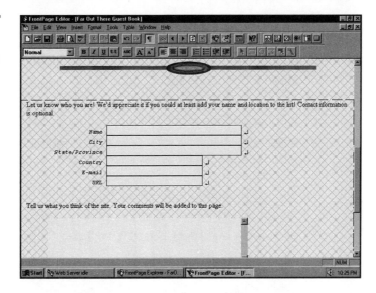

Figure 22.3.

The form is edited slightly to better suit the application.

Configuring the Guest Book Form Handler

Now you have to assign a form handler to your form. To do this, follow these steps:

1. Position your cursor anywhere in the form. Right-click and choose Form Properties from the pop-up menu.

2. Choose the Save Results bot as a form handler. Click the Settings button to configure the bot.

3. In the File for results field, enter guestlog.htm.

4. In the File Format field, choose HTML.

5. Make sure the "Include field names in output" checkbox is checked.

6. In the "URL of confirmation page" field, enter gstcfrm.htm and click OK. You'll be notified that the linked-to page doesn't exist yet. Answer Yes to link to it anyway.

7. Click OK to exit the Form Properties dialog box.

Adding the Include Bot for the Guest Log

When you configured the Save Results bot for the guest book, you assigned a form results page of guestlog.htm. This page is created automatically the first time a user submits his or her comments to your site. For you to include the comments on your guest book page, you need to insert the guestlog.htm page into your Guest Book page with an Include bot.

Follow these steps to continue with the Guest Book page:

1. Go down to the bottom of the page, where the divider and footer appear. Copy the divider into your Clipboard, and paste another copy above or below the existing divider.

2. Position the insertion point at the end of the top divider. Choose Insert I Bot, and select Include to open the Include Bot Properties dialog box.

3. In the "Page URL to Include" field, enter `guestlog.htm`, and then click OK to exit the Include Bot Properties dialog box. Your guest book page should now look like the one shown in Figure 22.4.

4. Save the Guest Book page to your Web site again. You can discard the normal page on which you originally created the form.

5. Remove the Guest Book page task from your To Do list.

Figure 22.4.
The guest log page is inserted into the Far Out There Guest Book page with an Include bot.

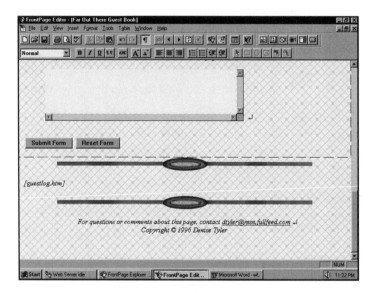

When you open your Guest Book in a browser that supports animated GIFs, you'll see the pages flipping in the guest book. The area behind the guest book won't be the blue color in the table when you view it in Internet Explorer. It will show the background image through it, as shown in Figure 22.5.

Figure 22.5.

When you view the header in a browser that supports animated GIFs, the pages of the book turn.

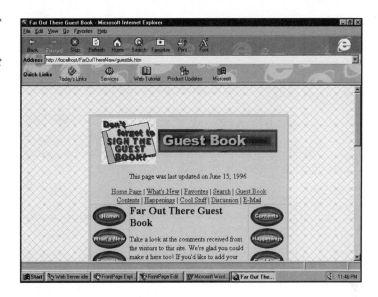

Creating the Guest Book Confirmation Page

You want to thank your site visitors for submitting their comments to your guest book and also let them know they can view their comments if they return to the Guest Book page and refresh it in their browser. Create a simple confirmation page as follows:

1. Choose File I New. Base the new page on the Normal page template.

2. Assign the Far Out There Web Colors page to the new page, using the File I Page Properties command.

3. Insert the `faroutsm.gif` (or `.jpg`) and `guestbk.gif` (or `.jpg`) images on the top line of the page. You can also add alternative text representations of "Small Header Graphic" and "Guest Book," respectively, for the two images.

4. Insert Heading 3 and enter the heading shown in the figure.

5. Press Enter and insert `divider.gif` (or `.jpg`) into the page, centering it with the Center button on the Format toolbar.

6. Position the insertion point at the end of the divider and insert an Address paragraph. Enter the text shown beneath the divider. The `[Name]` text shown in the figure is added with a Confirmation Field bot. This is how you'd enter the line:

   `Thank you,` (insert a Confirmation Field bot with `Name` as the form field to confirm), (add a space) `for adding your comments to our guest book.`

7. Insert a Normal paragraph and enter the following text:

   `The following information will appear in our guest book:`

8. Insert a horizontal line, using the default settings. Figure 22.6 shows the upper portion of the page, containing everything you've done to this point.

Figure 22.6.

The upper portion of your Confirmation Page should be complete.

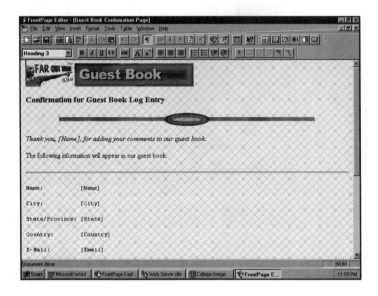

9. Insert a Formatted paragraph and enter each line of confirmation fields. A Confirmation Field bot is added for each form field in your Guest Book form. By using Formatted paragraphs, you can add spacing after all the form fields are added to align them perfectly. Here are the steps:

    Name: Insert a Confirmation Field bot called `Name`, and press Enter.

    City: Insert a Confirmation Field bot called `city`, and press Enter.

    State/Province: Insert a Confirmation Field bot called `state`, and press Enter.

    Country: Insert a Confirmation Field bot called `country`, and press Enter.

    E-Mail: Insert a Confirmation Field bot called `Email`, and press Enter.

    URL: Insert a Confirmation Field bot called `URL`, and press Enter.

    Enter Your Comments: on the current line and press Enter.

10. Insert a Confirmation Field bot called Comments on the line below the Your Comments line.

11. Insert a Normal paragraph after the Confirmation Field bot, and add some text that provides a link back to the Guest Book page. Let users know they need to refresh their browsers to see the comments added.

12. Press Enter and insert `divider.gif` (or `.jpg`) on the following line. Center the divider with the Center button on the Format toolbar.

13. Insert an Include bot at the bottom of the page, and include the Included Page Footer (`_private/footer.htm`). The lower portion of your page should now look like the one in Figure 22.7.

Figure 22.7.

The lower portion of your Confirmation Page is now complete.

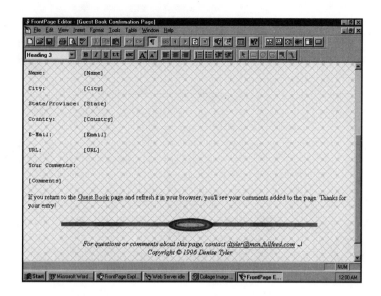

14. Save the page to your Web site with the following title and URL:

    Page Title: `Guest Book Confirmation Page`

    Page URL: `gstcfrm.htm`

 # Creating a Search Page

I decided to use what was already available to create a Search Page, so I combined the contents of the Far Out There Main Page template with the contents of the Search Page template. Here's how you can do that:

1. Minimize any pages you currently have open in the FrontPage Editor.

2. Choose File I New, and base the page on the Far Out There Main Page template.

3. Choose File I New again, and base the page on the Search Page template.

4. Choose Window I Tile to view both pages in the FrontPage Editor.

5. Replace the Annotation bot in the Far Out There Main Page Template with `search.gif` (or `.jpg`) from the book's CD-ROM.

6. Replace the Page Title bookmark with a title that reads Text Search.

7. Remove the divider and bulleted list from the page template, and replace it with the introductory text from the Search Page. When you get this far, your page should look like the one in Figure 22.8.

Figure 22.8.

The upper portion of your Search Page contains text from the Search Page template.

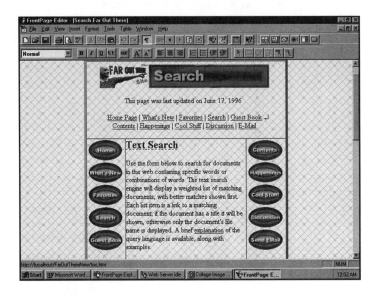

8. Position the insertion point at the end of the first divider beneath the table. Insert a table with the following properties:

Number of Rows:	9
Number of Columns:	2
Alignment:	Center
Border Size:	0
Cell Padding:	1
Cell Spacing:	2
Specify Width:	90 Percent

9. Insert a table caption, copy the Query Language bookmark from the Search Page, and paste it into the table caption. Click the Increase Text Size button to enlarge it a couple of increments.

10. Merge the two cells in the first row together with the Table | Merge Cells command. Paste the text from the original search page into the table, as shown in Figure 22.9. The figure also shows the content of the Search Page's Query Language section added to the table.

11. Continue to copy the contents of the Search Page into your page template until it looks like the one shown in Figure 22.9.

Figure 22.9.

The Query Language section from the Search Page template is moved into a table.

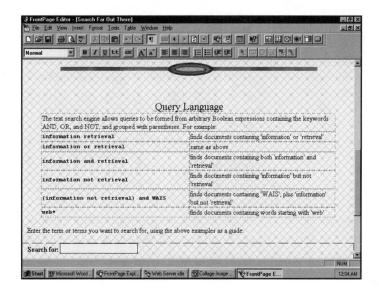

12. Remove the extra dividers and sections from the Main Page template, leaving only a divider and the footer at the bottom of the page. When you're finished, the lower portion of the Search Page looks like the one in Figure 22.10.

Figure 22.10.

The lower portion of the Search Page is complete.

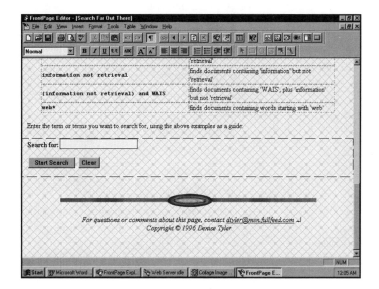

13. The Search bot is configured as follows:

    Label for Input: Search for:
    Width in Characters: 2

Label for Start Search button: Start Search
Label for Clear button: 0
Word List to Search: All
Additional Information: Score, File Date, and File Size

14. Save the page to your Web site with the following title and URL:

Page Title: `Search Far Out There`
Page URL: `search.htm`

When FrontPage asks whether you want to overwrite the existing file, answer Yes and then answer Yes to All to save all images to the current Web site.

15. Remove the task for the Search Page from your To Do list.

16. Close the untitled Search Page. When FrontPage asks whether you want to save the page before closing, answer No.

Creating the Discussion Group

You've created enough pages of your own now to get the idea of how to go about it, so now you'll use the Discussion Wizard to add a discussion group to your Web site because it's the simplest way to do this. After that, I'll show you what the settings are for each page in the discussion.

Follow these steps to add the discussion group to your site:

1. From the FrontPage Explorer, choose File I New Web. Make sure the Add to the Current Web option is checked, and choose the Discussion Web Wizard.

2. As you step through the Discussion Web Wizard, choose the following options:

❑ Include a Table of Contents, Search Form, Threaded Replies, and Confirmation Page.

❑ Name the discussion Far Out There Discussion. This places the discussion group articles in a subdirectory in your Web named `_fotd`.

❑ When you are asked to choose an appropriate set of input fields, choose Subject, Category, Comments.

❑ Select "No, anyone can post articles."

❑ Sort the articles from oldest to newest on the Table of Contents.

❑ The Table of Contents page is *not* the home page. This is important!

❑ For the search form, choose to report Subject, Size, and Date.

To create a discussion on a registered Web site, you have to create a new web for it, as discussed in Chapter 6, "Real-Life Examples."

❑ Leave the style sheet settings at the default choices. You'll be assigning your main style sheet to the discussion style sheet.

❑ Choose to create a dual interface frame set.

3. To generate the discussion group, click Finish. The new pages are added to your current Web site.

NOTE:
It might take some time for FrontPage to add these new pages to your current Web site. It might seem as though your computer is hanging, but be patient. Eventually the Web will refresh, and the new pages will appear in your Web site. Use the Tools | Web Settings command's Advanced tab to configure your Web site so that it shows pages in hidden directories. This allows you to see all the new pages.

The Discussion Wizard adds 14 new pages to your Web site; the settings on each page are described in the following sections when appropriate.

Pages You Won't Need to Change

The following pages for the discussion are okay the way they are, so you won't have to change them:

❑ `_fotd tocproto.htm` (`_fotd/tocproto.htm`)

❑ Far Out There Discussion TOC—Framed (`fotdtocf.htm`)

❑ Far Out There Discussion Welcome (`fotdwelc.htm`)

❑ Far Out There Discussion TOC (`fotdtoc.htm`)

❑ Included Article Footer for Far Out There Discussion (`_private/fotdaftr.htm`). This page is blank. You can add content to it, if you like.

Far Out There Discussion Web Colors (`_private/fotdstyl.htm`)

Open this page from your current Web, and use the File | Page Properties command to assign the Far Out There Web Colors page (`_private/faroutwc.htm`) to the page. Save the revised page to your current Web using the File | Save command.

`_fotd` Discussion Page (`_fotd/toc.htm`)

There are no changes to make to this page. However I wanted to point out something about it. At first, it appears as though there are no contents on this page. However, that is only a temporary situation. As a user submits articles or replies to your discussion, their titles are added to the _fotd/tocproto.htm page. That page, in turn, is included in this page through the use of an Include bot. Eventually, you will see a list of articles on this page, which will appear similar to that shown in Figure 22.11.

Figure 22.11.
The contents of the included page won't show until after a user enters an article in your discussion.

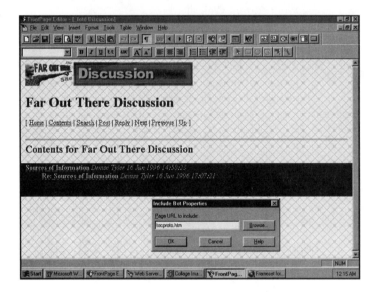

Frameset for Far Out There Discussion (fotdfrm.htm)

A completed example of the Discussion frameset is shown in Figure 22.12. The settings for the frame set are as follows in the Frame Wizard:

- ❏ The frameset contains two rows and one column. Two frames appear in this frameset.
- ❏ The upper frame is named contents and initially loads the Far Out There Discussion TOC (framed) page (fotdtocf.htm) into it.
- ❏ The lower frame is named article and initially loads the Far Out There Discussion Welcome (fotdwelc.htm) into it.
- ❏ The frameset uses the Far Out There Discussion TOC (fotdtoc.htm) for an alternative page URL, for those who don't have frame-compatible browsers.

Figure 22.12.

Your discussion articles and a table of contents appear in the frameset.

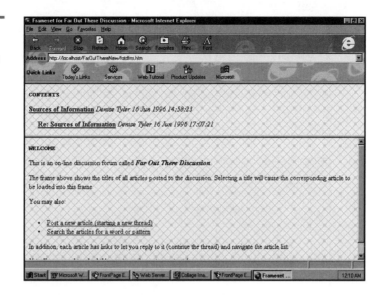

Far Out There Discussion Confirmation Form (`fotdcfrm.htm`)

The confirmation page a user receives when he or she submits an article to the discussion contains one Confirmation Field bot, which is shown in Figure 22.13. The confirmation field returns the subject of the article in the confirmation form.

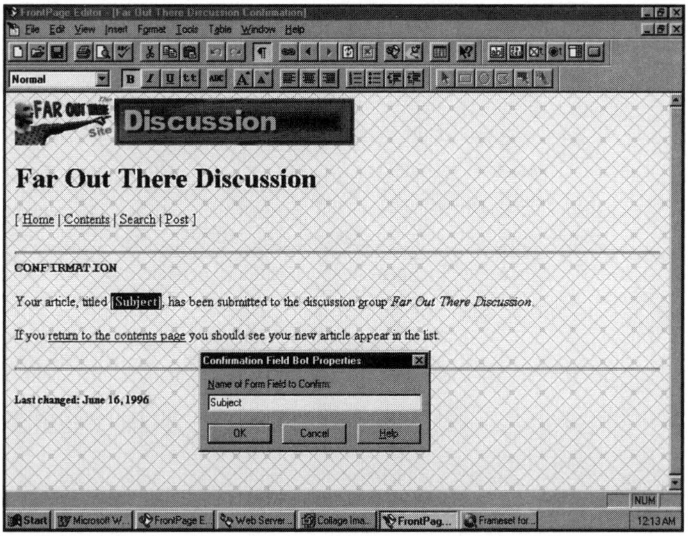

Figure 22.13.

The Discussion Confirmation Form contains one Confirmation Field bot.

Far Out There Discussion Search Form (fotdsrch.htm)

The Search Page for the Far Out There Discussion is configured to search through the articles in the discussion. This is done by assigning the discussion group's directory (_fotd) in the Search bot, where you specify the Word List to Search. The Search bot Properties dialog box is shown in Figure 22.14.

Figure 22.14.
The Search bot is configured to keep track of only the articles in the discussion.

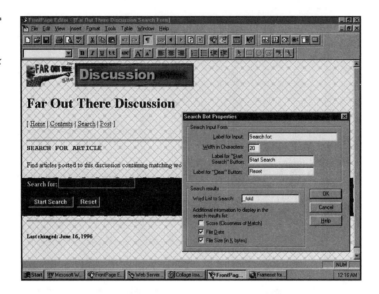

The settings for the Search bot on this page should be as follows (you can edit any settings you want, except the Word List to Search directory):

Label for Input:	Search for:
Width in Characters:	20
Label for "Start Search" Button:	Start Search
Label for "Clear" Button:	Reset
Word List to Search:	_fotd
Additional Information to Display:	File Date
	File Size (in KB)

Far Out There Discussion Submission Form (fotdpost.htm)

The Discussion Submission Form contains several form fields. You can add some of the other fields shown here to your discussion's confirmation form, if you like.

The settings for the Subject textbox are as follows:

Width in characters:	50
Maximum characters:	256
Password field:	No

You need to customize the settings for the Category drop-down menu, as shown in Figure 22.15. In the example I show, the choices in the drop-down menu were modified as follows:

Web Page Development	Selected = Yes
Creating Web Graphics	Selected = No
Adding Interactivity	Selected = No
Multimedia	Selected = No
Other	Selected = No

Figure 22.15.

The drop-down menu should be customized with topics of your choice.

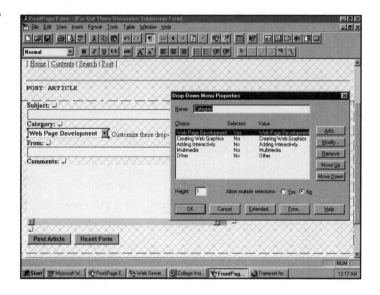

The From textbox is configured as follows:

Width in characters:	50
Maximum characters:	256
Password field:	No

The scrolling textbox for the Comments field is configured as follows:

Name:	Comments
Width in characters:	50
Number of lines:	6

The Post Article pushbutton field doesn't have a name. Add the following name in the Name field, and enter these other settings:

Name:	Enter Post here
Value/Label:	Post Article
Type:	Submit

The Reset Form pushbutton field also doesn't contain a name. Add the following name in the Name field, and enter these other settings:

Name:	Enter Reset here
Value/Label:	Reset Form
Type:	Reset

You also need to make a couple of minor changes to the Form Properties. Place the insertion point anywhere in the submission form, right-click, and choose Form Properties from the pop-up menu.

The Form Handler should already be set to Discussion Bot. Click the Settings button, and make sure the settings in the Discussion tab are the same as those listed here, shown in Figure 22.16. You'll need to add the title and check to display Time as an additional field:

Title:	Far Out There Discussion
Directory:	_fotd
Table Of Contents	
Layout fields:	Subject From
Additional form fields:	Date already checked; add Time
Get background and colors:	_private/fotdstyl.htm
URL of confirmation page:	fotdcfrm.htm

Click the Articles tab and make sure the settings are the same as the ones listed here. (See Figure 22.17.)

Header:	_private/fotdahdr.htm
Footer:	_private/fotdaftr.htm
Additional Information:	Time, Date, and Remote computer name are already checked; add User name.

Figure 22.16.
Configure the discussion in the Discussion tab.

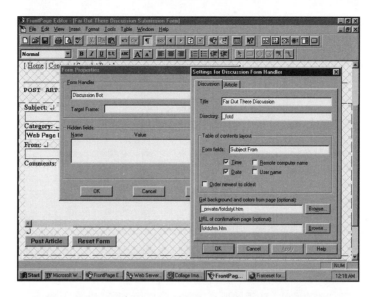

Figure 22.17.
Configure the discussion articles in the Articles tab.

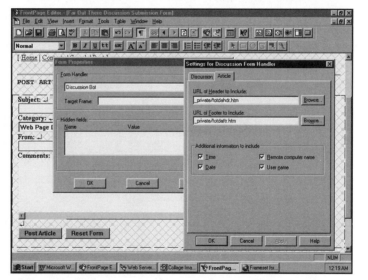

Included Article Header for Far Out There Discussion (`_private/fotdahdr.htm`)

You've probably noticed that my headers in the discussion pages have graphics and that I haven't told you to add them yet. That's because they're added in the headers for the pages in this section, and you're going to add them now. You also need to edit the link to the home page. To do this, follow these steps:

1. At the top of the page, insert the following two graphics:

   `faroutsm.gif` (or `.jpg`) from the current Web site

   `discuss.gif` (or `.jpg`) from the book's CD-ROM

2. Edit the link to the home page that appears in the text line. Choose the Far Out There Home Page (`index.htm`) from the pages in your current Web site.

3. Save the revised page to your Web site when it's finished.

The links on this page are assigned the following default target frames:

❏ The links to the main pages in the Web are assigned a default target frame of `_top`. When the user chooses to navigate to the main pages, the frameset is removed from the browser, and the main pages appear in a full browser window. This applies for links to Home, Contents, Search, Post, and Reply.

❏ The Next, Previous, and Up links are not assigned a default target frame.

You'll notice that this page contains some link types that haven't been covered so far. However, since you're working with them now, they're explained in the following paragraphs. An example of one of these link types is shown in Figure 22.18.

Figure 22.18.
Links like this one tell the Discussion bot what to do.

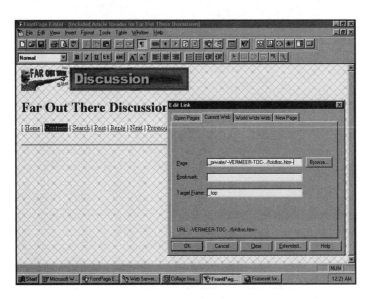

If you examine the link properties for the Contents, Reply, Next, Previous, and Up links on this page, you'll see links to some strange "pages" in your current Web site. These aren't pages—they're functions of the Discussion bot. If you design your own Discussion Group someday, without using the Discussion Wizard, here's what these special links do:

❑ The Contents link reads as follows:

`_private/--VERMEER-TOC-../fotdtoc.htm`

This entry instructs the Discussion bot to generate a current table of contents and place it into the `fotdtoc.htm` page before it displays.

❑ The Reply link reads like this:

`_private/--VERMEER-REPLY--`

This entry tells the Discussion bot to thread the reply with the article being replied to. The Discussion bot also opens the Discussion Submission form to allow the user to enter his or her reply.

❑ The Next link reads as follows:

`_private/--VERMEER-NEXT--`

This entry instructs the Discussion bot to display the next article in the discussion.

❑ The Previous link reads like this:

`_private/--VERMEER-PREV--`

This entry tells the Discussion bot to display the previous article in the discussion.

❑ The Up link reads as follows:

`_private/--VERMEER-UP--`

This entry instructs the Discussion bot to display the first (or top) article in the discussion.

Included Header for Far Out There Discussion (`_private/fotdhead.htm`)

The Included Header for the Far Out There Discussion is shown in Figure 22.19. Add the same graphics to this header as you did for the article header, and edit the link to the home page. To do this, follow these steps:

1. At the top of the page, insert the following two graphics:

   `faroutsm.gif` (or `.jpg`) from the current Web site

   `discuss.gif` (or `.jpg`), which should now exist in your current Web site

2. Edit the link to the home page that appears in the text line. Choose the Far Out There Home Page (`index.htm`) from the pages in your current web.

3. Save the revised page to your Web site when it's finished.

All links on this page have a default target frame of `_top`, meaning that the frameset will be removed and the target page displayed in a full browser window.

Figure 22.19.

Add the same graphics to the header for the main pages in the discussion.

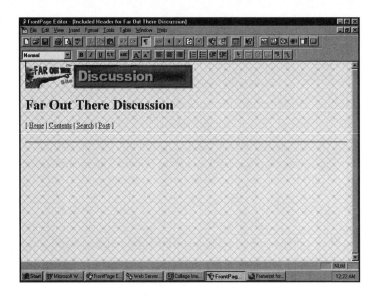

Included Footer for Far Out There Discussion (`_private/fotdfoot.htm`)

The timestamp on this page is set to update on the date this page was last automatically edited. By default, the date displays in the following format:

```
July 19, 1996
```

Choose the date and time format of your choice. The date options are as follows:

```
19 July, 1996
19 Jul 1996
19 July 1996
19/07/96
07/19/96
07.19.96
07.19.1996
19-Jul-1996
```

The default time choice is none. Additional time options are as follows:

```
05:13
05:13 AM
05:13 TZ
```

Editing the Links in Your Main Pages

You'll need to edit the links on your home page, and in the main navigation link page, to open the Far Out There Discussion Frame Set instead of the `disctoc.htm` page the links are presently assigned to.

Fortunately, there's an easy way to do this, and here are the steps:

1. Open the FrontPage Explorer. From any view, locate the Far Out There Discussion page (`disctoc.htm`). This is the page you created when you added all your links from the home page in Chapter 6.

2. Right-click the page, and choose Delete from the pop-up menu. FrontPage will ask whether you're sure you want to delete the page. Answer Yes.

3. Now, for the magic. From the FrontPage Explorer, choose Tools | Verify Links to open the Verify Links dialog box shown in Figure 22.20. The pages containing links to that `disctoc.htm` page (`index.htm`, `textnav.htm`, and `botmnav.htm`) appear in the list.

Figure 22.20.

Use the Verify Links dialog box to repair the links on your home and navigation pages.

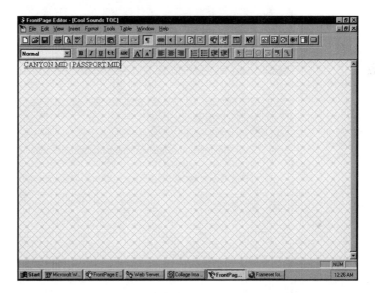

4. Select one of the pages that contain a link to the `disctoc.htm` page, and click the Edit Link button. The Edit Link dialog box shown in Figure 22.21 appears.

5. Enter the URL of the Far Out There Discussion frameset in the With: field:

   `fotdfrm.htm`

6. Select the Change all pages with this link radio button.

7. Click OK or press Enter. FrontPage repairs all the links for you automatically. Your Web refreshes and the broken links change to Edited status in the Verify Links dialog box, as shown in Figure 22.22. If you click the Verify button again, the links are removed from the list.

Figure 22.21.

Select one of the broken links to repair all of them.

Figure 22.22.

All the pages that contained the broken link have been repaired.

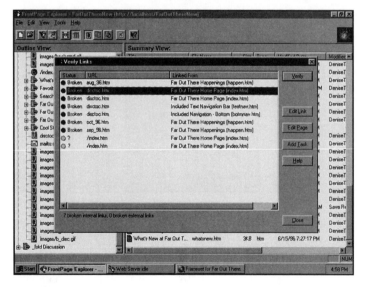

NOTE: To test the links in your browser or in the FrontPage Editor, refresh the pages on which the links originally appeared.

Adding Code into Your Cool Stuff Pages

The examples I'm giving in these pages are pretty basic, just to give you an idea of how to enter your own code into your FrontPage pages. I'll try to work with media you should already have on your computer, or at least have easy access to. If you want to hunt around on the Internet for public domain files that fall into the same category, you can generally start yourself off on the right track if you go to Yahoo! (http://www.yahoo.com). Do a search for the media type of your choice, and you'll come up with an endless list of links to choose from.

I'll start by adding a couple of sound pages into your Cool Stuff section. The two sounds you'll add come with Windows 95. I'm using these files only as an example; please keep in mind that they aren't public domain, so you don't want to use them on your site. If you have other MIDI files on your system that are original or public domain, replace the examples I'm using with your filenames.

The two sounds I used in my pages were CANYON.MID and PASSPORT.MID. If you installed all the multimedia options in Windows 95, you'll find both these MIDI files in the C:\Windows\Media directory. Import both these files into your Web site with the File | Import command from the FrontPage Explorer.

To add them to your Cool Stuff pages, follow these steps:

1. Open the Cool Sounds TOC (clsndtoc.htm) page in the FrontPage Editor.
2. On the first line of the page, enter the following text, as shown in Figure 22.23:

```
CANYON.MID ¦ PASSPORT.MID
```

Figure 22.23.

You'll create links to two sound files that appear on different pages.

3. Select the CANYON.MID text and create a link to a new page. Assign the following properties to the page in the Create Link dialog box's New Page tab:

Page Title:	CANYON.MID
Page URL:	canyon.htm
Target Frame:	main

Choose to edit the new page immediately and then click OK to create the page.

4. Base the page on the Normal template.

5. When the page opens, use the File I Page Properties command to assign the Cool Stuff Main Window Style Sheet (_private/csstyle.htm) for the page background and colors. In the Default Target Frame field, enter Main, and click OK.

6. Choose Insert I Bot, and select HTML Markup. The HTML Markup dialog box appears.

7. Enter the following in the Markup bot, as shown in Figure 22.24:

```
<BGSOUND SRC="canyon.mid" LOOP=2>
```

Figure 22.24.
The code for the background sound is added into your Web page with the HTML Markup bot.

8. Save the page to your Web site.

9. Return to the Cool Sounds TOC page, and repeat the steps again for the PASSPORT.MID file, replacing the page names and filename in the HTML Markup bot appropriately.

10. Save the Cool Sounds TOC page and the CANYON.MID page to your Web site.

Now give one of those marquees a try. Open the Cool Marquees TOC in the FrontPage Editor, and add a link to a page on which you will place a marquee.

To add a marquee to your Cool Stuff pages, follow these steps:

1. Open the Cool Marquees TOC (`clmartoc.htm`) page in the FrontPage Editor.

2. On the first line of the page, enter the following text:

   `Welcome Marquee`

3. Select the text and create a link to a new page. Assign the following properties to the page in the Create Link dialog box's New Page tab:

Page Title:	Welcome Marquee
Page URL:	`welmarq.htm`
Target Frame:	main

   Choose to edit the new page immediately, and then click OK to create the page.

4. Base the page on the Normal template.

5. When the page opens, use the File | Page Properties command to assign the Cool Stuff Main Window Style Sheet (`_private/csstyle.htm`) for the page background and colors. In the Default Target Frame field, enter `Main`.

6. Choose Insert | Bot and select HTML Markup. The HTML Markup dialog box appears.

7. Enter the following in the Markup bot (Figure 22.25 shows a partial example):

```
<FONT FACE="Arial" SIZE=4>
<MARQUEE
    ALIGN=MIDDLE
    BEHAVIOR=SCROLL
    BGCOLOR=WHITE
    DIRECTION=LEFT
    HEIGHT=40 WIDTH=350
    HSPACE=5 VSPACE=10
    LOOP=INFINITE
    SCROLLAMOUNT=10
    SCROLLDELAY=100>
    Welcome to the Cool Stuff Cool Marquees Pages!!!
</MARQUEE>
</FONT>
```

8. Save the page to your Web site.

9. Return to the Cool Stuff TOC page, and repeat the steps again for the `PASSPORT.MID` file, replacing the page names and filename in the HTML Markup bot appropriately.

10. Save the Cool Marquees TOC page and the Welcome Marquee to your Web site.

Figure 22.25.

The HTML code for the Marquee is entered in the HTML Markup bot.

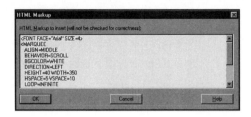

11. If you elected not to update your Cool Stuff Tables of Contents when a page was automatically updated, you'll need to open your Far Out There Cool Stuff page (`cooltoc.htm`) and save it to your Web site again to update the contents. Then choose the View I Refresh command from the FrontPage Explorer to update the pages for the Cool Stuff section. To view the new pages, you might also need to refresh the pages in your browser or empty the browser's cache.

The remaining Cool Stuff pages have yet to be completed, but learning the tasks and techniques to add content for those pages is a project I'll leave up to your imagination. I've tried to show examples of how you can add just about any type of code into the HTML Markup bots. Though I hate to cut you short on adding additional features, you'll soon learn how much more there is to learn! If I've succeeded in igniting that spark of creativity, then I've done my job. I'm sure you can take it from here!

Workshop Wrap-Up

With this last "Real-Life Examples" chapter, you know how to use all the features in FrontPage. The content of your Web site will change, I'm sure, as you learn more features and become even more familiar with the program. You've made a wise choice in choosing FrontPage for a Web authoring and Web management tool! Continue to learn and grow with it—you have lots to work with!

Chapter Summary

In this chapter, you have added interactivity and enhanced features to your site, using FrontPage's advanced bots. You added several different types of forms to your site and some additional code to attach sounds and Marquees to pages.

Next Steps

The chapters in the following part discuss how to maintain your Web site, how to work with the FrontPage Server Extensions, and how to test and publish your Web site.

❏ Refer to Chapter 23, "Web Maintenance and Administration," to learn how to make changes to your Web sites and how to configure your Webs.

❏ Refer to Chapter 24, "Working with the FrontPage Servers," to learn more about the FrontPage Server Extensions.

❏ Refer to Chapter 25, "Testing and Publishing Your Web," to learn how to publish your Web page on a FrontPage-enabled site or on one that doesn't have the FrontPage Server Extensions.

Q&A

Q: Can I configure a Search bot to place its results on a different page rather than on the same page?

A: At the present time, no. The Search bot places the results on the same page.

Q: Can I create a discussion group that has a different section for each topic, instead of using multiple topics in the same discussion?

A: Yes, you can, but remember that you'll be adding several pages to your Web site for each discussion when you do. Your web will be easier to maintain if you create multiple subjects in a single discussion group. On the other hand, if the discussion gets a lot of articles, it can be easier to locate specific subjects if you create several smaller discussion groups. Start with one and see how it goes!

Q: What's the best way to trim a discussion down when the article count gets too high?

A: One way to do it would be to periodically go through the discussion articles and select the best of the lot. Place the best articles on another Web page in an archive area, or zip the pages up into a file and provide a link to download the zip files of past articles.

PART

V

Putting It All Together

TWENTY THREE

Web Maintenance and Administration

A server administrator can get pretty busy, especially with keeping track of where pages are located. Sometimes changes have to be made to the Web. You might need to relocate, rename, or remove webs. New administrators, authors, and end users have to be added or removed, and passwords have to be changed. These are all tasks that require administrator authorization.

Changing the Default Home Page Name

By default, FrontPage uses a home page (or welcome page) name of `index.htm`. Your remote server may require that you use a home page with a different filename, such as `index.html`, `welcome.htm`, or `default.htm`. You can configure FrontPage to use a different home page name.

You can change the setting of the home page in a configuration file. If you installed FrontPage using the default installation, you can find this page in the following directory:

```
C:\FrontPage Webs\server\conf\srm.cnf
```

Within this file is a section where you specify your directory index. To specify a directory index file other than index.htm, add a line to this section. It should look similar to the last line shown below:

```
# DirectoryIndex: Name of the file to use as a pre-written HTML
# directory index. This document, if present, will be opened when the
# server receives a request containing a URL for the directory, instead
# of generating a directory index.
#
DirectoryIndex index.html
```

Changing Clickable Image Style

In Chapter 8, "Getting from Here to There," and in Chapter 17, "Real-Life Examples," you worked with clickable images—images containing hotspots that take the user to other pages in your Web site or other webs. If you or your service provider don't have the FrontPage Server Extensions installed, you will need to set a different clickable image style for your Webs.

There are two ways to approach clickable images—server-side image maps and client-side image maps:

Server-side image maps pass the coordinates of your hotspots to the server's image map handling routine. This requires additional processing time from your server to compute the target URL of the link based on its coordinates.

Client-side image maps encode the destination URL of each hotspot directly on the image map itself and pass the coordinates onto the user. This option doesn't require additional processing time from the server, so it's advantageous to use this option. The option is selected by default but can be changed.

You can instruct FrontPage to generate both client-side and server-side HTML by choosing the "Generate client-side image maps" option in the Web Settings dialog box and also by selecting a server-side image map style. That way you have both bases covered.

By default, FrontPage uses its own clickable image handler. You can change to one of four clickable image formats as follows:

1. From the FrontPage Explorer, choose Tools I Web Settings. The Web Settings dialog box shown in Figure 23.1 appears.

Figure 23.1.

Use the Advanced tab of the Web Settings dialog box to configure your image map handler and show documents in hidden directories.

2. Click the Advanced tab.
3. In the Style field, choose one of the following clickable image styles:

    FrontPage. This is the default setting and should be used if your Internet Service Provider (ISP) has the FrontPage Server Extensions installed on the remote server.

    NCSA. This setting uses the program `imagemap.exe` to handle the server-side clickable image maps when your ISP's server uses NCSA image maps.

    CERN. This setting uses the program `htimage.exe` to handle the server-side clickable image maps when your ISP's server uses CERN image maps.

    Netscape. This setting creates image map data for Netscape servers.

    None. If you select None, FrontPage will not generate any HTML that supports server-side image map processing.

4. In the Prefix field, enter the related URL of the server-side image map handler for the style you selected. If you choose an image map format other than FrontPage, you can accept the default value in this field or contact your service provider for its image map handler's URL.

If you choose FrontPage image maps, server-side image maps are handled automatically.

5. "Generate client-side image maps" is selected by default; it instructs FrontPage to generate HTML code that supports client-side image maps.
6. Click OK.

Displaying Documents in Hidden Directories

When you create discussion groups, the articles that visitors submit to discussions are contained in pages that get stored on your Web site, typically in hidden directories.

By default, FrontPage has these hidden directories turned off in the Web display. You can choose to view these hidden directories by following these steps:

1. From the FrontPage Explorer, choose Tools I Web Settings. The Web Settings dialog box appears.
2. Choose the Advanced tab.
3. Check the box beside Show Documents in Hidden Directories.
4. Click OK to apply the settings to your Web site and exit, or click Apply if you want to change additional Web settings.
5. FrontPage asks if you want to refresh the Web after the changes are made:

   ❏ Choose Yes to refresh the Web and update the directory trees to display the files in hidden directories.

   ❏ Choose No if you want to view the updated directories at a later time. The directories will show the next time you open the Web site or if you choose the View I Refresh command in the FrontPage Explorer.

Making Changes to Your Webs

Web administrators can make changes to webs. They can create new webs, copy them, delete them, and rename them; these tasks are all done through the FrontPage Explorer.

Copying Webs

You use the Copy Web command when you want to transfer your webs from your local server to your Internet Service Provider, or if you want to combine pages from multiple webs into a single Web site on your server. You can also use this command to add pages from one Web site to another.

NOTE: If your ISP doesn't have the FrontPage Server Extensions installed on your remote server, consider using the FrontPage Publishing Wizard, discussed in Chapter 25, "Testing and Publishing Your Web." It's much easier than using an FTP program to accomplish the same task.

When you copy a web, you can copy its contents to a new or existing web on your current server or to a web on a different server. To copy the current Web site, follow these steps:

1. Open the web you want to copy in the FrontPage Explorer.

   ❏ To copy the root web to the root web of another server, open the web named <Root Web>.

   ❏ To copy any child web to another server, open the web you want to copy.

2. Choose File I Copy Web. The Copy Web dialog box shown in Figure 23.2 appears.

Figure 23.2.

Use the Copy Web command to copy webs to other servers.

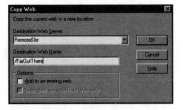

3. In the Destination Web Server field, select the server you want to copy your web to from the drop-down list, or enter the name in the field.

4. In the Destination Web Name field, enter the name of the destination web.

   ❏ To copy the current web to another server's root web, enter a name of <Root Web>. This will replace the server's root web with the web you currently have opened in the FrontPage Explorer.

   ❏ To copy the root web and all child webs to the other server, click Copy Child Webs. This option is enabled if you're copying to a root web.

   ❏ To copy your current web to a lower-level web on the destination server, enter the name of the Web site you want to copy to. By default, the Copy Web dialog box copies the web to a web that uses the same name.

   ❏ To add your current web to a web that already exists on the other server, check the Add to Existing Web checkbox.

NOTE: If you are copying a Web site to the same server you're currently working on, you must supply a new name for the Web site. FrontPage does not allow you to create a copy of a web over itself and prompts you to enter a different name for the destination web.

When you add a web to another web, the pages, files, and directories in the first web are copied to the second web. If the destination web has the same filenames as the web being copied to it, the files will be overwritten by those being copied.

5. Click OK to copy the Web site. FrontPage informs you when your web has been copied successfully.

Renaming Webs

You can change the name or title of a Web site by using the Tools I Web Settings command; just follow these steps:

1. From the FrontPage Explorer, choose Tools I Web Settings to open the Web Settings dialog box.

2. Click the Configuration tab, shown in Figure 23.3.

Figure 23.3.
Use the Configuration tab to assign a new name and title to your Web site.

3. Enter a new web name in the Web Name field. Web names are subject to the character and length restrictions of your server software or Internet Service Provider. Spaces and punctuation marks are typically not allowed, and text is case-sensitive.

4. Enter a new web title in the Web Title field. This title will display in the New Web dialog box the next time you open a Web site on your server with the File I Open Web command.

5. Click the Apply button to change the web name and continue with your web settings; then click the OK button to change the web name and exit the Web Settings dialog box.

Deleting Webs

To delete a Web site from your server, you have to be authorized as an administrator of the web. Also, you have to open the web before you delete it. Actually, this isn't such a bad idea, because you probably want to make sure it's the Web site you want to delete. You can't recover a Web site once it has been deleted.

To delete a Web site, follow these steps:

1. Open the Web site you want to delete in the FrontPage Explorer.

2. Choose File | Delete Web.

3. FrontPage asks whether you're sure you want to delete the Web site. Click Yes to delete the web (you can't retrieve it!) or No to cancel.

Administering Your FrontPage Webs

If you're using FrontPage to develop webs for your corporate intranet, you might be using multiple Web administrators and authors to develop your Web sites. You use the FrontPage Explorer to configure access for them and to add end-user permissions for restricted webs.

Who Has Access?

FrontPage allows you to assign access permissions in three categories—Web administrators, Web authors, and end users. Each Web site on your server can be assigned its own access permissions, allowing you to assign Web development and administration to a different team for each Web. End-user permissions are added if you have restricted webs on your server.

You can also assign address masks to your webs. These grant access permissions to a web through the use of an Internet address rather than by a name and password.

Administrators are allowed to perform the following tasks in FrontPage:

❏ Create webs and pages

❏ Delete webs and pages

❏ Designate other administrators, authors, and end users, and restrict end users from accessing certain portions of the Web site

Authors are allowed to perform the following tasks in FrontPage:

❏ Create pages

❏ Delete pages

By default, all end users have access to a Web site, but there might be instances when you want to restrict access to only certain individuals. For example, you might want to create a web to which only company employees have access. Another example might be a technical support site that requires a monthly subscription fee. On a personal level, you might want to allow access to only friends and family members.

Refer to Chapter 6, "Real-Life Examples," for an example of a web that is restricted to employees only.

Authorizing Administrators, Authors, and End Users

You must have administrator status to authorize another administrator. To add an authorization for a Web administrator, follow these steps:

1. From the FrontPage Explorer, choose Tools I Permissions. The Web Permissions dialog box appears, open to the Settings tab, as shown in Figure 23.4.

Figure 23.4.

Use the Settings tab in the Web Permissions dialog box to assign unique permissions for a child web.

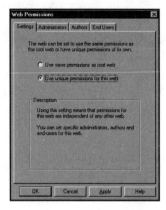

2. To assign unique permissions for the web (other than the root web), select Use unique permissions for this web. The current web will not inherit its settings from the root web.

3. Click Apply.

4. You can add permissions for administrators, authors, or end users as follows:

   ❑ To add an administrator, select the Administrators tab, shown in Figure 23.5.

   ❑ To add an author, select the Authors tab, shown in Figure 23.6.

   ❑ To add an end user to a restricted Web site, select the End Users tab, shown in Figure 23.7. Choose Registered Users Only.

Figure 23.5.

Assign permissions and address masks for administrators in the Administrators tab.

Figure 23.6.

Assign permissions and address masks for authors in the Authors tab.

Figure 23.7.

Assign permissions and address masks for end users in the End Users tab.

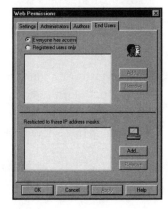

5. Click the Add button to add a new administrator, author, or end user and open a dialog box for each one. Figure 23.8 shows the New Administrator dialog box; the others are similar.

Figure 23.8.

Enter the name and password in the New Administrator, New Author, or New User dialog box.

6. Enter the name of the new administrator, author, or end user in the Name field.

7. Enter the administrator's, author's, or end user's password, and confirm it again in the Confirm Password field.

8. Click OK.

9. Click OK to add the administrator, author, or end user and close the dialog box. If you want to add additional permissions for the Web site, click the Apply button to continue adding permissions.

Restricting the IP Address

To restrict the IP addresses of Web administrators, authors, or end users, follow these steps:

1. From the FrontPage Explorer, choose Tools | Permissions. The Web Permissions dialog box opens to the Permissions tab.

2. To assign unique permissions for the web (other than the root web), select Use unique permissions for this web. The current web will not inherit the settings of the root web.

3. Click Apply.

4. You restrict the IP address for administrators, authors, or end users by clicking the Administrators, Authors, or End Users tab, respectively.

5. In the Restricted to these IP address masks section, click Add. The New IP Mask dialog box, shown in Figure 23.9, appears.

Figure 23.9.
Use the New IP Mask dialog box to assign IP address masks to the Web site.

6. In each of the four sections of the dialog box, enter either a number ranging from 1 to 256, inclusively, or a wildcard character (*). The wildcard character will cause any number to be accepted in that position of the IP address and can only come at the end if you're missing numbers and asterisks.

7. Click OK.

8. Click OK to add the IP address and close the dialog box. If you want to add additional permissions for the Web site, click the Apply button to continue adding them.

Changing Passwords

If you are an administrator or author of the current Web site, you can change your own password. Passwords can also be changed for end users. Simply follow these steps:

1. From the FrontPage Explorer, choose Tools I Change Password. The Change Password For *(name)* dialog box, shown in Figure 23.10, appears.

2. Enter the old password in the Old Password field.

3. Enter the new password in the New Password field and confirm it again in the Confirm Password field.

4. Click OK.

Removing Administrators, Authors, and End Users

To remove an administrator, author, or end user from a Web, follow these steps:

1. From the FrontPage Explorer, choose Tools I Permissions.

2. Click the appropriate tab for the individual you want to remove:

   ❏ To remove a Web administrator, click the Administrators tab. In the Administrators for this web field, select the name of the administrator you want to remove.

   ❏ To remove a Web author, click the Authors tab. In the Authors for this web field, select the name of the author you want to remove.

   ❏ To remove an end user, click the End Users tab. In the section labeled "Registered users only," select the name of the end user and click Remove.

3. To remove the administrator, author, or end user and return to the FrontPage Explorer, click OK. Click Apply to remove the name and continue adding or removing Web permissions.

Removing the IP Address

To remove the IP address of an administrator, author, or end user from a Web, follow these steps:

1. From the FrontPage Explorer, choose Tools I Permissions.

2. Click the appropriate tab—Administrators, Authors, or End Users—for the IP address mask you want to remove.

3. In the IP address masks section, select the IP address you want to remove.

4. Click Remove.

5. To remove the IP address mask and return to the FrontPage Explorer, click OK. Click Apply to remove the end user and continue adding or removing Web permissions.

Workshop Wrap-Up

FrontPage allows great flexibility, whether you're using it to develop your own personal Web site or using it in a corporate intranet environment. If you're working on your own Web site, you're already granted access permissions to perform administrative and authoring tasks. If you need to configure multiple administrators and authors, the capability is there for you to do so.

Chapter Summary

In this chapter, you have learned how to maintain and manage your Web sites and how to specify the name of your web's home pages. If your service provider doesn't have the FrontPage Server Extensions, you learned how to choose another format for handling the image maps. You have also learned how to make changes to webs and assign administrators, authors, and end users to your Web site.

Next Steps

In the next chapter, you'll learn more about the FrontPage Server Extensions and the files and directories that relate to them. You'll also learn what other server extensions are available.

In Chapter 25, "Testing and Publishing Your Web," you'll learn how to transfer your Web documents and files from your computer to your ISP.

Q&A

Q: Can multiple IP addresses be assigned to a single individual?

A: The IP address masks don't appear to be connected to an individual. You can enter multiple IP addresses.

Q: Do I have to copy the clickable image handler to my remote site if my Internet provider doesn't have the Server Extensions?

A: No, you define the path to the ISP's clickable image handler when you configure the image handler in your FrontPage web. The optional image handlers provided with FrontPage write the data that their image handlers expect to see. Refer to Chapter 25 for the files you'll need to transfer when your service provider doesn't have the FrontPage Server Extensions installed.

Q: Is there any way to specify copying only certain files when you use the Copy Web command?

A: Unfortunately not. It's currently an "all or nothing" command. You can use an FTP program to copy selected files to a remote Web site.

TWENTY FOUR

Working with the FrontPage Servers

The FrontPage Server Extensions are available for four different operating systems, covering a good range of commonly used server programs. When you work with FrontPage's Personal Web Server, you are using files similar to those found on servers in other platforms. For your FrontPage webs to use all the features in your web pages, the server extensions must exist on the remote server.

The Personal Web Server

Throughout this book, you have designed your pages while you were offline. You may not realize it, but by having the Personal Web Server installed on your local computer, you can actually connect to the Internet and use your local computer as a Web site while online. The best way to do this is to use a computer that you can dedicate to your Web site and also get a 24-hour connection to the Internet. You'll also need an extra phone line for that Internet connection if you want it to be a permanent connection.

In this chapter, you

- ❑ Learn how to configure the FrontPage Personal Web Server using the FrontPage Server Administrator

- ❑ Learn how to change the port number that the Personal Web Server uses

- ❑ Learn how to upgrade and check your server installation

- ❑ Learn how to enable and disable authoring on your server

- ❑ Learn how to add an administrator and IP address to your server from the FrontPage Server Administrator

- ❑ Learn how to assign a proxy server and specify other servers within firewalls

- ❑ Learn what other operating systems and server programs can use the FrontPage Server Extensions and where they can be downloaded

The Personal Web Server is intended for light usage. It uses only one port at a time (so it doesn't support multi-homing) and allows 12 child webs to exist on the server. If you need a server that's more robust, or one that supports multi-homing, this chapter covers the servers and operating systems for which other versions of the FrontPage Server Extensions are available.

The Personal Web Server is installed on your local computer when you choose one of the following installation configurations:

❏ When you install FrontPage using the Typical installation procedure outlined in the "Getting Started with Microsoft FrontPage" manual or Appendix A, "Installing FrontPage," of this book.

❏ When you install FrontPage using the Custom installation procedure and choose to install the FrontPage Server Extensions.

Appendix A explains how to perform a TCP/IP test to determine the host names you can use in the Personal Web Server.

Using the FrontPage Server Administrator

When you install the Personal Web Server on your computer, you use the FrontPage Server Administrator to configure your server, install or uninstall the FrontPage Server Extensions, enable authoring for a web, or add server administrators. The steps to perform each of these functions are listed in the following sections.

Changing the Port Number

When you install the FrontPage Personal Web Server, it gets installed to one of the following two ports:

❏ When you complete a new installation of FrontPage, the Personal Web Server uses Port 80.

❏ If you install FrontPage over a previous version (Version 1.0), your existing content continues to use Port 80. The new version of the Personal Web Server uses Port 8080.

To change the port number when using the Personal Web Server, you need to shut down your server, uninstall the server extensions from the existing port, and reinstall the server extensions to the new port.

To uninstall the server extensions from a selected port:

1. Shut down the server.

2. From the Start menu, select FrontPage Server Administrator to open its dialog box, shown in Figure 24.1.

3. In the Select port number field, choose the port number from which you want to uninstall the server extensions.

4. Click Uninstall. The Server Administrator notifies you that the server extensions will be removed, but that the content files will remain. This dialog box is shown in Figure 24.2. Click OK to uninstall the server extensions from your current port.

NOTE: When you remove the server extensions from a port, the following changes are made:

The `frontpg.ini` file, located in your Windows directory, is edited. The section for the selected port is removed.

The `_vti_bin` directory containing the server extension executables is removed.

The `_vti_txt` directory that contains the text index for the Web is removed.

Content files, such as Web pages, image files, and others, are maintained in the directories in your content folder.

5. Click OK to uninstall the extensions, or Cancel to return to the Server Administrator.

To install the server extensions to a new port on your server, follow these steps:

1. Change the port number for your server, following the normal procedures provided for that server.

NOTE: Be sure to use a port number higher than 1024. These numbers are reserved for well-known servers.

❑ If you are using FrontPage's Personal Web Server, the configuration file you want to use is in the `\FrontPage Webs\Server\conf` directory and is named `httpd.cnf`. The lines you want to edit will look similar to this:

```
# Port: The port the standalone listens to. 80 is the network
standard.
#
Port 80
```

❑ For the WebSite Server, use the Server Admin program furnished with WebSite to change the port number.

2. From the Start menu, select FrontPage Server Administrator to open its dialog box. Your server can't be running while you install the server extensions.

3. In the Select Port Number field, choose the port number to which you want to install the server extensions.

4. Click Install. The Configure Server Type dialog box shown in Figure 24.3 appears.

Figure 24.3.
Choose the server type you want to install to the selected port.

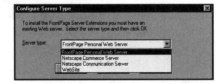

5. Choose your server type. The server type must be installed on your system, and its configuration file must exist in a directory on your hard drive. Choose one of the following server types:

FrontPage Personal Web Server (for Windows 95 or Windows NT)

Netscape Commerce Server (for Windows NT)

Netscape Communication Server (for Windows NT)

WebSite (for Windows 95 or Windows NT)

6. Click OK. The Server Configuration dialog box shown in Figure 24.4 appears. Enter the path and name of your server configuration file in the Server Config field, or use the Browse button to locate your server configuration file, as shown in Figure 24.5. Select the same file you edited in step 1.

Figure 24.4.

Specify your server configuration file in the Server Configuration dialog box.

Figure 24.5.

You use the Server Config dialog box to locate the server configuration file on your computer.

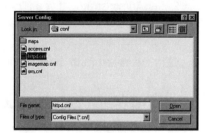

7. Click OK to install the server extensions. The Confirmation Dialog shown in Figure 24.6 appears. It lists the Server Type, Server Configuration File, Port, and Document Root for your server.

Figure 24.6.

The Server Administrator confirms your selections before the extensions are installed.

8. Click OK to install the extensions and return to the FrontPage Server Administrator. Click Cancel to cancel the installation.

Upgrading the Server Extensions

If you're upgrading FrontPage from a previous release, you need to update the server extensions in your existing webs. To do that, follow these steps:

1. Shut down the server.

2. From the Start menu, select FrontPage Server Administrator.

3. Choose Upgrade. The Server Administrator dialog box shown in Figure 24.7 appears and informs you that FrontPage will upgrade the extensions on the server. Click OK to upgrade the server extensions.

Figure 24.7.
FrontPage notifies you that the extensions will be upgraded.

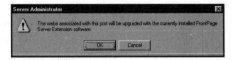

4. Click OK to upgrade the extensions, or Cancel to return to the FrontPage Server Administrator. If you click OK, the new versions of the server extensions are copied to your server and you are informed that the upgrade was completed successfully.

5. Click OK to return to the FrontPage Server Administrator.

Checking Your Server Configuration

If you're having problems with your server configuration, you can check the installation from the FrontPage Administrator. This application checks to see whether all the required DLLs and configuration files exist on your computer. To check your installation, follow these steps:

1. Shut down the server.

2. From the Start menu, select FrontPage Server Administrator.

3. Choose Check. If the check is successful, all the required files exist on your system. However, if the check isn't successful, you might need to reinstall the FrontPage Server Extensions from the installation disks.

Enabling or Disabling Authoring

To enable or disable authoring on your server, use the Authoring button in the FrontPage Administrator. The steps are as follows:

1. From the Start menu, select FrontPage Server Administrator.

2. Choose Authoring. FrontPage informs you whether authoring is enabled or disabled for the server.

3. Choose OK to change authoring status.

Configuring Security

You can add an administrator's password and restrict his or her IP address by using the Security button in the FrontPage Server Administrator. To configure security, follow these steps:

1. From the Start menu, select FrontPage Server Administrator.

2. Choose Security. The Administrator name and password dialog box shown in Figure 24.8 appears.

Figure 24.8.

Enter the administrator's name and password in the Administrator name and password dialog box.

3. Enter the name of the Web site you want to add the administrator to in the Web name field. By default, the root Web appears in this field. To add an administrator to the child Web, enter the Web name preceded by a forward slash, for example, /MyChildWeb.

4. Enter the administrator's name in the Name field. The name cannot contain any spaces or punctuation marks.

5. Enter the administrator's password in the Password field, and confirm it in the Confirm password field.

6. Click the Advanced button to restrict Web operations to only the administrator's IP address (optional). The Internet address restriction dialog box, shown in Figure 24.9, appears.

Figure 24.9.

Enter the administrator's IP address (optional) in the Internet address restriction dialog box.

7. Enter the IP address you want to restrict and click OK, or click Cancel to return to the Administrator name and password dialog box.

8. Click OK to add the administrator to the Web site. The Server Administrator confirms that the administrator has been added to the Web site you selected.

Using FrontPage with Proxy Servers and Firewalls

If your Web server uses firewalls and proxy servers, you can configure FrontPage to use the same configuration. Proxies are used any time the FrontPage Explorer or FrontPage Editor is used to access any Web pages outside your server, for example:

❑ When the FrontPage Explorer opens a link external to your web.

❑ When you use the Follow Link command in the FrontPage Editor to follow a link to a page outside your firewall.

❑ When you use the Open Location command in the FrontPage Editor to open a page outside your firewall.

Specifying a Proxy Server for a Web

To use a proxy server with FrontPage, choose the Tools I Proxies command to assign the server.

To specify a proxy server, follow these steps:

1. In the FrontPage Explorer, choose Tools I Proxies. The Proxies dialog box, shown in Figure 24.10, appears.

Figure 24.10.
Enter your proxy server and the list of servers within your firewall in the Proxies dialog box.

2. In the HTTP Proxy field, enter the name of the proxy server and its port.

3. In the List of Hosts without Proxy field, enter the names of the servers you want to use inside the firewall. The port number is optional. Separate the entries in the list with commas.

Server Configuration Files

There are three server configuration files installed in your server directory when you install the FrontPage Server Extensions. These files are located in the `\FrontPage Webs\server\conf` directory on your computer, and you can open them with a text editor such as Notepad or WordPad. The settings in each file are described in the following sections. It's best not to edit them unless you understand what the settings are there for.

ACCESS.CNF Configuration File

The access configuration file contains global access configurations. You assign access permissions to the directories in your webs in this file.

HTTPD.CNF Configuration File

The main server configuration file for the Personal Web Server has commands similar to those found in NCSA Server Version 1.3R. The configuration file contains a URL you can use when changing the settings in this file. In this file, you assign the following for your server:

Server root directory

The port the server uses

Timeout values

E-mail address of the server administrator

The location of the server's error log file

The location of the transfer log file

A host name sent back to clients if it's different from what the program would get (for example, using "www.myserver.com" instead of the value returned in the TCP/IP check)

The command-line template for CGI WinExec

The default image map configuration file

SRM.CNF Configuration File

The server resource configuration file settings control document layout and the files you want to make visible to users. Path defaults listed in this file are those related to the server's installation directory and should be given in UNIX format, using a forward slash instead of a backslash.

The following configurations are specified in this file:

Document (content) root directory

The default name of your index page

The default name of the access file permissions file

Aliasing and redirection names

MIME types

Automatic directory indexing

Files that the directory index should ignore

FrontPage Server Extensions: Other Platforms

If you're looking for a service provider that has the FrontPage Server Extensions installed, Microsoft keeps a list of them at the following URL:

`http://www.microsoft.com/frontpage/ispinfo/isplist.htm`

If your service provider doesn't have the server extensions installed, good news is in store. The FrontPage Server Extensions are also available for other platforms and operating systems. These server extensions are primarily intended for use by Internet service providers or those who are using FrontPage on corporate intranets. The server extensions are available for UNIX, BSDI, and Windows NT platforms.

General information on the server extensions and Web hosting can be found at the following URLs on Microsoft's Web site:

Microsoft FrontPage Internet Service Provider Information:

`http://www.microsoft.com/frontpage/ispinfo/`

Web Hosting Primer:

`http://www.microsoft.com/frontpage/ispinfo/primer/default.htm`

Web Hosting FAQ:

`http://www.microsoft.com/frontpage/ispinfo/hosting_faq.htm`

FrontPage Server Extensions:

`http://www.microsoft.com/frontpage/freestuff/fs_fp_extensions.htm`

At press time, the FrontPage Server Extensions are available for the following operating systems and Web servers:

Windows 95

Windows NT Workstation

Windows NT Server 3.5.1 (or Higher)

BSD/OS 2.1 (BSDi UNIX on Intel Architecture)

HP/UX 9.03 (Hewlett-Packard Computers)

IRIX 5.3 (Silicon Graphics Computers)

Solaris 2.4 (Sun Workstations, SPARC Architecture)

SunOS 4.1.3 (Sun Workstations, SPARC Architecture)

Windows 95

For Windows 95 users, the FrontPage Server Extensions are available for the following servers. Both are included in FrontPage:

❏ Microsoft FrontPage Personal Web Server (furnished with FrontPage)

❏ O'Reilly and Associates WebSite

Windows NT Workstation

For Windows NT users, the FrontPage Server Extensions are available for the following servers. All are included with FrontPage:

❏ Microsoft FrontPage Personal Web Server (furnished with FrontPage)

❏ Netscape Commerce Server. Does not support SSL.

❏ Netscape Communications Server

❏ O'Reilly and Associates WebSite

Windows NT Server 3.5.1 (or Higher)

For Windows NT Server users (version 3.5.1 or higher), the Microsoft FrontPage Server Extensions are available for the Microsoft Internet Information Server. You can download the Internet Information Server from the following URL:

`http://www.microsoft.com/infoserv/`

FrontPage Server Extensions are available from Microsoft's Web site. To download the server extensions, follow these steps:

1. Complete the user agreement form at the following URL:

   `http://www.microsoft.com/frontpage/freestuff/agreement.htm`

2. Download the `IISReadMe.txt` file, which contains general information about installing the FrontPage Server Extensions:

   `http://www.microsoft.com/frontpage/free/vt11/IISReadMe.txt`

3. Download the server extensions from the following URL:

   `http://www.microsoft.com/frontpage/free/vt11/Fpiisb2.exe`

4. Install and configure the FrontPage server extensions as outlined in the readme files that come with the server extensions.

BSD/OS 2.1 (BSDi UNIX on Intel Architecture)

For BSD/OS 2.1 users, the FrontPage Server Extensions are available for the following servers:

Apache
CERN
NCSA

Netscape Communications Server
Open Market Web Server

To download and install the FrontPage Server Extensions for BSD/OS 2.1, follow these steps:

1. Complete the user agreement form at the following URL:

   `http://www.microsoft.com/frontpage/freestuff/agreement.htm`

2. Download the server extensions from the following URLs. The `vt11.bsdi.tar` file is 6MB, and the `vt11.bsdi.tar.Z` file is 3.8MB:

   `http://www.microsoft.com/frontpage/free/vt11/vt11.bsdi.tar`
   `http://www.microsoft.com/frontpage/free/vt11/vt11.bsdi.tar.Z`

3. Install and configure the FrontPage Server Extensions as outlined in the readme files provided with the server extensions.

HP/UX 9.03 (Hewlett-Packard Computers)

For HP/UX 9.03 users, the FrontPage Server Extensions are available for the following servers:

Apache
CERN
NCSA
Netscape Communications Server
Open Market Web Server

To download and install the FrontPage Server Extensions for HP/UX 9.03, follow these steps:

1. Complete the user agreement form at the following URL:

   `http://www.microsoft.com/frontpage/freestuff/agreement.htm`

2. Download the `UNIXReadMe.txt` file that has general information about installing the FrontPage server extensions:

   `http://www.microsoft.com/frontpage/free/vt11/unixreadme.txt`

3. Download the Server Extensions from the following URLs. The `vt11.hp700.tar` file is 10.1MB, and the `vt11.hp700.tar.Z` file is 5.1MB:

   `http://www.microsoft.com/frontpage/free/vt11/vt11.hp700.tar`
   `http://www.microsoft.com/frontpage/free/vt11/vt11.hp700.tar.Z`

4. Install and configure the FrontPage Server Extensions as outlined in the readme files that come with the server extensions.

IRIX 5.3 (Silicon Graphics Computers)

For IRIX 5.3 users, the FrontPage Server Extensions are available for the following servers:

Apache
CERN
NCSA
Netscape Communications Server
Open Market Web Server

To download and install the FrontPage Server Extensions for IRIX 5.3, follow these steps:

1. Complete the user agreement form at the following URL:

   `http://www.microsoft.com/frontpage/freestuff/agreement.htm`

2. Download the `UNIXReadMe.txt` file, which contains general information about installing the FrontPage Server Extensions:

   `http://www.microsoft.com/frontpage/free/vt11/unixreadme.txt`

3. Download the server extensions from the following URLs. The `vt11.sgi.tar` file is 13.8MB, and the `vt11.sgi.tar.Z` file is 5MB:

   `http://www.microsoft.com/frontpage/free/vt11/vt11.sgi.tar`
   `http://www.microsoft.com/frontpage/free/vt11/vt11.sgi.tar.Z`

4. Install and configure the FrontPage Server Extensions as outlined in the readme files provided with the server extensions.

Solaris 2.4 (Sun Workstations, SPARC Architecture)

For Solaris 2.4 users, the FrontPage Server Extensions are available for the following servers:

Apache
CERN
NCSA
Netscape Communications Server
Open Market Web Server

To download and install the FrontPage Server Extensions for Solaris 2.4, follow these steps:

1. Complete the user agreement form at the following URL:

   `http://www.microsoft.com/frontpage/freestuff/agreement.htm`

2. Download the `UNIXReadMe.txt` file containing general information about installing the FrontPage Server Extensions:

   `http://www.microsoft.com/frontpage/free/vt11/unixreadme.txt`

3. Download the server extensions from the following URLs. The `vt11.solaris.tar` file is 8.2MB, and the `vt11.solaris.tar.Z` file is 4MB:

   `http://www.microsoft.com/frontpage/free/vt11/vt11.solaris.tar`
   `http://www.microsoft.com/frontpage/free/vt11/vt11.solaris.tar.Z`

4. Install and configure the FrontPage Server Extensions as outlined in the readme files that come with the server extensions.

SunOS 4.1.3 (Sun Workstations, SPARC Architecture)

For SunOS 4.1.3 users, the FrontPage Server Extensions are available for the following servers:

Apache
CERN
NCSA
Netscape Communications Server
Open Market Web Server

To download and install the FrontPage Server Extensions for SunOS 4.1.3, follow these steps:

1. Complete the user agreement form at the following URL:

   `http://www.microsoft.com/frontpage/freestuff/agreement.htm`

2. Download the `UNIXReadMe.txt` file that has general information about installing the FrontPage Server Extensions:

   `http://www.microsoft.com/frontpage/free/vt11/unixreadme.txt`

3. Download the server extensions from the following URLs. The `vt11.sunos.tar` file is 8.3MB, and the `vt11.sunos.tar.Z` file is 4.3MB:

   `http://www.microsoft.com/frontpage/free/vt11/vt11.sunos.tar`
   `http://www.microsoft.com/frontpage/free/vt11/vt11.sunos.tar.Z`

4. Install and configure the FrontPage Server Extensions as outlined in the readme files provided with the server extensions.

The Server Extension Files: Where They're At, What They're For

The FrontPage Server Extensions consist of three executable CGI files. When you install FrontPage on your server, the files and directories listed below are installed. For the

Personal Web Server, these files are in the `\FrontPage Webs\Server` subdirectories. For UNIX systems, the files are installed in the `/usr/local/frontpage` directory.

`/_vti_adm/admin.exe`	The CGI executable file that controls all administrator operations.
`/_vti_aut/author.exe`	The CGI executable file that controls all author operations.
`/_vti_bin/shtml.exe`	The CGI executable file that controls all browse-time behavior. All forms using Web bots refer to this file.
`/Bin/fpsrvadm.exe`	The FrontPage Server Administrator program, used to install and uninstall the server extensions.

The content directories (located in `\FrontPage Webs\Content` for Windows users) contain the following files and directories:

`/_private`	Used to store pages that aren't normally visible to browsers.
`/cgi-bin`	For executable pages and custom CGI scripts.
`/images`	The directory for storing Web images.

Each content directory containing pages also has the following subdirectories:

`/_vti_bin/`	This directory and its subdirectories contain the Front Page Server Extension executable files (described previously).
`/_vti_cnf/`	A corresponding `.htm` file exists for each page in the Web. These files use the same names as the Web pages in the Web. They contain any name/value pairs (such as author's name and registered users). If the file isn't present, it's re-created when necessary.
`/_vti_pvt/_x_todo.htm`	The Web's To Do List.
`/_vti_pvt/_x_todoh.htm`	The Web's To Do List history.
`/_vti_pvt/deptodoc.btr`	Dependency database for the Web.
`/_vti_pvt/doctodep.btr`	Dependency database for the Web.
`/_vti_pvt/service.cnf`	Meta-information for the Web, including information set with the Tools I Web Settings command.
`/_vti_pvt/services.cnf`	Contained in the root web only; has a list of subwebs.

`/_vti_shm/`	For each page containing Web bots, two files are kept. The source file is stored here. The expanded version is placed in the parent directory (the Web directory).
`/_vti_txt/`	Text indexes for the pages in the Web site are placed in this directory.
`/cgi-bin`	For executable pages and custom CGI scripts.
`/images`	The directory for storing Web images.

Workshop Wrap-Up

You now know some of the basics about the FrontPage Server Extensions. For additional information, visit Microsoft's site, where the most recent information about the server extensions are kept.

Chapter Summary

In this chapter, you have learned how to configure the FrontPage Personal Web Server, how to enable and disable authoring, how to assign server administrators, and how to add proxy servers. You have also learned about the other platforms and servers for which the FrontPage Server Extensions are available.

Next Steps

You can find the most recent information by following links to the MSOffice or FrontPage sections of the Web. Appendix C, "Directory of Resources," lists where you can find these directories, as well as other places you can go for help.

Q&A

Q: If my service provider doesn't have the FrontPage Server Extensions, do I have to keep all those other files and directories on my computer?

A: Yes, you probably should. The server extensions keep track of where things are located in your Web site, run the bots, assign authors and administrators, and maintain your directory relationships. They also keep track of the pages you're designing on your Webs and the FrontPage features used within them. Without the server extensions, the FrontPage Editor loses a lot of capability.

Q: If my service provider uses the FrontPage Server Extensions, do I need any files from its version on my local computer?

A: No, you don't. The server extension files are consistent from platform to platform, except that they're unique to the operating system used.

Q: When I transfer my web to my service provider's site, will my server extensions overwrite theirs?

A: No. When you copy a web to your remote site, the only files transferred are those in the /Content directories (your web pages, images, and other related files in your web). The server extensions reside in the /Server directories and aren't part of the transfer.

TWENTY FIVE

Testing and Publishing Your Web

It's time to give your Web page that final once-over before you get it out to the Web. You should check your spelling, check your links, check your directories, check *everything*. Fortunately, FrontPage keeps everything you have to do from start to finish in mind and offers a few tools that can help you, as well!

Links at a Glance

When you develop your pages with other types of editors, sometimes you can't tell, at a glance, if your links are working correctly. With FrontPage, you can tell quite easily from within the FrontPage Explorer. Look in Outline View or Link View, both shown in Figure 25.1, and you'll be able to tell whether the links between pages in your Web site need fixing. When you view your pages in Link View, you can expand the tree by clicking on any page icon that has a plus symbol (+) on it. That symbol tells you there are links to other pages contained in that page.

Figure 25.1.

Use Outline View or Link View to tell at a glance whether links to and from a page are working correctly.

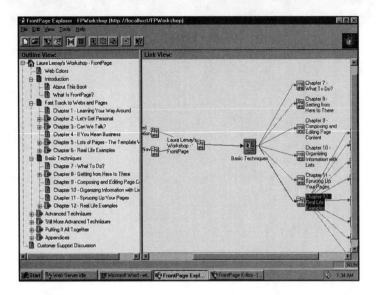

Viewing Links Inside Pages

Links inside pages are links from a page to itself, such as links to bookmarks that appear on the same page. In the example shown in Figure 25.2, the Hyperdocument page contains links to itself, as you can see more clearly in the Link View.

There are also a couple of broken links, represented by the torn pages, on this page that jump out at you, too. Notice also that some of the outgoing links are represented by arrows and others by circles. The arrows designate links to other pages (either in your web or to other webs). The circles represent links to items included in the current page—usually images or content that appears inside Include bots.

You can view links inside a page by using one of the following methods:

❏ From the FrontPage Explorer, choose View I Links Inside Page.

❏ Click the Links Inside Page button on the FrontPage Explorer toolbar. This is the icon that shows a page with a blue arrow coming out from and going back into the page.

To turn off the display of links inside pages, repeat one of those procedures.

Viewing Links to Images

You can use the FrontPage Explorer's Outline View or Link View to view links to images within your current Web site. Links to images are displayed with an icon of a picture in a frame, as shown in Figure 25.3.

Figure 25.2.

Use View | Links Inside Pages or its toolbar button to view links within a single page.

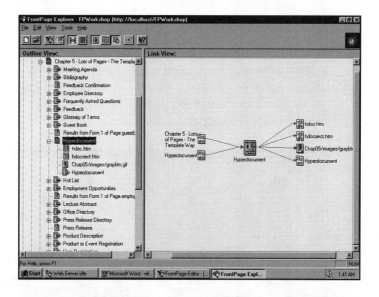

Figure 25.3.

View links to images in your pages by choosing the View | Links to Images command or toolbar button.

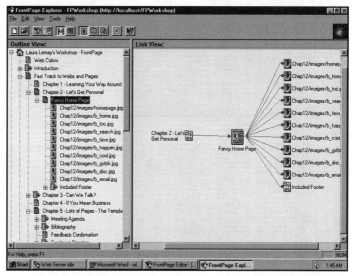

To view links to images, use one of the following methods:

❏ From the FrontPage Explorer, choose View | Links to Images.

❏ Click the Links to Images button on the FrontPage Explorer toolbar.

To turn off the display of links to images, repeat one of these procedures.

Viewing Repeated Links

You can use the FrontPage Explorer's Outline View or Link View to view repeated links to pages within your current Web site. Sometimes more than one link to the same page appears within your page. For example, you might have ten copies of the same bullet graphic on a page, or, as the example in Figure 25.4 shows, you can have links to your e-mail address in a couple of places on your Web page.

Figure 25.4.

View repeated links from your pages by choosing the View | Repeated Links command or toolbar button.

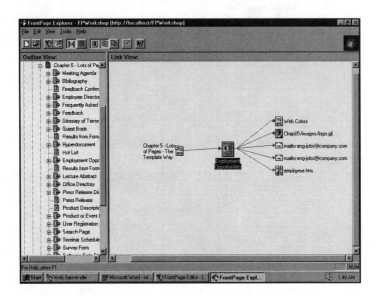

In most cases, you want to view links only once—but if you need to remove links to a particular page, you might miss the additional links on the page unless you choose this command.

To view repeated links, use one of the following methods:

❑ From the FrontPage Explorer, choose View | Repeated Links.

❑ Click the Repeated Links button on the FrontPage Explorer toolbar.

To turn off the display of links to images, repeat one of those procedures.

Better Check It: Verifying Links

What if you've got hundreds of pages on your site? You don't have to look at them all manually, do you?

Have no fear: There's an easy way to check the links on all those pages. Use the Tools | Verify Links command to both verify and repair internal and external links.

❏ To verify internal links, choose Tools I Verify Links to open the dialog box shown in Figure 25.5. All broken internal links are represented by a red circle.

Figure 25.5.

Broken internal links are represented by a red circle in the Verify Links dialog box.

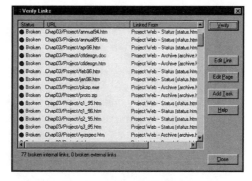

❏ To verify external links, you must be connected to the World Wide Web. Broken external links are represented by a yellow circle with a question mark beside it. Figure 25.6 shows lots of broken links (they are to fictitious sites).

Figure 25.6.

Broken external links are represented by a yellow circle next to a question mark.

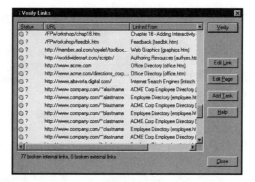

Once you establish an online connection, use the following procedure to verify external links:

1. Choose Tools I Verify Links. External broken links are listed after internal broken links, if any.

2. Click Verify to identify the broken external links. Each link is verified in sequence. It actually goes quite rapidly. Don't worry, it doesn't load the pages as the links are verified! The process only checks to see that the URLs are valid.

3. To stop verifying links before the list is complete, click Stop.

Fixing Internal and External Links

You might have some broken links inside your web, such as links you forgot to complete, links to pages you might have deleted from your web, or perhaps even links from pages imported into your web that you forgot to edit. You can easily fix them by using the Tools I Verify Links command in the FrontPage Explorer.

TIP: If you've got lots of broken links to look at, you can sort the list of broken links by one of three categories—Status, URL, or Linked from page. Click the headings above the list of broken links in the Verify Links dialog box.

To repair broken internal or external links, follow these steps:

1. From the FrontPage Explorer, choose Tools I Verify Links. The Verify Links dialog box appears. Internal links are listed first.

2. Select the broken internal or external link you want to repair.

3. Click Edit Link. The Edit Link dialog box shown in Figure 25.7 appears.

Figure 25.7.

Edit the broken link in the Edit Link dialog box. You can repair the link on any or all pages on which it appears.

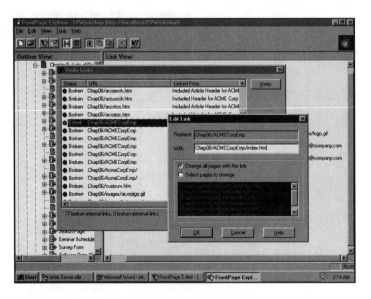

4. Enter the correct URL for the link.

5. Choose one of the following options:

   Change all pages with this link: Choose this option to change the link in all pages on which the broken link appears.

Select pages to change: Choose this option if you want to repair the broken link in a set of selected pages.

6. Click OK. The status of the repaired links changes to Edited in the Verify Links dialog box. After you repair your external links, click the Verify button again while you're online, just to make sure you fixed them all correctly.

TIP: Page URLs can change frequently on the Web or become outdated rapidly. If you run the Tools I Verify Links command on a fairly regular basis, you can delete or revise links when necessary and keep all the links in your Web site current.

You can also choose to edit the page on which the broken link appears. This doesn't automatically fix the other links on which the same broken link appears, but it does allow you to verify where you wanted that link to go. To edit the page on which the link appears, follow these steps:

1. From the FrontPage Explorer, choose Tools I Verify Links. The Verify Links dialog box appears.

2. Select the broken internal or external link you want to repair.

3. Click Edit Page. The page opens in the FrontPage Editor, and you can repair the link in the page.

4. Save the revised page to the Web site.

Fixing Page Errors

Refer to Chapter 7, "What to Do?" to learn how to add broken links to your To Do List.

If a bot is configured incorrectly, or if a page that a bot refers to is moved or deleted from your Web, you'll notice a small red triangle next to the page in the FrontPage Explorer's Outline View. You can determine why the error appears on the page by using the following procedure:

TIP: If you notice these red triangles after you import several pages that you know are linked correctly, choose the View I Refresh command. The error triangle might be there because of the order in which pages were imported to the web. Refreshing the web resolves some of these error messages.

1. From the FrontPage Explorer, select the page that has the error triangle.

2. Choose Edit I Properties, or right-click and choose Properties from the pop-up menu. The Properties dialog box appears.

3. Click the Errors tab to see a description of the page error, as shown in Figure 25.8.

4. Click OK to exit the dialog box and return to the FrontPage Explorer. Resolve the error as indicated by the dialog box.

Figure 25.8.

The Properties dialog box tells you why an error message exists on a page.

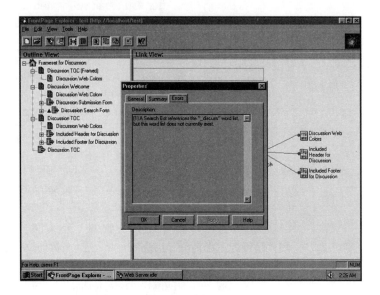

Getting Your Web Online

OK, your pages are linked, your spelling is checked, and your images are all nice, neat, and trim. You're ready to go on to the Web now.

There are three ways you can get your files onto the Web. If your service provider has the FrontPage Server Extensions installed, you can use the Copy Web command in the FrontPage Explorer to transfer your web files to their server. If your service provider doesn't have the extensions, you have a couple of alternatives. I'll take them one by one.

Using the Copy Web Command

Use the Copy Web command to transfer your web to a service provider that has the FrontPage Server Extensions installed. When you use the Copy Web command, you can copy the root web alone, the root web and all child webs, or any child web to the remote server.

NOTE: When you use the Copy Web command to copy your web pages from your local computer to a remote server, you will be prompted to enter a name and password. Enter the name and password you use to transfer content to your remote Web directory in the Name and Password Required dialog box.

To copy your web to the remote server, follow these steps:

1. Establish a connection with your Internet provider, using normal login procedures.

2. Open the web you want to copy to the remote server.

   ❏ Open the root web to copy just it or to copy it and all child webs.

   ❏ Open any child web to copy only the child Web to your remote server.

3. From the FrontPage Explorer, choose File I Copy Web. The Copy Web dialog box, shown in Figure 25.9, appears.

Figure 25.9.
Use the Copy Web command to copy webs to a remote server with the FrontPage Server Extensions installed.

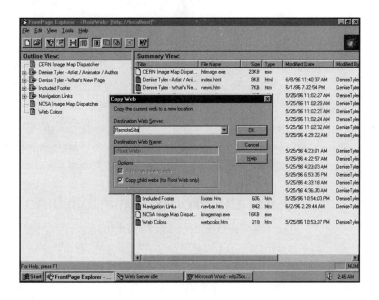

4. In the Destination Web Server field, select the server name or IP address that you use during remote connections.

5. In the Destination Web Name field, enter the name of the web to which you want to copy. By default, a name identical to the web you are copying appears in this field.

6. If you want to add your FrontPage Webs to a Web site that already exists on the server, check the Add to an Existing Web checkbox. Note that FrontPage will overwrite any files that already exist on the remote server if your new files have the same names.

7. If you are copying the root Web and want to include all child Webs in the Copy Web command, check the Copy Child Webs checkbox. This will copy all files and Web directories on your server to the remote site.

8. Click OK to copy the Web.

What happens after this? First, FrontPage checks to see whether the remote Web site has a web with the same name as the one you specified in the Destination Web Name field. If it does, it then checks whether you chose the Add to an Existing Web option. If you did, things proceed along just fine. If you didn't check that option, you'll get an error message.

Next, FrontPage gets the URL of the source web and creates the URL for the destination web. After that, FrontPage looks at each directory beneath the source web and creates each destination web. Directories that hold programs (such as the `cgi-bin` and `_vti_bin` directories) are marked as executable.

After the directories are created, FrontPage copies the contents into each directory. You'll see messages in the status bar as this occurs, indicating the percentage of completion.

FrontPage repeats this procedure for each child web beneath the root web, if you elected to copy all Webs on your server.

Once this process is finished, you should open the destination web in the FrontPage Explorer. Check to see whether there are any red triangles near any page names. If there are, follow the procedures outlined earlier in this chapter in "Fixing Page Errors."

Using the FrontPage Publishing Wizard

If your service provider doesn't have the FrontPage Server Extensions installed, you can use Microsoft's FrontPage Publishing Wizard to copy your pages to your remote site. This wizard has some advantages over using an FTP software package to transfer your files:

❏ The files you need to transfer to make your pages work are automatically selected and copied to your Web site.

❏ If your pages have any features that won't work without the FrontPage Server Extensions, the wizard warns you of that and gives you the option not to post those pages.

❏ The wizard keeps track of what you posted and gives you the option to post only the pages that have changed since the last time you posted.

You can download the FrontPage Publishing Wizard from Microsoft's site at the following URL:

```
http://www.microsoft.com/frontpage/freestuff/fs_fp_pbwiz.htm
```

When you use the FrontPage Publishing Wizard's setup program, the wizard is added to your Windows 95 Start Menu or to a program group. To use the Microsoft FrontPage Publishing Wizard, establish a connection with your Internet Service Provider and then choose the Microsoft FrontPage Publishing Wizard from your Start menu. The wizard guides you through your choices.

To use the FrontPage Publishing Wizard, follow these steps:

1. Choose the FrontPage Publishing Wizard from your Start menu or FrontPage program group. The introductory screen shown in Figure 25.10 appears. Click Next to continue.

Figure 25.10.
The introductory screen of the FrontPage Publishing Wizard.

2. The wizard asks for your publishing location in the screen shown in Figure 25.11. If you aren't sure what settings to enter here, check with your Internet service provider.

Figure 25.11.
Enter your FTP server and directory and the name and password you use to access this directory.

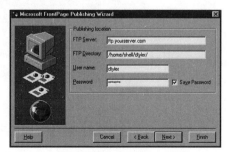

❏ In the FTP Server field, enter the URL of your service provider's FTP site—for example, `ftp.yourserver.com`.

❏ In the FTP Directory field, enter the home directory in which your Web pages are stored. Note that you don't use the HTTP address of your home page here. This is the directory assigned to you as your home directory, in which your home page is stored. Your entry should look similar to this:

`/home/shell/dtyler`

CAUTION: If you're transferring a web other than your root web, append the web name to the end of this entry. If you don't do this, the pages are copied to your home directory and overwrite any pages with the same names. For example, if you're transferring your /FarOutThere web, your entry should look something like this:

`/home/shell/dtyler/FarOutThere`

❏ In the User Name field, enter the name you use when you normally log into your FTP server. This may differ from the name and password you use to browse the Web.

❏ In the Password field, enter the password you use to log into your FTP server. If you want the FrontPage Publishing Wizard to remember your password the next time you publish, check the Save Password box.

Click Next to continue.

3. The FrontPage Publishing Wizard returns a list of the webs in your Content directory, as shown in Figure 25.12. Choose the web you want to post from the Web to Post list and click Next to continue.

Figure 25.12.
Select the web you want to post.

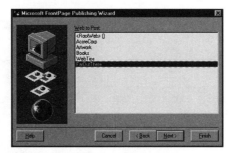

NOTE: If you select the root web in this wizard, it doesn't automatically copy the child webs to the server.

4. The wizard checks to see whether any of the pages in your selected Web site have features you need the server extensions for. If any are found, the Warning screen shown in Figure 25.13 appears. You are given the option not to post these pages on the next screen. Click Next to continue.

Figure 25.13.

The wizard checks to see whether any of your pages need the FrontPage Server Extensions and notifies you if any do.

5. The wizard asks which files you want to post and shows the number of pages in each category, as shown in Figure 25.14. Choose one of the following options:

   ❑ All files in the local web.

   ❑ Only files which changed since the last post.

   ❑ Choose the list of files to post: Choose this option to select from a list of pages in the web you want to post.

   ❑ If you received warnings from step 4, you can choose not to post the pages with warnings by checking the "Do not post pages with warnings" checkbox; however, it's disabled if no warnings are present.

Figure 25.14.

Choose the files you want to post and click Post.

NOTE: You'll receive warnings when your pages use any of the following features:

❑ Any of the FrontPage bots discussed in Chapter 20, "Runtime Bots: The Heartbeat of FrontPage Forms." The solution is to use custom CGI scripts or other scripting languages to design your forms.

❑ Using the default FrontPage image map handler. The solution is to use the Tools I Web Settings command to assign a different image map handler. Refer to Chapter 23, "Web Maintenance and Administration," for the procedure.

❑ Access permissions. If your FrontPage webs use pages or webs that require password authorization, you'll need to check with your service provider to determine how (or if) you can assign access permissions equivalent to those used in FrontPage. Also ask how you can use a hidden directory in your Web site.

6. Establish a connection with your Internet service provider, using the procedures you normally do when you log onto the Internet.

NOTE: The FrontPage Publishing Wizard logs on to your FTP site during the publishing process.

7. To post your pages, click Post. The FrontPage Wizard logs onto your FTP site and transfers the files. You are notified of the progress on the transfer screen.

Using an FTP Program

If you use an FTP program to transfer your pages to your remote site, this will give you an idea which files you should (or shouldn't) transfer for your Web site to work properly.

You should transfer the following files:

❑ Web pages and other files you included for download, which reside in your root and child web directories, including their subdirectories. You'll need to duplicate the same directory structures on your target server.

❑ All images in your Web site's /images subdirectory.

You *shouldn't* transfer these files:

❏ Directories that begin with _vti and their contents. These directories contain information used only with the FrontPage Server Extensions.

❏ Access control files. Don't transfer any files in your directories that begin with a period or the pound symbol (#).

The Final Test

After you transfer your files to your remote site, browse through the site to make sure all links work the way they should. If your server has the FrontPage Server Extensions installed, you can use the Tools I Verify Links command while logged into your remote site to verify the links quickly. Check your pages once again, using various browsers, to see if things look the way they should.

Publicizing Your Web

There are several ways you can publicize your Web site. One way is to post messages in newsgroups that relate to your topic of interest. If your site has information that will be of interest to those who frequent the newsgroups, post your URL so they can find your site.

I know you're excited about your new Web site and want to tell the world—but post your Web announcements sparingly, posting to only a handful of newsgroups at a time. Most who frequent newsgroups don't take too kindly to *spamming*—posting messages in dozens of newsgroups at the same time.

Another good way to publicize your Web site is to register your home page URLs with some of the many Web searches and robots, such as Yahoo!, AltaVista, Excite, Open Text, and others. Some of these search engines also provide links to sites from which you can send your URL to many other search engines at once.

Workshop Wrap-Up

Your web is complete and resides on your remote server. Now you can get to the task of getting the word out. You've come a long way since the day you first opened the FrontPage box. Congratulate yourself for a great accomplishment! *You're on the Internet!*

Chapter Summary

In this chapter, you have learned how to give your Web site the final once-over and how to publish it to a remote site. You have also learned three ways you can get your pages out to the world and which files you shouldn't transfer when your service provider doesn't use the FrontPage Server Extensions.

Next Steps

I hope I've succeeded in anticipating everything you need to know when you design your Webs. Sometimes it's difficult to consider all the questions that arise. I'll be maintaining a support site for this book at the following URL and will post answers to frequently asked questions, include more tips and tricks, and also include some graphics you can include in your pages:

`http://frontpage.flex.net/dtyler/FPSite/index.htm`

As far as where to go next, the sky's the limit. Keep tabs of the new features being developed for the Web. Learn how to use custom scripting languages to enhance your site even further. Continue to develop your Web design skills to keep up with the latest and greatest.

Q&A

Q: Are there any newsgroups I can join that concentrate on using FrontPage or the Server Extensions?

A: Yes, Microsoft has some newsgroups that might help. Subscribe to one of the following newsgroups to communicate with others who use FrontPage:

For the FrontPage Client (FrontPage Explorer and FrontPage Editor):

`news.microsoft.public.frontpage.client`

For Internet Service Providers using UNIX Server Extensions:

`news.microsoft.public.frontpage.extensions.unix`

For Internet Service Providers using Windows NT Server Extensions:

`news.microsoft.public.frontpage.extensions.windowsnt`

Q: Are there any other areas where I can get technical information?

A: The Microsoft Knowledge Base, located on their Web site, has articles that address technical questions. There is a link to the Knowledge Base on MSN (go MSSUPPORT if you're a member of the Microsoft Network). You can also find the Microsoft Knowledge Base at the following URL:

`http://www.microsoft.com/KB/`

P A R T

VI

Appendixes

A Installing FrontPage

This appendix leads you through the steps for installing FrontPage. Table A.1 describes the minimum system requirements. If you do not have an Internet connection, FrontPage guides you through the process of installing enough of Windows 95 or Windows NT networking to use FrontPage without connecting to the Internet.

Table A.1. System requirements.

Item	Requirement
CPU	486 or higher processor
Operating system	Windows 95
	Windows NT version 3.51 or higher
Hard disk space	15MB minimum (more required for your Web pages and images)
Physical memory	8MB (16MB recommended if you are using the Personal Web Server for Windows 95)
	16MB (24MB recommended if you are using the Personal Web Server for Windows NT)
Other	Winsock-compliant TCP/IP stack Winsock version 1.1 or later

The Setup Program

FrontPage installs in 15 easy steps. The following sections describe each step. Before you run the Setup program, save any data you are currently working on, and close all other applications.

Step 1: Run the Setup Program

Insert the setup disk into your floppy drive. To run the Setup program from Windows 95, choose Run from the Start menu. To run the Setup program from Windows NT, choose Run from the File menu. Enter A:\SETUP (replacing the drive letter with your drive if different). Choose OK or press Enter to continue.

Step 2: The Welcome Panel

The Welcome panel in the Setup program advises you to save all the data in your opened programs and to close all other applications. Choose Next to continue installation. The Destination Path panel appears.

Step 3: The Destination Path Panel

Use the Destination Path panel to select the drive and the folder where the FrontPage program will install. For Windows 95, the default installation directory is C:\Program Files\Microsoft FrontPage. For Windows NT, the default directory is C:\Microsoft FrontPage.

To change the drive or directory where FrontPage is installed, proceed to step 4. To install FrontPage to the default directory, skip to step 5.

Step 4: The Choose Directory Panel

To change the directory where FrontPage is installed, click the Browse button in the Destination Path panel. The Choose Directory panel opens.

Choose a new directory. In the Path field, type the directory and the path where you want to install FrontPage. Alternatively, in the Drives field, select a drive from the list of available drives, or choose Network to connect to a network drive. In the Directories field, select a new folder.

Click OK to exit the Choose Directory dialog box and return to the Destination Path panel. If you enter a new folder in the Path field, the Setup program asks if you want to create it. Answer Yes. To accept the destination directory, click Next. The Setup Type panel appears.

Step 5: The Setup Type Panel

The Setup Type panel enables you to choose how you want to install the program. The two installation options are Typical and Custom.

Choose Typical to install all three FrontPage components—Client Software, Personal Web Server, and FrontPage Server Extensions—on your system. Then click Next and skip to step 7.

Choose Custom to install only the components that you select. Then click Next and continue with step 6.

Step 6: The Select Components Panel

Use the Select Components panel to select any combination of the FrontPage components to install on your system. This panel displays the amount of disk space required to install the components that you select.

The Client Software component installs the FrontPage Explorer and FrontPage Editor, but not the Personal Web Server or FrontPage Server Extensions. Choose this option to reinstall the client software, or if you plan to use the FrontPage Explorer and FrontPage Editor with third-party server software. If you install only the FrontPage client software, click Next and proceed to step 10.

Choose the Personal Web Server component if you want to install the Personal Web Server. If the FrontPage Server Extensions do not already exist on your computer, select that option also. The Personal Web Server requires the FrontPage Server Extensions to operate correctly. Click Next and proceed to step 7.

Choose the FrontPage Server Extensions component to install the FrontPage Server Extensions. Extensions are provided for the Personal Web Server and other popular server software programs. You can install the FrontPage Server Extensions without the Personal Web Server if you are using other server software for which the FrontPage Server Extensions are available. Windows 95 users can use WebSite, by O'Reilly and Associates. Users of Windows NT 3.51 and above can use WebSite or Microsoft's Internet Information Server.

If you choose both the Personal Web Server and FrontPage Server Extensions, click Next and proceed to step 7. If you install the FrontPage Server Extensions without installing the Personal Web Server, click Next and proceed to step 10.

If you do not have enough disk space to install FrontPage, click the Disk Space button. The Available Disk Space dialog box appears. The Required field indicates the amount of disk space required to install the components that you select. The Available field indicates the amount of disk space available on the drive.

To change drives, select another drive in the Drive field. If you still do not have enough disk space to install FrontPage, click Cancel to close the Available Disk Space dialog box. Click Cancel again to exit the setup program.

Step 7: Setup Checks for Existing Software

After you select the installation options, the Setup program checks whether an existing version of FrontPage is installed on your hard drive. If you are installing FrontPage for the first time or if you are reinstalling the same version of FrontPage in the same directories, you will see the Choose Personal Web Server Directory panel. Skip to step 9. On the other hand, if you are installing FrontPage 1.1 to upgrade from FrontPage 1.0, you will see the Personal Web Server panel. Proceed to step 8.

Step 8: The Personal Web Server Panel

If the Setup program detects a previous version of FrontPage on your system, the Personal Web Server Panel appears. Choose one of the two options.

Choose Upgrade to install the new Personal Web Server over the previously installed version. The Personal Web Server is installed in the FRONTPAGE SERVER directory. If your current Personal Web Server is not installed in a folder with that name, it is moved to the new directory before it is upgraded. Your existing web content, which is installed in the CONTENT directory if you are upgrading from version 1.0, will be preserved. Click Next and skip to step 10.

Choose Install to install a new Personal Web Server in a directory separate from the previously installed Personal Web Server. When you install a second Personal Web Server, your original Personal Web Server continues to be configured to use TCP/IP port 80. The new Personal Web Server is assigned to TCP/IP port 8080. Click Next and proceed to step 9.

Step 9: The Choose Personal Web Server Directory Panel

By default, the Setup program installs the Personal Web Server in the \FrontPage Webs\Server directory and your web content in the \FrontPage Webs\Content directory.

To change the directory where the FrontPage Server is installed, click the Browse button. The Choose Directory panel opens. In the Path field, type the directory and path where you want to install FrontPage. Alternatively, in the Drives field, select a drive from the list of available drives or choose Network to connect to a network drive. Then select a new folder in the Directories field.

Click OK to return to the Choose Personal Web Server Directory panel. If you enter a new folder in the Path field, the Setup program asks if you want to create the new folder. Click Yes. To accept the destination directory for the server, click Next and proceed to step 10.

Step 10: The Select Program Folder Panel

In the Select Program Folder panel, you choose a program folder in which to include icons and shortcuts for FrontPage. By default, the icons are added to the Microsoft FrontPage program folder. After you choose a program folder or accept the default choice, click Next to proceed to step 11.

Step 11: The Start Copying Files Panel

The Start Copying Files panel displays the choices that you made during the setup procedure. Review the directories to make sure that everything will be installed where you want it to appear. If you want to change your choices, use the Back button to review your previous choices and revise as necessary. Keep clicking Next until you reach the Start Copying Files panel again.

To install the files, click Next. Insert the program disks when prompted and choose OK or press Enter to copy the files from each disk. The Setup program installs the files in the directories that you chose. After all the files are copied to your computer, proceed to step 12.

Step 12: Administrator Setup for Personal Web Server

If you installed the Personal Web Server, you must register yourself as a server administrator. You should set up an administrator name and password which uses the same name and password required to access the Web site on your remote server. FrontPage allows you to configure more than one administrator for each of your Webs, so you can use different configurations for local and remote Web development.

To register yourself as the administrator of the server:

1. Enter a name in the Name field of the dialog box. Use the account name required for your remote server, or a different name (optional) to develop your webs on your local computer. This name cannot contain spaces or punctuation marks.

2. Enter a password in the Password field. Use the password required for your remote server, or a different password (optional) to develop your webs on your local computer.

3. Confirm your password in the Confirm Password field.

Step 13: The Setup Complete Panel

After Setup configures the administrator name and password, the Setup Complete panel appears, telling you that you can run Microsoft FrontPage.

To complete the setup procedure and start the FrontPage Explorer, check the Start the FrontPage Explorer Now checkbox and click the Finish button. Then proceed to step 14.

To complete the setup procedure without starting the FrontPage Explorer, uncheck the Start the FrontPage Explorer Now checkbox and click the Finish button.

Step 14: Start the FrontPage Explorer

When you run the FrontPage Explorer for the first time, you are informed that FrontPage will try to determine your machine's host name and TCP/IP address and that the process might take several minutes. Click OK to continue.

A dialog box appears when the process is complete. It advises you of your machine's host name. Use this server name—or any of the others that are returned during the TCP/IP test—when you log into your server.

If you are installing FrontPage on a computer that does not have a modem or TCP/IP stack configured, FrontPage asks if you want help to install TCP/IP networking.

NOTE: You may be prompted to insert your Windows 95 Setup disks to install any drivers and DLL files necessary for TCP/IP networking. Have your installation disks or CD ready to insert when you are prompted for them.

The steps required to complete this setup in Windows 95 are as follows:

1. When FrontPage asks if you want help to install TCP/IP networking, choose OK. The FrontPage Networking Help Screen appears.

2. Click the arrow in step 1 of the Help Screen. The Network dialog box appears, opened to the Configuration tab.

3. Click the Add button. The Select Network Component Type dialog box appears.

4. Choose Protocol and click Add. The Select Network Protocol dialog box appears.

5. In the Manufacturers field, select Microsoft. In the Network Protocols field, select TCP/IP and click OK. You return to the Configuration tab in the Network dialog box.

6. Click the Add button again. The Select Network Component Type dialog box appears.

7. Choose Adapter and click Add. The Select Network Adapters dialog box appears.

8. In the Manufacturers field, select Microsoft. In the Network Adapters field, select Dial-Up Adapter and click OK. You return to the Configuration tab in the Network dialog box.

9. From the Configuration tab in the Network dialog box, choose Dial-Up Adapter from the list of installed network components, and click the Properties button. The Dial-Up Adapter Properties dialog box appears.

10. Click the Bindings tab. Verify that the TCP/IP->Dial-Up Adapter checkbox is checked. Click OK to exit the Dial-Up Adapter Properties dialog box.

11. Click OK to exit the Network dialog box. If you are prompted to restart your computer, click Yes.

After your computer restarts, you can run the TCP/IP test as indicated in step 15 to check your installation before you run the FrontPage Explorer.

Step 15: Run the TCP/IP Test Program

If you do not know what your server name is or if you need to enter additional information in the FrontPage Server Administrator, you can run the TCP/IP test program. It checks your system for a TCP/IP stack and reports back the server identifications that you can use on your system.

NOTE: If you don't have an Internet service provider, you should be able to use `localhost` as a server name if you followed the procedures recommended during setup to configure a TCP/IP stack.

To run the TCP/IP test program:

1. Establish a connection with your Internet service provider.
2. Click the FrontPage TCP/IP Test icon, which is located in the Microsoft FrontPage program group or your Start menu.
3. Click the Start Test button. FrontPage reports the results described below.
4. Click Exit to exit the FrontPage TCP/IP Test dialog box after the results are reported to you.

After you click the Start Test button in step 3, FrontPage reports the results that it finds. For a fully operational system, they should be

- ❏ **32-bit Winsock**: Reports Yes if a 32-bit version of Winsock resides on your computer.
- ❏ **16-bit Winsock**: Reports Yes if a 16-bit version Winsock resides on your computer.
- ❏ **127.0.0.1**: Reports Yes if you can use the `localhost` address. You can enter it as a server name while you develop offline.
- ❏ **Host name**: Reports the host name that you can use when you are online with your Internet service provider (for example, `www.myserver.com`). It reports No if you installed FrontPage without an Internet connection; use `127.0.0.1` or `localhost` for a server name in this instance.
- ❏ **IP address**: Reports the IP address that you can use when you are online with your Internet service provider (for example, `255.255.255.255`). It reports `127.0.0.1` if you installed FrontPage without an Internet connection.
- ❏ **localhost**: Reports Yes if you can use `localhost` as a server name while you develop offline.

If these results are not reported, click the Explain Results button. You are advised on how you can correct your configuration.

B

FrontPage References

This appendix provides information on keyboard shortcuts, icons, pointers, messages, and warnings.

Keyboard Shortcuts

The FrontPage Explorer and the FrontPage Editor have several keyboard shortcuts. Tables B.1 and B.2 list the shortcuts and the commands associated with them.

Table B.1. FrontPage Explorer shortcuts.

Command	Keyboard Shortcut
File I New Web	Ctrl+N
Edit I Delete	Del
Edit I Open	Ctrl+O
Edit I Properties	Alt+Enter or mouse right-click
Tools I Stop	Esc

Table B.2. FrontPage Editor shortcuts.

Command	Keyboard Shortcut
File I New	Ctrl+N
File I Open File	Ctrl+O
File I Print	Ctrl+P
File I Save	Ctrl+S
Edit I Bookmark	Ctrl+G
Edit I Clear	Del
Edit I Copy	Ctrl+C or Ctrl+Ins
Edit I Cut	Ctrl+X or Shift+Del
Edit I Find	Ctrl+F
Edit I Link	Ctrl+K
Edit I Paste	Ctrl+V or Shift+Ins
Edit I Properties	Alt+Enter or mouse right-click
Edit I Replace	Ctrl+H
Edit I Select All	Ctrl+A
Insert I Line Break	Shift+Enter
Tools I Back	Alt+Left Arrow
Tools I Forward	Alt+Right Arrow
Tools I Spelling	F7
Help	F1
Help cursor	Shift+F1
Bold text	Ctrl+B
Italic text	Ctrl+I
Underline text	Ctrl+U
Cancel dialog box	Esc
Previous window	Shift+Ctrl+F6
Next window	Ctrl+F6
Nonbreaking space	Shift+Space

FrontPage Icons and Pointers

FrontPage has several application-specific icons and cursors.

FrontPage Explorer Icons

The Outline View, Link View, and Summary View in the FrontPage Explorer have several icons that indicate the items and links that appear on pages.

Link View	Outline View	Summary View	Description
⊞	⊞		(On top of page icon) - Page can be expanded so you can see its links
⊟	⊟		(On top of page icon) - Page can be expanded so you can see its links
🖼			Current selected page (in center of Link View)
🖼	🖼		Broken link
🖼	🖼		Image appears on the page
🖼	🖼		Mailto Link on the page
🖼	🖼		A page in the current web
🌐	🌐		Link to World Wide Web in page
	⊟		The page has links
	🏠		The home page can be expanded so that you can see its links (red door)
	🏠		The home page has been expanded so that you can see its links (black door)
	📄		The page has been expanded
	⊟		An error has occurred in a page
	🖼		Page has been expanded elsewhere in Outline View
		🖼	Image file
		📄	HTML file
		⊞	Any other type of file other than HTML file

FrontPage Cursors

When you move the cursor over some objects on the page or perform some tasks in the FrontPage Editor and the FrontPage Explorer, you see various cursors.

Pointer Image	Name	When it appears	What it does
	Bot Pointer	The pointer is over a bot on the page.	
	Drop and Link Pointer	When you click and drag a page from the FrontPage Explorer to a page in the FrontPage Editor.	You can create a link by releasing the left mouse button.
	Drop and Open Pointer	Appears when you click and drag a page from the FrontPage Explorer to the FrontPage Editor and there is not an open page under the pointer.	You can open a page by releasing the left mouse button.
	Follow Link Pointer	Appears when the FrontPage Editor is opening a page or image by its URL.	
	Hand Pointer	Appears when you click and drag the left mouse button in the FrontPage Explorer's Link View.	Grabs the view and moves it as the mouse moves.
	Link Pointer	When you use the Ctrl key, the pointer becomes the link pointer when it is over a text or image link.	Click on the link to follow it.
	Selection Pointer	Appears only in the left margin of the page.	You select the list containing the current paragraph or an entire form by double-clicking when this pointer is visible.
	Can Not Open Pointer	You are dragging and dropping a page from the FrontPage Explorer to the Editor.	You are over another application or the desktop and can't open the page by dropping it.
	Draw Pointer		You can generate a geometric hotspot by clicking and dragging over an image.
	Transparent Color Pointer		You can click a color in an image to make it transparent.

C
Directory of Resources

This directory of resources is provided to help you find additional information on topics or FrontPage tools discussed in this book. Topics include FrontPage resources, general Web information, Web developer information, CGI and Perl scripts, graphics and multimedia, and sources for ideas.

An online version of this directory of resources will be kept current on the Internet support site for this book. The URL is as follows:

```
http://frontpage.flex.net/dtyler/FPSite/links.htm
```

FrontPage Resources

Many sites provide resources that help you get the most out of FrontPage. You can consult the support site for this book. Likewise, Microsoft has several sites with useful and relevant information.

Support Site for *Laura Lemay's Web Workshop: Microsoft FrontPage*

The support site for this book contains several sections which can assist you in developing and maintaining your Web pages using FrontPage. Among them are a User-To-User discussion group, a Tips and Tricks section, links to other helpful sites, graphics, and more.

```
http://frontpage.flex.net/dtyler/FPSite/index.htm
```

Microsoft's Home Page

Go to Microsoft's home page for up-to-date information and links to product information, support, downloads, Internet Workshop, and more.

```
http://www.microsoft.com
```

The FrontPage Home Page

The Microsoft FrontPage home page contains links to an overview of FrontPage, recent news, getting started, hosting and posting Web sites, Internet Service Provider information, and customizing FrontPage. Product information and support links are also provided.

```
http://www.microsoft.com/frontpage/
```

FrontPage Server Extensions

A download area for UNIX and Windows NT versions of the FrontPage Server Extensions, for the following servers: Microsoft Internet Information Server, NCSA, CERN, Apache, Netscape Communications Server, Open Market Web Server, and O'Reilly's Web Site.

```
http://www.microsoft.com/frontpage/freestuff/fs_fp_extensions.htm
```

Microsoft Internet Workshop

Contains information on creating and developing Internet pages. Includes information on authoring, editing, designing and creating, programming, site administration, planning and production, demos, and how-to sites.

```
http://www.microsoft.com/workshop/
```

Microsoft's Internet Service Provider Information

Information for Internet Service Providers, including a Web Hosting Primer, Frequently Asked Questions, and information about the FrontPage Server Extensions.

```
http://www.microsoft.com/frontpage/ispinfo/default.htm
```

ISPs That Use FrontPage Server Extensions

An up-to-date list of Internet Service Providers that host FrontPage Web sites.

```
http://www.microsoft.com/frontpage/ispinfo/isplist.htm
```

Free FrontPage Publishing Wizard

If your Internet Service Provider does not have the FrontPage Server Extensions installed, use this publishing wizard to upload pages to your site. The wizard allows you to upload an entire Web, or the pages which have changed since the past post. The wizard also warns you if any of your pages contain features which require the FrontPage Server Extensions. To obtain a free FrontPage publishing wizard for Windows 95 or Windows NT, go to

```
http://www.microsoft.com/frontpage/freestuff/fs_fp_pbwiz.htm
```

FrontPage Developer's Kit

If you're a programmer, you can use the FrontPage Developer's kit in conjunction with Visual C++ or Visual Basic to develop your own FrontPage Web and page wizards, Web templates, and bots. To obtain version 1.1 of the FrontPage Developer's Kit, go to

```
http://www.microsoft.com/frontpage/freestuff/fs_fp_sdk.htm
```

General Web Information

Here are just a few sites that provide general resources for the World Wide Web.

Boutell.com World Wide Web FAQ

This site contains an introduction to the World Wide Web, information on how to obtain and use browsers, and pages about Web servers, authoring pages, and other resources.

```
http://www.boutell.com/faq/
```

"Entering the World Wide Web: A Guide to Cyberspace"

This site, by Kevin Hughes, contains information about the World Wide Web and how it works. It also has some links to interesting places on the Web.

```
http://www.eit.com/Web/www.guide/guide.toc.html
```

Yahoo: Computers and Internet: Internet: World Wide Web

This site contains many links to sites that have information about the World Wide Web. Links to WWW authoring, the Best of the Web, books, browsers, caching, CGI, HTML, Java, JavaScript, page design, security, VRML, and more.

```
http://www.yahoo.com/Computers/World_Wide_Web/
```

Web Developer Information

Numerous sites provide information for developers. Many of them are described here. Categories include access counters, browsers, HTML standards and guides, and publishing and publicizing your web.

Access Counters

If you want to keep track of the number of times your pages are visited, you can include an access counter on the page. The following sites provide resources on how this can be accomplished.

Adding Access Counters to Your Documents

How do you keep track of how many times your pages are accessed? This is a tutorial that tells you what to do.

```
http://members.aol.com/htmlguru/access_counts.html
```

Yahoo: Computers and Internet: Internet: World Wide Web: Programming: Access Counts

This site provides links to all the counters you will ever need, and more.

```
http://www.yahoo.com/Computers/World_Wide_Web/Programming/Access_Counts/
```

Browsers

The following sites will help you keep track of the latest available browsers and the features which they include.

Browser Watch Browser List

A list of World Wide Web browsers and the operating systems (Windows, Mac, or UNIX) for which they are available.

```
http://www.browserwatch.com/browsers.shtml
```

Browser Watch Browser Stats

An extensive collection of browser statistics available for all browser types. Very thorough.

```
http://www.browserwatch.com/report-table-browsers.shtml
```

Browser Watch Plug-In Plaza

Links to all the browser plug-ins that are currently available or in development.

```
http://www.browserwatch.com/plug-in-big.shtml
```

Yahoo: Computers and Internet: Internet: World Wide Web: Browsers

Browser usage statistics, capabilities, comparisons, helper applications, public access Web browsers, VRML browsers, and Usenet browsers.

```
http://www.yahoo.com/Computers_and_Internet/Internet/World_Wide_Web/Browsers/
```

HTML Standards and Guides

The following sites will assist you in learning HTML standards and keep you informed of the latest features which can be incorporated into your Web pages.

Beginner's Guide to HTML

This contains an introduction to producing HTML documents, with information on getting started, publishing, HTML tags, and more.

```
http://www.ncsa.uiuc.edu/General/Internet/WWW/HTMLPrimer.html
```

HTML Reference Manual

Michael J. Hannah of Sandia National Laboratories has written an HTML reference manual. Very thorough and contains links to many other sources.

```
http://www.sandia.gov/sci_compute/html_ref.html
```

HTML Writer's Guild Home Page

This is the home page for the HTML Writer's Guild, the premier organization of WWW page authors and Internet publishing professionals.

```
http://www.hwg.org/
```

Introducing HTML 3.2

This is W3C's new specification for HTML, developed in conjunction with IBM, Microsoft, Netscape Communications Corporation, Novell, SoftQuad, Spyglass, and Sun Microsystems.

```
http://www.w3.org/pub/WWW/MarkUp/Wilbur/
```

Microsoft's Authoring Resources

This contains a list of imaging services, Web servers and utilities, HTML conversion tools, background image libraries, Microsoft Office document viewers, and ActiveX applications.

```
http://www.microsoft.com/Frontpage/productinfo/featuredetails/tools.htm
```

HTML Language Specification

This is a reference document which includes information on HTML basics and defining the characteristics of HTML text.

```
http://developer.netscape.com/platform/html_compilation/index.html
```

The Structure of HTML 3.2 Documents

This offers information on the structure of HTML 3.2 documents and contains a summary of the features of HTML 3.2 tags.

```
http://www.w3.org/pub/WWW/MarkUp/Wilbur/features.html
```

The Web Developer's Virtual Library

This site is an award-winning Webmaster's encyclopedia of Web development and Web software technology. It has a gallery, graphics, index, library, map, search, seminars, and Top 30 sites. Thousands of links and tutorials.

```
http://www.stars.com/
```

The Web Developer's Virtual Library: HTML

The HTML section of the Web Developer's Virtual Library contains several links to and about creating and using Web pages.

```
http://www.stars.com/Vlib/Providers/HTML.html
```

Webmaster's Resource Center: Note and Links for Webmasters

This is an excellent site that contains tools and references. Topics include HTML information, frames, books, Internet Service Providers, graphics, image maps, plug-ins, Java, JavaScript, browsers, CGI, Perl, publicizing, Web counters, and much more.

```
http://www.cio.com/Webmaster/wm_notes.html
```

Web Weavers Page

The Web Weavers Page contains general information about the World Wide Web, learning resources, standards and specifications, tools, advanced techniques, VRML and other Web 3D, building blocks, and more.

```
http://www.nas.nasa.gov/NAS/WebWeavers/
```

Yahoo: Computers and Internet: Software: Data Formats: HTML

This contains information on browser capabilities, extensions, forms, guides, tutorials, HTML 2.0, HTML 3.0, converters, editors, and much more.

```
http://www.yahoo.com/Computers_and_Internet/Software/Data_Formats/HTML/
```

The World Wide Web Consortium (W3C)

The World Wide Web Consortium is a group of individuals and organizations that support and develop the languages and protocols used on the World Wide Web. Their Web site contains information on HTML, graphics, 3D Web technology, fonts, style, SGML, and more.

```
http://www.w3.org/pub/WWW/
```

Publishing and Publicizing Your Web

Submit It! enables you to publicize a new Web site easily, to several Web searches and cataloging services at once. The site submits to Yahoo!, Open Text, InfoSeek, Web Crawler, Apollo, Starting Point, ComFind, BizWiz, Galaxy, What's New Too!, METRO-SCOPE, Lycos, InfoSpace, LinkStar, New Riders WWW Yellow Pages, Nerd World Media, AltaVista, and Mallpark.

```
http://www.submit-it.com/
```

CGI and Perl Scripts

If you want to learn more about using CGI and Perl scripts with your FrontPage Forms, these links will give you a good start. The links are arranged in two categories: sites that can help you learn how to develop scripts yourself and sites that have scripts you can use with your pages.

CGI Development

The following sites provide resources on CGI development.

The cgi-lib.pl Home Page

The cgi-lib.pl Home Page contains a standard library for creating Common Gateway Interface (CGI) scripts in the Perl language. The most up-to-date release of the library is found here.

```
http://www.bio.cam.ac.uk/Web/form.html
```

Decoding Forms with CGI

This is a technical discussion of how to use forms with CGI scripts.

```
http://hoohoo.ncsa.uiuc.edu/cgi/forms.html
```

Index of Perl and HTML Archives

Links to several sites that contain information on Perl and HTML, and using CGI and Perl scripts with Web pages.

```
http://www.seas.upenn.edu/~mengwong/perlhtml.html
```

The Common Gateway Interface

This is a primer on the Common Gateway Interface (CGI). Contains links to other pages about using CGI with forms.

```
http://hoohoo.ncsa.uiuc.edu/cgi/
```

Web Technology Expo CGI Scripts and Forms

This offers general information about using CGI scripts with forms.

```
http://forney.scinc.com/expo/cgi.html
```

Yahoo: Computers and Internet: Languages: Perl

This contains links and references about the Perl scripting language.

```
http://www.yahoo.com/Computers/Languages/Perl/
```

CGI Scripts That You Can Use

Here are many CGI scripts available for you to use. Check them out.

CGI Scripts for Windows NT/95 (Geocities Web Server)

CGI scripts by Ryan Sammartino include a hit counter, digital clock, simple guest book, and random image picker.

```
http://www.geocities.com/SiliconValley/6742/
```

Kamtec—Plug and Play Forms

These are public access CGI scripts. Forms you can use without the need to write CGI scripts. Sends the contents of the forms back to you in e-mail. Includes utilities such as Bounce, Search, Mail, Jump, and Random Link Supplier.

```
http://www.kamtec.com/public/
```

Matt's Script Archive

Here are many public domain CGI scripts. Includes a Guest Book, Free for All Link Page, WWW Board, Counter, Text Counter, Simple Search, Form Mail, Random Image Displayer, Animation, Countdown, and more.

```
http://worldwidemart.com/scripts/
```

Nuthin' but Links

Here are links to several sites that provide public domain CGI scripts.

```
http://rio.atlantic.net/~bombadil/nuthin/cgi.htm
```

Selena Sol's Public Domain CGI Script Archive

This is a nice site with several CGI scripts and instructions. Scripts for electronic outlets, music catalogs, forms processors, guest books, image maps, animation, Web chat, bulletin boards, and more.

```
http://www2.eff.org/~erict/Scripts/
```

Graphics and Multimedia

Graphics and multimedia are gaining popularity on the Web. The sites that follow will provide sources from which you can learn to develop graphics and multimedia for your Web pages. Categories include animated GIFs, clip art and image sources, retail and shareware graphics software support sites, Java and JavaScript, Microsoft ActiveX, Microsoft VBScript, and VRML/3D Web technology.

Animated GIFs

One way to provide animation on your pages is to develop animated GIF files. The site listed below provides a good start in learning to develop this type of graphic.

The Toolbox—GIF Animation on the WWW

For information on animated GIFs, check out the Toolbox. It is a resource for GIF animation on the Web and contains many pages and links which discuss creation and use of animated GIFs.

```
http://member.aol.com/royalef/toolbox.htm
```

Clip Art and Image Sources

There are several sites that provide clip art and images that you can use in your Web pages. The following sites contain a good collection of images or links.

Barry's Clip Art Server

Here are links to several sources of clip art for your Web pages. The clip art is available in a wide variety of categories.

```
http://ns2.clever.net/~graphics/clip_art/clipart.html
```

Microsoft's Multimedia Gallery

This offers free multimedia themes for your Web pages, including backgrounds, banners, navigation controls, images, sounds, and video clips.

```
http://www.microsoft.com/workshop/design/mmgallry/
```

Yahoo: Computers and Internet: Multimedia: Pictures: Clip Art

Here are links to several clip art collections available for use in your Web pages.

```
http://www.yahoo.com/Computers/Multimedia/Pictures/Clip_art/
```

Yahoo: Computers and Internet: Software: Data Formats: GIF

This offers technical information about the GIF file format and about the Unisys GIF/LZW controversy.

http://www.yahoo.com/Computers/Software/Data_formats/GIF/

Graphics Software—Retail

Here are some links for product information and support for some of the most popular retail graphics programs. Links include information on products by Adobe, Corel Corporation, Fractal Design Corporation, and MetaTools.

Adobe Systems Incorporated

Adobe Systems Incorporated, maker of a wide variety of graphics programs, has several pages which provide product information and support.

Adobe Systems Incorporated Home Page

The Adobe Systems home page provides links to product support and information. Products include Adobe Acrobat, Adobe After Effects, Adobe Type Manager, Adobe Dimensions, Adobe Illustrator, Adobe Photoshop, Adobe PageMaker, and more.

http://www.adobe.com/

Adobe Acrobat

This page is a download area for Adobe Acrobat and related items.

http://www.adobe.com/acrobat/

Adobe Acrobat Amber (Netscape Plug-In)

Download area for Adobe Acrobat Reader and related items, available in several software platforms.

http://www.adobe.com/acrobat/amber/

Adobe Photoshop

Adobe Photoshop is the graphics program of choice for many Web developers. You can find a product overview, details, help, and add-ons for Adobe Photoshop at this page.

http://www.adobe.com/prodindex/photoshop/main.html

Adobe-Compatible Plug-In Filters

For information on some of the most popular plug-ins available for Adobe Photoshop, or Adobe-compatible programs, refer to the following sites.

Alien Skin Software

Alien Skin Software is the creator of The Black Box, version 2.0, a very popular set of plug-in filters for Adobe Photoshop or compatible applications.

```
http://www.eskimo.com/~bpentium/skin.html
```

Andromeda Software

Andromeda Software is the creator of The Andromeda Series of plug-in filters for Adobe Photoshop or compatible applications.

```
http://www.andromeda.com/info/AndromedaSeries.html
```

Corel Corporation—CorelNet

Corel Corporation's presence on the Internet is located at the following URL. This site contains product information and support for Corel's wide variety of graphics and desktop publishing software programs.

```
http://www.corelnet.com/corelnet/corel/index.htm
```

Fractal Design Corporation

Fractal Design Corporation, creators of Fractal Design Painter and other ingenious graphics programs, has several useful pages which describe their products. Software updates and examples of artwork created with their software are also located here.

Fractal Design Corporation Home Page

Fractal Design Corporation's home page contains links to product information, art galleries, download areas, and product support.

```
http://www.fractal.com/
```

Fractal Design Painter 4

Product information for Fractal Design Painter 4, a natural-media graphics software package with incredible and inventive features. This is my graphics program of choice.

```
http://www.fractal.com/p4preview/
```

Fractal Design Poser

Fractal Design's figure design tool. This site contains an online Power demo (requires a JavaScript-capable browser), product information, a Poser art gallery, and more.

```
http://www.fractal.com/poser/poser.html
```

Fractal Design Dabbler 2

Fractal Design Dabbler 2 is a natural-media paint program that teaches you how to draw through the use of several tutorials. This site contains product information and more.

```
http://www.fractal.com/d2preview/
```

Fractal Design Sketcher

Fractal Design Sketcher is a program for creating original grayscale graphics with the look of natural media. Product information can be found at the following URL.

```
http://www.fractal.com/sketcher.html
```

MetaTools

MetaTools, formerly HSC Software, is the creator of Kai's Power Tools, a set of extremely powerful and inventive plug-in filters for Adobe Photoshop, Fractal Design Painter, and other Adobe-compatible applications.

MetaTools Home Page

The MetaTools Home Page contains links to new product information, what's new on the site, and an area for first-time visitors.

```
http://www.metatools.com
```

Kai's Power Tools

The following URL contains information on Kai's Power Tools 2.0 and 3.0, including KPT-related Web sites, product updates (Mac version), information on all the filters, and more.

```
http://www.metatools.com/kpt/
```

KPT Convolver

KPT Convolver is a series of advanced Adobe-compatible filters. This site includes a Frequently Asked Questions area, demos, exercises, hints, and more.

```
http://www.metatools.com/convo/
```

KPT Power Photos

KPT Power Photos are a collection of one-of-a-kind photographs, from which you can develop graphics for your Web pages. The site contains product information, a Frequently Asked Questions area, samples, demos, and catalog download area.

```
http://www.metatools.com/pphotos/
```

Shareware Graphics Programs

Some of the most popular shareware graphics programs for the Windows operating system are covered below. These sites will allow you to download the most current version of the software described.

Alchemy Mindworks

Alchemy Mindworks is the maker of several shareware graphics programs that can be of assistance in Web development. Most notable is the GIF Construction Set, which allows you to create animated GIFs. Graphic Workshop for Windows is also a very popular application.

Alchemy Mindworks Home Page

The Alchemy Mindworks home page provides links to software, books, and other resources about graphics development.

```
http://www.mindworkshop.com/alchemy/alchemy.html
```

GIF Construction Set for Windows

GIF Construction Set for Windows helps you create transparent and animated GIF files. The software is available in 16-bit and 32-bit Windows platforms.

```
http://www.mindworkshop.com/alchemy/gifcon.html
```

GrafCat for Windows

GrafCat for Windows prints a catalog of high-resolution thumbnails of your graphics. The program can print from 6 to 48 thumbnails per page.

```
http://www.mindworkshop.com/alchemy/gctw.html
```

Graphic Workshop for Windows

A shareware graphics program that allows you to view, manipulate, and manage your graphics. Includes support for TWAIN, PNG, MPEG, QuickTime, and multiple and interlaced GIF files.

`http://www.mindworkshop.com/alchemy/gww.html`

Lview Pro

Lview Pro is another popular graphics program for creating Web graphics. It is a 32-bit application for Windows 3.1 (requires Win32 Application Extensions), Windows 95, and Windows NT 3.51. The most current version of the software can be downloaded from this site.

`http://world.std.com/~mmedia/lviewp.html`

Macmillan Computer Publishing—Windows Graphics Shareware Library

The Macmillan Computer Publishing site contains a collection of Windows graphics shareware programs, screen capture programs, and icon editors. You can find this library at the following URL:

`http://www.mcp.com/65528152318075/softlib/windows-utilities/wgraph.html`

Java and JavaScript

There are several resources available on the Internet from which you can learn about using and developing applets and scripts with Java or JavaScript. The following sites provide a good start.

Sun Microsystems JavaSoft Page

What are people doing with Java? This site shows you what you can do, and also has information about the Java platform, JavaSoft news, products and services, and a developer's corner.

`http://java.sun.com/`

Java Resources

This Netscape site contains a library of Netscape-specific files, Sun Java documentation, the Java interface, applets, Java packages, security issues, language tutorials, developer's kits, and more.

`http://www.netscape.com/comprod/products/navigator/version_2.0/script/`

JavaScript Authoring Guide

This Netscape site contains information about authoring with JavaScript.

`http://home.netscape.com/eng/mozilla/Gold/handbook/javascript/index.html`

Andrew's JavaScript Index

This site provides links to several resources about authoring with JavaScript, as well as scripts you can learn from.

`http://www.c2.org/~andreww/javascript/`

Yahoo: Computers and Internet: Languages: JavaScript

This site contains a collection of several different pages and sites that provide information about JavaScript development, including scripts you can use.

`http://www.yahoo.com/Computers_and_Internet/Languages/JavaScript/`

Microsoft ActiveX

Microsoft ActiveX, the Web technology platform used for the upcoming version of Internet Explorer 3.0, provides the opportunity to make your Web pages come alive with interactivity and multimedia. You can find information on the following pages.

ActiveX Controls

This site contains information on the ActiveX controls, what they do, and how to use them.

`http://www.microsoft.com/intdev/inttech/controls/controls-f.htm`

ActiveX Scripting

This site contains detailed information about the ActiveX scripting language.

`http://www.microsoft.com/ie/script/default.htm`

Microsoft ActiveX ControlPad

This application allows you to quickly and easily develop Web pages that incorporate ActiveX features.

`http://www.microsoft.com/intdev/author/cpad/`

Microsoft HTML Layout Control

This application provides a means to lay out advanced Web pages, which incorporate features used in Microsoft Internet Explorer 3.0. You will not need to download this application if you already have the Microsoft ActiveX Control Pad, mentioned above.

`http://www.microsoft.com/ie/controls/layout/`

Microsoft VBScript

Microsoft VBScript, a subset of Visual Basic, provides a means to add interactivity to your Web pages. It is a cross-platform language with great extensibility.

Microsoft VBScript Home Page

The home page for Microsoft VBScript, with links to download areas, product support, and more.

`http://www.microsoft.com/vbscript/vbsmain.htm`

VBScript and Forms

Information on how you can use VBScript to develop Web pages that include forms.

`http://www.microsoft.com/vbscript/de/vbstutor/vbscntrl.htm`

Sound and Video

Here are some resources on sound and video.

Alison Zhang's Multimedia File Formats on the Internet: Movies

Alison Zhang's series on multimedia file formats on the Internet, with this section devoted to digital movies. Provides information on file formats, players, file converters, and links to sources.

`http://ac.dal.ca/~dong/movies.htm`

Alison Zhang's Multimedia File Formats on the Internet: Sound and Music

Alison Zhang's series on multimedia file formats on the Internet, with this section devoted to digital sound and music. Provides information on how computers play music, sound and music file formats, players, converters, and links to sources.

`http://ac.dal.ca/~dong/music.htm`

The MPEG FAQ

Contains information on what the MPEG standard is, as well as the differences between MPEG 1, MPEG 2, MPEG 3, and MPEG 4.

`http://www.crs4.it/~luigi/MPEG/mpegfaq.html`

Yahoo: Computers and Internet: Multimedia: Sound

Contains archives, MIDI sounds, MOD music format, movies, films and television, music software, speech generation, and Usenet links.

`http://www.yahoo.com/Computers_and_Internet/Multimedia/Sound/`

Yahoo: Computers and Internet: Multimedia: Video

Contains animations, collections, festivals, institutes, morphs, MPEG, QuickTime, software, and technical information.

`http://www.yahoo.com/Computers_and_Internet/Multimedia/Video/`

Sources for Ideas

There are several areas where you can find sources for ideas. One way is to keep track of the "Best of the Web" pages. Another way is to keep track of the types of sites that are getting the best ratings. Here are some links that can give you some ideas.

Best of GNN

Check out Global Network Navigator's "Best Of" Honorees. This site contains the GNN Best of the Net 1995 award winners. Categories include arts and entertainment, computers, food and wine, interactive sites, Internet navigation, K-12 education, literature, personal finance, sports and travel.

`http://www.gnn.com/wic/botn/index.html`

Cool Site of the Day

InfiNet's Cool Site of the Day includes their list of favorite Web sites. Links are arranged in Today's Cool Site, Iso-Topically Cool, and Still Cool (past cool winners).

`http://www.infi.net/cool.html`

What's Hot and Cool on the Web

This site provides links to several small, medium, and large sites. The sites are described as those with "strange, different, avant garde, and just plain weird" contents.

`http://kzsu.stanford.edu/uwi/reviews.html`

Other Books in the Laura Lemay Series

There are more books in the Laura Lemay series. All are published by Sams.net, unless otherwise noted.

- ❏ *Teach Yourself Java in 21 Days*. ISBN 1-57521-030-4. $39.99.
- ❏ *Teach Yourself Web Publishing with HTML 3.0*. ISBN 1-57521-064-9. $29.99.
- ❏ *Teach Yourself Web Publishing with HTML in 14 Days,* premier edition. ISBN 1-57521-014-2. $39.99.
- ❏ *Teach Yourself More Web Publishing with HTML in a Week*. ISBN 1-57521-005-3. $29.99.
- ❏ *Teach Yourself Web Publishing with HTML in a Week*. Sams Publishing. ISBN 0-672-30667-0. $25.00.

D

HTML Quick Reference

This HTML quick reference is different from most found in other HTML books. Because FrontPage has many HTML tags built in to the FrontPage Editor's features, you do not have to touch your HTML code very often. If you are familiar with HTML tags, you can use this quick reference as a guide to the commands and procedures that implement them.

All the tables except Table D.18 refer to an HTML tag and the attribute names and values that can be applied to it. Italic type indicates an attribute value that you must specify, such as a URL, a numerical value, or a filename. The source of the HTML tag is indicated when it is known. Included, as well, are the proposed tags for Internet Explorer 3.0 and the proposed tags for HTML 3.2. There is also a reference to the chapter that discusses the tag in more detail.

The final column in each table shows the name of the field or the choice you make in the appropriate dialog box. In most cases, the dialog box associated with the tag is also indicated. When this is not the case, the appropriate dialog box is listed for the tag.

The notation "Use extended attribute" indicates that a description of the function of the tag is given. Refer to the specific chapter for instructions on how to enter the extended attribute for the tag.

The notation "Use HTML markup bot" indicates that you should consult Chapter 21 for code examples for the tag.

Table D.1. Character styles and formatting.

Tag	Attribute name	Attribute value	Source	Chapter	Procedure or option to select in referenced dialog box
B			HTML 2	9	Advanced Styles, Bold (see also STRONG).
BASEFONT	SIZE	1			
		2			
		3			
		4			
		5			
		6			
		7	Netscape	9	FrontPage reads the BASEFONT tag but exports it as a FONT tag that includes a SIZE attribute. Specifies absolute font size.
BIG					Format toolbar, Increase Size button.
BLINK			HTML 2	9	Advanced Styles, Blink. Blink is surrounded by a green dotted-line in the FrontPage Editor.
CENTER			Netscape	9	FrontPage reads the CENTER tag. It is not interpreted as a paragraph break on import and centers a whole paragraph. Exports centering for paragraphs and headings as ALIGN=CENTER. Exports centering of PRE, LI, DD, and DT as CENTER.
CITE			HTML 2	9	Advanced Styles, Citation.
CODE			HTML 2	9	Advanced Styles, Code.
DFN			HTML 2	9	Advanced Styles, Definition.
EM			HTML 2	9	Regular Styles, Emphasis; or Italic Text button on toolbar (see also ITALIC).
FONT	COLOR	#rrggbb	Int. Exp.	9	Text Color button.
FONT	COLOR	colorname	Int. Exp.	9	Use extended attribute, or create custom color when using Text Color button.

Tag	Attribute name	Attribute value	Source	Chapter	Procedure or option to select in referenced dialog box
FONT	SIZE	1	Netscape	9	Font Size, 1 (8 pt). FrontPage exports absolute font sizes rather than relative font sizes.
FONT	SIZE	2	Netscape	9	Font Size, 2 (10 pt).
FONT	SIZE	3	Netscape	9	Font Size, 3 (12 pt). This is the default normal font.
FONT	SIZE	4	Netscape	9	Font Size, 4 (14 pt).
FONT	SIZE	5	Netscape	9	Font Size, 5 (18 pt).
FONT	SIZE	6	Netscape	9	Font Size, 6 (24 pt).
FONT	SIZE	7	Netscape	9	Font Size, 7 (36 pt).
I			HTML 2	9	Advanced Styles, Italic.
KBD			HTML 2	9	Advanced Styles, Keyboard.
LISTING			HTML 2	21	Use HTML markup bot.
PLAINTEXT			HTML 2	21	Use HTML markup bot.
S			HTML 2	21	Use HTML markup bot.
SAMP			HTML 2	9	Advanced Styles, Sample.
STRIKE			HTML 2	9	Regular Styles, Strike-through.
STRONG			HTML 2	9	Regular Styles, Strong, or Bold Text button on toolbar.
TT			HTML 2	9	Regular Styles, Typewriter Font; or Typewriter Text button on toolbar.
U			HTML 2	9	Regular Styles, Underlined; or Underlined Text button on toolbar.
VAR			HTML 2	9	Advanced Styles, Variable.
WBR			HTML 2	21	Use HTML markup bot.
XMP			Netscape	21	Use HTML markup bot.
FONT	FACE	name (name 2, name 3)	Int. Exp.	21	Use HTML markup bot.

Table D.2. Form-related tags.

Tag	Attribute name	Attribute value	Source	Chapter	Procedure or option to select in referenced dialog box
FORM	ACTION	URL	HTML 2	20	Form Properties dialog box.
FORM	METHOD	GET	HTML 2	20	Form Properties dialog box.
FORM	METHOD	POST	HTML 2	20	Form Properties dialog box.
INPUT	ALIGN	BOTTOM	HTML 2	19	Insert I Form Field I Image (align image source in Image Properties dialog box).
INPUT	ALIGN	MIDDLE	HTML 2	19	Insert I Form Field I Image (align image source in Image Properties dialog box).
INPUT	ALIGN	TOP	HTML 2	19	Insert I Form Field I Image (align image source in Image Properties dialog box).
INPUT	CHECKED	FALSE	HTML 2	19	Check Box Properties dialog box: Initial State.
INPUT	CHECKED	TRUE	HTML 2	19	Check Box Properties dialog box: Initial State.
INPUT	MAXLENGTH	n	HTML 2	19	Text Box Properties: Maximum Characters.
INPUT	NAME	name	HTML 2	19	Text Box Properties: Name Check Box Properties: Name Radio Button Properties: Name Push Button Properties: Name Image Form Field Properties: Name.
INPUT	SIZE	n	HTML 2	19	Text Box Properties: Width in Characters.
INPUT	SRC	URL	HTML 2	19	Insert I Form Field I Image Properties (select image source).
INPUT	TYPE	CHECKBOX			Insert I Form Field I Check Box.
INPUT	TYPE	IMAGE			Insert I Form Field I Image.
INPUT	TYPE	PASSWORD			Text Box Properties: Password Field = Yes.
INPUT	TYPE	RADIO			Insert I Form Field I Radio Button.
INPUT	TYPE	RESET			Insert I Form Field I Push Button.
INPUT	TYPE	SUBMIT			Insert I Form Field I Push Button.
INPUT	TYPE	TEXT	HTML 2	19	Insert I Form Field I One Line Text Box.
INPUT	TYPE	TEXTAREA	HTML 2	19	Insert I Form Field.

Tag	Attribute name	Attribute value	Source	Chapter	Procedure or option to select in referenced dialog box
INPUT	VALUE	value	HTML 2	19	Text Box Properties: Initial Value Check Box Properties: Value Radio Button Properties: Value Push Button Properties: Value.
OPTION		choice		19	Drop Down Menu Properties: Choice.
OPTION	SELECTED			19	Drop Down Menu Properties: Selected.
OPTION		VALUE		19	Drop Down Menu Properties: Value.
SELECT			HTML 2	19	Insert I Form Field I Drop Down Menu.
SELECT	MULTIPLE		HTML 2	19	Drop Down Menu Properties: Allow Multiple Selections.
SELECT	NAME		HTML 2	19	Drop Down Menu Properties: Name.
SELECT	SIZE		HTML 2	19	Drop Down Menu Properties: Height.
TEXTAREA				19	Insert I Form Field I Scrolling Text Box.
TEXTAREA	NAME			19	Scrolling Text Box Properties: Name.

Table D.3. Frame tags—Frames wizard.

Tag	Attribute name	Attribute value	Source	Chapter	Procedure or option to select in referenced dialog box
FRAME	ALIGN	TOP		21	Use HTML markup bot.
FRAME	ALIGN	MIDDLE		21	Use HTML markup bot.
FRAME	ALIGN	BOTTOM		21	Use HTML markup bot.
FRAME	ALIGN	LEFT		21	Use HTML markup bot.
FRAME	ALIGN	RIGHT		21	Use HTML markup bot.
FRAME	FRAMEBORDER	1	IE 3.0	21	Use HTML markup bot.
FRAME	FRAMEBORDER	0	IE 3.0	21	Use HTML markup bot.
FRAME	MARGINHEIGHT	n	Netscape	14	Screen 3 - Appearance: Margin Height.
FRAME	MARGINWIDTH	n	Netscape	14	Screen 3 - Appearance: Margin Width.
FRAME	NAME		Netscape	14	Screen 3 - Name.
FRAME	NORESIZE		Netscape	14	Screen 3 - Appearance: Check Not resizeable box.
FRAME	SCROLLING	YES	Netscape	14	Screen 3 - Appearance: Scrolling: Auto.
FRAME	SCROLLING	NO	Netscape	14	Screen 3 - Appearance: Scrolling: No.
FRAME	SRC		Netscape	14	Screen 3 - Source URL.
FRAMESET	COLS	%	Netscape	14	Screen 2 - Columns.
FRAMESET	COLS	n	Netscape	14	Screen 2 - Columns.
FRAMESET	FRAMEBORDER	1	IE 3.0	21	Use HTML markup bot.
FRAMESET	FRAMEBORDER	0	IE 3.0	21	Use HTML markup bot.
FRAMESET	FRAMESPACING	n	IE 3.0	21	Use HTML markup bot.
FRAMESET	ROWS	%	Netscape	14	Screen 2 - Rows.
FRAMESET	ROWS	n	Netscape	14	Screen 2 - Rows.
NOFRAMES			Netscape	14	Screen 4 - Alternate Page URL.

Table D.4. Heading tags—Paragraph Format dialog box.

Tag	Attribute name	Attribute value	Source	Chapter	Procedure or option to select in referenced dialog box
H1			HTML 2	9	Insert I Heading I Heading 1.
H2			HTML 2	9	Insert I Heading I Heading 2.
H3			HTML 2	9	Insert I Heading I Heading 3.
H4			HTML 2	9	Insert I Heading I Heading 4.
H5			HTML 2	9	Insert I Heading I Heading 5.
H6			HTML 2	9	Insert I Heading I Heading 6.
H7			HTML 2	9	Use HTML markup bot.
H1 thru H7	ALIGN	CENTER	HTML 3	9	Insert Heading, then press Center button.

Table D.5. Horizontal rule tags (Horizontal Line Properties dialog box).

Tag	Attribute name	Attribute value	Source	Chapter	Procedure or option to select in referenced dialog box
HR			HTML 2	11	Inserts a line that spans the entire page width.
HR	ALIGN	LEFT	HTML 3	11	Align: Left.
HR	ALIGN	RIGHT	HTML 3	11	Align: Right.
HR	ALIGN	CENTER	HTML 3	11	Align: Center.
HR	COLOR	#rrggbb	Int. Exp.	11	Use extended attribute. Specifies a color for the horizontal rule.
HR	COLOR	colorname	Int. Exp.	11	Use extended attribute. Specifies a color for the horizontal rule.
HR	NOSHADE		Netscape	11	Height: Solid Line (No Shading).
HR	SIZE	n	Netscape	11	Height: In Pixels.
HR	WIDTH	n%	Netscape	11	Width: Percent of Window.
HR	WIDTH	n	Netscape	11	Width: In Pixels.

Table D.6. Hotspot (image map) tags—image toolbar, circle, polygon, or rectangle.

Tag	Attribute name	Attribute value	Source	Chapter	Procedure or option to select in referenced dialog box
AREA	COORDS	x1,y1,x2,y2,z1,z2	Int. Exp.	8	Defines the hotspot area. This is defined when you draw a hotspot.
AREA	HREF	URL	Int. Exp.	8	Create Link dialog box (appears after you draw a hotspot).
AREA	NOHREF		Int. Exp.	21	Use HTML markup bot.
AREA	SHAPE	RECT or RECTANGLE	Int. Exp.	8	Image Toolbar I Rectangle.
AREA	SHAPE	CIRC or CIRCLE	Int. Exp.	8	Image Toolbar I Circle.
AREA	SHAPE	POLY or POLYGON	Int. Exp.	8	Image Toolbar I Polygon.
AREA	TARGET	window	Int. Exp.	14	Create Link dialog box - default target frame.
MAP			Int. Exp.		Specifies a collection of images for a client-side image map.

Table D.7. Image tags—Image Properties dialog box.

Tag	Attribute name	Attribute value	Source	Chapter	Procedure or option to select in referenced dialog box
IMG	ALT	text	HTML 2	11	Alternative Representations: Text.
IMG	ISMAP		HTML 2	11	Defines image as a clickable image map. See Image Map Tags.
IMG	SRC	URL	HTML 2	11	Image's source URL.
IMG	ALIGN	TOP	HTML 3	11	Alignment: Top.
IMG	ALIGN	MIDDLE	HTML 3	11	Alignment: Middle.
IMG	ALIGN	BOTTOM	HTML 3	11	Alignment: Bottom.
IMG	ALIGN	LEFT	HTML 3	11	Alignment: Left.
IMG	ALIGN	RIGHT	HTML 3	11	Alignment: Right.
IMG	ALIGN	TEXTTOP	Netscape	11	Alignment: Text Top.
IMG	ALIGN	ABSMIDDLE	Netscape	11	Alignment: Absmiddle.
IMG	ALIGN	ABSBOTTOM	Netscape	11	Alignment: Absbottom.
IMG	ALIGN	BASELINE	Netscape	11	Alignment: Baseline.

Tag	Attribute name	Attribute value	Source	Chapter	Procedure or option to select in referenced dialog box
IMG	HEIGHT	n	HTML 3	11	Use extended attribute. Defines image height in pixels. Image is stretched to fit. Used in conjunction with WIDTH attribute.
IMG	WIDTH	n	HTML 3	11	Use extended attribute. Defines image width in pixels. Image is stretched to fit. Used in conjunction with HEIGHT attribute.
IMG	CONTROLS		Int. Exp.	11	Use extended attribute. If a video clip is present, a set of controls is displayed beneath the clip.
IMG	DYNSRC	URL	Int. Exp.	11	Use extended attribute. Specifies the address of a video clip or VRML world to be displayed in a window.
IMG	LOOP	n	Int. Exp.	11	Use extended attribute. Specifies how many times a video clip will loop when activated. If n=-1 clip will loop indefinitely.
IMG	LOOP	INFINITE	Int. Exp.	11	Use extended attribute. Video clip will loop indefinitely.
IMG	START	FILEOPEN	Int. Exp.	11	Use extended attribute. Video clip plays as soon as file is opened. When used in conjunction with the MOUSEOVER attribute, it will play as soon as it opens and thereafter when the user moves the mouse.
IMG	START	MOUSEOVER	Int. Exp.	11	Use extended attribute. Video clip plays when cursor is moved over animation. When used in conjunction with FILEOPEN attribute, it will play once as soon as it opens and thereafter when user moves the mouse.
IMG	USEMAP	mapname	Int.Exp.		Specifies the map name for a client-side image map.
IMG	ALIGN	ABSBOTTOM	Netscape	11	Alignment: Absbottom.
IMG	ALIGN	ABSMIDDLE	Netscape	11	Alignment: Absmiddle.
IMG	ALIGN	TEXTTOP	Netscape	11	Alignment: Text Top.
IMG	ALIGN	BASELINE	Netscape	11	Alignment: Baseline.
IMG	BORDER	n	Netscape	11	Layout: Border Thickness.
IMG	HSPACE	n	Netscape	11	Layout: Horizontal Spacing.
IMG	LOWSRC	URL	Netscape	11	Alternative Representation: Low-Res.
IMG	VSPACE	n	Netscape	11	Layout: Vertical Spacing.

Table D.8. Line break tags—Break Properties dialog box.

Tag	Attribute name	Attribute value	Source	Chapter	Procedure or option to select in referenced dialog box
BR			HTML 2	9	Insert I Line Break.
BR	CLEAR	LEFT	HTML 3	11	Clear Left Margin.
BR	CLEAR	RIGHT	HTML 3	11	Clear Right Margin.
BR	CLEAR	ALL	HTML 3	11	Clear Both Margins.
NOBR			Netscape		Use HTML markup bot.

Table D.9. Link tags—Edit Link dialog box, unless noted otherwise.

Tag	Attribute name	Attribute value	Source	Chapter	Procedure or option to select in referenced dialog box
A	HREF	URL	HTML 2	8	World Wide Web tab.
A	HREF	filename	HTML 2	8	Open Page tab or World Wide Web.
A	NAME	name	HTML 2	8	Edit I Bookmark, Bookmark Properties dialog box.
A	REL	relationship			Specifies a relative relationship.
A	REV	revision			Specifies the revision number.
A	TARGET	window			Loads the link into a targeted window. Window name must begin with an alphanumeric character.
A	TARGET	_blank			Loads the link into a new blank window.
A	TARGET	_parent			Loads the link into the parent of the document the link is in.
A	TARGET	_self			Loads the link into the same window the link was clicked in.
A	TARGET	_top			Loads the link into a full window.
A	TITLE	name			Specifies the title that appears when a hyperlink is selected.

Table D.10. List tags—List Properties dialog box.

Tag	Attribute name	Attribute value	Source	Chapter	Procedure or option to select in referenced dialog box
DD			HTML 2	10	Insert I Definition I Definition.
DIR			HTML 2	10	Insert I List I Directory. FrontPage allows nested directory lists.
DL			HTML 2	10	Insert I Definition I List.
DL	TYPE	COMPACT	HTML 2	10	Use extended attribute. Creates less white space around the definition list.
DT			HTML 2	10	Insert I Definition I Term.
LI			HTML 2	10	Insert I List (defines a list item).
MENU			HTML 2	10	Insert I List I Menu List. FrontPage allows nested menu lists.
OL			HTML 2	10	Insert I List I Numbered List.
OL	START	number	Netscape	10	Use extended attribute. Specifies a starting number for the list. Default number is 1.
OL	TYPE	A	Netscape	10	Use extended attribute. Uses large letters in the list.
OL	TYPE	a	Netscape	10	Use extended attribute. Uses small letters in the list.
OL	TYPE	I	Netscape	10	Use extended attribute. Uses large Roman letters in the list.
OL	TYPE	i (this should be a small l)	Netscape	10	Use extended attribute. Uses small Roman letters in the list.
OL	TYPE	1	Netscape	10	Uses numbers in list. Default when you choose a numbered list.
UL			HTML 2	10	Insert I List I Bulleted.
UL	TYPE	DISC	Netscape	10	Use extended attribute. Uses disc-shaped bullets in bulleted list.
UL	TYPE	CIRCLE	Netscape	10	Uses circular bullets in bulleted list. Default when you insert a bulleted list.
UL	TYPE	SQUARE	Netscape	10	Use extended attribute. Uses square bullets in bulleted list. Also default for second, third, and so on, levels in a nested bulleted list.

Table D.11. Marquee tags.

Tag	Attribute name	Attribute value	Source	Chapter	Procedure or option to select in referenced dialog box
MARQUEE	ALIGN	TOP	Int. Exp.	21	Use HTML markup bot.
MARQUEE	ALIGN	MIDDLE	Int. Exp.	21	Use HTML markup bot.
MARQUEE	ALIGN	BOTTOM	Int. Exp.	21	Use HTML markup bot.
MARQUEE	BEHAVIOR	SCROLL	Int. Exp.	21	Use HTML markup bot.
MARQUEE	BEHAVIOR	SLIDE	Int. Exp.	21	Use HTML markup bot.
MARQUEE	BEHAVIOR	ALTERNATE	Int. Exp.	21	Use HTML markup bot.
MARQUEE	BGCOLOR	#rrggbb	Int. Exp.	21	Use HTML markup bot.
MARQUEE	BGCOLOR	colorname	Int. Exp.	21	Use HTML markup bot.
MARQUEE	DIRECTION	LEFT	Int. Exp.	21	Use HTML markup bot.
MARQUEE	DIRECTION	RIGHT	Int. Exp.	21	Use HTML markup bot.
MARQUEE	HEIGHT	n	Int. Exp.	21	Use HTML markup bot.
MARQUEE	HEIGHT	n%	Int. Exp.	21	Use HTML markup bot.
MARQUEE	HSPACE	n	Int. Exp.	21	Use HTML markup bot.
MARQUEE	LOOP	n	Int. Exp.	21	Use HTML markup bot.
MARQUEE	LOOP	INFINITE	Int. Exp.	21	Use HTML markup bot.
MARQUEE	SCROLLAMOUNT	n	Int. Exp.	21	Use HTML markup bot.
MARQUEE	SCROLLDELAY	n	Int. Exp.	21	Use HTML markup bot.
MARQUEE	VSPACE	n	Int. Exp.	21	Use HTML markup bot.
MARQUEE	WIDTH	n	Int. Exp.	21	Use HTML markup bot.
MARQUEE	WIDTH	n%	Int. Exp.	21	Use HTML markup bot.
MARQUEE			Int. Exp.	21	Use HTML markup bot.

Table D.12. Applet, script, and object-related tags.

Tag	Attribute name	Attribute value	Source	Chapter	Procedure or option to select in referenced dialog box
APPLET	ALIGN	LEFT	HTML 3.2	21	Use HTML markup bot.
APPLET	ALIGN	RIGHT	HTML 3.2	21	Use HTML markup bot.
APPLET	ALIGN	CENTER	HTML 3.2	21	Use HTML markup bot.
APPLET	ALT	alternate text	HTML 3.2	21	Use HTML markup bot.
APPLET	CODE	appletFile	HTML 3.2	21	Use HTML markup bot.
APPLET	CODEBASE	codebaseURL	HTML 3.2	21	Use HTML markup bot.
APPLET	HEIGHT	n	HTML 3.2	21	Use HTML markup bot.
APPLET	HSPACE	n	HTML 3.2	21	Use HTML markup bot.
APPLET	NAME	appletInstanceName	HTML 3.2	21	Use HTML markup bot.
APPLET	PARAMNAME	AttributeName	HTML 3.2	21	Use HTML markup bot.
APPLET	VSPACE	n	HTML 3.2	21	Use HTML markup bot.
APPLET	WIDTH	n	HTML 3.2	21	Use HTML markup bot.
EMBED	HEIGHT	n	HTML 3.2	21	Use HTML markup bot.
EMBED	NAME	name	HTML 3.2	21	Use HTML markup bot.
EMBED	OPTIONAL PARAM	value	HTML 3.2	21	Use HTML markup bot.
EMBED	PALETTE	FOREGROUND	HTML 3.2	21	Use HTML markup bot.
EMBED	PALETTE	BACKGROUND	HTML 3.2	21	Use HTML markup bot.
EMBED	SRC	data	HTML 3.2	21	Use HTML markup bot.
EMBED	WIDTH	n	HTML 3.2	21	Use HTML markup bot.
OBJECT	ALIGN	BASELINE	HTML 3.2	21	Use HTML markup bot.
OBJECT	ALIGN	CENTER	HTML 3.2	21	Use HTML markup bot.
OBJECT	ALIGN	LEFT	HTML 3.2	21	Use HTML markup bot.
OBJECT	ALIGN	MIDDLE	HTML 3.2	21	Use HTML markup bot.

continues

Table D.12. continued

Tag	Attribute name	Attribute value	Source	Chapter	Procedure or option to select in referenced dialog box
OBJECT	ALIGN	RIGHT	HTML 3.2	21	Use HTML markup bot.
OBJECT	ALIGN	TEXTBOTTOM	HTML 3.2	21	Use HTML markup bot.
OBJECT	ALIGN	TEXTMIDDLE	HTML 3.2	21	Use HTML markup bot.
OBJECT	ALIGN	TEXTTOP	HTML 3.2	21	Use HTML markup bot.
OBJECT	BORDER	n	HTML 3.2	21	Use HTML markup bot.
OBJECT	CLASSID	url	HTML 3.2	21	Use HTML markup bot.
OBJECT	CODEBASE	url	HTML 3.2	21	Use HTML markup bot.
OBJECT	CODETYPE	codetype	HTML 3.2	21	Use HTML markup bot.
OBJECT	DATA	url	HTML 3.2	21	Use HTML markup bot.
OBJECT	DECLARE		HTML 3.2	21	Use HTML markup bot.
OBJECT	HEIGHT	n	HTML 3.2	21	Use HTML markup bot.
OBJECT	HSPACE	n	HTML 3.2	21	Use HTML markup bot.
OBJECT	NAME	URL	HTML 3.2	21	Use HTML markup bot.
OBJECT	SHAPES		HTML 3.2	21	Use HTML markup bot.
OBJECT	STANDBY	message	HTML 3.2	21	Use HTML markup bot.
OBJECT	TYPE	type	HTML 3.2	21	Use HTML markup bot.
OBJECT	USEMAP	url	HTML 3.2	21	Use HTML markup bot.
OBJECT	VSPACE	n	HTML 3.2	21	Use HTML markup bot.
OBJECT	WIDTH	n	HTML 3.2	21	Use HTML markup bot.
SCRIPT	LANGUAGE	scriptLanguage	HTML 3.2	21	Use HTML markup bot.

Table D.13. Paragraph tags—Paragraph Format dialog box.

Tag	Attribute name	Attribute value	Source	Chapter	Procedure or option to select in referenced dialog box
ADDRESS				9	Insert I Paragraph I Address.
BLOCKQUOTE			HTML 2	9	Sets apart quotation in text, indents both left and right margins.
P			HTML 2	9	Insert I Paragraph I Normal.
P	ALIGN	LEFT	HTML 3	9	Align Left button on toolbar, or Left Alignment in Paragraph Format dialog box.
P	ALIGN	CENTER	HTML 3	9	Center button on toolbar, or Center Alignment in Paragraph Format dialog box.
P	ALIGN	RIGHT	HTML 3	9	Align Right button on toolbar, or Right Alignment in Paragraph Format dialog box.
PRE			HTML 2	9	Insert I Paragraph I Formatted.

Table D.14. Sound tags.

Tag	Attribute name	Attribute value	Source	Chapter	Procedure or option to select in referenced dialog box
BGSOUND	SRC	URL	Int. Exp.	21	Use HTML markup bot.
BGSOUND	LOOP	n	Int. Exp.	21	Use HTML markup bot.
BGSOUND	LOOP	INFINITE	Int. Exp.	21	Use HTML markup bot.

Table D.15. Table caption tags—Caption Properties dialog box.

Tag	Attribute name	Attribute value	Source	Chapter	Procedure or option to select in referenced dialog box
CAPTION	ALIGN	LEFT	HTML 3	21	Use HTML markup bot.
CAPTION	ALIGN	RIGHT	HTML 3	21	Use HTML markup bot.
CAPTION	ALIGN	CENTER	HTML 3	21	Default when you insert a table caption.
CAPTION	ALIGN	TOP	HTML 3	13	Insert I Caption.
CAPTION	ALIGN	BOTTOM	HTML 3	21	Use HTML markup bot.

Table D.16. Page-related HTML tags—Page Properties dialog box.

Tag	Attribute Name	Attribute Value	Source	Chapter	Procedure or option to select in referenced dialog box
! (comment)				21	Indicates a comment. Text between the tags is ignored unless it contains HTML code. Use HTML markup bot to include comments on your pages if desired.
!DOCTYPE			HTML 3.2		Specifies the HTML version used in the document. Required element for HTML 3.2. Use HTML markup bot.
COMMENT				21	Indicates a comment. Text between the tags is ignored unless it contains HTML code. Use HTML markup bot to include comments on your pages if desired.
ISINDEX			HTML 2		
META	NAME			11	
BASE	HREF	*URL*	HTML 2	11	Full URL of Current Document.
BODY			HTML 2	11	Indicates where a document begins and ends. Tag is automatically applied to a new page.
BODY	BACKGROUND	*URL*	HTML 3	11	Background Image.
BODY	BGPROPERTIES	FIXED	Int. Exp.	11	Use extended attribute. Specifies a watermark (a background that does not scroll).
BODY	LEFTMARGIN	*n*	Int. Exp.	11	Use extended attribute. Specifies a left margin which overrides the default. When set to 0, the left margin is exactly on the left edge of the page.
BODY	TOPMARGIN	*n*	Int. Exp.	11	Use extended attribute. Specifies a top margin which overrides the default. When set to 0, the top margin is exactly on the top edge of the page.
BODY	ALINK	*#rrggbb*	Netscape 1.1	11	Active Link Color.
BODY	ALINK	*colorname*	Netscape 1.1	11	Use extended attribute, or create custom color as shown in Table D.18 when using Text Color button.
BODY	BGCOLOR	*#rrggbb*	Netscape 1.1	11	Background Color.

Tag	Attribute Name	Attribute Value	Source	Chapter	Procedure or option to select in referenced dialog box
BODY	BGCOLOR	colorname	Netscape 1.1	11	Use extended attribute, or create custom color as shown in Table D.18 when using Text Color button.
BODY	LINK	#rrggbb	Netscape 1.1	11	Link Color.
BODY	LINK	colorname	Netscape 1.1	11	Use extended attribute, or create custom color as shown in Table D.18 when using Text Color button.
BODY	TEXT	#rrggbb	Netscape 1.1	11	Text Color.
BODY	TEXT	colorname	Netscape 1.1	11	Use extended attribute, or create custom color as shown in Table D.18 when using Text Color button.
BODY	VLINK	#rrggbb	Netscape 1.1	11	Visited Link Color.
BODY	VLINK	colorname	Netscape 1.1	11	Use extended attribute, or create custom color as shown in Table D.18 when using Text Color button.
DIV	ALIGN	LEFT			Use HTML markup bot.
DIV	ALIGN	CENTER			Use HTML markup bot.
DIV	ALIGN	RIGHT			Use HTML markup bot.
HEAD				11	Encloses the head of the HTML document.
HTML				11	Encloses the entire HTML document.
META	CONTENT	n	Netscape	11	Use Meta Variable tells the browser to reload in n seconds.
META	CONTENT	URL	Netscape	11	Use Meta Variable tells the browser to load the URL after the specified time has elapsed. If no URL is specified, it will reload the current document.
META	HTTP-EQUIV	REFRESH	Netscape	11	
TITLE			HTML 2	11	Defines the title of the document. Automatically applied to a page.

Table D.17. Table tags—Table Properties or Cell Properties dialog box.

Tag	Attribute name	Attribute value	Source	Chapter	Procedure or option to select in referenced dialog box
TABLE	BORDER	n			Table Properties - Layout: Border Size.
TABLE	FRAME	ABOVE	HTML 3	13	Use extended attribute Table Properties. Displays a border on the top side of the table frame.
TABLE	FRAME	BELOW	HTML 3	13	Use extended attribute Table Properties. Displays a border on the bottom side of the table frame.
TABLE	FRAME	BOX	HTML 3	13	Use extended attribute Table Properties. Displays a border on all sides of the table frame.
TABLE	FRAME	HSIDES	HTML 3	13	Use extended attribute Table Properties. Displays a border on the top and bottom sides of the table frame.
TABLE	FRAME	LHS	HTML 3	13	Use extended attribute Table Properties. Displays a border on the left side of the table frame.
TABLE	FRAME	RHS	HTML 3	13	Use extended attribute Table Properties. Displays a border on the right side of the table frame.
TABLE	FRAME	VOID	HTML 3	13	Use extended attribute Table Properties. Removes all outside table borders.
TABLE	FRAME	VSIDES	HTML 3	13	Use extended attribute Table Properties. Displays a border on the left and right sides of the table frame.
TABLE	RULES		HTML 3	13	Use extended attributeTable Properties. Removes all interior table borders.
TABLE	RULES	ALL	HTML 3	13	Use extended attribute Table Properties. Displays a border on all rows and columns.
TABLE	RULES	BASIC	HTML 3	13	Use extended attribute Table Properties. Displays horizontal borders between the table head, table body, and table foot.
TABLE	RULES	COLS	HTML 3	13	Use extended attribute Table Properties. Displays horizontal borders between all table columns.

Tag	Attribute name	Attribute value	Source	Chapter	Procedure or option to select in referenced dialog box
TABLE	RULES	ROWS	HTML 3	13	Use extended attribute Table Properties. Displays horizontal borders between all table rows.
TABLE	WIDTH	n		13	Table Properties: Width, Specify in Pixels.
TABLE	WIDTH	n%		13	Table Properties: Width, Specify in Percent.
TBODY			HTML 3		
TFOOT			HTML 3		
TH, TR, or TD	ALIGN	BOTTOM		13	Cell Properties - Layout: Vertical Alignment: Bottom.
TH, TR, or TD	ALIGN	CENTER		13	Cell Properties - Layout: Horizontal Alignment: Center.
TH, TR, or TD	VALIGN	LEFT		13	Cell Properties - Layout: Horizontal Alignment: Left.
TH, TR, or TD	VALIGN	MIDDLE		13	Cell Properties - Layout: Vertical Alignment: Middle.
TH, TR, or TD	VALIGN	RIGHT		13	Cell Properties - Layout: Horizontal Alignment: Right.
TH, TR, or TD	VALIGN	TOP		13	Cell Properties - Layout: Vertical Alignment: Top.
TH, TR, or TD	BACKGROUND	URL	Int. Exp.	13	Use extended attribute. Defines an image for the background.
TH, TR, or TD	BGCOLOR	#rrggbb	Int. Exp.	13	Use extended attribute. Specifies background color for cell.
TH, TR, or TD	BGCOLOR	colorname	Int. Exp.	13	Use extended attribute. Specifies background color for cell.
TH, TR, or TD	BORDERCOLOR	#rrggbb	Int. Exp.	13	Use extended attribute. Defines border color.
TH, TR, or TD	BORDERCOLOR	colorname	Int. Exp.	13	Use extended attribute. Defines border color.
TH, TR, or TD	BORDERCOLORDARK	#rrggbb	Int. Exp.	13	Use extended attribute. Defines darker color for 3D-appearing border.
TH, TR, or TD	BORDERCOLORDARK	colorname	Int. Exp.	13	Use extended attribute. Defines darker color for 3D-appearing border.

continues

Table D.17. continued

Tag	Attribute name	Attribute value	Source	Chapter	Procedure or option to select in referenced dialog box
TH, TR, or TD	BORDERCOLORLIGHT	#rrggbb	Int. Exp.	13	Use extended attribute. Defines lighter color for 3D-appearing border.
TH, TR, or TD	BORDERCOLORLIGHT	colorname	Int. Exp.	13	Use extended attribute. Defines lighter color for 3D-appearing border.
TH, TR, or TD	COLSPAN	n		13	Cell Properties - Cell Span, Number of Columns Spanned
TH, TR, or TD	ROWSPAN	n		13	Cell Properties - Cell Span, Number of Rows Spanned.
TH, TR, or TD	WIDTH	n		13	Cell Properties - Min. Width, Specify Width in Pixels.
TH, TR, or TD	WIDTH	n%		13	Cell Properties - Min. Width, Specify Width in Percent.
THREAD			HTML 3		

Table D.18. Color formulas that can be used in place of the Internet Explorer color name attribute values.

Color	Hex Value	Red	Green	Blue
BLACK	#000000	0	0	0
NAVY	#000070	0	0	112
BLUE	#0000F0	0	0	240
GREEN	#007000	0	112	0
TEAL	#007070	0	112	112
LIME	#00F000	0	240	0
AQUA	#00F0F0	0	240	240
MAROON	#700000	112	0	0
PURPLE	#700070	112	0	112
OLIVE	#707000	112	112	0
GRAY	#707070	112	112	112
SILVER	#B0B0B0	176	176	176
RED	#F00000	240	0	0
FUCHSIA	#F000F0	240	0	240
YELLOW	#F0F0F0	240	240	0
WHITE	#F0F0F0	240	240	240

E

What's on the CD-ROM

Microsoft-Related Products and Utilities

- ❏ Internet Explorer 2.0
- ❏ Microsoft Internet Information Server
- ❏ Internet Assistant for Microsoft Word for Windows 95
- ❏ Internet Assistant for Microsoft Excel for Windows
- ❏ Internet Assistant for Microsoft PowerPoint for Windows 95
- ❏ Internet Assistant for Microsoft Access for Windows 95
- ❏ Internet Assistant for Microsoft Schedule+ for Windows 95
- ❏ Microsoft Word Viewer for Windows 95
- ❏ Microsoft Excel Viewer for Windows 95
- ❏ Microsoft PowerPoint Viewer for Windows 95
- ❏ Microsoft PowerPoint Animation Player for Windows 95

Internet/HTML Utilities

- ❏ CuteFTP
- ❏ HotDog Pro Web Editor from Sausage Software
- ❏ HTML Assistant from Brooklyn North Software Works

Graphics/Editing Programs

- ❏ Paint Shop Pro from JASC., Inc.
- ❏ Thumbs Plus from Cerius Software
- ❏ Snagit32 from TechSmith Corp.
- ❏ Map This
- ❏ UltraEdit-32

Web Servers

- ❏ WebSite from O'Reilly & Associates

Perl 5

- ❏ Perl 5 for Win32 from Hip Communications

Java/JavaScript

- ❏ Sun's Java Development Kit, Version 1.02
- ❏ Sample Java Applets from the Web
- ❏ Sample Java Scripts from the Web

Compression Utilities

- ❏ Winzip from NicoMak Computing

INDEX

C

Laura Lemay's Web Workshop: Netscape Navigator Gold 3

Laura Lemay & Ned Snell   *Internet/General*

Netscape Gold and JavaScript are powerful tools for creating and designing effective Web pages. This book discusses design elements and how to use the Netscape Gold WYSIWYG editor. CD-ROM includes editors and all the source code from the book. Teaches how to program within Navigator Gold's rich Netscape development environment. Explores elementary design principles for effective Web page creation. Covers Web Publishing.

Price: $39.99 USA /$53.99 CDN   User Level: Casual–Accomplished
ISBN: 1-57521-128-9   400 pages   7 3/8 × 9 1/8   06/01/96

Laura Lemay's Web Workshop: VRML 2.0 and 3D Graphics

Laura Lemay & Karl Jacobs   *Internet/Graphics/Multimedia*

This book is the easiest way for readers to learn how to add three-dimensional virtual worlds to Web pages. It describes the new VRML 2.0 specification, explores the wide array of existing VRML sites on the Web, and steps the readers through the process of creating their own 3D Web environments. CD-ROM contains the book in HTML format, a hand-picked selection of the best VRML and 3D graphics tools, plus a collection of ready-to-use virtual worlds. Contains complete coverage of VRML 2.0! Teaches how to create 3D worlds on the Web. Covers the Internet.

Price: $39.99 USA /$56.95 CDN   User Level: Casual–Accomplished
ISBN: 1-57521-143-2   400 pages   7 3/8 × 9 1/8   09/01/96

Laura Lemay's Web Workshop: Creating Commercial Web Pages

Laura Lemay & Daniel Bishop   *Internet/Business*

Filled with sample Web pages, this book shows how to create commercial-grade Web pages using HTML, CGI, and Java. In the classic clear style of Laura Lemay, author of the bestseller *Teach Yourself Java,* this book shows how to create the page and apply proven principles of design that will make the Web site a marketing tool. CD-ROM includes all the templates in the book, plus HTML editors, graphics software, CGI forms, and more. Teaches how to use HTML, CGI, and Java. Illustrates the various corporate uses of Web technology: catalogues, customer service, and product ordering. Covers the Web.

Price: $39.99 USA /$56.95 CDN   User Level: Accomplished
ISBN: 1-57521-126-2   400 pages   7 3/8 × 9 1/8   09/01/96

Laura Lemay's Web Workshop: Graphics and Web Page Design

Laura Lemay & James Rudnick   *Internet/Online/Communications*

With the number of Web pages increasing daily, only the well-designed will stand out and grab the attention of those browsing the Web. This book illustrates, in classic Laura Lemay style, how to design attractive Web pages that will be visited over and over again. CD-ROM contains HTML editors, graphics software, and royalty-free graphics and sound files. Teaches beginning and advanced-level design principles. Covers the Internet.

Price: $39.99 USA /$56.95 CDN   User Level: Accomplished
ISBN: 1-57521-125-4   425 pages   7 3/8 × 9 1/8   08/01/96

Laura Lemay's Web Workshop: JavaScript

Laura Lemay   *Communications/Online/Internet*

Readers will explore various aspects of Web publishing—whether CGI scripting and interactivity or graphics design or Netscape Gold—in greater depth than the Teach Yourself books. CD-ROM includes the complete book in HTML format, publishing tools, templates, graphics, backgrounds, and more. Provides a clear, hands-on guide to creating sophisticated Web pages. Covers CGI.

Price: $39.99 USA /$56.95 CDN   *User Level: Casual–Accomplished*
ISBN: 1-57521-141-6   *400 pages*   *7 3/8 × 9 1/8*   *09/01/96*

Teach Yourself Web Publishing with HTML 3.2 in 14 Days, Professional Reference Edition

Laura Lemay   *Internet/Web Publishing*

This is the updated edition of Lemay's previous bestseller, *Teach Yourself Web Publishing with HTML in 14 Days, Premier Edition.* In it readers will find all the advanced topics and updates—including adding audio, video, and animation—to Web page creation. CD-ROM included. Explores the use of CGI scripts, tables, HTML 3.2, Netscape and Internet Explorer extensions, Java applets and JavaScript, and VRML. Covers HTML 3.2.

Price: $59.99 USA /$81.95 CDN   *User Level: New–Casual–Accomplished*
ISBN: 1-57521-096-7   *1,104 pages*   *7 3/8 × 9 1/8*   *06/01/96*

Teach Yourself Web Publishing with HTML in 14 Days, Premier Edition

Laura Lemay   *Internet/Web Publishing*

This book teaches everything about publishing on the Web. In addition to its exhaustive coverage of HTML, it also gives readers hands-on practice designing and writing HTML documents. CD-ROM is Mac- and PC-compatible and includes applications that help readers create Web pages using graphics and templates. Readers will learn how to upload their page to a server and how to advertise. Covers HTML 3.0.

Price: $39.99 USA /$53.99 CDN   *User Level: New–Accomplished*
ISBN: 1-57521-014-2   *840 pp.*   *7 3/8 × 9 1/8*   *09/01/95*
Design, create, and upload your Web page to a Web server for the world to see!

Microsoft FrontPage Unleashed

William Stanek, Kelly Martin Hardebeck   *Internet/Web Publishing*
& Susan St. Maurice

FrontPage technologies has recently been acquired by Microsoft, who immediately reduced its retail price from a staggering $695 to $150, making FrontPage affordable for thousands of hackers and professionals. Microsoft is also launching FrontPage as its point technology for its suite of Internet products, which will undoubtedly increase demand. With that new demand in mind, this book gives readers of all levels the information they need to succeed in Web publishing with FrontPage. CD-ROM includes all the examples and source code from the book. Explains how to add interactivity to Web sites. Shows how to integrate CGI scripting with FrontPage.

Price: $49.99 USA /$70.95 CDN   *User Level: Casual–Accomplished*
ISBN: 1-57521-140-8   *800 pages*   *7 3/8 × 9 1/8*   *09/01/96*

Add to Your Sams.net Library Today
with the Best Books for Internet Technologies

ISBN	Quantity	Description of Item	Unit Cost	Total Cost
1-57521-128-9		Laura Lemay's Web Workshop: Netscape Navigator Gold 3 (Book/CD-ROM)	$39.99	
1-57521-143-2		Laura Lemay's Web Workshop: 3D Graphics and VRML 2.0 (Book/CD-ROM)	$39.99	
1-57521-126-2		Laura Lemay's Web Workshop: Creating Commercial Web Pages (Book/CD-ROM)	$39.99	
1-57521-125-4		Laura Lemay's Web Workshop: Graphics and Web Page Design (Book/CD-ROM)	$39.99	
1-57521-141-6		Laura Lemay's Web Workshop: Scripting and Interactivity (Book/CD-ROM)	$39.99	
1-57521-096-7		Teach Yourself Web Publishing with HTML 3.2 in 14 Days, Professional Reference Edition (Book/CD-ROM)	$59.99	
1-57521-014-2		Teach Yourself Web Publishing with HTML in 14 Days, Premier Edition (Book/CD-ROM)	$39.99	
1-57521-140-8		Microsoft FrontPage Unleashed (Book/CD-ROM)	$49.99	
		Shipping and Handling: See information below.		
		TOTAL		

Shipping and Handling: $4.00 for the first book, and $1.75 for each additional book. If you need to have it NOW, we can ship product to you in 24 hours for an additional charge of approximately $18.00, and you will receive your item overnight or in two days. Overseas shipping and handling adds $2.00. Prices subject to change. Call between 9:00 a.m. and 5:00 p.m. EST for availability and pricing information on latest editions.

201 W. 103rd Street, Indianapolis, Indiana 46290

1-800-428-5331 — Orders   1-800-835-3202 — FAX   1-800-858-7674 — Customer Service

Book ISBN 1-57521-149-1

CD-ROM
What's on
the CD-ROM

The companion CD-ROM contains an electronic version of the book, plus all the sample projects from the book. Also included are the Java™ Developers Kit from Sun Microsystems and many useful third-party tools and utilities to complement Microsoft's FrontPage.

Windows 95 Installation Instructions

1. Insert the CD-ROM disc into your CD-ROM drive.
2. From the Windows 95 desktop, double-click the My Computer icon.
3. Double-click the icon representing your CD-ROM drive.
4. Double-click the icon titled Install.exe to run the installation program.
5. Installation creates a program group named LLWW Frontpage. This group contains icons to browse the CD-ROM.

NOTE: If Windows 95 is installed on your computer and you have the AutoPlay feature enabled, the Install.exe program starts automatically whenever you insert the disc into your CD-ROM drive.

Windows NT Installation Instructions

1. Insert the CD-ROM disc into your CD-ROM drive.
2. From File Manager or Program Manager, choose Run from the File menu.
3. Type *drive*\install and press Enter, where *drive* corresponds to the drive letter of your CD-ROM. For example, if your CD-ROM is drive D:, type D:\INSTALL and press Enter.
4. Installation creates a program group named LLWW Frontpage. This group contains icons to browse the CD-ROM.